BREAK-SHOT

A LIFE IN THE 21ST CENTURY AMERICAN MAFIA

S0-BMR-045

KENNY "KENJI" GALLO
MATTHEW RANDAZZO V

POCKET STAR BOOKS

New York London Toronto Sydney

Pocket Star Books
A Division of Simon & Schuster, Inc.
1230 Avenue of the Americas
New York, NY 10020

Copyright © 2009 by Matthew Randazzo V and Phoenix Books, Inc.

Published by arrangement with Phoenix Books, Inc.

All rights reserved, including the right to reproduce this book or portions thereof in any form whatsoever. For information, address Phoenix Books, Inc. with offices at 9465 Wilshire Boulevard, Suite 840, Beverly Hills, CA 90212.

First Pocket Star Books paperback edition December 2010

POCKET STAR BOOKS and colophon are registered trademarks of Simon & Schuster, Inc.

For information about special discounts for bulk purchases, please contact Simon & Schuster Special Sales at 1-866-506-1949 or business@simonandschuster.com.

The Simon & Schuster Speakers Bureau can bring authors to your live event. For more information or to book an event, contact the Simon & Schuster Speakers Bureau at 1-866-248-3049 or visit our website at www.simonspeakers.com.

Designed by Esther Paradelo
Cover design by John Vairo Jr., all images by Shutterstock

Manufactured in the United States of America

10 9 8 7 6 5 4 3 2 1

ISBN 978-1-4391-9583-3
ISBN 978-1-4391-9585-7 (ebook)

MRV:
To Melissa & Jeannie.

Kenji:
In memory of
Jerry Lee Lawrence
(murdered, 1984)
Catherine Anne Lawrence
(murdered, 1985)
Jose "Joey" Avila
(murdered, 1987)
Lee Matthew Clyde
(murdered, 1989)
Perry Ross
(murdered, 1992)
Osvaldo Blanco
(murdered, 1992)
Shannon "Savannah" Wilsey
(suicide, 1994)
Randy "Cal Jammer" Potes
(suicide, 1995)
Karen "Alex Jordan" Hughes
(suicide, 1995)
Israel Gonzalez
(suicide, 1997)
Herbert "Fat Herbie" Blitzstein
(murdered, 1997)
William "Wild Bill/Billy Fingers" Cutolo
(murdered, 1999)
Elroy Jenkins
(suicide)
Chester "Jon Dough" Anuszak
(suicide, 2006)
Charles "Buck Adams" Allen
(heart attack due to prolonged drug abuse, 2008)
Justin Levens
(suicide, 2008)
Sarah McClean-Levens
(murdered, 2008)

And last but not least:
Kenneth Gallo, also known as Kenny Gallo,
Kenji, 健児, Kenny G., Kenji Kodama, Ramon Gomez,
Ramon Gonzalez, Kenji Kodama, Ken Calo
(disappeared, 2004)

Authors' Note

Kenny "Kenji" Gallo is an FBI-protected informant against New York's Colombo Mafia Family and the Lucchese Mafia Family who currently lives under an assumed identity somewhere in the United States. Since Gallo began his work with the Federal Bureau of Investigation, the Colombo Family has placed a contract on his head, leading to one confirmed assassination attempt, another suspected plot presumably foiled by law enforcement, and hundreds of death threats. Though FBI-protected witnesses usually have a normal life expectancy, two former members of the American Mafia interviewed by co-author Matthew Randazzo V stated that the Colombo Family vendetta against Gallo is so extreme that his life is in serious danger.

Breakshot is Kenny Gallo's story as told to Matthew Randazzo V over four years of near-daily phone calls, e-mails, letters, and in-person interviews. All assertions, memories, and opinions expressed by the narrator in *Breakshot* thus belong solely to Kenny Gallo and Kenny Gallo alone. Archival research and interviews conducted by Randazzo of civilian eyewitnesses, law enforcement officers, members of organized crime families, and pertinent members of the judicial system have broadly confirmed Gallo's story.

We expressly note each instance in which a name has been changed to protect one of Gallo's victims or accomplices. All dialogue that is not directly lifted from material records such as wiretaps, police transcripts, or newspaper articles should be considered reconstructions from Gallo's memory. Unless otherwise attributed, the direct quotations at the beginning of each section are drawn from Randazzo's independent interviews with other principals in Gallo's story.

Contents

BREAK-SHOT

ONE

Sunday Sauce with Uncle Manny

*"The closer Kenny comes to death,
the more alive he feels."*

Anthony "The Animal" Fiato
Made Man in the Milano Mafia Family,
Street Boss of L.A.'s breakaway Rizzitello Family

*New York City,
January 2002–October 2004*

"After 9/11, our business went in the toilet," Emanuel "Uncle Manny" Garofalo, my mentor in New York City's Colombo Mafia Family, once told me as I sat in the passenger seat of his Porsche. "Suddenly, all the labor unions and construction projects in the city were stopped dead in their tracks. The stock market went to shit. Bookmaking and gambling returns were the pits. Everyone got jumpy and trigger-shy with all the feds all over the Five Burroughs like fleas and maggots. It was the worst—like the Great Depression. Good, hardworking guys who lived week to week were getting cleaned out.

"Y'know, deep down, nobody wanted to get involved with the whole Ground Zero thing," Manny continued in his thin, reedy accountant's voice. A small, tan, paunchy man with short silver hair and a small manicured hand on the steering wheel, Manny had none of the flash or physical presence that most Americans would expect from one of New York's most powerful gangsters. "It was like, y'know, in poor taste and very dangerous, very high-profile. It was just an ugly thing to have to make a living from . . . You know what I mean, Kenny?

"But . . ." Manny raised his black eyebrows, cocked

his head, and shrugged with a pragmatic, none-too-troubled expression. "It's business . . . you gotta do what ya gotta do. It's the Life. The feds were handing out billions of dollars of contracts, employing tens of thousands of union guys, and it was a long job; you'd be bringing home the bacon for a decade or two if you got a foot in the door. You'd be an asshole not to take advantage . . . if you do what we do, y'know. This isn't the Golden Age; beggars can't be choosers." Manny smiled like a cocky attorney resting his case and looked out of the driver's side window of the $100,000 Porsche Cayenne Turbo SUV, which I was told had been expense-accounted for his use by a telecommunications company controlled by the Colombo Family.

Manny was appointed steward of the telecommunications business after his allies in the Colombo Family murdered the previous owner, Colombo underboss "Wild Bill" Cutolo, and buried him on a farm in East Farmingdale, New York. Wild Bill's body would only be found in October 2008, nine years after he disappeared and his Mafia "family" had robbed his widow and son of their inheritance. In the Colombos, it's not uncommon to get lynched from the family tree.

"Besides, it's not like I'm being greedy," Manny continued in a self-satisfied tone that told me he thought I admired him and bought his bullshit wholesale. "After all, all I'm getting right now from the union work is $12,000 a week with a little bit in the pension fund," he said with a smirk.

Manny was a street millionaire who acted like $12,000 a week—over $600,000 a year—was pocket change, a little extra to make the ends meet. Manny's job at Ground Zero as a union "oiler" of heavy machinery in reality consisted of Manny taking naps in Wild Bill's old office and pleasure-cruising around the empty streets in a golf cart, looking for places to eat. At night, Manny and his goons stole tons of raw materials from the cleanup and reconstruction projects, which they would resell on the black market to many of the same mobbed-up construction firms that had originally bought the materials with federal money.

Manny and I were driving through Manhattan to a doctor's office near Ground Zero to get medically cleared to access the toxic ruins of the Deutsche Bank Building, one of the buildings destroyed by the 9/11 attacks. The collapse of the WTC South Tower showered the adjacent Deutsche Bank Building with tons of steel and mortar debris, ripping open a twenty-four-story wound in the building's façade. Doused by fire sprinklers and exposed to the toxic air, the gash in the building festered with poisonous black mold. Before long the entire structure was permeated with dozens of lethal toxins, including dioxin and asbestos.

The obliteration of the Two Towers transformed the Deutsche Bank Building into a monolithic mass grave. Dozens of people were blasted clean over Liberty Street, spray-painting the ruins red and lodging bone in the walls like shrapnel. As late as 2006, splattered human remains were still being found on the roof of the forty-story building.

The history of the Deutsche Bank Building was irrelevant to Manny, who was absolutely cynical when money and power were involved. Manny was a sentimental teddy bear when it came to his beloved wife, two sons, and Bruce Springsteen, whom he almost homoerotically worshipped, but he was born without the moral gag reflex that would have made a normal man reluctant to profit from the misery of the 9/11 victims and their families. As boss of the Colombos' construction rackets and their representative on the New York Mafia's labor commission, Manny saw Ground Zero as a demolition site to be ransacked and pillaged like any other.

For Manny, bidding on the massive federal contract to demolish the Deutsche Bank Building was an opportunity to control millions of dollars in embezzled funds, stolen materials, fictitious cost overruns, and money-laundering "no-show" union jobs that allowed mobsters to justify their illicit wealth to the Internal Revenue Service. If Manny succeeded, he would become one of the most powerful criminals in America, the underworld equivalent of the chairman of the House or Senate Appropriations Committee: a pork-barrel kingpin who could steer unimaginable federal largesse to whomever he wished.

As we sat in a doctor's waiting room with other contractors, demolition artists, and construction workers, Manny was giddy speculating about the potential windfall if he entered a bid for the demolition job and won. "Kenny, this would be big," Manny whispered, his eyes darting around the room to see if anyone was eavesdropping.

"Real big. Let's say they accept my bid of $42 million. Minimum—and I mean minimum—we could steal $7 million from the deal, pure profit. And that's before I even get a real good look at what I'm dealing with. Given time to do a thorough job, we're looking at a lot more."

I knew the sort of thorough job the Colombos did with a big-money demolition project—I had an asbestos poisoning scare from visiting their last big score. Retail giant Target was building its first-ever store in the Bronx, and, through his usual mixture of charm and influence peddling, Manny obtained the subcontract to

demolish the buildings that occupied the space on the
Major Deegan Expressway. Displaying the usual Mafia
contempt for the safety of civilians and subordinate wiseguys alike, Manny sent his crew to the site on a beautiful
sunny afternoon without a permit, without the proper
equipment, without properly surveying and preparing
the site, without taking the most basic preliminary safety
precautions, and without warning either the police or the
local residents about the dangers of the demolition they
were about to perform.

I watched with my roommate, porn star Dayton
Raines, as one of Manny's sons illegally stopped traffic while Colombo cavemen haphazardly ripped these
buildings apart like kids dismembering Lego sets. In an
eerie echo of 9/11, the buildings tumbled, and this Bronx
neighborhood—one of the most densely populated areas
in the United States—disappeared without warning beneath suffocating clouds of dust and pollutants.

When one of Manny's "guys" screamed through the
dust storm to warn me as a fellow wiseguy that the building was heavily contaminated with asbestos and "Lord
knows what else," Dayton and I ran to my car with
our hands over our mouths. Since the Colombos had
plenty of experience demolishing rotten old buildings,
we trusted his claim about the asbestos without need for
further verification.

A few months later, Manny called and told me to
watch the NY1 News that night. I was awestruck: there
was Manny Garofalo, convicted Mafia leader, standing
next to New York City mayor Mike Bloomberg at the
ribbon-cutting of the first Target in the Bronx. Manny was
beaming, inwardly laughing. He thought he was smarter
than everyone.

I was thinking of the ramifications of such a "thorough"

demolition job on the most toxic building in America as we waited for Manny's name to be called. Finally, his turn came, just as Manny was laughing about the time he had his son escort my ex-wife, porn star Tabitha Stevens, on a VIP tour of Ground Zero. Wearing a hard hat and miniskirt, Tabitha was swarmed by cleanup workers begging her to pose for sexy pictures amid the death and destruction. As Manny stood up, he suddenly realized that the doctor might ask him to strip—meaning that it might be wise to unload his incriminating Mafia paraphernalia.

In a frenzied display that amused some of the more plugged-in contractors in the waiting room, Manny handed me a preposterous cabbage-sized wad of cash (I counted about $10,000 as I waited) and his day planner notebook, which contained all of his racketeering, Mafia payoffs, and loan-sharking notes.

While Manny had his checkup, I leafed through his "big black book." There were notes, in our personal code, about the due dates for tribute payments to the Colombo leadership, loan shark interest payments, and payouts on business deals at Wild Bill's old telecommunications company. I lifted my camera phone to my face as if checking a text message, the lens poised over the open book on my lap. I took pictures, one after the other, page after page. The FBI was going to love this.

I was a rat, an undercover government informant by the code name of BREAKSHOT, derived from my ability to singlehandedly knock the Colombo Family leadership pyramid into disarray like the first shot in a game of pool. That is why I can't finish the Deutsche Bank story. My agreement precludes me from divulging certain details crucial to ongoing investigations and prosecutions, so I can't say if Manny won the demolition bid. What I can say is that he was medically cleared.

I can also say that on Saturday, August 18, 2007, a fire on the fourteenth floor of the Deutsche Bank Building brought the New York Fire Department back down to Ground Zero. The standpipe that the firemen would normally use to pump water up into the building was inexplicably disconnected, violating safety protocol and regulations. The firemen charged into an inferno, only to discover that they had no water with which to extinguish it. Two helpless firemen were killed in the blaze.

Their deaths raised red flags for a lot of Mafia observers. The Deutsche Bank Building exhibited two trademarks of a Mafia project: flagrant safety violations and mysterious fires that spontaneously erupt on the weekend—when the job site is empty of wiseguys.

I've done a lot of things in my life that I regret, but flipping on Manny Garofalo isn't one of them.

> *"Are you kidding me? When those buildings went down on 9/11, you knew the big contracts were coming down, and you know those guys in the Colombos would be all over it."*
>
> William "Billy" Cutolo, Jr.
> Ex–Colombo Family mafioso,
> son of slain Colombo Family
> underboss William "Wild Bill" Cutolo

It took years for Manny to suspect that I had become a government informant, even though I should have seemed like the most obvious turncoat imaginable. First of all, I wasn't from the Colombo family network; in addition to being the most murderous of New York's storied "Five Families," the Colombos are also the closest to being an actual family. Many Colombos are related by blood or marriage, with the crime family's leadership generally hailing from an insular circle of intermarried Brooklyn families centered in the neighborhood of Bay Ridge. All of the Colombo bad apples tend to fall from the same family tree. Other wiseguys often called the Colombos "inbred," a diagnosis that fits many of the cross-eyed, evolutionary-chart escapees I worked with in Brooklyn.

So how did I, of all people, become a Colombo? I wasn't from New York or New Jersey, and I certainly wasn't related to any of those zoological monstrosities. I didn't come from a central-casting, blue-collar, goombah background, either; I was born into a publishing family in Orange County, California, where I grew up a straight-A student. My upbringing alone should have disqualified me from joining the Colombos: the ability to read and speak like an adult aroused suspicion in Bay Ridge.

Even more suspicious than my wealthy background was my ethnicity. Though Manny introduced me to everyone as his beloved cousin, "Kenny Gallo," I am Japanese-American. I have some Italian blood, but my father was Japanese; I was born with a Japanese name; I look Japanese. Despite my Italian pseudonym, Gallo, I have hardly hidden my heritage since my nickname on the streets for a quarter century has been the hardly Sicilian-sounding Kenji (in Japanese: 健児).

At any other time in Mafia history, the concept of a pivotal Mob leader like Manny Garofalo making an "overeducated California chink" his Number Two, his aide-de-camp and "cousin," would have been impossible. But today's desperate, depleted Mob welcomed me. In past eras, I would have been used to make a quick buck and executed as a matter of course. In the venomously racist New York Mafia, outsiders were considered informants-in-training. We had little to gain by staying loyal to mobsters who had a long record of killing loyal non-Italian associates just to "be sure" they kept their mouths shut.

But Manny didn't suspect me, not for the longest time. I came highly recommended from previous work under Mafia legends John "Sonny" Franzese and Vincent "Jimmy" Caci, two Golden Age relics with unimpeachable credentials and connections. I had made a considerable reputation from my teenage exploits as one of California's top cocaine dealers, the stone-crazy wildcat who survived half-a-decade in the orbit of Pablo Escobar's Medellín Cartel. My name carried weight in Orange County, Los Angeles, Palm Springs, and Las Vegas with the police and gangsters alike; my references checked out, and my credentials stretched back two decades.

Most importantly, Manny liked me. We were incredibly similar: two savvy guys who could have made it as legitimate businessmen who nonetheless chose the outlaw life because it was fun, exciting, empowering, and never boring. We were two men with hyperactive minds fixated on power and destruction; we needed the Life to keep us occupied and fulfilled, to keep us from turning our predatory mania inward.

Manny used to tell me all the time that we weren't crooks—we were "racketeers." We weren't "street people" like the other Colombos. We were the professionals. We were among the last of the Mob's "finesse" criminals, con men who could mastermind crimes so subtle and complex that our fellow mafiosi had to take our word that they worked. We specialized in James Bond villain crimes, like hijacking millions of dollars of telecommunications bandwidth and selling it to corrupt companies in Cambodia or laundering millions in illicit profits through federally funded construction projects.

The antithesis of the dumb goombah mobster, Manny was both a meticulous businessman and a charming, sophisticated operator. In public, Manny was polished and driven like a politician; he projected the type of fierce pride you often see from blue-collar millionaires who are exceptionally sure of themselves because they earned every cent of their fortune. Every morning at seven o'clock, Manny would be dressed in his tasteful clothes and reading the *New York Post* and New York *Daily News* one after the other, front to back. By 8 a.m., he would grab his worn leather day planner and start rushing to dozens of construction sites around the city, inspecting the work and poring over budget invoices. Unlike most lazy and unemployable wiseguys, Manny relaxed rarely, only taking it easy at Ground Zero, where he was paid $600,000 a year largely to hang out.

I was at Manny's side every day: a muscular thirty-six-year-old Asian man in jeans, sneakers, and a cheap T-shirt covered with aliens—a hard hat over my shaved head, a cell phone to my ear, and a wiseass smile on my face. Following Manny was the closest I had ever come to a real, honest job; I felt like an executive VP at a huge construction firm with a casual dress code. I kept Manny's appointments in order, picked up cash for him, relayed messages, strong-armed guys who were getting out of line, programmed computers, and balanced budgets.

We were Uncle Manny and his cousin Kenny, the two most unorthodox mobsters in New York: one a masterfully composed businessman and gentleman who happened to have a perfect Brooklyn wiseguy pedigree, the other a hyper-educated Asian-American from California with a high-profile past as a porn producer and cocaine smuggler.

Because I made Manny so much money, and because

we were so alike, Manny convinced himself that I would be loyal to death. Not that he took it for granted: Manny relentlessly schemed to isolate me from the rest of the Colombo Family and make me feel like a dependent part of the Garofalo family instead. Manny insisted that I attend the Garofalo family's Sunday dinners, and if I didn't show up he would get on my case, asking what could have possibly been more important than the "Sunday Sauce."

He even attempted to make his Mob nickname, "Uncle Manny," literal in my case: he discussed sealing our alliance by marrying one of his young nieces to me like a Renaissance prince. Since the Garofalos claimed to have some Finnish lineage that made them look "a little Asiatic," Manny thought I would fit right into his mongoloid brood. Manny hinted that I was his one true friend, the one wiseguy he could trust not to rob his family in case anything happened to him. The others in the Colombo leadership were disloyal thieves who regularly defrauded the families of any wiseguy who went to jail or the grave for the family.

Manny wanted me to think of him as my father or at least my favorite, most indulgent uncle, and, to an extent I found disturbing, his plan worked. A scam artist like me hates the feeling that another scammer is "working" him, but I couldn't help it: Manny and I became close. Even at the end, when the FBI hinted daily that the Colombo leadership was considering whacking me out, I still felt safe with my Uncle Manny.

It was six o'clock on a prematurely dark evening in October 2004, when I received a phone call from Manny asking me to meet him at his favorite diner. He wanted to repay me for the $2,700 I lent him one day when the stack he was carrying was short. I drove to the familiar

diner off the Belt Parkway en route to Coney Island.
When I entered the restaurant, the hostess pointed to a
roped-off room used for large catering events. Looking
in, I saw only the back of Manny's square head; he was
sitting all by himself, hunched over, staring through the
window at the parking lot. He had been watching me
when I walked into the restaurant.

I sat down with Manny, and I could immediately
tell he wasn't in his normal pleasant, measured mood. I
asked him about my money. Scowling, he grumbled, "I
don't have it for you." For a Mob hierarch like Manny,
there was no possibility he didn't have the scratch to
settle our debt; he need only order an underling to give it
to him. If Manny wasn't paying me, it was to send a message. I thought to myself: Maybe he thinks I'm headed to
a shallow grave like Wild Bill; maybe Manny just doesn't
want to give the gravediggers a $2,700 tip.

"Kenny, did you tell Edward that I laundered money
for you?" His normally measured voice seethed with
paranoia and rage. The Edward in question was his own
nephew, Eddie Garofalo, the Colombo soldier who gave
him the nickname "Uncle Manny." Regardless of the
blood link, it was strictly against the rules for me to talk
to Eddie about any business I had with his uncle. Manny
was his own man in the family, an autonomously operating criminal who reported only to the Boss and his acting
boss on the street; his rackets were not Eddie's business.
It would have counted as a violation of the Mafia omerta
code of secrecy to reveal Manny's affairs to Eddie, a
transgression punishable by death.

"Uh, no, Manny. I've never told Eddie anything."
Uncharacteristically, I was being honest; Manny turned
on me for just about the only act of betrayal I didn't
commit. This demonstrates how dangerous a life with

the Colombos can be without the protection of intricate chain mail links of Brooklyn blood relations and diplomatic neighborhood marriages. One groundless rumor and Manny forgot all my weekends with the Garofalo family, all that "Sunday Sauce" and flirting with his nieces, all that affectionate "Uncle Manny" bullshit.

"Well, Kenny," he continued, "I heard you said that. I heard you told Edward. *Let's see who's fucking lying.*" This was an unmistakable threat; there was no "innocent until proven guilty" and there was no way Manny would believe me over his nephew Eddie. I thought, *If only I could whip out my FBI audio recorder and play my conversations with Eddie: "Here, dumbfuck, I was talking to the FBI, not Eddie. Good guess, though!"*

"I thought what we had was between us, Kenny," Manny growled, blinking incessantly. "Look at me when you answer me! I am not going to jail over you, Kenny. *Look* . . . in my eyes . . . and *tell me* you didn't tell Edward I was laundering money for you." Manny apparently thought that his eyes were intimidating enough to rob a hardened felon of his ability to lie.

"Manny, sincerely, no bullshit, no!" I said with a shake of my head and a hint of smile, amused by the irony. It was as if Manny had caught me in bed with his wife and, not noticing, proceeded to falsely scold me for stealing change from his car's cupholder.

"Don't you fucking lie to me with that smirk on your face!" Manny erupted. I guess he could see I was laughing at him. The normally placid and composed businessman was a drooling, fuming Mob-movie hothead, fangs out and ready to kill. I was stunned; I was scared shitless. Unlike some Mafia families, the Colombos do not hesitate to murder, regardless of whether the FBI is guaranteed to catch them or not. The Colombos are the ghetto gangbangers of the Mafia: they talk a lot of shit, drop bodies over nothing, and hold their family reunions in prison.

"If you sit there, Kenny," Manny gasped, sputtering with rage, "looking . . . at *me* . . . with that *smirk* . . . for one more *fucking* second . . . I'm going to punch you in your *fucking* face."

The idea of an out-of-shape senior citizen punching me, a semi-professional martial artist for over twenty years, was hilarious. Unlike in the movies, Mafia membership doesn't bestow super-badass powers on fat, slow, pasta-slurping, middle-age guidos. You don't need a kryptonite fist to knock out a wiseguy. I was still scared for my life, but I couldn't help but laugh in Manny's face. He took his own bullshit image seriously, something wiseguys started doing ever since the movies convinced them they were world-class tough guys and outlaw celebrities. Manny was a yuppie with a potbelly, not Mike Tyson, and he'd sooner shit an exact copy of the *Mona Lisa* than slap me in the face.

Manny's arrogance triggered the dominant class clown aspect of my personality. I enjoy annoying people; I *love* annoying people. I couldn't resist mocking Manny, making this lifelong criminal realize that he was a straight-up *bitch* compared to me. I have trained in martial arts since I was a kid; I learned how to handle myself on the streets from legendary drug smugglers and hit men; I was taught how to use firearms in military school and how to deploy explosives by an FBI-trained urban warfare expert. And now some aging Brooklyn civilian like Manny was going to threaten to slap me around? *Please.*

"Manny, not for nothing, but you are *not* going to punch me in the face," I said, shaking my bald head.

"Say one . . . more . . . thing, Kenny," Manny said, glowing bright red, "and I promise you, I will fucking punch you."

This was too easy. *Say one more thing? Okay, Manny, you dumb prick.*

"What?" I screamed as if I had tuned out and missed what he had said.

I waited. Then said it again: "What? I can't hear you, Uncle Manny! Speak up!" I laughed, barely restraining myself from pointing at him like the fat kid on the playground.

"I'm going to fucking kill you, Kenny! I'll fucking kill you!" The outburst silenced us both. We stared at each other; not quite a Mexican standoff, but more like two guys who had gotten carried away and were unsure what to do next. Had I been thinking, I never would have disrespected Manny to the point where he could never trust me again and had no choice but to kill me. I was leaving my life in Brooklyn tonight.

I was terrified: a soft-touch guy like Manny surely had a backup crew waiting in ambush to be this forward, and my gun was in my car. Until I reached my car, I was, therefore, in fatal danger. After a minute of uneasy staring, Manny started to talk in a calm and lucid way, playing the levelheaded good guy who wants to cool the tempers of two friends who said things they didn't mean.

This was the worst sign of all. I was being calmed down so I could be ambushed. I had to get out of that diner, now. I just stood up and started walking, fast, to my car, to my gun, to parity.

Manny chased after me, his serpentine voice reassuring me that I was overreacting, turning an innocent misunderstanding into a life or death crisis. "C'mon, Kenny, let's end this now. Let's not take this any further. Let's clear all of this up; come with me and visit Edward at the truck lot so we can clear all this up."

It was the worst pitch imaginable. If Manny wanted to persuade me to get into his car, suggesting that we visit his burly, born-killer nephew Eddie at his infamous truck lot in Staten Island was not a wise strategy. More than any other place I've ever visited, that truck lot smelled of death. The lot was a post-apocalyptic ruin of concrete and wrecked cars where the Colombo Family's heir apparent, Eddie's partner Teddy Persico, held court surrounded by a slapstick gang of high-school-dropout bodybuilders and cokeheads, all of them heavily armed, slack-jaw stupid, and eager to kill anyone, anytime to burnish their meathead, Brooklyn street rep. The last time I saw Teddy at the truck lot, he bragged to me that he was eager to "put bodies on the street" and that the lot "would be a great place to whack someone."

Teddy was sincere: he once deputized me as a member of an improvised hit team, placing a rusty gun in my hand and dragging me across town to kill a former friend of mine over a decade-old beef in broad daylight. As soon as I heard Manny's invitation to Teddy and Eddie's truck lot, I quickened my pace; I knew for sure that Manny intended to have me killed.

Realizing that I would jeopardize his freedom if I fled and turned rat, Manny followed with uncharacteristic speed; his thighs must have been rubbing together furiously. He grabbed hold of my arm and began desperately wrenching me to his car, all the while trying to seduce me with incongruently gentle assurances of his friendship. Manny was losing it. I saw it in his eyes: panic, terror, berserk survival instinct.

Manny saw the end of the decades-long lucky streak

that kept him out of serious jail time. Some mobsters thought of Manny as if he was the Faust of Brooklyn, the beneficiary of some demonic bargain that allowed him to walk through a storm of indictments without getting wet, effortlessly stepping between the raindrops. Now the devil was coming for his due.

As Manny pulled me toward his Porsche, I saw what he had been hiding. In two cars parked across the street sat a group of Bay Ridge goombah idiots who did strong-arm work for the family. Manny *had* brought backup—but we were still right in front of the restaurant, where we were regulars. There was no way for them to jump me in plain sight without getting caught.

With no other choice, I muscled away from Manny and ran to my car. I climbed into the front seat and grabbed my pistol: *relief,* an unbelievable deluge of endorphins, the closest I've ever come to attaining ex-istential peace. There was no more suspense; even with a ten-on-one advantage, Manny and his goons weren't going to take out an armed Kenny Gallo.

I was going to be okay. Unlike most modern mob-sters, I had *real world* gunfight experience, not just Staten Island truck-lot target practice. Worst case sce-nario: I'd have some bloodshed to explain to the FBI, and it wouldn't be my blood on the Belt Parkway. I drove off with a defeated Manny Garofalo in my rearview mirror, his hands upturned at his side, an awful broken look on his face. I think Manny was seeing his future: jail, his family tossed out of their home, public ridicule, "The 9/11 Mafioso" splashed across newspaper front pages.

I drove off, changing my route to lose any cars that might be tailing me. As far as the New York Mafia was concerned, I drove off the edge of the Earth that night, clean off the planet. Kenji—mobster, drug lord, and porn kingpin for twenty-five years—died, to live on only in the nightmares of the mobsters who had the misfortune of incriminating themselves in my company. This is the posthumous memoir of Kenji, a terrible character, who in ceasing to exist has done the world the favor. This is also the memoir of another man, a nameless man, who is trying every day to figure out how to live contrary to his nature.

> *"An organized crime copper told me—I am paraphrasing—*
>
> *'Your boy really gets around. [Kenji] has done very, very, bad things.'*
>
> *Bottom line, in the eyes of law enforcement, Kenji Gallo was seen as a man of evil reputation."*

Anthony "The Animal" Fiato

- Cocaine Trade of Mid-1980s California
- U.S.-based Colombian smuggler has a kilo shipped directly from Colombia for $7,000
- Colombian smuggler sells kilo to California dealer for $12,500
- American dealer breaks up, whacks up, packages, and sells kilo piecemeal for $35,000
- American dealer smuggles kilo to Hawaii and sells it for $47,500

People like to make excuses for evil fucks like the man I used to be because it is too scary to accept the truth. Society needs to think criminals are warped by unhealthy environments and bad upbringings and can therefore be prevented. I laugh at psychiatrists and cops who suggest that I embraced crime in response to textbook emotional scars from my childhood, or environmental influences, or peer pressure. I don't make any excuses. I became a crook because I get high from danger, pain, and violence. I committed crimes for the same reason I used enormous amounts of illegal drugs: it felt good.

Violent crime has always made me giddy. There was nothing in the world funnier to me than a weeping hood wetting his pants and pleading for mercy as I held a gun to his head. As a teenager, I had to stuff my mouth with toilet paper to stop from laughing uncontrollably whenever I went out to stick up a drug dealer, break into a house, do a drive-by, or plant a bomb under a competitor's car. I had to take this precaution or I'd ruin my fearsome appearance by giggling like a little girl.

Even when I am outwardly calm, my body and mind are abuzz with nervous energy, a full-body, full-psyche static assuaged only through perilous aggression, sometimes followed by sedatives like marijuana or GHB. I need chaos to be calm; violence to feel safe. Even had I been born into a different time, place, and family, I would have inevitably discovered this kink in my psyche and entered the underworld, the only place where I could scratch this perverse existential itch.

I was known as a smiling bandit on the streets—a happy-go-lucky neurotic, a joyrider of my psyche's rollercoaster twists and turns. I would ruin people's lives with the can-do attitude and sunny disposition of a motivational speaker or toothy infomercial host. I was one of those people who you can immediately tell just *loves* his job, who practically hops out of bed every morning because he's so enthusiastic to start his day. I was the guy who would threaten to kill you with loose body language and a beaming smile on his face—and mean it.

It's not that I wasn't scared when I was in mortal danger; any violent crook who says he was never scared is a liar or a certified lunatic. I was always scared, but I would be tripping on that fear, driven to a primal hysteria that felt so *good*. I was a chaos addict, a freak who worked himself up into an ape-like fury and attained inexplicable serenity at the edge of insanity.

Violent expression has been a compulsion for me since puberty, a base necessity like food or water. Now that I'm no longer on the street, I train in full-contact martial arts every day, 365 days a year, fighting younger and larger men for hours to exhaust that malignant energy and establish any sort of mental and emotional stability. And you can ask my sparring partners: I still laugh and smile when I fight, even when I'm getting my ass kicked.

Without that daily dose of violence, I gradually lose my self-control and moral restraint like any other junkie jonesing for his fix. I was such a junkie for crime and violence that for years I wondered whether I was a crook by choice or due to a pathetic inability to resist. Now that I have been strictly crime-free for nearly five years, there is no other reasonable conclusion: I was a horrible, exploitative monster by choice, because I was happiest inflicting pain, misfortune, and humiliation on others. I have no alibi, no excuses—I committed crimes for pleasure.

Though I am in most ways an unusual criminal, I ironically am something of a stereotypical native of Orange County, the cradle of California country-club privilege and wealth. Once known as one of the most oppressively Caucasian areas in California, by my adolescence Orange County was starting to be invaded by a semi-assimilated horde of Asian immigrant professionals. The natives viewed my generation as a suburban "Yellow Menace" of Asian kids who, under the merciless pressure of their striving immigrant parents, slaughtered the local kids in the battle for academic supremacy and admission to top universities.

The only difference between my fellow O.C. ricers

and me is that, whereas they displayed superhuman Old World discipline pursuing 4.0 grade point averages and perfect SAT scores, I focused with quiet, scary intensity on becoming a gangster. In my 1986 senior class yearbook, next to all of my classmates basking in their academic achievements, you can see me waving a thick roll of drug money and proclaiming "God Bless Yayo [Cocaine]!"

I was a criminal prodigy. When my fellow sophomores at University High in Irvine were studying for Honors Geometry tests, I was robbing $150,000 worth of uncut cocaine from Pablo Escobar's Medellín Cartel. When my friend Babar was taking pre-law classes at UCLA, I was smuggling hundreds of pounds of marijuana from Hawaii in hidden Plexiglas compartments built into speedboats.

I was a pot dealer at thirteen, a cocaine user at fourteen, a stickup kid and coke dealer at sixteen, a coke smuggler for a Mafia drug trafficker at seventeen, a car-bomber and drive-by shooter at eighteen, the leader of a major narco-trafficking crew and an undercover FBI witness at nineteen, a club owner and accused murderer at twenty, and a porn producer at twenty-one. Orange County had never seen the likes of me.

My poor family was flabbergasted, completely at a loss. I could not have come from a less criminally minded family. I was the product of a mixed-race marriage, my mother a rich white plantation belle from the South and my father a poor first-generation Japanese immigrant. As a small child, my father emigrated from Japan to Spokane, Washington, with his farmer parents. Unsurprisingly, I come from a family of moneymakers and hustlers: within a few years of their arrival, my grandparents owned multiple orange groves and delivery trucks.

This American Dream ended when the Imperial High Command decided to bomb Pearl Harbor. The United States government responded by taking my father and his family into custody and confiscating their businesses, their home, and all of their belongings. FBI head J. Edgar Hoover allegedly fought against the widespread internment of Japanese citizens in concentration camps during World War II; ironically, the Japanese were the one minority race he found trustworthy.

My father's family and around 10,000 other innocent Japanese-Americans were transported like livestock to a fortified camp in Idaho where they lived in makeshift barracks. When he arrived, my father was told that if he were seen anywhere near the barbed wire fences encircling the camp he would be shot on sight—no trial, no jury, no appeal.

Few Japanese-Americans were killed with bullets in these camps. Most were murdered by willful neglect. Refused medical care, my grandmother died of pneumonia surrounded by countless other ill, destitute, desperate American citizens in a fenced-in pigpen. When an army recruiter approached my teenage father and offered him a reprieve from camp life if he joined the military, my father calculated a better chance of survival fighting the Nazis than living as a POW in the U.S. government's race war.

My father's military career ended with a bang—a grenade shattered his teeth, busted his eardrums, and shredded his right arm. The white doctor who was assigned to treat his injuries took one look at him and dismissed him with the recommendation that he hold his rifle with the other arm. Decades later, the government offered my father $20,000 as restitution for confiscating all of his family's property, interning them in a concentration camp, killing his mother, and nearly killing him by refusing to treat the wounds he suffered fighting for his country.

After the war, my father was a great success in the magazine business, first as a graphic artist and then as an entrepreneur in golfing magazines. He met my mother, a cerebral southern brunette with glasses, on the staff of *TV Guide* in the late '60s, where she was a respected businesswoman; shortly afterwards they married. In 1968 I was born to these accomplished, artistic, and ahead-of-their-time parents, the sort of mixed-race yuppie couple that would become a trademark of Orange County.

I was a bright and energetic kid, the kind of pushy little bastard that today would be diagnosed with attention deficit disorder and "cured" with a payload of pharmaceuticals. In the late '70s, I was a student making straight A's and getting behavioral reports that would have made a Hells Angel proud.

I've always bored easily, and in my twenty years as a con man and criminal, I've never met more tiresome fools and frauds than the jackass teachers who wasted my time as a kid. So I was a "bad" kid—a bored kid, a smartass. My parents spent a fortune sending me to the most expensive private schools and invested thousands more on counselors, tutors, athletic coaches, and summer camps. I was just another Asian-American O.C. brat on his chauffeured way to Stanford or UCLA.

Then my parents got divorced and my mischievous bullshit became a pressing crisis. I hadn't changed, but my family had; I was living with a new parent, a stepfather named Jack. Jack had been a hot-shit bomber pilot in World War II and clung to his *Top Gun* self-image even though he'd become a tubby chiropractor living in Pasadena. Then he married a woman with a wiseass half-Jap kid who hated his guts. My antics infuriated Jack, and

I took pleasure in flouting the tight-ass discipline he attempted to enforce in our household. To Jack, my boyish misbehavior was insubordination, a challenge. So he sent me to military school, and like my father, I entered adolescence in military barracks.

I was thirteen when I was dumped at the Army and Navy Academy in Carlsbad, one of the most prestigious and hard-ass military schools in the United States. My life underwent a *Lord of the Flies* shift toward the deranged and cannibalistic. I was just a suburban class clown who liked to annoy people; my sparring partners were harmless ultraliberal private-school teachers and my soft-touch yuppie parents. I was now an inmate of a prison for the most delinquent spawn of California's upper class.

Most of my fellow cadets were sociopaths and, worse, upperclassmen: seventeen- and eighteen-year-old jocks, juiced-up malcontents warped by the environment of sadism and abuse at the academy. I was an undersize thirteen-year-old Japanese kid, a nerd by their standards, and I immediately learned how it felt to get my ass kicked by thugs three times my size. I was hazed relentlessly and with incredible ingenuity and innovation.

When the cadets weren't abusing me, the staff took their turn with the normal boot camp brutality: shaved heads, thousands of pushups, endless drilling, holding your heavy rifle over your head until you pass out. Being trapped in a holding pen administered by jackboot-sniffing military cretins triggered my survival instinct. It was the beginning of my criminal career. I've always loved annoying people, but military school taught me to enjoy hurting people.

I was taught in excruciating sensory detail the power of ridicule, terror, and violence—and that the only antidote to these means of dominance was *better* ridicule, terror, and violence. Surrounded by sociopaths and criminals, I adapted by absorbing and perfecting their behavior. Military school taught me a way of life governed by a simple and all-encompassing ideology: a man should use any means at his disposal without hesitation to obtain dominance over everyone he meets. The only cure for weakness was strength. I believed that aggressive, unprovoked shows of force were always justifiable as self-defense. All that liberal humanist bullshit I was taught in my Orange County private school was supplanted by the law of the jungle: fuck or be fucked.

The miserable and cruel parallel universe of the academy twisted my psyche and alienated me from my family, society, and my assumptions about the fundamental decency of people. My parents and military school superiors taught me a poisonous distrust and loathing for authority, which was always arbitrary, exploitative, and corrupt. No one with a working brain who goes through boot camp should graduate with a molecule of belief in the fairness and competence of the police, the military, or any government that would use such crude instruments to promote its interests. If I could not trust my own mother to protect me from the abuse of the idiots and thugs at military school, then I certainly couldn't trust the nanny state in Washington, D.C., or the local police to protect me from abuse.

My time at military school convinced me that I was alone. Forming a sincere and honest relationship with anybody became impossible. I guess you could say my "normal" emotional and social development stopped at military school, when I was thirteen; I stopped developing as a healthy adult citizen and, first out of self-defense and then out of pleasure, began honing my skills as a predator.

It was my own fault; it was my conscious decision to become a predator. I don't blame my mother or military school or God. I take sole responsibility for my life. There comes a time in any man's life when he will be victimized, and there are two responses: he can embrace the Golden Rule and decide that being victimized is more honorable than victimizing others, or he can decide that he would rather leave a trail of bruised, bloodied, cold bodies in his wake than take shit from anyone ever again. After the academy, I joined the second camp. Fuck everybody but me.

The school that was supposed to reform my delinquent tendencies streamlined and disciplined them; I went from being a disorderly brat into an orderly outlaw. Under the suffocating surveillance of my military school superiors, I learned invaluable street smarts. Every day was a crash course in criminal behavior taught by my barracks comrades, a guerilla army of deranged juvenile criminals intent on flouting authority and smuggling contraband. What hope could the police ever have when I had sharpened my skills getting away with crimes in confined spaces under twenty-four-hour military supervision?

The fact that even my classmates' most brash and reckless misbehavior evaded the notice of the authorities taught me the great immutable rule of the criminal trade: it's extremely easy to get away with crimes as long as you are confident and don't let your nerves telegraph your guilt. Good criminals are all "confidence artists": confidence is ninety percent of a gangster's skill set.

In a frantic, confused, free-for-all world, anyone who convincingly acts like he is doing what he is supposed to be doing will rarely be bothered. It is easy to be believed if you lie with conviction; it's easy to inspire fear when you're fearless; it is easy to avoid arrest if you can credibly portray a man who is unafraid of the cops and their punishments. In my career, I don't think I was investigated, let alone caught, for one out of every 5,000 felonies I committed.

People always ask me how an average-looking Japanese guy could gain entry to the toughest corners of the underworld and be taken seriously by the scariest mafiosi, bikers, and Colombian drug traffickers in America. The answer is simple: I always acted like I belonged. I never acted scared. The only thing crazier than a sophisticated guy like me being tough enough to hang with the underworld's most infamous predators was the idea I could fake that comfort level. Even the best actor can't trick a room full of killers into believing that he's one of them when he isn't. Real recognizes real.

On my very first night at the Army and Navy Academy, my roommate, Sammy, had barely introduced himself before whipping out a tray of cocaine and snorting a line right in our bedroom. I was waylaid with shock—I had no idea what the fuck I had just witnessed. Pretty soon, Sammy and my new friend Frank, a devious Serbian kid, taught me how to make money and win credibility by selling pot.

I started peddling skunk weed, mostly for the buzz and the cred—the monetary returns were shit in that market and at that volume. I would buy a few ounces and break it up into dime bags and make maybe $100, all off a crappy product I had to sell like a door-to-door salesman. It didn't give me a glamorous impression of the criminal trade. When I was fourteen, however, Frank let the genie out of the bottle by slamming my face into a line of cocaine and forcing me to snort. *Holy shit. If this is illegal, I have no interest in being legal.* The die was cast; cocaine convinced me that I wanted to be a professional criminal.

This was 1982, long before crack ghettoized the drug wars. It was very chic, very cool to do cocaine; it was the only drug that made the junkie glamorous. It wasn't bulky, didn't smell, sold itself, and made the user feel awesomely self-confident and cool.

Cocaine was the Midas drug for dealers. Anyone who had a steady supply became enormously rich very quickly. A vagabond punk could become a sultan within months of getting into the coke trade, and his supply of magic white powder made him the hottest guy at every party, allowed him to bypass the line and swagger right into the VIP section of the elite clubs, and turned him into the best friend of socialites and celebrities. Striving to be cool in my new surroundings, I saw that coke was my shortcut to social dominance, money, girls, and power—to escaping my shitty life.

My mom completed her abandonment of me by moving to the East Coast after a couple years, and my father was able to get me released from military school. Instead, I was enrolled at University High School, an ultra-competitive Ivy League farm team. University High was located in Irvine, an incredibly boring, wealthy, and quiet suburb of Orange County that the FBI once rated as the safest city in America.

There is no place in America less suited to aspiring teenage criminals than the conformist, uptight, honor-student heaven of University High, where every moment of every day is lived for the sole purpose of creating the perfect college transcript. It was the most oppressively white place imaginable, with all the successful immigrant families pressuring their children to behave, kiss ass, and get into the right college. It strangled all the joy out of jumpy, easily bored teenage delinquents like me.

The elite California student body naturally included some future celebrities. I was friends with Zack de la Rocha and Tim Commerford, who would go on to form the band Rage Against the Machine. Comedian Will Ferrell was my buddy on the school dance team and started the school reptile club, of which I was a charter member. Will was infamous for applying blackface when the dance team performed at other schools. He later claimed in an interview that his comedy is a product of Irvine being so "safe, master-planned" that he had to be funny to avoid going insane from boredom.

I chose a different outlet. I started looking for trouble by any means necessary. I wanted to be a coke dealer and sought like-minded teenagers, which meant hanging out with a group of no-hope, teenage punk rockers from Santa Ana destined for prison and trailer park life. I was headed for a life in the gutter of criminality when my straitlaced father, of all people, plugged me into California's underworld elite. He wanted the best for me, and little did he know that he was indirectly granting my wish: a place in the Colombian cocaine trade.

Without telling me, my father got me a job as a busboy at a new Japanese restaurant called Setoya—his way of teaching me discipline and keeping me out of trouble. Setoya was an upscale restaurant and club in the Back Bay area of Newport Beach run by a member of the respected Avila restaurant family. The Avila family ran and owned the very successful El Ranchito Mexican restaurant chain, which had a great local reputation. El Ranchito was one of Richard Nixon's favorite restaurants and catered some of his events, which is quite a recommendation considering that the quality of its food had to overcome his contempt for Mexicans. "They steal, they're dishonest" was Nixon's opinion of Mexicans in his White House tapes.

In Joey and Sal Avila's case, Richard Nixon was right: they did steal—up to ten million dollars' worth of cocaine at a time. My father had unwittingly found the best mentors an aspiring gangster could ever have.

Identical twins Joey and Sal Avila grew up middle-class, the heirs to a small family restaurant. As teenagers in the 1960s, they became hell-raising surfers with a taste for narcotics, free love, and gunplay. Joey was the charismatic and ambitious twin, Sal the spaced-out pothead twin. Their identical Julio Iglesias–style Latin heartthrob looks, bad-boy reputations, and incredible surfing skills netted the Avila boys plenty of girlfriends, whom they secretly shared by exchanging wardrobes and identities.

That stopped when a guy whose wife Joey was fucking shattered his face with a beer mug at the El Ranchito in Newport Beach. Joey then hired a Mexican hit man named Lalo, who will become a major character in my story, to shoot the disgruntled husband. The husband survived the shooting, but it left him fidgety and paranoid; Lalo made a point of yelling "Gunshot!" whenever we saw him around.

The Avila Twins were put into business in the 1970s by a group of drug traffickers in Laguna Beach called the Brotherhood of Eternal Love, a drug cartel and legally licensed, registered religion dubbed the "Hippie Mafia" by *Rolling Stone* and known on the streets simply as the Brotherhood. Created and led by '60s counterculture icon Timothy Leary, the Brotherhood ran an international drug-smuggling operation out of a Laguna Beach head shop that reached all the way to Afghanistan, Sri Lanka, and Guatemala. The Brotherhood was probably California's top importer of hashish, LSD, and cocaine from the late '60s to the mid-'70s, a drug empire run by devoted hippie dropouts, Hare Krishnas, flower-children-turned-jaded-criminals, and assorted mercenaries who were just in it for the cash and easy free-love sex. When Timothy Leary himself was jailed along with dozens of Brotherhood members, the group stayed cohesive enough to engineer Leary's escape with help from the militant leftist terrorist organization, the Weather Underground.

Of course, Timothy Leary went on to have a wonderful third career as an FBI informant. After all, Timmy was a smart guy and died a free man. Timmy knew the secret: The Game Is Rigged.

A massive federal and local law enforcement campaign gradually dismembered the Brotherhood, which had already lost its sense of brotherly love as more guns, money, and coke got involved. The remnants of the group retained the connections to hook up the Avila brothers with wholesale volumes of any drug they wanted.

Though Joey and Sal liked to present themselves as laidback hippie surfers who dealt a little grass and a little blow to subsidize their surf-and-party lifestyle, they were in reality major narco-traffickers who smuggled huge amounts of marijuana, cocaine, and heroin into the United States. An uncle in the Mexican federal police, the notoriously corrupt *federales*, ensured that Joey and Sal had no trouble smuggling drugs over the Mexican border. They were suspected of being involved in more than a few shootings, and they would later be accused of stealing somewhere between 400 and 800 kilos of cocaine from Pablo Escobar's cartel—a heist worth over ten million dollars.

Sal Avila, an inscrutable character who became a

theoretically devout Jehovah's Witness, has amused me for the past twenty years with his extremely bad job of pretending that he was just an innocent bystander to his wilder brother Joey's gangster antics. If you believe Sal, all he ever did was surf, pray, and chase pussy while his brother imported heroin from Afghanistan, got into fire-fights with Colombian cartel goons, and nearly got his innocent identical twin brother killed on a weekly basis.

For example, Sal once told me about a surfing trip in Hawaii when a gangster named Bobby Ochoa burst into his place with a shotgun-wielding hit man and held Sal and his friends hostage.

"Where the fuck is Sal Avila and the kilos?" the Ha-waiian gangster asked as he waved his pistol, referring to ten kilos of cocaine that had randomly come into Sal's possession. This was in the late 1970s, when ten kilos of cocaine might net you $500,000 or more in Hawaii.

Having nothing to hide as an upstanding Christian, Sal courageously responded in his best Mexican stoner voice, "Sal Avila? He ain't here, and we don't know noth-ing about no kilos." As Sal said this, a clean-cut civilian friend who had slept through Bobby Ochoa's arrival woke up and asked, "What the fuck's going on?" Bobby Ochoa answered the groggy surfer's question by shooting him in the skull at close range and tossing his body in the ocean. "When you see Sal, tell him that was for him," said Bobby after pulling the trigger.

Sal told me this story decades later as if it were an ev-eryday occurrence for people to come into half a million dollars' worth of coke and have Hawaiian drug-runners hunt them down by name and kill their friends.

Sal then recounted how he had later been held hos-tage at an El Ranchito by *another* cocaine smuggler and hit-man duo. The smuggler threatened to kill Sal the

Innocent if he did not convince Joey to return three kilos of cocaine he had requisitioned as payment for securing the return of a larger shipment of stolen kilos. Luckily for Sal, who claimed to be "just going about my business," Joey saved the day by arriving with a pistol stuffed under his waistband and two vanloads of shotgun-brandishing Hawaiians as backup. According to Sal, Joey made his entrance into El Ranchito by grabbing the gun tucked into his jeans, kicking open the door, and announcing his willingness to "shoot it out right here"—reckless behavior that Sal, with a theatrical *"¡ay Dios mio!"* look to the heavens, claimed was very traumatic for him to endure.

In reality, both Sal and Joey were gangsters for nearly two decades—though, in Sal's defense, he was always the less competent, less dangerous, and less determined of the two. By 1977, Joey was a major cocaine and heroin smuggler, organizing his cadre of surfing buddies into a cartel and appointing his *federale* uncle in Mexico as his liaison with the nascent Colombian cartels. Joey was so respected on the streets that, when rumors began circulating that he would go to war against Alfredo Tavera, another Southern California drug kingpin, the chief of the Newport Beach Police Department humbly requested a meeting through Joey's father and, in the company of Sal and Alfredo, respectfully pled for Joey to exercise restraint. Alfredo and Joey squashed their beef, becoming good enough friends that Joey for a time named the club above Setoya "Tavilas," a play on their names.

Another sign of Joey's standing was the level of firepower that the local authorities retained when they had no choice but to confront him. In the '70s, the Avila brothers scandalized Orange County with the lifestyle they cultivated at their ranch in Costa Mesa. Dubbed the "Animal Farm," the Avilas' ranch became the party bunker and headquarters for the dealers, addicts, bikers, and outlaws of Southern California. When the police finally felt compelled to search the Animal Farm, they called in a detachment of Marines from Camp Pendleton to help them storm the compound. It's not every day that the police call in the United States Marine Corps to lay siege, so it was great street PR for Joey and Sal.

Though the Avilas were active everywhere from Afghanistan to Anaheim, their main business involved buying cocaine in Peru and Colombia and shipping it via Tahiti to Hawaii. In Hawaii, the cocaine would be packaged and shipped to the mainland or allegedly sold to the Black Trunk Gang, a tough group of surfer gangsters led by a wild Brooklyn kid named Edward "Fast Eddie" Rothman. Today, Fast Eddie is a legitimate millionaire, the founder of the Da Hui surf club and its successful apparel brand and the father of professional surfers.

The Avilas' operation in Hawaii with the Black Trunk Gang was exposed when a car transporting ten kilos of cocaine worth about $500,000 crashed and was discovered by law enforcement. A massive DEA investigation was initiated to bring down the entire network. The feds managed to flip an instrumental player in the Avilas' crew and transferred him into Witness Protection, but he was soon found shot dead right in front of Joey's Newport Beach restaurant.

This was more than the tame local scene could handle, causing pandemonium on the streets, with all manner of drug-fueled panic and paranoia. When I was growing up, there were a lot of conspiracy theories and rumors swirling around Joey, including stories about murders and one instance where a member of Avila's crew nodded off and drove his Stutz Bearcat with over a million dollars' worth of heroin in the trunk off the road.

Spooked by the rumors of an imminent cartel melt-down, the feds went ahead and pressed charges against Joey and his crew with an uncharacteristically less-than-airtight case. The DEA dubbed Joey's operation the "Tahitian Connection" and trumped it onto front pages across California. They wanted Joey's head for the murdered witness.

The now very rich and connected Avila family knew how to give battle on the government's own terms. The brothers hired F. Lee Bailey, the high-powered attorney of Richard Nixon, Patty Hearst, the Boston Strangler, and later O. J. Simpson, to defend them at trial. According to Joey, the cost included $150,000 in off-the-books payoffs delivered discreetly in a duffel bag to Bailey's office. The Avilas also enlisted the expert help of a paralegal whose specialty was poking holes in drug trafficking cases; within a decade, that paralegal would be the biggest cocaine dealer on the West Coast. His name was Michael Marvich, a wizened Californian ex-con with a rap sheet that stretched back to the Great Depression. As I would learn, "Big Mike" Marvich tended to win at anything he decided was worth contesting.

The prosecution of the Avila brothers was a decisive rout; the judge threw out the case. Joey returned to holding court at his various restaurants. Setoya replaced the Animal Farm as the headquarters and favorite hangout of every local drug dealer and trafficker in Orange County. *This* was the restaurant where my dad got me a job bussing tables for $1.75 an hour. His attempt to keep my nose clean succeeded: at the age of fourteen, my nose was getting a nightly polish from the purest uncut cocaine in America.

Outwardly, Setoya was a nondescript, strip-mall sushi bar in a rich neighborhood. On the side of the strip mall was an El Ranchito location, which allowed Sal and Joey to watch over two businesses at once. They lived nearby, one twin inside a wealthy gated community and the other twin just outside the gates. From the street, there was little indication that the second floor of Setoya was a rollicking dance club or that the sushi bar was a den of international organized crime. As far as I knew, I was showing up to be a busboy at a very boring yuppie restaurant.

I remember the day I started working at Setoya. Following my father's stereotypical Japanese businessman advice, I arrived ridiculously early. Joey, being a playboy cocaine trafficker, was in no rush to get to the job, and his staff knew his habits well enough to show up late as well. I was left standing alone for hours in the tiny parking lot waiting for someone to unlock the doors.

A brand-new blue Cadillac glided into the parking lot and smoothly purred into a spot. Out stepped Joey Avila in a dark sport coat and silk shirt, looking every bit the Latin movie star. He was about 5'10", with brown eyes, a charismatic smile, and this loose, indifferent stride that radiated confidence. He walked up to me, flashed a cinematic smile, shook my hand, and led me into the restaurant. I liked him immediately; everybody liked Joey. He possessed an innate charm that was almost hypnotizing; I would have followed him into battle within ten minutes of meeting him.

A few weeks after I started at the restaurant, Joey, a congenital playboy, announced to an audience full of rolling eyes that he was getting married. It was impossible to take him seriously. On his wedding day, I walked into his office to discover him fucking a waitress on his desk. He had his share of marriages and more than his share of girlfriends—some gorgeous, some ugly, some mass murderers, some the wives of mass murderers. He wasn't particular.

Joey and I quickly bonded. We were very much alike: two smart guys from comfortable minority backgrounds who were insensibly attracted to the criminal lifestyle. Like a mischievous older brother who gets off on telling his younger brother *only* the things that he shouldn't, Joey enjoyed being a bad influence on me, pulling me aside and telling me tall tales of his criminal career and teaching me all the little tricks he had learned. Since Joey and I also shared a love for boxing and martial arts, we were always talking about my training in Jeet Kune Do and Joey's background as a boxer. Occasionally, I'd bring some training mitts to Setoya, and we'd spar a little out back.

I idolized Joey; he was by far the coolest person I had ever met. He was like James Bond to me. He seemed to have achieved the impossible aspiration of every teenage boy, to be both the most feared and the most popular badass around. Even more incredible to me was that Joey and Sal honestly seemed like two nice, friendly dudes who would rather have fun with someone than rob or exploit him. They weren't mean or vindictive; the drug trade was just a game to them. Joey made it look like I could be a gangster *and* a good person, taking away any lingering misgivings I may have had about following in his footsteps. Watching Joey swagger through life with his hot girlfriends, gangster buddies, new sports cars, and ever-present entourage dispelled any notion I had of being a normal civilian. I wanted to be a playboy gangster just like Joey Avila, and I pursued that goal with all of my abilities.

Seeing that my talent was wasted as a busboy, Joey recast me as Setoya's booze and cigarette gopher. Since the restaurant had no liquor license, it became my job to go around to all the crooks and take their orders for booze and cigarettes from the liquor store in the strip mall. This job allowed me to network with basically the entire Orange County drug trade, so it took me only a few weeks to secure my entry into the cocaine business.

I earned a mere $196 a month working for minimum wage at the restaurant, so the money I made dealing coke was mind-boggling. I had a steady supply from a hardened dealer nicknamed Roach with jaundiced killer eyes and half his face gone from a gunshot wound, and the price was right because he moved heavy weight.

I would buy these flat slabs right from a kilo with very little powder in the bag—the finest coke available in America. Good cocaine is flaky, like pearl shale, almost translucent, slightly pink, very soft. I would test it by rubbing it between my index finger and thumb; if the coke was good, my skin would absorb it and any cut would fall off like chalk. I used to buy ounces and then add maybe two grams of filler or "cut" to an ounce of cocaine to increase profits, a process called "whacking up" or "stepping on" the cocaine.

I was never too greedy, so my cocaine stayed comparatively pure, and I quickly built up a regular clientele. I would buy an ounce of coke for $1,200 and four or more ounces at $800 apiece; I made about $2,000 for every ounce I sold, so the profits were great. In those days, the life was a lot slower; there were no pagers, and pay phones cost a dime, so I used to carry rolls of dimes to make all my calls. There weren't even ATMs back then! People today would go crazy if they couldn't reach their dealer or withdraw cash right away. In those days dealers like me were used to staying put so that we could always be found.

At fifteen, I thought I was a big-time coke dealer and decided that I needed a gun. I bought my first pistol, an old, beat-up .32 semiautomatic, from a guy in Santa Ana. I had only five bullets, but it was a pistol, the start of an arsenal that would one day reach absurd proportions. I was beginning to realize that I had a real fetish for weapons and violence.

> *"Everyone was terrified of Kenny in high school. They all knew the type of crimes he committed, and they thought he was just cold-blooded and crazy. Not stupid crazy, but diabolical crazy. He was known as the last person you ever wanted to make your enemy."*
>
> "Chuck Browntooth"
> Road captain of the Vagos outlaw motorcycle gang

I was hanging out with a lowlife punk gang from Santa Ana called the League, and they gave me a tip about a guy in San Pedro who had a half-pound of cocaine that we could rob. Without even giving it much thought, I decided that I'd lead the group to rob the guy since I had a piece. I was too young, stupid, and reckless to think twice about the huge personal risk I was embracing by becoming a stickup kid. At that point, crime just seemed so *easy*—it felt stupid not to take any opportunity that came to me.

I got a brown UPS windbreaker, a clipboard, and a parcel with a hole in the bottom in which to hide my gun. As I approached the door, I thought happy thoughts so that I would present a harmless civilian face to the guy looking through the peephole. He would just see a young Asian kid working for UPS. When he opened the door, I asked if he was Tom, and he said yes; that was all

I needed to hear. I dropped the package and slammed my pistol in his face. Oh, God, I still remember how good it felt when the steel smacked his forehead. That's when I first learned I would need to stuff toilet paper in my mouth to plug up my laughter.

Tom wilted and whimpered as I erupted into a fit of giggles. I pushed him inside while my backup, a jacked-up skinhead named Kurt, came inside behind me. Kurt slapped the guy and asked who else was in the house. Tom told us that his brother was in a downstairs room, so we made him lead us to his brother while I covered him with the pistol. Kurt socked the brother in the face as soon as we walked into his room, and I jammed my pistol into his mouth.

We must have made a good first impression because he immediately gave up $12,000 worth of cocaine and a load of cash and jewels. We celebrated the score by holding parties for our friends all summer long in hotel rooms, far from our parents and the local beat cops looking to meet their quota hassling teens for juvenile delinquency misdemeanors like underage drinking, loitering, pranks, and brawling.

It was the beginning of a major disconnect in my life. I was a baby kingpin at night and a suburban high school student by day. To my friends, I was an aspiring Pablo Escobar; to my father, I was destined to be a doctor or lawyer. He already had my spot picked out at the New Mexico Military Institute; my future at that university was the one thing my estranged parents still agreed on.

I was a thick, muscle-bound kid with a lot of street-fight experience and martial arts training; I earned the nickname "Kenji Snaps" because of my habit for settling any disagreement or problem with sudden outbursts of violence. I gave off such a chill, easygoing vibe that my thunderous fits of rage came as a shock to most people; hence the "Snaps." It was eventually shortened to "Kenji" (健児), a Japanese derivative of my birth name, Ken, as my social circle became accustomed to these fits. I had learned that I could get anything I wanted through violence. All I ever had to do was flash my gun, maybe throw in a pistol whip or two, and anything I wanted was mine.

Ask around Orange County underworld circles; the name Kenji is still good. It still carries muscle.

The Irvine beat cops weren't prepared for serious criminal misbehavior and, though I was harassed, I mostly got away with everything. Even the few times I got caught, the small-time juvenile repercussions were nowhere near heavy enough to make me back away from the fun I was having. For example, I was sentenced to home arrest when I was fifteen for beating up a twenty-one-year-old in one of my rages. Being sentenced to chill in my room and smoke blunts for a couple weeks didn't deter me from nonstop partying and violence.

Once I returned to the street, I hung out every night at Joey's restaurant as a customer, using a fake ID to drink and party with the guys there as an equal. I even lost my virginity to the same waitress I had caught Joey fucking on his wedding day, a pretty Japanese part-time model who would go on to be some rich guy's trophy wife. Things were already crazy, but it was only the beginning.

My first real promotion in the criminal world came when I started working for a major drug dealer from Miami named Kenny DiMartini. Kenny was a stereotypical Miami guido drug dealer: short, skinny, temperamental, fast-talking, eager to display his gold chains and hairy chest, quick to flash his piece—a real asshole. Kenny was always bragging with wired eyes about his uncle, a made guy in the Colombo Family who got killed for saying the wrong thing about boss Carmine "The Snake" Persico. It was the first time I had heard the name "Persico," and the story should have served as a warning. It's funny: everything I'd ever heard about the Colombos was atrocious, yet it only drew me to them further.

Kenny was stupendously rich from his coke business, with all the typical coke-dealer perks: the sports cars, the electronics, the big fat gaudy mansion, the drug dealer–size pool, the sexy-ass wife. Kenny was also crazy and extremely volatile from all the coke he snorted. Kenny saw that I was fearless, tough, and, best of all, demographically desirable, an eager drug smuggler who looked like a studious middle-class Asian kid.

Since you could travel in the '80s without having to show your identification, I would buy a plane ticket under a stranger's name. I packed light: nothing but my backpack. Hiding Kenny's kilos beneath pencils, pens, and books in my backpack, I would dress casually and read books as I waited for my plane. The security checks were a joke; all they looked for were guns. Once I deplaned at my destination, I'd spend an hour or two distributing DiMartini's uncut kilos to a few prearranged dealers, picking up anywhere from $20,000 to $50,000 per kilo, depending on the market. With the tightly bound blocks of cash in my backpack, I'd head right back to the airport and fly home.

Since I could pass for a local, I smuggled and distributed cocaine throughout Kenny's Hawaiian market without drawing any attention. In my senior year of high school, Kenny hired me full-time. He would purchase the drugs from Colombian wholesalers in California, and I would distribute them in Colorado, Hawaii, and countless places in between. While the rest of my class was graduating and taking their senior trip to Jamaica, I was in Hawaii dropping off kilos of cocaine and picking up fifty-pound bags of marijuana. My parents' plan to enroll me at the New Mexico Military Institute for college was aborted.

The Hawaiian marijuana route was one of my favorites. Normally, I would fly into Maui with a kilo of Kenny's cocaine and drive to Lahaina, the biggest tourist town in West Maui, where I'd sell the kilo at an enormous profit thanks to the scarcity of cocaine in Hawaii.

However, I would occasionally take my kilos to the Big Island and drive from Hilo to a sleepy village called Pahoa. This tiny Polynesian community was devoted almost entirely to the harvest of elite marijuana. It was hardly a secret: the local females would throw raucous parties organized around the communal clipping of the marijuana leaves, laughing, singing, telling bawdy stories, dancing, and gossiping all the while. It was a family atmosphere, very pre-colonial and innocent. I would drive to Pahoa with a couple of kilos and drive away with garbage bags stuffed with harvest-fresh, high-quality purple marijuana leaves, with all the little buds packed in as well.

Unlike most pot smuggling, which yielded very low returns, the Pahoa shipments were real moneymakers thanks to the huge volume and world-class quality of the pot. Kenny had a clientele of older and mainly Jewish lawyers and doctors who would pay $4,000 per pound for our gourmet Pahoan weed. Since Kenny could exchange a kilo of Colombian cocaine in Hawaii for about fifteen pounds of pot, his $12,500 cocaine purchase in California could be flipped for $60,000 of Hawaiian marijuana with the only expenses being my cut of the money and my airfare.

One of the most interesting locals in Pahoa was a South African gang leader and speedboat manufacturer who I'll call "Ben." Ben was the boss of a paramilitary crew of former army and secret police toughs who fled South Africa when it became clear that Apartheid would end. As soon as terrorizing blacks was no longer part of their job description, these Boer thugs followed Ben to Hawaii, where they took up marijuana farming and distribution. Ben's crew was looking for a trading partner on the mainland who would be willing to exchange bulk amounts of quality uncut cocaine for dump-truck-size shipments of plentiful Hawaiian *daga* (Afrikaans slang for pot). In Kenny DiMartini, Ben found his trading partner.

Kenny liked the idea of expanding the Pahoa pot trade because it combined great profits with a lower law enforcement profile, lower potential jail sentences, and far less murderous competition than the cocaine trade. After Ben reached out, Kenny sent his hot blonde, coke-banshee wife, who I'll call "Diane," to Hawaii with me to work out the details. Ben's plan for overcoming the logistical challenges that came with trafficking huge volumes of marijuana was brilliant: he would package hundreds of pounds of Pahoan marijuana into airtight Plexiglas compartments within the speedboats he built and have the speedboats shipped to California. Diane and I agreed to the deal immediately and spent the rest of our "business trip" drinking and partying.

Kenny, being a paranoid coke dealer, was still worried that law enforcement could detect the pot in Ben's boats. To prove that the acrylic glass would prevent anyone from finding the pot, Ben packaged fifty pounds of it into glass containers and sent it through the rigorous drug-screeners at FedEx to California; the majority of the marijuana was delivered without any questions. If his packages could pass through FedEx without trouble, the chances of anyone finding marijuana in the bow of a speedboat was infinitesimal. Kenny agreed to the deal.

Had Kenny DiMartini been a competent criminal, the deal would have made him millions—today Ben's guys are all retired multimillionaires who own surfing and home fitness companies. They didn't make that money with Kenny, however, because Kenny's business almost immediately began to fall apart.

Years of success had transformed him into the usual '80s *Scarface* stereotype, constantly sweating and screaming and gritting his teeth and panicking from using too much of his own stash. He got sloppy and was caught in the Miami Airport with coke. He had endless trouble with Diane, who was turning into a rampaging coke princess with a million-dollar-a-year shopping addiction and a flare for shit-talking her husband at every opportunity. With felonies, a bad addiction, and a demon wife wearing him down, Kenny made a mess of his business.

Meanwhile, I was learning the trade and expanding my business. Kenny trusted me not only to handle his distribution network in Hawaii but also in Denver, Aspen, and Dallas. I made great cash with him, and he sold me coke for my clients at extremely low prices, which made it effortless for me to build up my own customer base and network. Though I snorted a lot of coke and drank a lot of booze, I was young and fresh enough to keep it under control, unlike my ragged, bug-eyed boss.

Besides, the drugs and booze helped me overcome the anxieties of my inexperience; cocaine made me crazy, daring, and fearless. I was getting away with it, getting a big head, and I began to think that Kenny wasn't worthy of being my partner, let alone my boss.

I decided to break away from Kenny and go out on my own. My first step was to take down one of his affiliates, a guy named Tim who stored over 100 pounds of Kenny's pot in his Orange County garage—a mammoth score at the prices Pahoan pot commanded. The challenge was that Tom's garage was situated directly across the street from the O.C. Sheriff's substation.

I had learned how to pick locks from some of my sleazy friends, so I brought my picks and a group of young accomplices to the garage one night. I was nervous, thinking about the squadron of police sitting at their desks right across the street, but I managed to maintain my cool and pick the lock in under four minutes. After that, it was too easy; we simply grabbed the bales of pot and stashed them in a large truck we had brought to carry it away. But our luck wasn't as good as it first looked; instead of the pristine Hawaiian bud I expected, the pot was crappy Mexican dirt weed, 120 pounds of it.

One hundred and twenty pounds of Pahoan weed at $4,000 a pound would have sold for half a million dollars; I was barely able to squeak out a couple thousand selling my share of this crap weed at $125 a pound. In retrospect, it was still great for ten minutes of work. I got away with it, but my Mexican-American friend, Babar, refused to follow my advice and sell his share immediately, and he was caught at his UCLA frat house with this huge bag of pot. With a glittering career as a criminal defense attorney in his future, he sold me out to the cops to minimize the charges, but I forgave him for the sake of my social life and street income. Babar was not always a reliable friend, but he was a reliable partier and money-maker.

In a trend that would continue for the rest of my criminal career, the woman I was seeing would give me a huge break on the streets. When Kenny's wife, Diane, finally left him, Kenny spent all of his free time chasing Adena, a tall chica with dark brown hair and a killer body who used to live with Tim, the drug dealer I had just robbed. I would drive Adena home each night after Kenny failed to seduce her, even after throwing rolls of cash at her over dinner. One night on our way to the Newport Beach home where she was staying with a friend, we stopped so she could buy some booze. Adena suggested that I keep her company while she drank, which seemed like a good idea to me; I ended up fucking her all night long on her friend's floor.

Little did I know that many of my friends were fucking Adena too. She may have had a thing for teenagers—or anyone besides Kenny DiMartini. I apparently did her the best, however, because Adena decided to hook me up (and me alone) with one of Kenny's big cocaine suppliers.

Gladis was a Colombian woman in her forties who moved bulk shipments of cocaine to a number of heavy California dealers. One day Adena and I called Gladis from a pay phone at Fashion Island in Newport Beach to set up an introduction, and she called back right away and agreed to come down and meet me. Gladis had great coke at great prices, and better yet she would front me a kilo at no charge to get started. Had I been a jerkoff like a lot of reckless '80s coke dealers, I would've partied away all the coke myself and been left owing Gladis and her Colombian friends money. Instead, thanks to military school, I was disciplined and efficient, making huge profits and always maintaining cash reserves and a steady cash flow. With Gladis on my side, I no longer needed Kenny.

I was in business.

"Kenji's crew, man, well, there was Kenny [Gallo, Kenji], Babar, Frank, Phil, Keith, Clyde, y'know. Babar was like Kenny's main guy since Babar never left his side. He never left the dude alone. He would follow Kenny around like a dog. Babar was like his right-hand flunky. When Kenny got a new Rolex, he gave Babar his old one, and it was like the honor of that dude's life. Frank was just a rich little spoiled kid who could scam and make money. Keith was a construction guy, loved to party, just a crazy dude who would talk a lot of shit to people and then get his ass whooped. Guy always needed backup because he was a fuckup machine. Clyde was obsessed with weapons, a big, thick, tough dude. He always loved to talk about guns and weapons and things. He was the toughest dude—besides me, no doubt, no doubt."

Greg Benjamin
Convicted of murder while in Kenji's crew

"Clyde and Greg were big, tough guys, but Keith was really tough in his own right. Keith was completely crazy—I mean crazy—and loved to fight. I remember one time we were at a party where someone talked to Keith's girlfriend, and drunk Keith, who was just a jealous as hell guy, picked the dude up and just put him through a wall. The guy was down, but, though Keith's head had been the first thing to go through the sheetrock, he just walked back through the hole in the wall, brushed the sheetrock off his head, and asked for another beer like nothing had happened."

Frank

"You know, looking back, we were just crazy, man. Crazy. It's insane all the drug deals, robberies, fights, car bombings, drive-bys that went down. We were completely out of our minds, bro. All I wanted was money and pussy, and I got lots of both."

Babar

"I was a drunk, a junkie, a mess. I wasn't alone; all of us were on drugs—teenagers on drugs. We were all a mess. That shows you how brilliant a leader Kenny was: he took these misfits and turned them into a tight crew."

Phil

With my own steady supply of cocaine, I could now delegate business to my friends and expand my criminal operations. In the words of a local police document I own, I created "a semi-organized crime outfit," a euphemism for a drug cartel of reckless teenage cokeheads. We were an Orange County crime family: wealthy, educated, multicultural, and possessed of an arrogant belief that suburban kids like us were immune to the law, which existed mainly to punish ghetto street criminals.

My first recruit was my friend from military school, Frank, to whom I owed my fascination with cocaine and crime in the first place. Frank was a tall, medium-build Serbian kid who grew up in what seemed to me a literal palace; his family was filthy rich even by Orange County standards. Despite the privileged background and the most supportive parents imaginable, Frank was still a congenital fuckup. A born petty crook, Frank was a ruthless, devious little shithead with a knack for making quick money and spending it quicker. Frank was the type of short-money crook who would discover a goose that laid golden eggs, beat the shit out of it for laying the eggs too slowly, and then microwave it for lunch.

Phil was another half-ass crook with drug, alcohol, and girl problems. Phil was funny because his mom was the real criminal talent in the family. That woman was *lowdown*—she referred dealers and smugglers to us, drove me to drug deals, and would cover for me when I was under house arrest so I could leave and commit crimes.

Phil's mom was a tiny, squat, clay-red Mayan gnome, while her son was this strapping Ken Doll model with a frosted blond mullet. It was no great mystery why Phil looked like Robert Redford while his parents looked like Yucatan jungle savages. I always told Phil that he was adopted, though the family denied it vehemently, as if two kangaroos could give birth to an eagle. I had a lot of fun busting Phil's balls over his miraculous conception.

"Babar" (name changed to protect the guilty) was my drug crew's token Latino, the Dr. Gonzo in my teenage *Fear and Loathing in Las Vegas*. An undergraduate at UCLA with aspirations of becoming a really shitty attorney, Babar was the type of Chicano lothario whose *telenovela* good looks let him get away with being a complete sleazebag and degenerate. Fueled by a diet of cocaine and designer drugs, Babar was an insatiable, indiscriminate pussy hound who earned himself many, many well-deserved beatings from furious boyfriends. Despite his relentless tough-talk and self-mythologizing, Babar was a vag who froze up whenever things became life-or-death. I didn't hold Babar's lack of muscle against him: there were plenty of niches in the underworld ecosystem, and Babar was a passable dealer and burglar. He didn't need to be a badass to be useful.

If anything, I had a surplus of badasses in my crew. My unholy trinity of violent sociopaths was Keith, Greg, and Clyde. Keith was freakishly ugly, a muscular 220-pound kid with a prematurely balding head and a face like Lon Chaney's *Phantom of the Opera*. We called Keith "Alcoholic Popeye": when he got drunk, Keith's muscles popped, his eyes turned red, and he suddenly became preposterously strong, aggressive, and immune to pain. Keith was just ridiculous; he was *that* guy who always got too drunk and ruined every party. It was impossible to control or even contain Keith when he was on a bender.

Since we couldn't hope to stop Keith's rampages, we learned to enjoy them. They added an edge of danger and slapstick hilarity to every night on the town, since we were all just waiting for the Incredibly Drunk Hulk to arrive. We even had a dead-accurate method of timing Keith's blowups: the second Keith became too drunk to hold his head upright, and his chin started bouncing off his chest, then it was mere moments before someone, *anyone*, was going to get hurt.

Joining Keith somewhere in the lower reaches of the human evolutionary scale was my Crip caveman Greg. Greg was a 6'3", 240-pound black kid with elite amateur wrestling, high school football, and tae kwon do credentials who had close ties to the Shotgun Crips black street gang. He was just an awesome physical specimen, a jacked-up, Bo Jackson–style athlete whose mere presence would cause white dealers to shit themselves.

Greg's specialty was just wrecking guys, beating them until they were concussed, toothless, and half-blind. Physically, Greg was a juggernaut; mentally, however, he was pretty much hopeless. Because he was the one black kid in my crew, we gave him a lot of shit; we treated him like a feral jungle beast granted the gift of speech. Don't get me wrong, Greg was the sort of barbaric thug who would fuck people up for their shoes or slap someone around for a free Big Mac and fries. When Mike Tyson was at his peak as undefeated heavyweight boxing champion and Scariest Man on the Planet, Greg promised to find Tyson and kick his ass if we paid him $500. Greg was great muscle, completely fearless and obedient, but he needed to be very carefully supervised.

Besides me, the only member of my crew who needed neither supervision nor backup was my best friend, Lee Matthew Clyde, whom we all called Clyde. Clyde was another Marine friend from military school, a big, bloodthirsty, corn-fed motherfucker with a black belt who could fight, shoot, and party as hard as anyone. I had admired Clyde dating back to when, at the age of fourteen, he repeatedly stabbed a man in the chest at a McDonald's for trying to beat him up—a case of "self-defense."

That same year in military school, Clyde became a legend as the freshman who, in the course of beating the crap out of a senior, somehow managed to kick both himself and the senior *through a window.*

One of my favorite stories about Clyde happened when he went to a party with Greg. This was a chilled-out party full of rich college kids, so when a drunk preppy started bragging about how tough he was, he could not have imagined that he was seconds away from receiving *the* beatdown of his life. Offended that anyone would talk shit in their presence, Clyde and Greg matter-of-factly began to deliver a professional, scrupulous, award-winning asskicking; they didn't leave a tooth unchipped or a rib uncracked. This wasn't a suburbs beatdown; this wasn't even a ghetto beatdown; this was a Gestapo jackboot beatdown.

The Republican trust-fund kids at this party were stunned, to say the least. After the asskicking was well and truly finished, Clyde announced that the party was fucking lame anyway and left with Greg.

This is where the story gets funny: Clyde's pistol slipped out of his pants while he was beating the kid. As he and Greg were driving away, Clyde noticed it was gone and started to panic. Any pistol Clyde owned for more than a few days saw *action;* one that fell from his pocket into the hands of a police forensic team might solve a dozen cold cases. Minutes after they had left, Clyde returned to the party and kicked down the door of the house brandishing a sawed-off, 12-gauge shotgun. Those kids did not see this *Terminator* shit coming. Clyde and Greg held the party hostage, threatening to kill everyone unless someone ratted out the person who took Clyde's gun. Eventually they realized it had fallen—unnoticed—under the couch. Greg and Clyde made a fence-jumping, mad-dash escape seconds before the police stormed the house.

Clyde loved guns, loved bombs, loved to fight, and loved to go balls-out on the street; he did a number of bombings and drive-by shootings for me. He was an incredible presence, six feet and two inches of animosity and muscle, but he was also as nice, smart, and loyal a guy as you could ever meet. He'd probably be a decorated Marine if things had turned out differently; his friend in my crew, Phil, turned into a war hero after he cleaned himself up. Clyde was just a great guy who loved violence.

Then there was me: the laughing smartass with a pistol in my hand and a burgeoning passion for violent hijinks. Though I was small by my crew's standards—only about 5'8" and 160 pounds—I was the most dangerous member of my crew for two simple reasons: I was the smartest, and I enjoyed hurting people the most. I mean I *really* enjoyed hurting people—as in laugh-about-it-to-this-day enjoyed it, borderline-erotically enjoyed it.

I never rushed violence. I took my time to make sure it was *special*. I relished the opportunity to inflict pain so much that I spent my time in school daydreaming new and ingenious ways to fuck someone up.

For example, I used to mix kerosene or turpentine with food coloring until it looked like Mountain Dew, then poured it into plastic Mountain Dew bottles. When someone crossed me, I'd unscrew the cap, splash him in the face, and toss my ignited lighter at him. You make a reputation quickly when you set motherfuckers on fire.

And, believe it or not, my tactics were hardly the most ruthless in Orange County in the '80s. In fact, I was an amateur. The most vicious, cruel, and prolific murderer in the history of the Colombian cocaine trade was not only in town but also a frequent visitor of Setoya . . . and Joey Avila's bed.

Griselda Blanco de Trujillo was the queen of the California cocaine trade, an international legend as feared as any man. Growing up as a starving South American street urchin, Griselda immigrated to New York City and in 1971 started one of the first cocaine trafficking networks in America. A rapacious bisexual, her preferred smuggling method was to use pretty female mules to carry her drugs through customs in special lingerie; her preferred method of handling street business was to kill at the first sign of trouble, dismember the bodies, and dump the remains on the side of the road, sometimes in gift-wrapped boxes.

The DEA directly tied Griselda to over forty homicides, many by her own hand; she is rumored to have ordered hundreds and hundreds more. She can take credit for inventing the standard M.O. for cocaine-cowboy killings: two men on a motorcycle, one driving the bike and the guy behind him firing a MAC-10 machine pistol. In the late '70s, Griselda moved her operation to Miami, where she would earn international infamy.

In Miami, Griselda trained a paramilitary squad of hit men to impose her will on the local drug trade. To enter her crew, each prospective hit man was required to kill someone and bring back a body part to Griselda as proof. Griselda recruited only the most feral, unhinged, violent sociopaths for her personal army; she wanted killers who slaughtered on command, no matter how dubious the reason or how sympathetic the victim. She offered bonuses for killing women and children, and once ordered a top hit man to stab an enemy in the middle of an airport with a bayonet—just because the idea amused her.

Griselda's magnum opus was the 1979 Dadeland Massacre, the infamously sloppy and over-the-top hit at a Miami mall that brought the Colombian coke cartels to national prominence. Griselda's hit men took a white Ford Econovan, inscribed the motto "Happy Time Complete Party Supply" on its side, steel-reinforced the walls and outfitted them with gun ports, and drove it to the liquor store where Griselda was supposed to meet two rival dealers. Instead of Griselda in all her Miss Piggy glory, the dealers were met by two Colombian commandos with machine guns and bulletproof vests who pounced from the van and sprayed them with bullets in broad daylight. Then the two coked-out Colombians, for whatever reason, thought it would be a wise tactical move to shower the civilian-filled parking lot with 100 or so rounds of ammunition while screaming hysterically in Spanglish.

Griselda's Dadeland Massacre created America's fascination with the "cocaine cowboys" of Miami and inspired both *Scarface* and *Miami Vice*. However, her stupendously bloody business practices soon attracted far too much heat in Miami, so she moved her cartel and four sons to Irvine to lie low. Her sons were no better: they had once sawed off a man's head at their mom's request.

Griselda was already a legend by the time I met her. Some called her "The Black Widow" since she had killed three of her husbands; some called her "The Godmother" because she loved *The Godfather* so much that she named one of her sons Michael Corleone. My crew was unsatisfied with these names and dubbed her "Betty"; later we adopted the nickname that competing cocaine kingpin Mike Marvich gave her, "Mama Coca." Everyone besides Mike Marvich was terrified of Mama Coca; she'd kill over absolutely anything, and her history showed that she'd go after you with incredible firepower if you even vaguely challenged or annoyed her.

According to numerous people I trust, the only person to really get close to Mama Coca was Joey Avila—he got close enough to fuck her. Joey didn't want Griselda's body; he wanted the "preferred customer" discount on Griselda's cocaine. That goes to show how much a *dog* and a daredevil Joey Avila was. The man who could get any model or Hollywood actress chose to fuck the most dangerous woman in the world—a fat mass-murderer with a penchant for killing her lovers. Though cocaine definitely played a part, knowing Joey, I think a big factor was probably just the thrill, the danger, the showoff stupidity of it. Joey was wild and lowdown and, for a while, really lucky.

I'd see Mama Coca and two of her sons, Osvaldo

and Dixon, all the time at the club above Setoya. They met there with other cocaine dealers and gangsters. They were just a few of the luminaries that Joey attracted to his underworld Studio 57; at Setoya you would regularly see everyone from L.A. Mafia boss Michael "Mike Rizzi" Rizzitello and Orange County's resident mafioso "Fat Bobby" Paduano to Griselda to the Medellín Cartel's local viceroy, Mike Marvich.

My favorites were the Colombians, all dressed up in thousands of dollars' worth of the best *Miami Vice* villain fashions, driving around in their sports cars with Florida license plates. Griselda would waddle around Setoya looking like a jowly Mexican maid—picture Danny DeVito after a sex change operation. Squat, mannish, beady-eyed Griselda seemed totally out of place among the flashy Colombian gangsters, but everyone was terrified of her. I remember when one of my stupid drunk friends goofed off and asked Griselda why she carried around such a huge purse; the answer, of course, was that she carried a big fucking pistol with her at all times. I remember the look she gave us and, more so, the embarrassment and abject terror I felt.

Osvaldo was a constant terror at Setoya, an effeminate little viper who looked like the Latino version of Prince. As murder-happy as his mother, Osvaldo was a compulsive bully and sadist who picked on me at every opportunity to show off in front of other dealers. Since Osvaldo was the murdering son of a mass-murderer, and I was *fifteen* when the abuse started, this was pretty traumatic for me—not to mention a good way to temper my nerve as a criminal.

One night at Setoya when I didn't *immediately* deliver Osvaldo the cigarettes he demanded, he lost his mind. "I fucking told you to get me some cigarettes, you little dickhead!" Osvaldo screamed as he flounced around and attempted to kick me. A guy I'll call "Tommy Thornton," an imposing local who worked as Joey Avila's bodyguard and a freelance muscle in the cocaine trade, stepped between us at the last second and told Osvaldo I was Joey Avila's boy. Within a couple years, Tommy would cease to be Joey's and my protector and become a mortal threat to our lives.

THREE
Officer Jerry

"Sergeant Jerry ———— began his law enforcement career with the Tustin Police Department
in 1981. In 1983, Jerry transferred to the Irvine
Police Department. Jerry has worked a variety
of assignments, including as a field training
officer in Patrol, as a narcotics detective and
auto theft detective in the Investigative Bureau,
and as the departments training officer in the
Office of Professional Development. In addition
to his recent appointment to Sergeant, Jerry is
currently the Team Leader for one of the
departments [sic] two SWAT teams. He has also
instructed SWAT tactics to law enforcement and
military personnel throughout the United States
and in 15 foreign countries."

Website for the City of Irvine, California
November 25, 2008

My loved ones had the best intentions and the worst
track record when it came to helping me become a law-
abiding member of society. My mother wanted to make
me a well-behaved and obedient child, so she sent me to
the military school that trained me to become a criminal
cokehead. My father wanted to teach me the dignity of
an honest day's work, so he sent me to work for drug
lord Joey Avila. My beloved girlfriend Tara only wanted
me to stay away from drugs and marry her, but it was
thanks to her that I met the criminal mastermind who
would teach me how to become a playboy cocaine millionaire who holds monogamous romantic relationships
in contempt.

Tara was my naïve Newport Beach princess with long blond hair, freckles, blue eyes, a gleaming wall of ivory teeth, and a lean beach-bunny body. Tara was innocent, mild, and kind, a ray-of-sunshine California sweetheart whose girlish charms stripped me of my criminal pretensions and reduced me to a doting, pining teenage boy. I lavished my cocaine profits on her, bought her diamond rings, spa manicures and pedicures, weekend vacations at luxury hotels with champagne and room service, and a movie star's wardrobe full of tacky '80s clothes. I even offered to buy her a Mercedes, but she had no use for any car besides her cute green Volkswagen Rabbit Cab.

I felt insensibly protective of Tara; I took her virginity, and she steadfastly believed in my decency throughout my sociopathic teenage years despite all available evidence. In all of California, she was the only "innocent civilian" whose inviolability I recognized.

One night shortly after I turned eighteen, Tara accidentally triggered a street war. That night, I had decided to rob some small-time pot dealers with a friend. Small-time pot dealers, coke dealers, bookies, whatever; they were all favorite targets. With dealers, I'd give them a call and set up a buy, show them the money and ask to see the merchandise, and then put the drugs and the cash in my pocket. When they'd ask for the money, I'd laugh.

"What, you don't get it?" I'd ask with a big cocky smile on my face. "What goes into my pocket does not come out. Once it's in my pocket, it's gone. If you want it, you're going to have to kill me."

"Dude, seriously. Give me the cash."

"Ha, you *really* don't get it," I'd say and shake my head. "Bro, you just got robbed. The good news is, if you shut your mouth, you might walk out of here alive." At this point, I'd flash my piece. No small-time Orange

County pot or coke dealer was ever prepared to shoot it out; this wasn't the movies. "Also, from now on," I'd continue, "I might be calling you from time to time for a 'loan,' you know, just to make ends meet, so don't be a stranger."

The robbery of the pot dealer that night was easy as usual, and afterward I met Tara and some friends at a Carl's Jr. fast-food joint down the street. I was having a good time, high off adrenaline and happy to see Tara, whom I worshipped.

We were walking to our car when two guys Tara knew made a disrespectful comment to her—in my presence. I was just beginning to dispense an asskicking with three of my friends when four other guys jumped out of a nearby van. Now it was six of them on four of us, with Tara and everyone else watching a ridiculous *West Side Story* brawl unfold.

I was lucky: one of my buddies was driving by the parking lot, saw the fight, and got out of his car with a club. That was the turning point; one maniac wailing in every direction with a blunt object is quite the tide-turner in a fistfight. With six dumbshits bleeding on the asphalt, I told my crew to get into their cars and leave before the police arrived.

I was starting my engine when one of the idiots who didn't have the sense to stay down lurched at me through the open driver's side window. I started driving away, but he ran along with the moving car, strangling me through the window while I repeatedly punched him in the face. My friend in the passenger's seat put my .45 caliber pistol in my hand, which I hammered into the attacker's face.

Still the punch-drunk zombie wouldn't let go, hanging onto my throat for dear life as his blood drenched my hair and eyes. Then one of his dipshit friends—who must have been huffing something serious that night—jumped in front of the car to block the exit to the parking lot. I just stepped on the gas. The would-be speed bump moved out of the way at the last second, but I swerved into him anyway, launching him over the roof of my car.

Even *that* didn't persuade his friend to let go of my throat. I was on the street before he finally lost his grip, and I laughed as I watched him tumble away in my rearview mirror. I knew I was in deep shit—there were a lot of witnesses at Carl's Jr. and the adjacent supermarket parking lot. Shockingly, I didn't catch any heat and basically forgot about it. (That shows what an exciting life I was leading, when I could write off something like drilling a civilian with my brand-new Mitsubishi Starion Turbo.)

Months later I went to Hawaii for Kenny, picking up over forty grand for him and taking home a one-day cut of $12,000 for myself. When I returned, I stashed the money in a bag in my bedroom and tried to sleep off the jet lag. My enforcer Greg was living at my house at the time.

Living with Greg was a great insurance policy if my enemies dropped by, but he was a serious liability in any other situation. The Irvine cops knocked on my door as I slept, and Greg didn't ask if they had a search warrant or even why they were there. He just invited them inside and led them to my bedroom.

I woke up surrounded by a squad of Irvine police pointing their guns at me; I had no idea what was going on. I figured I was finally getting arrested for coke dealing. I nearly died when they told me they were arresting me for assault with a deadly weapon. I had no idea what specific assault they were referring to, though I assumed

I was guilty of whatever they had in mind since there were so many legitimate cases they could have made against me.

The cops let me get dressed, cuffed me, and started searching my room. I had maybe $1,200 in my pocket, and they took that as some kind of evidence. I had a small Jennings .22 caliber semiautomatic hidden in my stereo that they missed, along with a fortune in drug money in various hiding spots. They drove me to the Irvine Police Department, where I was fingerprinted and booked.

I was sitting in a holding cell when a familiar face approached me, a villain whom I would unhesitatingly call the most evil person I've ever met, worse than every Mafia boss and Colombian coke trafficker, worse even than Mama Coca. By defending Tara's honor, I set off a chain of events that would end with me making a deal with the devil—and, for the first time, law enforcement.

I recognized the cop who walked over to my cell from his days patrolling my area of Irvine when I was just a young juvenile delinquent. He was the type of guy who makes an impression: tall, handsome, stylish, tan, and recklessly cocky, a player like Joey Avila. He was now working in undercover narcotics and asked to speak with me. Since I considered my situation desperate, I decided to listen to his pitch, even if he was a pig.

He surprised me immediately: I was being arrested for running that guy over with my car! It had happened so long ago that it never occurred to me, and I had committed so many more assaults with a deadly weapon since then.

With an easygoing charm, the cop told me he could sweep the case under the carpet if I cooperated with him. The young cop delivered this offer with this degenerate slacker attitude that let me know he personally didn't care whether I died in jail or went on a killing spree as long as it didn't inconvenience him.

I liked the cop's too-cool-to-care delivery, and I appreciated that, unlike every other cop I knew, he didn't claim to hold any moral high ground or advantage in maturity. He talked to me in the straightforward "use me and I'll use you" language of a hood, and I responded to his line of bullshit because he made no attempt to hide that he was bullshitting. Eager to avoid charges, I agreed to cooperate and help out this undercover cop's career if he helped mine.

His name was Jerry. To this day, he's still a cop in the Irvine Police Department despite a thousand attempts by other policemen to investigate and convict him of his numberless crimes. The cops in Irvine call him the Teflon Cop because nothing sticks to him even though everyone knows he's crooked, reckless, and evil. Sworn to protect and serve, Jerry has smuggled and robbed. Jerry is the definitive gangster with a badge.

According to Jerry, he became a cop only because a fellow surfer dared him. In a lot of ways, Jerry was like Joey Avila—they were both stone-cool surfers with a voracious appetite for women, cocaine, and cash. Jerry thought he was Sonny Crockett from *Miami Vice*. He dressed, talked, and looked the part—tall, handsome, with long hair and a great tan, a police-issue gun in his holster, and all the money and coke you could ever want. Girls lusted after him. He was cool, devilishly cool—Joey Avila with more edge, a sadistic streak, and the ability to arrest anyone at will.

Jerry had been trained by the FBI in Virginia and was on the SWAT team. He was an expert with explosives, surveillance, forensics, money laundering, and false identifications, and a crack shot with any weapon. In other words, he was the ideal mentor for the next phase of my criminal career. As long as I was his informant and scored him drugs for his partying, it was in Jerry's best interest not only to keep me on the streets, but to make me as successful a gangster as possible so that the quality of information I could give him would be correspondingly more valuable.

The Game Is Rigged. It's in the cops' best interest to aid the lawbreaking of their best informants and then ensure that they are never punished so that the investigations they assisted are not compromised.

So Jerry taught me everything: how to really shoot a pistol, avoid surveillance, protect my profits, avoid DEA busts, get the best fake ID, monitor my enemies, find untraceable weapons and get away with using them—even how to pick up beautiful women. He used his connections in the DEA, FBI, and Irvine PD to keep me aware of ongoing investigations, other informants, and new federal tactics and technology.

Jerry taught me how to manipulate the DMV to get an ID for any name I wanted; in the mid-'80s, all you needed was a baptismal certificate to get a driver's license, and the Catholic Church's safeguards against counterfeiting schemes were nonexistent.

My deck of authentic California driver's licenses was invaluable to me as both a drug smuggler and underage partier. I collected IDs like baseball cards, racking up fake names: Ramon Gomez, Ramon Gonzalez, Kenji Kodama, Ken Calo, and the name that would stick with me until the end of my criminal career, Kenny Gallo, a combination of my real first name with the last name of infamous New York City rebel gangster "Crazy" Joe Gallo. For most of my life, no one knew my real name;

if you knew me on the streets, you either knew me as Kenny Gallo, Ken G., or Kenji.

I had mastered a rigged game: I had a get-out-of-jail-free card, the best info, the best strategies, and I could get anyone I wanted busted and put away for a couple decades. Under Jerry's tutelage, I developed into a professional criminal with friends in law enforcement and the ready firepower to kill.

Twenty years before Baghdad jihadis introduced American soldiers to the horrors of urban guerilla warfare, Officer Jerry taught me how to rig untraceable IEDs (improvised explosive devices) to destroy cars, houses, and anything else smaller than a sports stadium. Judging by his casual expertise in the art of bomb construction, I assumed at the time that Jerry had plenty of experience blowing people up on the streets, though I doubt, in the end, that he was as prolific as I was in my coked-out, jacked-up teenage terrorist years. After all, Jerry farmed out a few IRA-style bombings to me, including the firebombing of a LSD dealer's car on Sequoia Tree Lane as a "message" for him to ditch the neighborhood.

It deserves repeating: Officer Jerry is still an Irvine policeman.

With Jerry's help, I embarked on a plan to take care of Kenny DiMartini. I had tried to be patient with him, but Kenny was consuming so much cocaine that he could no longer conceive of himself as a mortal man vulnerable to bullets or the fed cases hanging over his head. Nothing I could say would convince that swaggering junkie vampire that I sincerely intended to kill him if he had a problem with me going out on my own and occasionally stealing his property.

The coke-crazed divorcé became so incensed by my

refusal to kick up a portion of my profits that he decided to teach me a lesson. If this had been Mama Coca or Jerry, I would have been dead.

Luckily, I was dealing with an idiot. Get this: DiMartini *confronted* me outside of my apartment with some goombahs wielding baseball bats. How quaint! In a cocaine market ruled by Colombian psychopaths to whom "diplomacy" meant car bombs and drive-by shootings with MAC-10s, gentleman DiMartini and his chaps were going to threaten me with an old-fashioned 19th-century drubbing.

While they talked shit, flexed, and posed as badasses, I took the opportunity to retrieve the AK-47 from the trunk of my car. Imagine the smirk on *my* face! That was just the sort of outdated, hapless dealer DiMartini was, the type who would bring a couple bat-wielding guidos to a gunfight. Needless to say, Kenny and his *Scooby Doo* goons fled in terror of my 20th-century weaponry.

Kenny's Victorian-style ambush, though ineffective, convinced me that I should kill him just in case he ever learned how to pull a trigger. At this point I was so intoxicated with the criminal life that I didn't hesitate to consider murder—if anything, I was excited, geeked to see what a fat cokehead looked like when he exploded. I was actually *going to blow a motherfucker up*.

Working off a recipe from Jerry, I started by assembling a souped-up pipe bomb and tossing it over the wall of Kenny's mansion. It sank to the bottom of his swimming pool and caused only minor damage to the house. Imagine the firepower of a bomb that sinks to the deep end of a pool and still inflicts some harm on a nearby house when it detonates.

Then I attached a bomb to the bottom of his car, which I figured would do the job; miraculously, the bomb fell off before it detonated. I felt like Wile E. Coyote chasing the Roadrunner. Soon, with Jerry's help, I was making so much money and having so much fun that I decided I'd rather let Kenny self-destruct than risk my freedom and cash flow over a harmless old dealer.

From the beginning of my cooperation agreement, Jerry inserted himself into my teenage crew's social circle. It was a perfect fit for Jerry: he liked teenage girls, and no one older than us could keep up with Jerry's marathon partying.

Babar, Frank, and I idolized Jerry and imitated his lifestyle. He was just so cool, the ultimate rebel to a teenage criminal: this degenerate gangster surfer and master seduction artist who pretended to be a cop so he could rape and pillage with impunity. In imitation of him, I purchased an entire wardrobe of neon-colored tank tops and pastel sports coats with specially tailored easy-to-roll-up sleeves. I completed the *Miami Vice* look with a gold Rolex "Presidential" watch and a valiant Asian kid attempt at manly stubble. My sorry imitation of Jerry's Don Johnson stubble eventually shamed him into letting me in on his secret—the "Miami Device," a special beard trimmer that delivered the "three-day stubble" look.

Each night Jerry would pick me up in his Porsche, already blitzed from the bottomless bag of policeman coke he carried everywhere. Jerry was always driving drunk *and* high whenever we partied, flying down the road at 100 miles per hour in the suburbs. When I got in his car he'd usually greet me by whipping out his badge, flashing a TV-ready smile, and announcing, "Master Badge: never leave home without it," lampooning the '80s American Express commercials. Jerry's badge meant we could bypass any lines at any club and party as wild as we wanted without ever being hassled. There was no end to the fun we had using Jerry's badge. We got away with *everything*. The cops once arrested Jerry and my enforcer Keith for beating a fellow drunk halfway to death and fleeing from the arresting officers. Jerry's badge worked like the memory-wiping device in *Men in Black*: one flash and the other cops suddenly forgot why they were arresting them and let both Keith and him go.

On his own, Jerry accounted for half of the $75 bar tab the four of us would run up in a couple hours at the $1-drink-nights at the Red Onion bar in Huntington Harbor. After Jerry had earned his buzz downing shots of hard liquor, he'd whip out a line of cocaine longer than my arm, hoover it up, and then the party would *really* begin.

Jerry and my crew would hit all the big places in Newport Beach: Tiffany's, Promises, and Pompeii (Joey Avila's club above Setoya, the former Tavilas). We were able to do business while moving freely about after we discovered pager technology. We were the first dealers in town with pagers, which cost about $500 apiece at the time. They were primitive call-in answering service pagers, not display pagers, so they were just a step above waiting by a pay phone. Nonetheless, we could "work" at any club or bar in the city, an advance that made our easy life unthinkably more decadent.

Within seconds of sitting down at a club, Jerry would start yammering, "I got a bad case of TSB. I need a cure for my TSB immediately." TSB was *toxic sperm buildup*. Jerry was always horny, always prowling.

Since Jerry was incredible at picking up girls, and we had an endless supply of cocaine, women were never a problem. We would set these huge pagers on the table as soon as we arrived at a club or a restaurant. They were our homing beacons. Any plugged-in girl would walk by and know we sure as hell weren't doctors, so the instant they saw the pagers they started angling for coke.

Jerry was a master seduction artist. Even if the crowd didn't include many party girls, Jerry always got what he wanted. He had two simple and all-encompassing rules: hit on every girl you find attractive enough to fuck and appeal to the lowest common denominator.

Watching Jerry on the prowl made me a misogynist. It was impossible to take women seriously after seeing how effortless it was for this sleazebag to convince smart women to go home with him.

Let me tell you some of the caveman antics Jerry used to seduce women, and then ask yourself if you could have grown up a well-adjusted modern gentleman if you had spent your formative years watching these routines work *again and again*. Jerry would approach a girl and, with a friendly smile, ask her if she wanted to see a photo of him as a baby. Then he'd hand her this snapshot of a baby with a freakishly large penis—that's it. Within seconds Jerry would have his hands down the girl's blouse.

Another of Jerry's reliable pickup lines was, "What is the difference between a roll of Lifesavers and a man? A roll of Lifesavers comes in five flavors; a man only comes in three: salty, saltier and lumpy." What an irresistible hunk, huh ladies?

Perhaps Jerry's favorite opening salvo was, "Why do cavemen drag their women by their hair instead of their feet? So they don't fill up with dirt!" There was no way to interpret that joke as anything but a declaration of open contempt, yet women would swoon.

Much to my chagrin and the chagrin of the whole human species, Jerry's intelligence-insulting gimmicks, if executed with confidence, *worked*. Jerry's method was easy: be upfront, be disarmingly confident, and appeal to women's primal sexual impulses and illogical attraction to having their sexuality "challenged" by a condescending asshole. Jerry taught me that women are attracted by contempt. They thrive on rejection and a feeling of insecurity that they can overcome only by seducing a guy.

It was easy for me to play a condescending, contemptuous asshole: after watching Jerry, I honestly believed that, besides Tara, all women *were* beneath me. I have never lacked a bedmate since those days with Jerry.

I applied this lesson to other gangsters as well. Since most major gangsters are constantly surrounded by lackeys and wannabes, the way to get their attention is to act like you don't give a shit who they are and you're too busy doing your own thing to need them. Mob bosses aren't used to guys like me playing hard-to-get, so it draws them in, makes them want my approval, and makes them susceptible to a condescending asshole in the same way as models and porn stars and actresses. Of course, it never hurt that, after Jerry, I always had elite arm candy by my side as bait. Whenever I went to a new area and wanted to meet the underworld boss, I'd just go to his hangout with three knockout broads and ignore him. He'd come to me.

I was often Jerry's wingman, which was a funny team: a thirtysomething surfer cop and a teenage Japanese-American drug dealer. Nonetheless, thanks to Jerry's direction, we had a lot of success. One time, after Jerry and I spent a night meticulously macking on two stewardesses at a club in Hawaii, I found myself rolling around on the beach with the blond one. Before I really got anywhere, though, Jerry came over and, standing over us, told me that he was "finished" with the brunette, and it was thus time to go. Without saying goodbye, I stopped kissing my blond stewardess and hightailed it, kicking up sand in her face.

She was just a girl.

"Frank was a spoiled rich kid—we all had money, being from Orange County, but Frank's parents were especially loaded. Frank was always on drugs and getting bailed out by his parents. Frank cashed in his trust fund, bought a new Corvette, and immediately crashed it. Unfortunately, there were some binds that Frank's parents could not help him out of."

Greg Benjamin

To ensure my success in the narcotics racket, Jerry procured a DEA memo for me, which detailed how the agency profiled drug traffickers at airports and at roadside customs stations. I was still traveling to Hawaii regularly, where the money was still incredible due to cocaine's scarcity. In California, the cocaine I didn't sell to other dealers I would break down into smaller quantities without whacking it up because I liked to sell high-quality shit—it attracted high-quality, no-stress customers. The profit margin was naturally huge; I was making $10,000 a kilo, $20,000 per front, and that's taking theft and my crew's personal usage into account.

It's hard for people who were not in the coke trade during the 1970s and '80s to believe how much money I made as a teenager. For example, I remember spending hours with Jerry counting $100,000 in small bills on the living room floor of a condo in Park Newport. Though I recall counting the cash, I don't remember why or how we had specifically earned it; it was no big deal, just a routine score. The money was such an afterthought to us that, when we left midway through the count for happy hour, we forgot to close the door to the condo. When we returned hours later, we found the sliding glass door wide-open, clearly displaying a pyramid of banded cash to anyone who may have passed by the apartment.

My crew made millions of dollars while most of us were still too young to drink. We hid our multi-kilo slabs of cocaine in customized hidden compartments within cars we bought using cash and fake IDs and parked in inconspicuous suburban locations. Sometimes, we'd keep our kilos in a storage unit or in a paid-off civilian's house. My cash was constantly shuffled between bank safe deposit boxes, hidden safes, and hollowed out crannies in walls, ceilings, closets, and even electrical appliances. I lost track of some of it; tens of thousands of dollars are probably napping behind a loose tile at some stash house or apartment of mine from 1987.

The challenge was breaking down the uncut kilos for sale in packaged form without drawing attention or leaving traces. We had only triple beam scales back then, which were huge and hard to work with, so breaking down and packing the product was the most vulnerable part of our operation. Hotel rooms, an old standby, had become a bust thanks to hotel clerks and competitors who would tip off the local PD as soon as we showed up. Instead, I would find someone in Irvine who was not a criminal or junkie and pay to use their house as a coke lab.

One of my guys would pick up the kilos from one of our stash cars, and then shake off any possible surveillance before heading to the civilian's house. My crew would take a couple hours to bust up the cocaine and package it in ounces, all of us wearing gloves and masks so that we wouldn't get high from the powder. We would then clean the place up, wiping everything down, washing the kilo wrappers in the shower, and then dumping them in random trash containers around town. Finally, we'd call Jerry, and we'd party.

Though cocaine was our main business, like any good criminal crew we adapted to whatever moneymaking opportunities came our way. For a while, one of our most profitable sidelines was counterfeiting. I once stole a huge stash of decent counterfeit bills, over a half million dollars' worth, but the score was deceptive. It's very hard to circulate hundreds of thousands of dollars in easily traceable fake cash without attracting the attention of the police and Secret Service, and federal prosecution for counterfeiting is accompanied by all sorts of auxiliary felony charges and huge jail terms. Besides, why would I want to risk attracting the interest of a *competent* law enforcement agency like the Secret Service?

I knew not to spend the fake cash until I could do so with the lowest profile and the maximum short-term value possible. Once the money was in circulation, I needed to distance myself from it. The ideal plan was to trade in the fake cash for a dozen kilos of cocaine from an outside smuggler. If the coke trafficker discovered that our cash was shit, he would never report it to the cops and, most likely, he'd be dumb enough to spend it anyway and take the fall when the Secret Service traced it back to him. "Another drug dealer paid me with fake cash!" was not the most winning defense at trial.

Unfortunately, this half-million-dollar score was derailed by this kid I'll call "Sid Johnson," a rat-faced punk rocker and raging coke fiend who did flunky work for my crew. This blond-haired dildo lived next door to Tara and thought his proximity to her granted him immunity from me fucking his shit up. Since he seemed harmless, I let him crash at a stash house where I kept some of the fake money. I didn't worry about Sid because I figured that he knew, from being around me, that I would not hesitate to set him on fucking fire if he screwed with my business. I was wrong: the dirtbag stole some of my coke.

When I found out, he acted real laidback and California cool, like "Dude, chill," he said, "I'll pay you back a little at a time. I don't have anything for you now. Just give me time, bro. I was just really aching for some and couldn't control myself"—bullshit like that. I hated bullshit excuses for misbehavior; I was as laidback as any other SoCal surfer, but I was as humorless as a Nazi when it came to my drug money. I didn't care what his excuse was; I just wanted money for the blow he stole. I wanted it now—and didn't care if he had to rob a convent or sell his anal virginity on a street corner.

Sid was hard to communicate with under normal conditions, and his natural imbecility was made impenetrable by his binge consumption of my cocaine. With a tornado of coke scrambling his thoughts, Sid came to the conclusion that since I didn't *immediately* kill him, no harm would come from stealing *more* of my property. Partnering with Frank, my best friend from military school, Sid dumped huge rolls of my counterfeit cash all over California, and within days I saw Xerox copies of the bills in every store I passed on the street. With the Secret Service swarming into Orange County, I had to dump the rest of my cash if I wanted to avoid federal jail time. I made it rain $420,000 in good fake bills over the freeway. Obviously, I intended to collect $420,000 worth of pain from Sid Johnson.

First, I needed to deal with Frank for blindly following Sid. When sober, Frank was a reliable hustler. However, after a couple years in the drug business, Frank got hooked on freebasing cocaine, which transformed him into a sniveling, thieving, impulsive junkie pussy with a penchant for latching onto obnoxious junkie girls.

Junkie Frank was amusing at first. In one legendary story, his multimillionaire-contractor father entrusted him to deliver irreplaceable architectural blueprints worth $40,000 to a client, only for Frank to make a "pit stop" and disappear. When the odd-couple rescue crew of Frank's panicking Serbian dad and I finally discovered Frank after *two days*, he didn't remember anything about the previous forty-eight hours or what had happened to the blueprints.

My best friend's transformation into a senseless, freebasing force of nature explained his otherwise inex-plicable decision to go along with Sid Johnson's suicidal plan to rob me even though he knew better. I was very patient with Frank, dangerously patient according to the rest of my crew. Instead of just killing him for stealing my money and dope, I tried to reach him through tough love. I went to his junkie girlfriend's place, pistol-whipped Frank with my revolver when he opened the door, and drove him back to his parents' house, lecturing him along the way.

His girlfriend, not being too smart, called the cops on me and reported a kidnapping. This really pissed me off—as far as I was concerned, she owed me from a previous act of kindness: I had stolen a car and used it to run over the dealer who, against my orders, had been supplying the two helpless, self-destructive junkies. The poor kid looked like Freddy Krueger after I drove over his face. When I saw him years later, one of his eyes seemed to be taking orders from a different brain than the rest of his body.

Failing to appreciate my concern for her well-being,

the girl got a new dealer, kept Frank high, and had the temerity to call the police on me. Though I considered myself a committed gentleman and defender of the fairer sex, my chivalry had limits. I had my friend Lee Clyde shoot up her car while it was parked in front of her house. In a mortal panic, she fled, and the grieving Frank clung to me for support.

Clyde did great work.

"2 Men Arrested After Shotgun
Fired at Garage"

The suspects, Jeffrey Mikia Okuda, 23, of Irvine, and Lee Matthew Clyde, 20, who listed addresses in Orange and San Diego, were stopped after they ran a red light about 1:50 a.m. Tuesday in Newport Beach, police in Irvine and Newport Beach said. One of the men was attempting to hide a sawed-off shotgun under his jacket, police said.

Los Angeles Times
October 19, 1988

Since Clyde was my most reliable muscle, I decided to send him against Sid Johnson. I had already tried blowing him up for stealing my fugazi cash, but the bombing was botched and only his house was damaged.

My next thought was to collect his debt with a Clyde Special: a drive-by shooting of his house, which would either kill him or scare him into paying me. To insulate myself from the purchase of the vehicle, I gave a friend the cash to buy a used motorcycle from a kid named Chris.

The plan was textbook Colombian narcoterrorism: another military school friend, Marine deserter Jeff

Okuda, would drive the motorcycle to Sid's house with Clyde on the back; Clyde would scare the shit out of the entire neighborhood by unleashing a few cannon blasts from a sawed-off 12-gauge; and then they'd ditch the bike five miles away, where Clyde's truck would be waiting as the getaway car.

Clyde, as always, did his job perfectly, but during the getaway Jeff got cocky and coasted the bike down a hill like a jackass, attracting the attention of a Newport traffic cop. Instead of outrunning the pigs on the faster and more maneuverable motorcycle—that was the *point* of using a crotch rocket in the first place—Jeff *stopped* and let the cop pull them over. Clyde, who was carrying a fucking sawed-off shotgun a few miles from a shooting, nearly followed his impulse to kill both Jeff and the cop on the spot. Instead, they were both arrested, and the bike was impounded.

Clyde and Jeff refused to talk, putting the cops in a rough situation. They had captured a thug on a getaway motorcycle carrying a sawed-off shotgun; it was clear that Clyde had committed or was about to commit a crime, but the police had no idea what. If they charged him for possession of the gun, it would be a misdemeanor, and Clyde would go free. Instead, the cops charged Clyde with armed robbery—without any specific robbery in mind. They just wanted to keep Clyde in jail long enough for Jeff to flip, which he did when they threatened to turn him over to the Marines for going AWOL. Luckily for Clyde, Sid Johnson and his family had no interest in testifying about Jeff's story.

Though Clyde was released on the imaginary robbery charges, he was going to be nailed for driving a "stolen" bike unless I could produce papers for it. I had a friend ask Chris for the paperwork so I could clear Clyde and get the bike back. When Chris heard what had happened, he told my friend "Tough shit!" and refused to give him the papers. "If you don't like it, you can talk to my step-dad. He's a cop."

Chris was lucky I didn't blow up his pig step-dad. I felt compelled to teach him some respect, and this time I decided to impart the lesson personally. As a result, I almost blew myself up.

I rigged a bomb and deputized my friend Moses to drive me to Chris's neighborhood one night. The bomb lay on my lap during the drive over, and when we parked a few blocks from Chris's house, I told Moses to open my door for me so I could get out carefully with the bomb in my hands. Thanks to the attention-span-shortening wonders of cocaine, however, in the time it took Moses to walk to the passenger side, I had forgotten about holding onto that bomb on my lap. When I stood up, the bomb took a hard fall on the sidewalk.

My heart clenched up too tight to beat; my ears zapped out completely. Deaf, instantly soaked with cold sweat, and unable to breathe, I watched the bomb bounce three times and stop. No explosion.

I was surprised Moses didn't shit himself. Without hesitating further, I scooped up the bomb and hustled it over to Chris's house, where I planted it under his car. After I set the timer, we rushed back to our car and waited for news of the explosion to come over my police scanner. When ten minutes passed without any word, I realized that I must have broken the timer when I dropped the bomb. I rushed back to the car, stuffed a short fuse into the bomb, lit it with my lighter, and ran like hell. Seconds later, I was deaf again, and for a split second all the darkness evaporated from the sleeping neighborhood and there was daylight. A part of the car rocketed clean through a house and nearly disemboweled an innocent civilian. Collateral damage.

This demonstration of my insanity persuaded Chris to hand over the paperwork for the bike. As for Sid Johnson, I'd deal with him later.

Of course, the only reason I got away with such reckless, ostentatious criminal behavior was because my protector, Jerry, was leaking me tips and running interference at the police department on my behalf. Jerry was hardly selfless, so I had to pay him back twice over, being both his enforcer and his informant, delivering the big cases for him at the Irvine PD and later with the FBI.

I knew this guy Dave who was dealing cocaine in southern Orange County, so I set up a two-kilo deal with him for the Irvine police. It was nothing personal; instead of robbing him like usual, I just decided to set him up. The deal was to go down at the Holiday Inn, so Jerry and I booked adjoining rooms along with a Newport Beach narcotics officer. We became bored while we were waiting for Dave to bring us the cocaine, so we ordered a room-service feast. I was drinking illegally with two police officers when Dave called from the lobby and told us he was on his way up.

Dave and his guy came into our suite to see Jerry and me innocently eating room service; the police were listening in the adjoining room. Jerry showed them the $56,000 in cash and let them count it as I took the cocaine into the bedroom. Happy with the deal, the two smiling idiots left the room and were tackled by ten Irvine cops. The police left the cocaine for us to bring back to the station; I requisitioned five ounces for myself as a bonus.

Things stepped up when Jerry became attached to the FBI narcotics squad for a new case they were opening called "ORCO"—Orange County Cocaine. I consecrated Jerry's new gig by offering up as a sacrifice the Black Trunk Gang, the group of Hawaiian big wave surfers who traded heavy loads of pot for blow and were suspected of some murders. Jerry and I traveled to Hawaii with an undercover FBI agent named Carl to set up Fast Eddie, the leader of the Black Trunk Gang.

Carl was a fuckup. Shortly after our arrival in Hawaii, Jerry and I watched in disbelief as Carl wildly chased the airport shuttle bus for fifty yards because he had carelessly left his badge, his gun, and the "buy money" the FBI provided on his bus seat. Insisting that Carl was too square and incompetent to take undercover, Jerry and I traveled by ourselves to Pahoa, the "grower's town" where the pot was harvested, to handle the sting, and we had a good laugh when we noticed new, expensive four-by-four trucks parked at every ramshackle hut. Like ghetto and redneck dealers in California, Hawaiian dealers were just fine living in horrendous conditions as long as they could upgrade their rides.

This successful operation established my credibility with the FBI, who, in exchange for my future cooperation, began paying me around $4,000 a month plus the rent for my apartment. Adding this loot to the profits from my unimpeded cocaine business, I was making so much cash that it became meaningless to me. Since I could buy everything I ever wanted with disposable drug cash, I was living in a world where everything in effect was free.

I was grossing millions without any repercussions, a government-protected coke dealer with elite Colombian connections and a hardened crew of teenage smugglers, car-bombers, drive-by shooters, and all-round sociopaths at my disposal. In addition to my criminal life, I also had a gorgeous and kind girlfriend who had no idea how I really made my money. I felt like the toughest, smartest, and luckiest guy in the world, a sly fucker who could get away with anything without suffering any consequences. I had "won" at life.

If this is starting to sound like Act I of a Greek tragedy, that's no accident. Like everything cocaine touched in the '80s, my life collapsed; one day I went to bed in heaven and woke up in hell. Some of my closest friends would die, and I would be in handcuffs for one of their murders.

FOUR
Big Mike

> _"There are some people you just can't fuck._
> _There's one thing about this business you've got_
> _to keep in mind: Fucking with people's money_
> _is the fastest way to get clipped."_
>
> Jack Dragna
> L.A. Mafia Boss

The first person I would lose was Tara, my girlfriend, the love of my life. I lived a Clark Kent lifestyle with Tara; she thought I was just a good kid who bussed tables at Joey's club, ran a profitable little auto detailing service called Quick Shine on the side, and was friends with a charismatic young cop named Jerry. Like any good rich California girl, she loved the lines of cocaine I chopped out for her, but actually _dating a dealer_ was out of the question. This was a good girl, an O.C. princess—not a drug moll.

Our relationship was founded on the lucky break that Tara was not exactly the most observant or inquisitive person you'd ever meet. She was sweet, innocent, and confused by the world, like a kitten. Sometimes, she'd get her feelings hurt because I could not help but laugh at her ignorance of basic American history and current affairs; she was the type of girl who wasn't sure if the man on the Monopoly box was a former U.S. president.

Once, out of the blue, Tara turned to me with this bedeviled look and asked me _where bread came from_. Until her nineteenth year, it had never occurred to her to inquire about the origins of bread. I told her that it grew by the loaf on trees, an answer that she repeated to her friends as if it were a well-known fact. She was pretty pissed when they told her I was lying.

Another time, I took her to a swap meet where she noticed a hot dog stand advertising "Polish Dogs"; with a furrowed brow, she asked me how exactly you polish a hot dog. I could just tell she was picturing a hot dog vendor with a squeegee and a bottle of Windex.

Tara also spent a great deal of money taking her cat Tilly to a pet psychologist, who diagnosed the feline with a psychological disorder arising from spending too much time with other women. I came closer to dying (from laughter) when I heard that diagnosis than I ever did feuding with Kenny DiMartini.

I know I'm sounding mean, but I loved Tara exactly as she was. I *liked* that she was simple; it was a relief to deal with someone so sincere, trusting, and transparent. I still love Tara; she's the most special person I've ever known. I'd give up all the fun I've had in the porn and crime rackets just to be able to have a pleasant one-hour lunch with her, to laugh and smile and get back to that special place with her for a little while. She meant so much to me that I couldn't have expressed it then and certainly cannot now.

Under the threat of death, everyone in my crew covered up my criminal career and philandering around Tara. As our relationship became more serious, the pressure to protect her from the rest of my world began to wear on me. At any moment with Tara, we could run into the wrong people, and she'd be dead before she even understood why.

A slightly more reassuring scenario was Tara simply having her heart broken when she realized that I was a sociopathic, coke-dealing, compulsive liar and attempted murderer. I was eviscerated with guilt and anxiety every time those blue eyes looked at me. Violating Tara's trust was the only thing in the world that activated my conscience. The last thing a criminal needs is a conscience; having a sense of moral awareness gravely imbalanced my gangland judgment. The pressure on my psyche was exacerbated by a kid I knew who was actively trying to steal Tara away from me, which was near-irresistible temptation to commit a murder that could not possibly escape Tara's attention. I had to maintain my self-control and let this twerp chase after my girl, which drove me mad with insecurity and stifled rage.

In addition, it seemed increasingly inevitable that my crew would succumb to the coke dealer cliché and end up flipping on or massacring one another. I was partly to blame: my leadership and decision-making abilities became grossly impaired after I discovered anabolic steroids.

Steroids weren't illegal when I started my habit, and most people didn't know how to use them properly. My friend Chuck Browntooth, who worked for me as a dealer and later became a road captain for the Vagos outlaw motorcycle gang, suggested that we get into steroids and weightlifting to help distract him from a recent breakup. I dug the idea—why shouldn't a gangster be as strong and intimidating as possible? Naturally, once we became steroid users, we became steroid dealers.

Steroid trafficking was easy: Chuck and I would go to Mexico, purchase about 4,000 little blue Dianabol anabolic steroids tablets at the pharmacy at one fifth of the American price, and drive back over the border in a truck. We'd just stuff them in our shoes, down our pants, and in our jacket pockets.

Even when steroids became illegal in 1988, the penalties were a joke. One night a gang of tooled-up Customs agents ambushed us at the border. It was comical when they frisked us: we produced so many pills from so many places that it seemed like a magic act. As punishment for discovering a few thousand pills on us, the agents made us write essays attesting to our remorse for trafficking in steroids.

While Chuck furiously scribbled on a notepad and kissed ass, I did my usual best to infuriate authority. "I love steroids!" my essay began. "I use tons of steroids because I want to be the best that I can be!" Chuck glanced at my notepad and got pissed, begging me to play nice and feign repentance so that we would be let off. Speaking as loud as I could to ensure that the agents would hear, I told him, "These jokers ain't gonna do shit! They're chickenshit!"

I was right. They let us go after we turned in our essays, and the next afternoon I returned to Mexico and just walked another shipment over the border. Soon I would be bench-pressing around 350 pounds, twice my body weight.

We were smuggling thousands of pills a week, so I had an ample supply to gulp down when I was lifting. As a result of my steroid abuse, my temper became volcanic. On the best of days, I was already a violent drug dealer; now I was a volatile, irrational, raging beast with a stupendous arsenal of automatic weapons and explosives at my disposal. I was a rabid, jacked-up idiot who was entrusted with the lives of my crew and the operation of a multimillion-dollar cocaine business.

Befitting anyone who would trust me with their lives, my crew was even less reliable than I was: paranoid, alcoholic, whoremongering coke addicts to a man, some of them still in the throes of puberty. When you mix the gangster lifestyle with drugs and alcohol, somebody is going to die, and it increasingly felt like our partnership was degenerating into a circular firing squad. The best indication of our rapidly deteriorating solidarity was that my own crew was obsessed with killing my oldest friend.

The problem was simple: Frank, the little devil on my shoulder, had gone fucking nuts from his addiction to freebasing cocaine. Any organized drug operation is one weak link away from federal prison or slaughter at the hands of competitors, so the presence of a pathetic, crumbling basehead cannot be tolerated within a cartel. Frank had to go, and quick; our paranoia and precarious position in the middle of the most competitive, murderous drug trade in America meant we either had to kill him or frame him so that he would be imprisoned in Mexico, where the lazy authorities would have no interest in flipping him.

Everyone in my crew insisted that we simply kill him; they were persistently reminding me of my duty to sacrifice anything that got in the way of our business. I could say "no" only so many times before they would take it into their own hands. After all, if Frank flipped or fucked up under pressure, their lives would be on the line as well. More to the point, there was too much fucking cash at risk. Our lives were one thing, but my crew didn't let anyone fuck around with our cash. I let Frank live only because the moneymaking fool replaced every dollar he lost me five times over.

I kept dropping hints to Frank that it would be in his best interest to get the hell out of town, but he was a stubborn, oblivious junkie. My only choice was to frame him in Mexico so that he would be put away until he cleaned up, but I couldn't quite pull the trigger. We had great connections with the federal police in Mexico, so it would have been easy to do. If we didn't give Frank to the Mexican cops, it was only a matter of time until he'd stumble into the custody of the American cops.

Thanks to our increasingly arrogant, sloppy way of doing business, the Irvine Police were finally onto us. As they closed in on my crew, Jerry was too distracted with the FBI to run interference. The heat from the cops was all over us, and the other drug groups knew it. They were looking to set us up for a fall and take our market share. I felt helpless as the vultures circled overhead.

I was mulling things over at one of the Avila family's El Ranchito restaurants in Laguna Hills. I had recently begun my first attempt to quit drinking, since the mixture of booze and steroids was not conducive to survival. While I was eating dinner there, I ran into an extremely dangerous Mexican dealer and hit man named Lalo, the same Lalo who bragged about shooting the cuckolded husband who hit Joey Avila with a mug.

Edward "Lalo" Ugalde was pure muscle, a prison-tattooed, greasy, dead-eyed hombre who looked like a Tijuana prison escapee. Lalo was a remorseless killer, a psychopath, a hardcore Vietnam vet who got his mind *all sorts* of fucked up in the jungles of Southeast Asia. Even though he worked for the Avilas, Sal warned me about him: "Watch out, Kenny. Lalo's sick. That boy got no conscience. None at all." Sal and Joey consorted with lots of killers, so warning me that Lalo was *morally reprehensible* even to them made a big impression on me—I wanted to talk to Lalo even more! I was just a teenager; I wanted to be as close to the flame as possible.

Lalo and I were talking, and I mentioned that I was having trouble with the dickhead who was trying to seduce Tara. Lalo, without hesitating, just said, "I tell you how you handle him. Kill him. It's easy."

Lalo then produced a vial of pure China White Horse

heroin and told me a story about a guy named Renny who ripped him off for some cocaine. In retaliation, Lalo dosed him with a fatal quantity of China White Horse, put a bottle of pills under his body, and left Renny on the couch. "It was great that Renny had a lot of problems," Lalo explained, trying to catch his breath from laughing at his own luck. "Man, he was so upset over his parents getting divorced and his girlfriend breaking up with him. Poor dude just got 'fucked up on drugs,' y'know," he said with a smile.

I still don't think the police have officially solved that homicide since I can't remember Renny's real name. Lalo left Renny's body to decompose in the California summer heat until the neighbors called the cops to complain about the smell.

Though I was disgusted by Lalo's story and felt, deep down, that the dumb kid didn't deserve to *die* for wanting to date Tara, I took the heroin just in case. As long as Tara was in my life, I retained *some* mercy and decency; I let the kid go about his business unscathed. Out of curiosity to see what type of character I was really dealing with in Lalo, I asked Jerry to test the heroin to see if it was for real. It turned out to be ninety percent pure: as fatal as a shotgun blast to the brain. Lalo was the real thing, which impressed me at the time and motivated me to befriend him.

My friendship with Lalo would teach me that one pitfall of associating with homicidal maniacs is that they will occasionally murder your friends.

Soon after I met Lalo, I was bored and followed pussy-chaser extraordinaire Babar to a house party in Irvine. The party sucked, but we stuck around to mack on the girls. We were drinking outside in the street with some cooze when, suddenly, ten members of this punk gang who was beefing with my crew drove up. Their leader, a shithead I knew named Jimmy P., came at me brandishing a beer bottle, spitting "Jap" and "gook" in my face; I told him he was making a mistake. He didn't listen and continued to pull my bitch card. He gave me no choice: "Okay, one on one, right now."

To remove the possibility that it would fall into the wrong hands, I took out my Walther PPK pistol and handed it, along with my cash and Rolex, to Babar. I remember wishing it was Clyde, or at least Chuck or Phil, who was with me instead of Babar, but you can't always pick your sidekicks.

Without wasting more words, I charged at Jimmy, easily disarmed him, and commenced beating him unconscious. Between punches, I thought of the racial slurs he had thrown at me in front of all those girls, consulting my steroid-raging brain, and decided that a mere asskicking was insufficient; I needed to *kill* Jimmy.

By the third or fourth time I slapped his forehead against the concrete in an attempt to crack it open like an egg, his crew swarmed over me brandishing beer bottles. Infuriated that they weren't honoring my right to finish the fight on my own terms, I erupted into a wild roid-raging tornado of haymakers and kicks. I turned my fury on everyone within range, even if they were not involved; one bystander who screamed "I'm not in this, Kenny!" was grabbed by the hair, pulled over to the house, and thrown through a window anyway.

I don't remember what happened next; according to Babar, I blacked out after two beer bottles to the head. Never the most timely or reliable accomplice, Babar jumped into the fray only when I lay face-down on the asphalt next to Jimmy. Waving my gun in every direction, he scared the hyenas away from my defenseless body.

Awakening to the sound of sirens, I brushed the dirt and blood from my eyes, snatched the Walther PPK from Babar's hands, and ran.

After I buried the gun in some dirt, I turned myself in. The cops were everywhere, and I figured I had no reason to risk running away since I looked like the bloody victim of a hate crime. Acting on the information provided by some witnesses, they asked if I had a gun: "If I had a gun, would I look like this?"

After they searched my car and found nothing more suspicious than $4,000, they let me go on the condition that I went to the hospital to get stitched up. At the hospital, the doctors told me I had suffered a severe concussion and needed to be under medical supervision, but I immediately checked myself out. While I was recuperating over the next few days at home, Jimmy P. and two goons showed up at my dad's house to finish the job; I chased them down the street with an Uzi. Putting my family in danger was a provocation that required a massive, devastating response.

I engineered an unremitting campaign of violence and psychological torment against this punk gang. They didn't deserve to relax, sleep, have fun, enjoy themselves, or do anything at all besides hide and worry that they were in mortal danger at all times. I firebombed some of their cars and rigged bombs to others; I randomly fired shotgun and machine gun rounds into their homes at all hours of the day and night; I ambushed them while they were out enjoying themselves; I beat them up until they cried and begged for mercy.

For a little bit of cash, Greg physically *wrecked* a few dudes from Jimmy's gang; they permanently surrendered control of some of their bodily functions. Frank and Clyde shot up another punk's house.

When one girl tried to pull drunk nutball Keith off her boyfriend, Keith matter-of-factly punched her in the face and told her to mind her own business. When the bleeding girl ran to her car, she accidentally ran over Keith's foot, so we made a point of hunting down her car *that night* and firebombing it. Her oblivious parents hired a private investigator who quickly sniffed us out and got in my face, so I had him thrown down a flight of stairs.

Jimmy P.'s crew must have felt like they had crossed Satan himself. I systematically terrorized every facet of their lives until some fled the county and others lost their minds. Twenty years later, the mention of my impending arrival at his office caused one of the former gang members to hide under a desk, crying; he was still positive I'd kill him on sight for that fight in high school. When I found out, I felt this beaming sense of satisfaction at a job well done; even all those years later, he didn't deserve any peace of mind.

After my fire-and-brimstone campaign, the Orange County Sheriff's Department finally decided that they had to put me away or drive me into exile. Two detectives specifically wanted my head at all costs: Tom Carney and Tom Dove. The "Two Toms" double-checked every case that landed on their desk to see if they could pin it on me or someone associated with me. The pair of assholes had me shadowed at all times, badgered me constantly, and tried to intimidate me. I wanted to stick around just to spite the Two Toms, but the heat was just too much. I swallowed my pride and fled Irvine, relocating across Orange County to Newport Beach in what was admittedly a feeble attempt to shake them.

A few months before, I had thought I was the king of Orange County: a miniature mobster with my own arsenal, my own crew, my own cocaine ring, a paycheck from the FBI, total immunity from the cops, and the best girlfriend in the world. Now I was on the run, away from home with a vial of lethal heroin that I briefly considered using on Frank. The love of my life was being wooed by another guy, my crew was falling apart, and my criminal career was almost surely winding down to a long-overdue jail sentence. My luck was evaporating— the luck of my entire circle of friends was evaporating. Our lifestyle was to party through the most vindictive, bloodthirsty, lawless era of drug trafficking in American history. We were helpless prey for a predator far more ruthless, calculating, and painstakingly professional about the business of crime than we could ever be.

That predator was Michael "Big Mike" Marvich.

"Leaping over a railing in Superior Judge Blake's court yesterday just before he was called up for sentence [sic] for the theft of an automobile, Mike Marvich, 16-year-old youth, yesterday nearly escaped by running down eight flights of stairs."

Los Angeles Times
June 9, 1931

"It is argued that [Marvich and his accomplice] could not be expected to know the meaning of the word 'rob' and thus were not given notice as to the offense for which they must stand trial. . . . It is next contended that the district attorney was guilty of prejudicial misconduct in trying to prove that Marvich had attempted to escape from jail . . . a cellmate testified that while confined in jail Marvich secured a file and pliers from a trusty and made active preparations for an escape; that

> *he loosened the screws on a ventilator, filed a part of the door and removed bolts; and that he had seen him take bolts out of the door and go into another part of the building at night."*
>
> People v. Israel (1949)
> Mike Marvich acting as his own attorney

> *"Michael P. Marvich, now 77, says he was a bed-ridden old man helping out a friend in need when police burst into his sprawling, five-bedroom house one night three years ago. He had no idea, he says, that his friend, an ex-con on parole, had stashed 23 pounds of high-grade marijuana in his closet and in a child's swing-set box in the attic. Or that he had more than 3 kilograms of meth-amphetamines, blasting caps and an explosive device. . . . 'Looks can be deceiving,' said Orange County Deputy District Attorney Mike Lubinski."*
>
> *Orange County Register*
> January 31, 1993

Of all the criminals I've known, no one has ever given less of a fuck than Mike Marvich. He robbed and killed with perfect disinterest in the potential for gangland reprisals, police investigations, public infamy, karmic retribution, or even catastrophic emotional damage to his immediate family members. If he thought it would expand his already unimaginable wealth and power, Mike Marvich would have personally strangled the Pope on Christmas Day and sold the papal corpse to a coven of necrophiliacs. If Mike stood to profit from your death, then you were dropped as if he were unloading a few shares of penny stocks. I've never encountered a more brilliant, daring, or nonchalant mass murderer.

Mike was not a danger-junkie like me; his actions were always precisely calculated and chillingly rational. While homicidal freaks like Griselda Blanco or Lalo would let their egos and perverse love of inflicting pain dictate their behavior, Mike was sincerely indifferent to violence and murder. To kill or not to kill was never a question that affected his peace of mind; he once bragged to me that he had no trouble sleeping while splattered with the brains of his own murdered wife. The conscientious pursuit of his business interests was all that mattered; the same man who could peacefully nap next to his wife's corpse would be too outraged to sleep if you shorted him a few dollars on a deal.

Big Mike was an old-school gangster: everything was just business. By the time I knew him in his old age, Mike was just a disembodied, predatory instinct expertly hunting for the sake of hunting. He didn't care about money or material things, just the power they signified. Mike at one point had tens of millions of dollars in cash yet lived in a trailer park because, to him, comfort and conventional social status held absolutely no value. He attained a level of criminal nirvana that other crooks only aspire to; hundreds of millions of dollars passed through his hands to what appeared to be blissful cosmic indifference.

This cosmic indifference extended to Mike's own life. Unlike your average hotheaded and impulsive crook, Marvich's self-control and discipline were godlike. When wronged, Mike was capable of willfully suffering humiliation and suppressing his desire for revenge for *years* until he could derive the maximum benefits from striking back. I got the feeling that if I pulled a gun and shot him mid-conversation, Mike would have just laughed and continued talking until his breath ran out. Kill you, kill him: same bullshit, different direction. Mike wasn't bothered. Already in his seventies when I met him, Mike figured that he would be dead of natural causes one day soon anyway, so why stress out over the bullshit details.

Mike was a gangland genius. He was stealing cars and launching daring courtroom escapes from police as a pubescent newsy during the Great Depression. As a young man, he made his bones as an armed robber and burglar with a reputation for violence. When an elaborate *Shawshank Redemption*–style escape from prison was narrowly thwarted, Marvich sought an escape route in the prison's library. The poorly educated hood spent months inching through every sentence of every available legal textbook. Within a couple of years, he was defending himself at trial and arguing his case up to the Supreme Court of the United States. Upon his release from jail, Mike almost immediately established himself as one of the preeminent experts of the criminal justice system of California, a high-priced paralegal with a unique mastery of both sides of the law.

Although he told me that he continued to traffic in weed and arms, Mike the paralegal established himself as a perfectly respectable member of Orange County society in the 1960s and '70s. Mike quickly developed favor-trading friendships with the most powerful defense attorneys, government prosecutors, judges, and police officials in Southern California by lending out his dual expertise as an underworld veteran and legal researcher. As a specialist in narcotics law, Mike also formed close relationships with high-profile drug traffickers like Timothy Leary and Joey Avila, which naturally gave him connections and inside knowledge that would be priceless advantages if he were running a drug cartel.

When Orange County succeeded Miami as the cocaine hotspot in the '80s, Big Mike was already in his late sixties. Decades had passed in a relatively lawful fashion, but Mike was still a predator. Most importantly, he was a far more disciplined, experienced, patient, efficient, and calculating predator than the psychotic, illiterate, backwater village idiots from Colombia who ran the drug trade at the time. With only the shitty tail-end years of his life left to lose, Big Mike couldn't resist the opportunity to become fabulously wealthy and powerful. He reentered the underworld and coolly began to outmaneuver, humiliate, and crush the competition.

Besides his own qualities, Big Mike's decisive advantage over every other criminal in California was his close relationship with Jose Gonzalo Rodriguez Gacha, one of the most powerful crime bosses in world history. Rodriguez Gacha was a Colombian warlord who acted as the most trusted enforcer of Medellín Cartel boss and fellow billionaire Pablo Escobar. His personal turf included Colombia's capital Bogotá and the surrounding countryside, a vast feudal fief that he ruled with a private mercenary army and an Israeli-trained team of assassins so formidable that they openly made war against the Colombian government military and *won,* until America intervened.

Colombia's cocaine crops were transported to the western half of North America from Rodriguez Gacha's totalitarian narco-state within Colombia using his private fleet of state-of-the-art boats, planes, helicopters, and sports cars. If you snorted a line of coke anywhere west of the Mississippi in the 1980s, you were ultimately a resident of Jose Rodriguez Gacha's drug turf and a customer of his cartel.

In recognition of his control of the Californian, Mexican, and Texan cocaine trade, *Forbes Magazine* in 1988 estimated that Rodriguez Gacha's personal fortune amounted to as much as $3 billion, which made him many times richer than the Queen of England. Rodriguez Gacha was one of the world's richest and most powerful people, and Big Mike Marvich was one of his favorite people.

When one of Rodriguez Gacha's most beloved cousins was tried on drug charges in Los Angeles in the late '70s or early '80s, Mike Marvich was retained to salvage an otherwise hopeless case. After helping to secure the acquittal of Gacha's cousin, Mike further ingratiated himself with the Medellín Cartel by daringly smuggling the Colombian over the border in the face of another federal indictment.

In return for Mike's loyal and ingenuous service, Rodriguez Gacha arranged for Mike to join him in his Colombian principality. While being lavishly entertained at one of Gacha's palatial compounds, Mike received from Gacha Rodriguez a special token of his thanks: a baroque golden cross inlaid with emeralds. That wasn't the only honor Gacha bestowed upon Big Mike; soon afterwards, Big Mike the elderly paralegal was importing more cocaine than anyone else in California.

Mike Marvich the ruthless legal professional made an easy, elegant transition to the profession of murderous drug kingpin. With his finely honed street instincts, legal expertise, and unparalleled connections to both law enforcement and the Medellín Cartel, Big Mike was the unstoppable force in the Californian underworld. The local Colombians couldn't touch him because Mike had more juice back home than they did, and the Californians couldn't begin to compete with his firepower, unlimited war chest, and brilliant strategic ability. Mike was the boss of Orange County and easily more powerful than any traditional mafioso anywhere in the western United States.

> *"The report also alludes to Marvich's 'Colombian drug smuggling connection' and alleges Marvich's 'colorful criminal past includ[ed] at least two alleged "hits" Marvich made on a former girlfriend and an associate.' . . . Of course [Customs Agent Cari] Hennen . . . had been told Marvich kept a gun by his easy chair and had been involved in several murders. Hennen had heard Marvich was implicated in the murder of an attorney and Lawrence's parents. Apparently, there was insufficient evidence to try Marvich for the killings."*
>
> People v. Collin Lee Quick et al. (1997)

The first time I blundered into Mike Marvich's life should have been my last: I accidentally robbed him! I was just a kid bussing tables at the time when Sal and Joey Avila's most trusted accomplice, Elroy, approached me. Elroy was a legendary character, a red-haired surfer who looked like a nerd but became Dirty Harry in a shootout. Authentically insane and fearless, Elroy was a deadly twerp with a volcanic temper and a vicious Napoleon complex who took care of Joey's dirty work. When he wasn't blasting the competition away, Elroy specialized as a liaison to the Afghani heroin market, making millions for the Avilas by arranging for tons of heroin to be sent in consignments of scissors to his fictitious office supply company.

As a young crook, Elroy bungled a robbery of the famous Jack's Surf Shop in Huntington Beach. Although he remembered to wear a mask, he forgot to disguise his voice. Recognizing the voice of his frequent customer, the cashier said, "Hey, Elroy, what the fuck do you think you're doing?" and chased him down the street and kicked his ass. In later years, Elroy would have just shot the cashier, but he was young and inexperienced at the time.

A couple decades later, when Elroy had been reduced to a crippled, wheelchair-confined skeleton by muscular dystrophy, he told Sal Avila that he had made a deal to act as the *muscle* in a bank robbery. Sal looked at his friend's gnarled, shaking hands and said, "Elroy, how you can act as the muscle when you don't have any left?"

Elroy explained how he would be wheeled into the bank with a sawed-off shotgun taped to his hands. When Elroy's body proved incapable of going through with this scheme, the lifelong crook lost his reason to live and committed suicide by overdosing.

At the time Elroy approached me, he was still in his prime, but he was nonetheless one man short on a caper. Joey had told him that I was an eager little crook who wouldn't second-guess anything. Otherwise, I would have realized that any scheme a connected guy like Elroy planned in which I was the most capable accomplice was probably something of a suicide mission. I could never have imagined that I would be stealing from the most dangerous cocaine trafficker in California, a ghoul that even the "Black Widow," Griselda Blanco, hesitated to cross.

I was told only that we were breaking into a businessman's office in Santa Ana. I was so young I couldn't even drive to the caper; I had to take a bus! When we arrived at the office, we realized that our original plan to quietly mine through the wall was unnecessary. No one was around, so Elroy just pried open the door with a crowbar. We rushed in, rifled through the file cabinets, found the cabinet that had the distinct chemical smell of good cocaine, and grabbed the five kilos of block-wrapped white powder inside. I was so relieved when I found that cocaine: I was just a kid, a sophomore in high school with a skittering heart and a loopy mind.

Elroy gave me $2,500 and some coke for my work—by far the biggest score of my life at that time. This was back when I was lucky to make $93-a-week at Setoya's. Shortly afterwards, a blanched and sweating Elroy pulled me aside and told me we had made a huge mistake. "Grind that coke I gave you, whack it up, repackage it. Sell it in small quantities. Don't let anyone know you got a big score," Elroy warned me. "We're going to be killed if Mike Marvich finds out we robbed him."

When I asked around about Mike Marvich, I couldn't believe what I heard. I had fucked over the *Medellín Cartel.* I had screwed over one of the handful of people in the world with the power and willingness to kill absolutely anyone who wasn't under constant Secret Service protection. But the stories about Mike Marvich's daring and power seemed too fantastical to be true. I would need firsthand evidence to take Mike's James Bond–villain reputation seriously.

I would be converted. Later I learned that Mike told the Colombians that *fifty* kilos, not five, but *fifty kilos* had been stolen and would need to be replaced. This fucker was so fearless that he used the burglary of five kilos of cocaine (worth roughly $150,000 chopped up) as an excuse to scam $1,500,000 worth of cocaine from Pablo Escobar. By robbing him that night, I made Mike Marvich more money than I made in a year as a cocaine trafficker.

At his height, Big Mike's operation, which included his own private squadron of planes and boats, was making over a million dollars a week. I read those figures from one of Mike's own private ledgers, so that's not an inflated DEA estimate. Since Mike was active in the cocaine trade for over a decade earning around $50 million a year, he could finance the sort of firepower that no one else in California could even hope to match. Mike was so heavy that, among the Colombians, he outranked and commanded more fear than Griselda Blanco, who practically invented the coke trade. Mike openly dismissed Griselda as "Mama Coca"—an insult that the indiscriminately homicidal Griselda let slide. Griselda was nuts, but she wasn't *that* nuts.

Besides cash, Mike also had at his disposal Rodriguez Gacha's mercenary assassins and decades of accrued favors from every lawyer, judge, sheriff, and politician in California; he could have made millions of dollars without worrying about anyone trespassing on his turf or getting his hands dirty. The problem was, Big Mike *wanted* to get his hands dirty. He was a grizzled old monster with the money and muscle to trample everyone else in O.C., and he wasn't going to let that power go to waste.

Big Mike was an old-school gangster, and to old-school gangsters crime was abstract, a gypsy way of life more than a profession. That's one reason why Mike kept dozens of over-the-hill ex-cons on his private welfare roll. They had done business the right way, and as the hand-picked viceroy of one of the world's top crime bosses, Mike was upholding traditional underworld values by rewarding them for it. Mike rewarded the good crooks and killed the half-ass wannabes who did business like assholes.

It was the principle that mattered to Big Mike. Even if a gangster had all the material things and money he could ever desire, it was his duty to uphold the gangster's code of conduct. That gangster's code was simple: fuck anyone weak enough to be fucked, don't take shit, and get as much money as you can—even if you can't spend the money you already have. In the same way, a lion surrounded by easy, defenseless prey will just keep on killing long after it's no longer hungry; killing is just what it does.

Mike could have had a billion dollars in the bank, but he would risk losing everything just to make sure that anyone who shorted him got what he deserved. I saw Mike drop off hundreds of thousands of dollars to his attorney and then threaten to kill someone over a late payment on a tiny loan. It was one of those comparatively inconsequential debts that would kill Joey Avila.

Surfer party-boy Joey Avila was tough enough for the Orange County of the 1970s, but by the late 1980s he was a rich playboy restaurateur on the brink of a Hollywood midlife crisis. Joey didn't have that hunger or viciousness anymore; he even found Jesus. Though he still dealt drugs and hung with heavy gangsters, it was just a pastime, posturing, something he did to aggrandize and amuse himself. It wasn't life or death for Joey; the game was just a game.

Joey's example taught me one of the immutable laws of the street: the quickest way to get killed is to dabble in crime. You can't be a part-time hood; you can't be half yuppie, half killer. Since the underworld is basically a business community organized around the exploitation of mankind's weaknesses, no allowances are made for a crook who does not aggressively defend his interests at all times. The tiniest bit of hesitation, mercy, complacency, or laziness in a gangster's game will be sniffed out by a rival predator and exploited with usually deadly results.

Joey was such a waste. If he had had any common sense or self-control, he would have seen his scrape with the federal justice system in the Tahitian Connection case as a sign to retire from the drug game. He could have lived luxuriously off the profits from his restaurants and nightclub as he partied for years and years with his playboy friends, aging gracelessly until he became a leather-skinned, Botox-enhanced L.A. pussy hound with a facelift and frosted hair. Or he could have turned out like Sal, a mellowed-out, brain-fried old hippie surfer with a beautiful family, a dozen ex-wives, and an easy life. To this day, people still want to talk with Sal and me about Joey. He wasn't the type of guy you forget, especially with his identical twin still bumbling around like a low-budget independent film remake of a big-budget Hollywood blockbuster.

For such a wonderful guy to get pumped full of bullets for no better reason than he liked to play gangster was ridiculous, shameful. Joey's son is fatherless—for what? When I was still working at Setoya years before Joey died, an incident occurred that should have made a bigger impression on me. Freddy, a smuggler who had once made a deal to rat on Joey only to renege and save his life, visited the restaurant to find Joey sitting at a table with his behind-the-scenes lover, Griselda Blanco, and some other mass-murdering Colombian heavyweights.

Freddy pulled Joey aside and asked him, "Joey, do you have any idea what you're doing? These guys are *real* gangsters. They will *kill* you."

I was eighteen when Joey was killed. He was still larger than life to me, my idol; he had introduced me to a world of incredible excitement and fun, and I admired how he lived every day with such style and bravado. As far as I was concerned, there was no such thing as death. Everyone in our circle had lived so recklessly for so long that death seemed like a trap for suckers, something you'd have to be a fool or asshole to fall for. Even as my own luck started to rot, it never really occurred to me that all the bloodshed happening *out there* could infiltrate our privileged little bubble.

Don't forget: I was a rich O.C. kid. People like me didn't die like ghetto dealers. The heat would eventually die down, the crises of today would work themselves out tomorrow, and we'd be back to living the high life. I was still only a teenager, a teenager whose mind was warped by an inordinate amount of success, luck, and drugs. My brain's daily diet of adrenaline, coke, hormones, and steroids programmed me to feel invincible at all times. I had no reason to know better.

Joey had ample reason to know better. He had known that Mike Marvich was a heavy-duty guy going back at least a decade; the Avilas confided to me that, in the late '70s, they had gone to Mike to "take care of" a creep who had attempted to rape Sal's wife, and Mike had apparently done the job. Joey also knew from Griselda, and the contempt with which Mike treated her, that you might as well be talking to Pablo Escobar himself when you talked to Mike.

Joey didn't care what Mike thought, or what Pablo Escobar thought for that matter. Joey had gotten away with murder for too long to fear anything or anyone. The guy who happily got into bed with the Black Widow unhesitatingly fucked the Medellín Cartel and its viceroy, Mike Marvich—and Mike Marvich's wife.

In retrospect, it's almost comical to review how insistently the Avila family was paging the Reaper. Arrogant verging on suicidal, they did everything within their power to volunteer for a chalk outline. They so thoroughly disrespected Mike Marvich that they gave him a simple choice: start killing or be disgraced.

The trouble started when Joey Avila recognized a prime target for seduction in Mike's thirty-years-younger trophy wife, Cathy Lawrence. Beautiful, friendly, and sociable, Cathy was neglected by her workaholic husband and compensated with a bottomless bankroll to spend as she pleased. Seeing the potential but not the peril, Joey effortlessly scooped Cathy up and fucked a no-interest, no-timeframe $200,000 loan out of her, which he used to build the dance club over Setoya known first as Tavilas and then as Pompeii.

At the same time as Joey was pilfering Mike's money and fucking his wife, the Avila twins' *federale* uncle was infuriating Rodriguez Gacha and Pablo Escobar by shaking down the Medellín Cartel's cargo planes as they refueled in Mexico. More oblivious than brashly defiant like his twin brother, unreformed Jehovah's Witness Sal was casually throwing a bone to Mike's beloved daughter, Leslie. Lastly, Joey's right-hand Elroy and I robbed Mike's office.

The Avilas gave Mike Marvich exquisite justification to kill their entire family, but Mike did nothing for years. Like the FBI, Mike moved methodically and struck with pinpoint precision and devastating force. Unlike the typical mobster, who is sentimental and hotheaded in equal proportions, Mike was patient, ruthless, and absolutely calculating. He only acted when he stood to gain the maximum return.

He was smart: his first target was not Joey or even Cathy, but Cathy's ex-husband, Jerry Lee Lawrence. A pot dealer and founder of the Church of Cannabis Sativa, Lawrence had famously run for Orange County Sheriff in 1974 while under indictment for possession of sixteen pounds of marijuana. In June 1984, the pot pastor was discovered in the trunk of his car at Ontario International

Airport, his brain splattered across the carpet. Mike would later tell me that Ontario Airport was where his top smuggling pilot kept his planes.

Jerry Lee Lawrence was survived by Cathy and their kids, who received all the insurance and inheritance that was coming to them—which Mike Marvich would then inherit along with the kids in case Cathy were to expire.

Which she did: after a decent six-month interval, Cathy "accidentally shot herself" while lying in bed next to her husband, who apparently was not awoken by the gunshot or the soaked bedsheets and slept through until morning. Mike claimed that she kept a gun under her pillow and accidentally set it off in her sleep—he never explained to me how a gun lying horizontally under a pillow would shoot directly *upwards* into Cathy's head instead of sideways. She was thirty-eight; Mike would get her children and her assets. Though the police obviously suspected Mike of the murder, he had done just enough to deprive them of the evidence needed to prosecute.

Next came Joey—Mike informed him that he knew about his dearly departed wife's $200,000 loan, and, tacking on a few years' interest at shylock rates, he was there to collect the full amount owed to the Marvich estate: $400,000. My assumption is that Joey, still marginally sane, paid him in dribs and drabs over the next two years, begrudging Mike the humiliation of paying another hood tribute. Mike was satisfied to leave Joey alone until there was no more cash left to extort.

In 1987, this awkward truce was broken, incredibly, by the Avila family. The uncle continued to rip off the Medellín smugglers in Mexico, and, though I don't know the details, Joey was indirectly involved in the robbery of another stash of Medellín coke. I suspect Elroy or Lalo was probably involved. According to Mike, the

Colombians were getting apoplectic over the Avila inter-ference in Mexico and wanted to send a message.

It is at this point, I believe, that Mike pulled off a double-cross that to this day leaves me awestruck in its ballsiness and strategic brilliance. Realizing that he had a ready-made scapegoat in his pal Joey Avila, I believe Mike arranged to make the maximum profit from what he had intended to do all along. A few years earlier, Mike had transformed the five kilos Elroy and I had stolen into *fifty* so he could get forty-five free kilos when the cartel sent a substitute shipment. In 1987, with Joey and his uncle already on the hook with Medellín for stealing, between 400 and 800 kilos of Mike's cocaine suddenly disappeared—a stash worth tens of millions of dollars.

This ploy served Mike's interests in a multitude of ways. Obviously, he made millions and millions of dollars without having to do any work whatsoever. Mike also gained an ironclad justification for killing Joey that had nothing to do with Cathy, the humiliating adultery rumor, or the galling idea that Setoya was built with Mike's money. Finally, there would be no doubt that the cartel, already in a rage over the Avilas, would accept Joey as the culprit, taking the heat off Mike for the theft and improving his rep when he clipped Joey for the rob-bery.

Big Mike Marvich showed up at El Ranchito to say goodbye to Joey in May 1987. He was accompanied by influential cocaine kingpin Mark Ruiz, who smuggled tons of coke through his private fleet of shrimp boats in Mexico and provided useful misdirection for any law enforcement investigators eavesdropping on this meeting. When Big Mike arrived, I was dumbstruck; the stranger radiated power and menace like no one I had ever en-countered before or since in my life.

Big Mike was tall, very old, and very strongly built. He wore his clothes and his hair in an identical fashion to the mafiosi I would later meet who, like him, made their bones in the mid–20th century underworld. Like my future Mafia mentors and his convict contemporaries John "Sonny" Franzese, Vincent "Jimmy" Caci, and Anthony "Big Tony" Peraino, Marvich regularly dressed in immaculately pressed slacks and a dress shirt with a short-billed gangster/cabbie hat over his neatly trimmed silver hair. The effect was very impressive: a couple members of my crew would later believe rumors that Marvich was a protégé of Mafia icons Lucky Luciano or Meyer Lansky, though Big Mike himself would never spread such fabulous tales.

Marvich's thin, callow face betrayed no emotion as he walked through Joey's restaurant. As he slightly nodded and shook hands with me, I noticed that he had very large, very thick, very worn hands—tough guy hands, giant calloused catcher's mitts. For a moment, he fixed his eyes on me with a brief intensity that made me feel like he had just memorized my entire genetic code.

Acting like the big boss, Joey sent Sal and me out of his office so he could talk with Marvich and Ruiz alone. From what Joey told Sal, Mike started demanding more money, and I would assume he did so in a condescending, emasculating manner tailored to raising Joey's ire. Within minutes, Joey, with his Latin machismo, was screaming at Marvich for insulting him by shaking him down in his own establishment. Though we heard bits of Joey's apeshit meltdown, I don't recall hearing any response from Mike. That silence was ominous.

Big Mike was not the type of guy to make a scene or even argue. Mike was so much smarter than all the hothead cocaine cowboys; he knew that words meant

nothing and that temper tantrums would dare his enemies to make the first move. Mike smoothly ignored Joey's bratty tirade without saying a word, calmly opened
the door, and walked out of the restaurant with a blank
face.

Joey apparently didn't think much of it. He just told
Sal and me that we had to do something about Big Mike
one way or the other. Sal responded that he had to hurry
because Mike was going to kill him. "I'm going to die any
day now, anyway," Joey said with a shrug.

I wasn't worried, and within moments neither was
Joey. After all, we both always came out winners in the
end. I remember feeling proud that Joey told off the most
powerful criminal in California and sent the guy fleeing
with his tail between his legs! I was so clueless. So was
Joey—even Sal the Space Cadet was perceptive enough
to take a break from knocking on doors and distributing
The Watchtower to let Joey know that Mike was going to
kill him if he didn't kill Mike first.

Looking back, it's clear to me that Joey was an out-
of-his-depth amateur *despite* the millions he earned in
the drug trade. And Mike knew this: he counted on it by
letting Joey live so long. By the end of his life, Joey was
a gangster for recreation, for profit. Mike Marvich was a
gangster by *nature;* his predatory behavior was disconnected from whatever material benefits he derived from
it. Mike killed and exploited because it was the existential purpose of his life.

The day after Mike's visit, a pair of unfamiliar Colombians shouldered past the hostess at El Ranchito, scanned
the restaurant intently, and, finding what they were looking for, ripped some photos of Joey off the wall. Around
the same time, an Avila-affiliated dealer named Jim,
who was rumored to be involved in stealing Marvich's

cocaine, had his house invaded by a two-person Colombian hit team and barely escaped. Acting on a tip about Jim's hiding place, the assassins tried again, knocked on the wrong door, and shot up an innocent family.

On the night of the murder, even I could tell there was something palpably wrong. I remember feeling nauseous, uneasy, and anxious for no apparent reason. It was as if I could sense that our little bubble of invincibility had been popped. Frank and I were drinking tequila shots at El Ranchito's bar in Back Bay; I still remember the sound of the blenders whirring as the bartender whipped up margaritas, the phones ringing, people laughing. We were both very drunk and very high on coke. Regardless of any workout routine or diet regimen I was on for martial arts and bodybuilding, I couldn't always resist a half-dozen shots and a couple lines at Joey's place, the temple of the Orange County coke and booze cult.

After getting wasted, Frank and I went outside to talk with Joey before he left for the night. Joey was standing next to his shiny black Porsche Carrera with the vanity license plate "BBBBBad," in the same strip-mall parking lot where I had met him five years earlier on my first day as a busboy.

Joey had his cinematic smile turned on to its full intensity, but, even drunk and flying on coke, I was still weighted down with foreboding. I asked Joey if everything was all right, breaking the rhythm and tenor of our usual who-gives-a-fuck, ball-busting guy talk.

Though he understood my intent, Joey didn't take me seriously. He told me that everything was fine and that he was going to meet his girlfriend at a restaurant in Irvine. Over the years, I have reviewed and dissected that night over and over to see what I did wrong, what I could have done, but there was nothing. Joey was the same age as I am today, forty.

The one thing I'm sure I wouldn't have done is what Joey did: drive off in his Porsche, happy as usual, completely unprotected, and oblivious to the danger he was in. This was Joey the Gangster in a nutshell: he kept his one pistol in the *trunk* of his car. Mike Marvich wasn't Kenny DiMartini; if he struck, Joey would have no time to exit his car, run to the trunk, open it, find his gun, and fire. There would barely be time to scream.

Around midnight, Joey's Porsche was speeding along the curves and turns of Irvine Boulevard, with Newport Beach and Back Bay to his left and gorgeous beach homes to his right. He was listening to a sermon by local evangelical pastor Tim Timmons, who was in the process of converting Joey to a sect of born-again Christianity whose teachings must not have conflicted with organized crime and cocaine trafficking. Joey and Sal disagreed on every major tenet of Christian doctrine except the one condoning the drug trade. Those two kooks would traffic kilos of coke and smack while engaged in endless verbal slap fights over the finer points of the Sermon on the Mount.

While Timmons preached, a high-speed motorcycle silently followed Joey's Porsche. Joey began to turn onto Santa Isabel Avenue when someone he knew appeared on the street corner and waved him over. Slowing down, Joey began to lower his window, probably so he could crane toward the person and flash his famous smile. Just then, the motorcycle pulled up to the driver's side of the black Porsche and a burst of .45 caliber slugs shattered Joey's window and ripped into his torso. The motorcycle swung in front of Joey's car; the passenger wielding the MAC-10 submachine gun dismounted. According to witnesses in the nearby houses, the killer spoke to Joey (some said he yelled) before unleashing another burst of concentrated gunfire from his tiny automatic pistol. Joey's life drained out of fourteen bullet wounds.

A small Honda sports car zoomed up to the intersection, and all three men—Joey's "friend," the motorcyclist, and the shooter—got in and fled the scene. The police in the rich beachfront neighborhood arrived within five minutes. The hit team was gone, but the cops discovered a brand-new, abandoned motorcycle and an idling black Porsche containing the corpse of Joey Avila. A police helicopter noisily circled the scene. A background check on the motorcycle showed it had been purchased a week before in South Bay; unsurprisingly, it had been bought with cash and registered to a fictitious person who lived at a vacant lot.

My phone rang at five in the morning. I was still very asleep and very drunk, so I was not pleased by the disturbance. It was Officer Jerry wishing me a good morning: "Hey, I guess we won't be doing anything with Joey anymore."

"Why? Did he get busted?" I asked, groggy and pissed that he was calling so early.

"Nope, he can't hold water anymore. He's too full of holes!" Jerry was being a sleazy bastard as usual, but I was too sleep-drunk to understand.

Jerry made it simple: "Joey was killed last night." He said it with no preamble and no feeling in his voice. Suddenly I was very awake. Jerry, no fan of Mexicans, added, "That's one less pepper-belly."

I started to ask questions but Jerry simply cut me off and said, "Drive by his house" and then hung up. Perhaps no story better encapsulates Jerry's depravity than how he took malicious joy in telling an eighteen-year-old kid that his idol had been shot to death. A week before, Jerry had partied with us in Joey's office, laying out lines of coke for everyone and laughing; now Joey was just a punch line to him. A few days later, Jerry made some copies of the crime scene photos to show me, to rub my nose in the gore so he could see my reaction.

As I was getting dressed, I received another telephone call, this time from a strange number. I picked up the phone to immediately hear an unfamiliar voice: "Well, that's the end of the Joey Avila problem!" Dial tone. Maybe Mike had heard about my visit to his office years back with Elroy; maybe he knew my reputation as a lunatic who idolized Joey.

I was so panicked that I began to feel numb and disoriented, as if my head were trapped inside a melting ice cube. When I drove past Joey's house, it was still dark, but the police had lit up the entire place like a movie set. There was plastic laid out all around Joey's Porsche; cops huddled everywhere. Though I couldn't see anything clearly, I knew Joey was dead, and that made me suddenly realize that I was no adult. I felt helpless. I was brokenhearted and had none of the maturity or life experience to know how to deal with it.

For the safety of everyone around me, I knew I needed to get out of the business. I was leading the life of a cannibal, feeding off the suffering, misery, and weakness of other people. I should have retired, especially since I still had Tara, who deserved to be pampered, loved, and protected, who was worth the shallow fun and excitement I would give up by leaving the drug trade.

At that point, I could have walked away; although the Two Toms had a tag-team hard-on for me, I wasn't important enough for them to chase forever. My family could easily have arranged my admission to a good college and internships at good companies; I was four years of easy schoolwork away from straitlaced yuppie success. With my interest in electronics and computers, I probably would have made it rich in the Silicon Valley tech boom. Tara could have stayed home at our mansion and baked bread all day.

I had options; I always had options. Every choice I made was entirely my fault. I wouldn't say I was addicted to the criminal lifestyle, but it was the only thing I knew, the entire basis of my social life, value system, and ambitions. My entire concept of me had been founded on violence, exploitation, and misbehavior ever since I was in military school. I can blame no one else. Normal college and cubicle life just seemed like it would suck ass in comparison to the excitement and freedom of life as an outlaw; it wasn't any more complicated than that.

The very day Joey died, I was back doing what I always did. My only good influence was Tara, and I had to keep her at a distance. She took note of Joey's death, read my body language when we talked about it, and began to realize the truth. I tried to put off the inevitable argument with her—kept slithering away at just the right moment. I had experience being cagey.

While I tried to cope, I was getting increasingly impatient phone calls from Lalo and another muscle guy I knew from Joey's restaurant, Tommy Thornton, asking me to meet them.

Tommy was a giant white dude with a huge garlic-bulb head, a bad toupee, a wardrobe full of awful, ill-fitting '70s-style suits, and eyes that were just inhumanly *cold*. When Tommy talked to you with his deep Grim Reaper voice, he gave you the unshakeable feeling that you lived at his discretion.

To this day, Tommy is a California underworld legend.

Anyone from the 1970s and 1980s who claims not to have been afraid of Tommy is either a liar or a stranger. Even Colombian hit men and 300-pound Hells Angels will admit to being scared shitless of Tommy. An undercover cop who worked in close quarters with criminal heavyweights from all over the world once told me that Tommy (by that point an old man) was the only crook whose mere presence filled him with dread. I've seen Tommy destroy younger men, even in his seventies.

And, one on one, you were defenseless against Tommy, no matter who you were. He was more badass than most movie heroes. In addition to his incredible size and accompanying superhuman strength, Tommy was one of the five or six most dangerous men in the world in hand-to-hand combat. A grand master in kenpo karate with a tenth-degree black belt, Tommy racked up a 33–0 (31 by KO) record in elite full-contact martial arts competitions and opened a chain of martial arts dojos throughout California. Hired by the U.S. State Department for security work, Tommy trained military and law enforcement personnel in counterterrorism and hostage rescue tactics.

With his James-Bond-meets-Bruce-Lee credentials, Tommy stomped around California like he was always looking for a fight, a white Mr. T wearing a huge golden chain with an eagle pendant given to him by Elvis Presley when he was the King's bodyguard.

After Elvis died, Thornton got a job as Joey's bodyguard, which naturally flattered Joey's perception of himself as a glamorous celebrity. When Joey had been kidnapped in the wild Tahitian Connection days, Tommy supposedly rescued him in *Rambo* fashion, earning Joey's lifelong gratitude. When Joey had been beefing with rival dealer Alfredo Tavera, it was Tommy who kidnapped the defenseless Sal and held him under armed guard in a safe house. Sal eventually lost his temper at being isolated against his will from all of California's pussy and parties and picked a fight with Tommy. He threw a sucker punch at Tommy, and in one fluid motion Tommy rotated with the force of the punch and knocked Sal out with a roundhouse kick.

In addition to being a physically terrifying presence on the Avilas' side, Tommy was also their biggest weakness. Tommy was with the Avilas for the same reason he had been with Elvis—for the cash, and as with every other mercenary in the cocaine trade, Big Mike and his bottomless bankroll ultimately owned Tommy. Despite Tommy's unstoppable-killing-machine reputation, he clearly wanted *nothing* to do with pissing off Marvich under any circumstances.

Knowing that Thornton was a stone killer and that Lalo had a habit of murdering friends over chump change, I wasn't exactly eager to put my safety in their bloodstained hands when they asked for a meeting. Nonetheless, I had no choice; it's not like I was going to volunteer to get on Tommy Thornton's bad side. I eventually agreed to meet with them at a crowded ice skating rink.

At the skating rink they told me that Big Mike wanted to speak with me, which was both terrifying and exciting. Even after Joey's assassination, I was still too caught up in the coke trade not to be a little awed by the prospect of a personal meeting with one of the most powerful cocaine smugglers in America, the Medellín Cartel's viceroy for Southern California. Of course, I was still scared shitless.

I was brought to Mike's house in Costa Mesa, a modest two-story home planted close to the curb on the edge of a park and a golf course. My family grew up in a nicer house than this; my friend Frank's house was the Taj Mahal by comparison. Although Mike owned boatyards, planes, apartment buildings, and construction companies, it was clear that money didn't matter to him, aside from the power it represented and the crimes it could subsidize. When I got to know Mike better, he would brag to me that he'd move to a trailer park before he died just to show how little money mattered to him, which he eventually did despite having—at the very least—tens of millions of dollars tucked away in investments.

Lalo and Tommy escorted me, smirking, into the house's Oriental-themed foyer. Mike was plopped in a La-Z-Boy recliner next to an antique reading lamp; before I knew it, Lalo and Tommy were gone, and I was alone with Mike. I walked to a couch next to his recliner and sat. Years later, I learned that he kept a gun hidden in his recliner. He was quiet, still.

Big Mike wore his little gangster cap inside his own home. He was very cold; without warning he grunted, "How do you feel about Joey's death?"

Before I could answer, he asked what Joey's family thought. While I tried to think of a diplomatic way of answering that wouldn't get anyone killed, Mike stuck his chin out, bugged his eyes, and spoke as if to an idiot, "Maybe they should pay me back the money they owe me, right? Get what I'm saying?"

Mike continued asking me questions without remotely paying attention to my answers; he just stared me down hard. Finally, he waved his hand and asked in the most nonchalant voice if I had heard that his wife killed herself right next to him in their bed for no apparent reason. "Isn't that strange, Kenji? I didn't hear a thing!"

I realized that the rumors were true: Big Mike was bragging that he'd killed his wife and slept with her corpse until the morning to arrange a credible alibi. No villain I've ever seen in a movie even comes close to the menace in Big Mike's eyes as he reclined in his La-Z-Boy. Finally, his point made, Big Mike loosened up and told me, smiling, "You do know, if you were in that car with Joey that night, you'd have had to go, too, you understand?"

When he wanted, Mike could be personable and easy to talk to, so much so that his inflection was somehow *charming* when he told me he wasn't bothered by the idea of murdering me. I just looked at him, and he continued telling me, in a very soothing voice, that, since I happened to still be living, from now on he wanted me to work with Tommy and his friends. When I told him I was working with some other people, he ignored my answer and patiently repeated that he wanted me to work for Tommy and his guys. He was used to people being scared stupid in his presence. I nodded. Big Mike grunted and shrugged in the direction of the doorway. I left, shaken. I wasn't as tough as I had thought, not with people like Big Mike Marvich in my neighborhood.

Shortly afterwards, Mike let Sal know he was coming into El Ranchito to see him. Sal, showing unusual mental clarity, deduced that if Mike leaned on him the way he had leaned on Joey, then he might as well kill Mike, because he was as good as dead anyway. Sal took his .38 to work that day and arranged for his enforcer Elroy and another associate, a heavyweight Colombian wholesaler named Martha, to be in the bar and watch his meeting with Mike. He needed backup, and he'd need witnesses to say the shooting of his brother's murderer was self-defense.

Mike ambled in with his gangster cap, sat at a table, and ordered some food. A tense, terrified Sal—who never had his identical twin's swagger or balls, which goes to show that neither are genetic—sheepishly listened to Joey's murderer ramble on about nothing. Mike hadn't come to threaten Sal—Joey's death had been the threat—but to revel in Sal's powerlessness and to feel him out face-to-face, the way he had felt me out. While Mike made small talk, he took a bite of food and swallowed without chewing. Mike Marvich began to choke and turn blue.

Watching from over Mike's shoulder, Martha jumped up and started waving at Sal not to do anything. Here was the perfect opportunity to kill Mike and possibly get away with it. Sal thought to himself, *Oh, Jesus, thank you for this blessing* . . . and then lost his mind. Watching the helpless, pathetic old murderer slowly die before his eyes, Sal picked the absolute worst scenario in which to abandon his normal hypocrisy and actually embrace his Christian faith. Sal jumped up and saved Mike Marvich's life with the Heimlich maneuver.

Within minutes, Mike went back to extorting the Avila family. Soon afterwards, Mike entered legal proceedings against Joey's estate demanding the rest of the money. Mike put an incontrovertible motive for killing Joey down on paper and filed it with the United States government; *that's* how pathological he was about getting his money, and that's how little he appreciated Sal's mercy.

In a way, the Avilas deserved what they got; they got into the ring against a tougher, meaner, stronger, and bigger fighter and tried to fight a good, clean, fair Christian fight. What a fucking joke! There's a reason Jesus wasn't born in Miami or Medellín.

According to Sal, who claims to have heard it from the paramedic who treated Big Mike, the last words Mike Marvich said before he died of natural causes at the age of eighty-three were, "JOEY! JOEY MADE ME DO IT!" I think Sal's lying to console himself; at the moment of his death, I think the only thing Big Mike was thinking about was who on the planet still owed him money.

> *"When I stepped out of Kenny's dad's condo, it
> looked like something out of* Hill Street Blues.
> *There were 200 guns pointing at me, the SWAT
> team positioned all over, twenty sheriff's cars
> parked all around, a surveillance Winnebago, six
> unmarked cars. . . . It was crazy. I was, like,
> what the hell happened?"*
>
> Greg Benjamin

My meetings with Mike Marvich made me realize that
I was *not* a gangster; I was just a teenager smuggling
and dealing drugs with my friends. I was in far over
my head; I was paralyzed from making any move since
I lost the confidence in my ability to outthink and
outmaneuver someone like Marvich. I was coasting,
trying to avoid confronting all of my problems: my fear
of Big Mike and his attempt to co-opt our operation,
Tara's dawning realization that I was a criminal, the
impending war in my crew caused by Frank's freebasing, the Two Toms' continuing plot to put me in jail,
and my own impossible-to-process despair at Joey
Avila's death.

   Patiently waiting for Fate to take care of my problems
was the worst possible strategy. If I had moved quickly
to reestablish discipline in my crew and adapt our operations to exploit the considerable advantages of working
with Big Mike, I believe I could have become his primary
heir and lieutenant. In retrospect, the eighteen months
I wasted by attempting to maintain business as usual
against contrary conditions was my fatal mistake—I lost

my momentum and fell behind. I would never be so close to kingpin status again.

My decision to try to indefinitely preserve my 1987 business model as an independent mini-cartel would prove to be a catastrophic strategic mistake that I continue to pay for to this day. The cost would be high: the life of my best friend and the love of Tara.

The kickback began in February of 1989, shortly after I had returned to Orange County from a trip to Hawaii with Clyde. Raj, another buddy from military school, had invited me to visit him in Hawaii during his vacation from active duty. Since a run to Hawaii with a kilo of cocaine was always profitable, I decided to use Raj's visit as an excuse for a business vacation. Clyde and a flunky of ours named Darren accompanied me.

After we met Raj at our luxury hotel in the middle of Honolulu, I had Clyde rent a Jeep so I could get the coke deal out of the way and have fun. I called Freddy, the laidback hood who had warned Joey about dealing with "real gangsters," and drove up to the North Shore the next day with Clyde, Darren, and some brand-new surfboards in tow. I dropped off Clyde and Darren at the pipeline so they could have fun, and drove alone to Freddy's beautiful beach house on Sunset Beach. He hooked me up with a buyer who asked for the whole kilo, but I decided to keep an ounce for later to impress Hawaiian party girls and have a little fun. Fred's buyer paid me $34,000 in cash and told me to move to Hawaii and become his regular supplier, which would have been an easy way to make a fortune. I told him I'd think about it.

With $34,000 to spend and an ounce of coke to snort, I had Clyde scour the classified ads in the newspaper to pick us up some MAC-10 machine guns, which you could buy and sell without ID, registration, or any bill of sale in those days. Clyde came back with a .25 caliber automatic for me—*Scarface* shit for any trouble that I stirred up with the Colombians or Mike Marvich back home. Our professional responsibilities dispatched, we turned our attention to partying. We visited Pearl Harbor, the famous volcanoes, the best surfing beaches, and all the hottest clubs, having one of the best times of my life. It was like a flashback to the carefree, fun times before Joey's death. After two weeks, we returned to reality, which was like a demonic parody of our idyllic trip to Hawaii.

The news reports and rumors swirling around Joey's death had gradually blown my cover. Tara *finally* realized that I was a depraved liar and a criminal; I was such an obvious gangster that I couldn't hide it from the girl who believed that bread was harvested by the loaf from bread trees. Despite the devastation I inflicted on her trusting heart, Tara loved me enough to come to me and offer me another chance if I quit the gangster lifestyle. I blew off her request and told her to get used to my career.

To give you an idea how much Officer Jerry's teachings had warped my mind, I was truly shocked that Tara actually left me! Where did she get off? Even though I had lied to her for years and told her point-blank that my criminal lifestyle was more precious to me than her love, I never really considered the possibility that she would dump me. Women weren't supposed to reject and break the hearts of coke-dealing badasses like me. More importantly, Jerry shamed me into trying to convince Tara and myself that her absence meant nothing to a hardened player like me, which made the situation much more painful for both of us.

My mentors, my parents, my friends, the cops, and

even the FBI had let me get away with being an evil prick. Only a cute O.C. beach bunny had the backbone and moral authority to hold me accountable for my crimes. Tara may not have been brilliant, but she had integrity and strength of character, which is more than I can say for every woman dumb enough to date a dog like me since.

I met Greg, Clyde, and my untrustworthy buddy Lalo at a bar one night to discuss how to deal with Frank for the thousandth time. They were drinking and snorting lines in between insisting that we needed to kill Frank. Lalo helpfully suggested that we take him down to Mexico to cap him to make it more low key; after all, a junkie like Frank skipping town wasn't going to arouse anyone's interest if they didn't find a body. Since Lalo was living part-time down in Playas, just south of Tijuana, he was close with the local police and could bribe them to cover it up.

Of course, I didn't particularly trust Lalo, both because of his loathsome personality and what I saw as him setting me up with Big Mike. Greg also kept chiming in that we should kill Frank, but I just told him to shut the fuck up every time he opened his mouth. No matter my emotional state, I would never be so desperate that I'd entrust matters of life and death to the judgment and discretion of savages like Greg and Lalo. If it had to be done, Clyde was the person I would have trusted to dispatch Frank, but he had nothing to say about the matter. He was comfortable waiting for me to give the word to act.

But I was not ready to kill Frank; I told them all to stop being paranoid and that I was in control of things. I honestly wasn't sure what to do, but I wasn't comfortable killing Frank so soon after Joey's death . . . though I

considered it, discussed it, and rehearsed it. Often. I just
did not have the self-confidence to make *any* move that
serious.

After drinks, they decided to go to Frank's drug pad
hotel room in El Toro to "party" by cleaning out his
mini-bar, stealing his drugs, and trashing his room. I followed along since I had nothing else to do and wanted
to keep an eye on these idiots. I gave Lalo a ride in my
Corvette; on the way, he showed off his leather satchel
full of tequila, cocaine, pistols, and *crystal meth.* I was
baffled: crystal meth? Meth at that point was an obscure
dirthead drug—cracker crack, biker speed. It was cheap,
nasty, trailer park shit. Looking into Lalo's demented
bag of tricks, I began mulling over how to dispose of this
Mexican asshole before he killed one of us.

When we got to the hotel, I immediately had another
bad feeling like the one I'd had the night Joey died. I
didn't like the idea of these three violent, coked-up,
shitfaced idiots smoking crystal meth and horseplaying
with weapons around Frank. An "accident" could all too
easily happen, and it would be executed in the sloppiest,
most shitfaced way imaginable; we'd go to jail for it. Even
though I had no intention of partying, I felt like I had no
choice as a conscientious criminal but to supervise this
volatile situation. I hadn't been in the mood for booze
or drugs ever since Joey's death and my recent breakup
with Tara.

While my coke-fiend friends partied, I watched a
weepy chick flick on TV, *Terms of Endearment,* and repeatedly dialed Tara's number. I was in a pathetic state.
I badly wanted to leave, but just as I was about to bolt,
Greg started following the oblivious Frank around with
a .38 RG blue-steel revolver pointed at the back of his
head, "joking."

As exhausted as I was with Frank's bullshit, the idea of Greg doing a sloppy, shitty hit in a hotel room pissed me off. If Frank needed to go, we'd take care of him in Mexico—where no one cared and real police didn't exist—just like Lalo suggested. After all, Lalo was a murderer; he knew what he was talking about.

Even if I stayed at the hotel, I soon realized, this situation was only going to deteriorate once the booze and drugs took effect, so I forced everybody to leave Frank's hotel room. After a stop at the Black Angus steakhouse across the street for last call, we drove Lalo to the train station in San Juan Capistrano around 1:30 a.m. so he could go back down to Mexico.

Lalo was creeping me out on the entire drive down. I was positive there was something crooked with his behavior: why was a coke dealer who made thousands off every kilo wasting his time with meth? I knew the likely answer: for people who have built up a tolerance for cocaine, meth gets them geeked up like coke once did. Meth makes a criminal a rampaging silverback, a focused killer who can harm others without troublesome fear, anxiety, or guilt. I didn't want to guess what type of low-down, dirty task a subhuman shithead like Lalo needed to be blitzed on tequila and rabid on meth to execute.

At the station, I ordered Clyde and Greg to stay away from Frank's hotel room and made them promise to obey. I had a horrible vibe about those two human wrecking machines getting any more drunk or high in the presence of fragile, infuriating Frank and his annoying girlfriend. They should have listened. I even followed them to the El Toro Road freeway exit to make sure they listened before I took off to Newport in search of Tara. I've been responsible for a lot of things, but what ensued in that hotel room is not on me.

As I walked up to Tara's window, a police car drove by, and out of congenital paranoia I hid from it. I would have been far better off had I let that cop establish my whereabouts. Once he drove away, I played Romeo to little effect, standing outside Tara's window and pleading with her to believe that I wasn't a criminal or involved in drugs anymore.

When I finally got home, I was so exhausted that I passed out on my floor. It was 5 a.m. My phone rang at 5:30. I answered it and heard another anonymous voice say, "You better get to that hotel room fast, Kenji." Still haunted by my last early-morning phone call, I nearly lost my mind; my heart skittered out of control. It had happened again.

> *I was really drunk, blackout drunk. Clyde and I were partying with Frank and Teresa, and I remember Lalo coming back to the room, and then—that's it. The next morning I woke up in San Juan Capistrano, it's daylight, and I don't know where I'm at. I call a cab, head to Kenny's dad's condo, got to sleep, and the next thing I know Kenny is waking me up and telling me Frank's dead.*

Greg Benjamin

I immediately suspected that I was being set up. After all, I still had Big Mike looming over me. I was getting some of my cocaine and business through Tommy Thornton, but nowhere near all of it as Marvich had requested. The only gun I had on me was a cheap, piece-of-shit CZ-75 that jammed after one shot, but I didn't have time to visit my arsenal before heading back to the hotel. I had to make sure my first shot was a good one.

I was there within ten minutes; with my CZ-75 tucked into the waistband of my pants, I took the elevator to the fourth floor. The floor was very quiet, peaceful, but the door to Frank's room was slightly ajar.

I had my hand on the pistol as I slid through the door into the dimly lit, torn-up room. There was no sign of forced entry. I was surprised to see Clyde's huge body asleep on the floor, his arm crossing his eyes as if to keep the light out. There was a tequila bottle on the floor. So those assholes *had* sneaked back to Frank's hotel room! Had Clyde killed Frank?

I took another step and saw blood; when I shook Clyde, his arm fell away and I saw the gory crater where his right eye used to be. Since it was a two-room suite, I charged through the door to the other room. The room appeared empty; then, in the darkness, I heard a sound. To my relief, Frank and his willowy junkie girlfriend were huddled together in a closet, weeping, petrified. I felt the same way; only my emotional response was mixed with a bitter anger at Clyde for being so stupid as to disobey my direct order. Well, he paid for it.

Worst of all, he died like a chump: defenseless, oblivious, and most likely deep in a shitfaced slumber. The toughest kid I knew didn't die like a man, like a gangster; he died like Joey, too stupid and reckless to know he was in danger. Clyde went out like a joke—a dumb, high, passed-out frat boy lying on a stained hotel room carpet. Clyde's mom lost her son because he couldn't resist another couple hours partying in Frank's freebase pad.

Frank and Teresa were incoherent, too fucked up to know what happened. I got them up and firmly instructed them to help me clean the room before we all got busted for drugs. After I painstakingly flushed the pot and coke down the toilet—there was so much cocaine that it formed a hard plaster in the toilet bowl—I had Frank and his bird-brained soul mate clean up the rest of the place and make sure to get rid of any evidence. I thought of telling them to make a run for it, but two weepy, panicked junkies fresh from witnessing a murder were not going to last long on the streets. I told them to wait for the cops.

When we were finished with our makeshift cover-up, I dialed 9-1-1. This is from the Orange County Sheriff's Department transcript of that phone call, 8:57 a.m., February 20, 1989:

> Operator: Sheriff's Emergency.
> Kenji: Yes, I'd like to report a murder.
> Operator: A murder?
> Kenji: Yes.
> Operator: When did it happen?
> Kenji: Ahm, it's at the Quality Suites, Room 402. . . . I don't know what happened, the guy's dead. Someone murdered him.
> [. . .]
> Operator: Are you calling from the, are you an employee there?
> Kenji: No, I'm here. I, it's my friend. My name is Ken [Gallo].
> Operator: Okay Ken, are you in the room?
> Kenji: Yes. And I'm going to leave right now, it's making me sick.

Though theoretically there were countless people who wanted Clyde dead—he was an enforcer for a coke trafficker—the main suspects had to be Lalo and Greg. Lalo's tequila and meth were in the room, and Frank remembered seeing Greg later that night with Clyde.

An outsider going to the hotel alone to seek revenge for Clyde's crimes seemed highly unlikely; though Clyde had done loads of dirty work for my crew, we always got away with that type of thing. Besides, there was no sign of forced entry; no matter how high or drunk Clyde was, he wouldn't have opened the door and fallen asleep with a competitor in the room. This had been done by someone Clyde trusted, with the assistance of someone already in the room: Lalo or Greg.

As I drove away from the hotel, my CZ-75 in my waistband, I realized two very important things. The first was that the Orange County Sheriff's Department, without a doubt, was going to pin this murder on me. It wouldn't take the Two Toms five minutes to connect this to me: Clyde was my enforcer who was seen partying with me the night of the murder, I was spotted driving to and from the hotel twice later that night, and I made the 9-1-1 call. I also had an obvious motive: Clyde had committed so many serious crimes on my behalf that I would clearly be safer if he were unable to incriminate me. Clyde's arrest over the botched drive-by with Jeff Okuda had yet to be adjudicated, so even though that burglary case was fictitious, the cops already had a charge against Clyde that they could say was making me nervous enough to kill him. As soon as the Orange County Sheriff's Department found me, I had no doubt that I would be cuffed and charged with first-degree murder.

In a panic, I had handed the police Frank and his girlfriend, the only witnesses, and I had little reason to believe that they had my interests at heart. If Frank got nailed with an accomplice or conspiracy charge, then a jonesing, mentally crumbling junkie like him would surely sell me out to escape jail time. I was on my way to death row. The electric chair was waiting. The Two Toms both had a good grip on the lever, one Tom's hand lovingly placed on top of the other Tom's hand.

The second realization was that the gangland slaying of my good friend Clyde in the very hotel room in which I had partied with him—the same hotel room from which I had repeatedly called Tara—would seal the coffin on Tara's and my relationship. His autopsy would show cocaine and alcohol levels that would kill a rhinoceros; my fingerprints would be all over the room; I would be arrested for first-degree murder; and, if I wasn't smart, they'd take me in with a CZ-75 pistol under my belt. Whatever bullshit Tara believed about my fundamental decency would become transparently preposterous, and she would never be able to trust me again.

We were done. Tara, the last thing holding me back, the only thing that civilized and humanized me, the only person who could have saved me, was gone. I had nothing precious left; everything human inside of me became bestial and merciless. The second I felt Tara's love drain from my body, the second I knew that my future was going to be nothing but a lonely, savage continuation of the depraved life I was leading, a series of reenacted gangster movie clichés—that's when a delinquent teenager became a psychotic monster with nothing to lose. The paralysis and insecurity caused by Joey's death immediately ended: I became recklessly confident because nothing was at stake. I simply didn't care if I lived or died anymore.

I was twenty years old, armed, raging on steroids, totally alone, a cornered animal. The murder hanging over my head might as well have been the Mark of Cain; I was exiled forever from normal life. I was surrounded by pitiless predators, and the only way I could survive was by fighting my way out, by becoming more ferocious, unpredictable, and ruthless than the mob of backstabbing cannibals that encircled me. Big Mike, Lalo, the Two Toms, Greg, Jerry, the Colombians, Sid Johnson, whoever killed Clyde, even Frank—I was going to throw myself at my problems gun-first. I wasn't going out like a bitch; I wasn't going out like Joey or Clyde.

A cornered animal attacks.

"It should be noted that [Kenji] made one or two telephone contacts with a subject named Jerry while at or near or in possession of the RG revolver at the Rimhurst address, and, after leaving [Kenji] went to a pay phone where he called Jerry again. [Kenji] seems to protect and be vague about two people, one of which is Jerry. [. . .] Who he seems to be protecting: Jerry=[Officer] Jerry, Irvine Police Department."

"[Kenji] said he came into control of the gun some time prior to giving the gun to Benjamin from a friend that said to [Kenji]—'Here is a good gun to do the murder.'"

Orange County Sheriff's Department
Files on the Murder of Lee Matthew Clyde

Gun in hand, I drove across town to visit the first suspect in Clyde's murder: Greg. That Neanderthal was too unsophisticated to be trusted: anyone could manipulate him into doing their dirty work. Hell, I did all the time! The night before, he shoved his gun to the back of Frank the oblivious junkie's head hours before Clyde got killed, and he left with Clyde after we dropped off Lalo in Mexico. I wasn't sure that Greg was the killer, but I was sure that he was capable of it and that I would kill him if he was responsible.

I took my tinkertoy CZ-75 over to my dad's condo where Greg was crashing, confident that my junk pistol would be able to fire the one round I'd need to put the dimwitted giant back to sleep if he looked at me the wrong way when he woke up. I was positive that I could read his face: if he lied, I'd know it, and I'd kill him without hesitation. There was no way that this barely functional thug would be able to credibly feign shock and confusion; if he already knew, his acting would be as believable as a kindergarten production of *Macbeth*.

Greg looked like Blackenstein with his 1989 hip-hop flattop haircut, stretched out on my dad's couch and snoring in his deep drunk sleep. With the CZ-75 at the ready, I woke him up and told him that *Frank* was dead—for some reason I felt like I could get a more accurate reading on what he knew via this misdirection. Greg seemed unmistakably shocked that anyone was dead, no doubt about it—so he lived. Looking into Greg's eyes, I knew there was no way he had the balls it would take to shoot my best friend Clyde in cold blood and then take a taxi across town to fall asleep at my dad's condo. He knew me too well; he knew I would be hunting for him. So Greg was innocent; one way or another, Lalo had to be involved.

My next concern was tooling up. A rinky-dink CZ-75 was enough to protect me against Greg, but if I ran into Lalo and Thornton or Big Mike's Colombians, I'd need considerably heavier ordnance. Greg and I tried to break into the apartment of my soldier Keith, who I knew had a Mossberg pump shotgun stashed in his room since I had set him up with Jerry to buy ammunition for it. Unfortunately, Keith was a skilled carpenter. By reinforcing his door to prevent a drug robbery, he thwarted his own crew's attempt to break in.

Without any other weapons close at hand, I had to take the only other gun available: I told Greg to get me the .38 Special he had stuck to Frank's head. It was a tense moment, but he obeyed, and I was careful not to grab it with my hands. The gun used to be mine; I had bought it for $40 from a guy who became a Costa Mesa cop. Its selling point was not its quality (it was a shit gun), but its purity: it was "clean"—an untouched, un-used, untraceable gun that I could use for a crime. When I had first showed it to Greg, he impulsively reached out and picked it up, staining the spotless gun with his fin-gerprints. Furious, I told him to just keep the damn thing since it was no longer of any use to me. Now I was taking it back out of necessity, reluctant as I was to be tied to whatever Greg did with it in the interim.

Since Greg had already gotten me arrested once by letting the police into my apartment, I already knew he was going to be worse than useless to me while I was trying to evade a police manhunt. I left him there at my dad's condo. In retrospect, I should have told the likely murder suspect to vacate my family's property, but I was pretty distracted at that moment. Needless to say, I told Greg to keep his fucking mouth shut no matter what hap-pened, and to stay out of the way of the police.

The next step was obvious: call Jerry. There was no better time to have a mole in the police department than when I was looking at a manhunt and murder charges. I drove out to Irvine and called Jerry on a pay phone. As with Joey Avila's death, Jerry took Clyde's in stride; his reaction was a mixture of predatory exhilaration and self-interested worry, as if the gangster side of him liked chaos and fresh blood, whereas the policeman side of him was concerned that my crew would get leaned on and rat out our relationship with him. He told me to meet him at Boomer's.

Boomer's was a ridiculous place for a life-or-death sitdown: it was an arcade and miniature golf course. It served our purposes because it was a public place, easily accessible by the 405 Freeway, and completely innocuous, the last place the police would ever look for me. I met Jerry in the arcade, which was overrun by hordes of screaming kids and exasperated parents thronging in every direction. Jerry was wearing nice jeans and a pea-green shirt; his hair was immaculate. He looked sharp, relaxed, and well rested, a player.

I looked like I had just escaped from a POW camp: my short spiky hair was an unwashed mess, my face was greasy, I was sweating, and my eyes were red and raw. After the terrifying 5 a.m. phone call, I had quickly dressed in whatever I picked up off the floor: beat-up high-top Reeboks, some dirty jeans, and a wrinkled gray-collared shirt that could only have been worn in the '80s. I must have looked seriously strung out because Jerry pulled me over to the booths where the families were eating pizza and told me to calm down and order something to drink. I ordered a Diet Coke.

All around us kids played and gobbled down shitty pizza while Jerry asked me to slowly, calmly tell him everything I could remember about the murder scene so he could advise me, the top suspect, on how I could evade getting convicted. Whether I killed Clyde was irrelevant to Jerry as long as it couldn't be proven. If I faced a life sentence or the electric chair, however, Jerry knew damn well that a crooked cop was my trump card to freedom. That's why I met him in public and why I brought Greg's pistol: I didn't trust that Jerry, my mentor in the art of ratting, hadn't considered putting a just-to-be-safe bullet in my brain. He well knew how devastating an informant I could be.

Jerry's questions focused on Lalo. We both figured he was the killer. The evidence seemed strong—Lalo was a known murderer connected to Mike Marvich and some Colombians who hated us. Lalo had claimed that he was going to take a 2 a.m. train that we now realized didn't exist, and a tequila bottle like the one he had been carrying the night before was found in the hotel room. Jerry asked if I had the gun that Greg had pointed at Frank. When I told him that I did, he took a condescending tone and asked, "You didn't touch it, did you?"

"Am I fucking stupid?" Even amidst the horror of the last few hours, I was still offended that Jerry could think so little of me as a criminal that I would put my fingerprints all over a possible murder weapon. Even if Greg hadn't killed anyone with that gun, there was a fair likelihood *I* would have to kill someone with it if things continued to go the way they were going. And I wasn't a rookie; Jerry had taught me well. There would be no fingerprints, and no one would find the weapon.

"Well, regardless, the cops are going to be looking for you. They're going to get you," Jerry said without a surplus of sympathy. It was an uncomfortable situation for him to have his drug trafficking partner cross-examined in the dark, dank room known as "the Box" in the OCPD homicide unit. "You should let me bring you in," Jerry said. It made sense: a prolonged manhunt would make me look guilty, and this way Jerry would get the credit for the arrest. Since I had so much money invested on the street in Orange County and hadn't given up on scamming my way back into Tara's arms, I didn't want to go on the lam, especially for a murder charge that would never go away. I agreed.

"Listen, Kenny, ask for a lawyer immediately if it looks like trouble. And . . . ," Jerry hesitated, looking uncharacteristically grim. "If they bring me up, tell them they have to talk to me. No matter what they ask—they have to talk to me about it." Laughing inwardly at Jerry's unwavering self-interest, I nodded.

With that, Jerry took out his raccoon-size cell phone and called the O.C. Sheriff's Department telling them he was going to bring me in. As we walked to Boomer's parking lot, he asked for Greg's gun. Although I knew that giving up the gun meant I was going to be in the car with Jerry alone and unarmed, I had no choice. If I hesitated or refused, Jerry would have known I didn't trust him and therefore wasn't trustworthy. Officer Jerry wrapped the gun in a plastic bag and stuffed it in the trunk of his car.

I climbed into the passenger seat of Jerry's spotless white Porsche Cabriolet, which he had confiscated as a trophy from a competing cocaine dealer. I felt intensely vulnerable—I had no idea if he had really called the cops to tell them he was taking me in. He might have been talking to the Psychic Friends Hotline for all I knew, and no one would ever know I had been with him if something happened to me. As he was driving, Jerry turned and sliced me up and down with this scrutinizing look, like I was a meek and undersized pit bull about to get tossed into a dog fighting ring. "You sure you're up to this? They're going to tear you up in there."

"Yeah, I can handle it," I responded with a hard stare, knowing not to show weakness. Shortly afterwards, we pulled into a gas station in South County, and there was Tom Dove with a detachment of deputies waiting for me. Well, at least Jerry had told the truth. He left me in the car and walked over to them with Greg's gun in the plastic bag. As Jerry talked, they looked over to me in the passenger's seat of Jerry's Porsche, squinting and sizing me up just like Jerry had. Suddenly Tom Dove nodded, and Jerry walked back. "I told them you hadn't eaten all day and needed to eat before you were interrogated."

I smiled—there were benefits playing for the home team. I had them take me to a sandwich shop for a turkey sub since I needed some protein. I didn't want a murder investigation to get in the way of my muscle gain, nor did I want the D-Ball and Equipoise steroids I was taking to go to waste. I wasn't planning on missing any reps at the gym over Clyde. Clyde wouldn't have wanted me to go soft on his behalf.

When the cops arrived at the hotel to find Frank and his scrawny girlfriend waiting for them, they told the police that Greg had come back to the hotel the night before with Clyde. The last thing either of them remembered before nodding off was Clyde and Greg drunkenly karate-chopping furniture and screaming "Hi-YAH!" followed by Greg telling Clyde to "wake up" and a tiny, indistinguishable pop. When Frank and Teresa woke up in the morning, Clyde was dead.

SoCal police don't take much convincing to arrest a black guy with a rap sheet, but they were too scared to simply knock on the door of my dad's condo because of my crew's reputation as gunslingers and bombers. They had reason to be scared: not only had Greg been carrying that .38 caliber, but we also had flak jackets and 7.62x39 military ammo for an AK-47 stashed there.

A team player to the end, I was relieved that the cops' first concern was Greg, not me, and I happily offered my services toward apprehending him. When I finished my turkey sub, the other cops took custody of me and drove me to an enormous mobile home they were using as a command center for the SWAT team that was staking out my dad's condo. They wanted me to draw Greg out of the apartment and into a public space so the SWAT team could cover him from all angles before they took him into custody. Since my dad's condo was already surrounded, and Greg would only get himself killed if left to his own King Kong devices, I cooperated. I called and paged Greg repeatedly, trying to get him on the line to talk him out of the apartment, but he never picked up the phone or called back.

Worried, the cops ordered the SWAT team to envelop the complex from every angle; imagine the FBI closing in on the Branch Davidian compound in Waco, Texas, to get an idea of the big operation they were launching to take down Greg. The SWAT team spent the next few hours positioning and repositioning, scoping out the building, playing a heavily armed game of chess with Greg—who, it turned out, was fast asleep the entire time.

Finally, the big oaf woke up and answered the phone, so I handed it to the cops. They promised to "light up" Greg if he didn't strip down to his underwear and slowly walk outside with his hands up. As soon as Greg stepped outside, the SWAT team gored him to the ground, right onto the hand he had recently broken when he was punching a guy in a car and accidentally hit the door. Greg screamed and writhed on his broken hand, causing the SWAT team to brutalize him for "resisting."

With Greg in custody, the cops no longer had a reason to play nice with me. I was taken from the command center to the Santa Ana police headquarters to be interrogated. Upon arrival, I was informed that I was still a top suspect in Clyde's murder; the cops ordered me to hold out my hands and, instead of handcuffs, they shoved plastic bags over my fists. This, I was told, was to keep my hands uncontaminated for when they tested them for gunpowder residue.

I think I may have actually laughed when the cops explained to me what they were doing: these idiots were trying to stop me from contaminating any evidence on my hands half a day after the crime and *hours* after Jerry first brought me in. I had eaten and used the restroom unattended, which gave me ample opportunities to wash my hands with bathroom soap or Neat Feet, the harsh foot scrub that Jerry had taught me to carry whenever I planned to fire a gun since it erased any traces of gunpowder residue. The Two Toms' sloppy work reassured me that I was smarter than they were after all, and it made me even more arrogant than usual for the interrogation.

I was escorted with my bagged hands to the Box, a small room with peeling gray paint, a steel table, and a two-way mirror. My chair faced the two-way mirror and two other chairs across the table. I was left alone for a short while, ostensibly to psych me out. I was eventually joined by Tom Carney; this was my official confirmation that the Two Toms had leapfrogged whoever was ahead of them in the rotation to grab Clyde's case for themselves. They wanted any case that had anything to do with my circle, both out of personal dislike for me and to avenge their failure to solve Joey's murder.

Tom Carney sat across from me; he was a tall, chubby, fifty-something guy with a *Leave It to Beaver* 1950s-style square haircut. He looked like an ex–football player, a big corn-fed redneck who let himself go in his middle age. Carney was the older, more straitlaced, and less fun of the Two Toms. He gave me the uptight pastor talk: "You're in trouble, Kenny. This is serious business we're talking about here. This is a *murder*—we don't care about the drug dealing or counterfeit cash. That is small potatoes in comparison. You're in serious trouble!"—that sort of suburban middle-age dad talk. I just sat there with the goofy bags on my hands acting carefree and thinking of new ways to scandalize or piss him off.

The transcripts of Tom Carney interrogating me read like excerpts from a comedy sketch. Some selections from the transcripts:

Carney: When is the last time you touched [Clyde's] wallet?
Kenji: I don't even remember touching it. I think maybe you guys found Greg's wallet, not Clyde's.
Carney: Clyde's?
Kenji: I took Greg's wallet the day before, and I wrote this type, this fake driver's license thing on a piece of paper. It said, you know, "[Greg Benjamin], 38 Watermelon Road, Spooksville, North Carolina." Stuff like that.
Carney: Um-huh.
[. . .]
Carney: Did, was there any money in [Clyde's] wallet?
Kenji: Nope.
Carney: Did you, ah, you didn't take anything out of it yourself?
Kenji: No. I don't need the money. Money's not my problem. I got plenty of it. [laughs]
[. . .]
Kenji: [After seeing Clyde's corpse] I got to Frank, and then I go, "What the fuck you mean you didn't know [if] he's breathing?" Frank told me [Clyde] just went to sleep and he didn't wake up. I go, "He's got a fucking bullet hole in his head you dickhead!" And so I started yelling at Frank.

Next came Tom Dove, the cool Tom; he was younger, taller, more easygoing, and handsome. He had a nice head of black hair flecked with gray. Tom Dove attempted to level with me, appeal to my sense of reason and self-preservation. As before, I just ran my mouth. I didn't give a shit what these assholes thought of me because they had nothing on me. Being interrogated is easy work as long as you're not stupid (like Greg), a junkie (like Frank), a braggart (like Babar), or an unhinged lying psychopath (like Lalo)—in other words, anyone in my crew but me. Everyone else was a huge liability in the Box.

Eventually the cops' patience waned, and I was told that my opportunity to make a deal and get off easy had passed. "Well, we're going to have to read you your rights," one of the cops said with a snarl as he stood up and stepped away from the table, as if saying "We gave you a chance to play ball, so now it's time for us to fuck you up."

Just to be an asshole, I refused to sign the paper the cops gave me confirming that I had been read and understood my rights. Figuring there was no point holding back, I also informed them that I had a lawyer on retainer, which forced them to reconsider their plan of grilling me for hours on end to wear me down through attrition.

After a short delay, Tom Carney returned to the Box with a Mexican girl carrying a fisherman's tackle box—it was time for the GSR test. She carefully removed the plastic from my hands and blotted them with round sponges. Though I don't expect anyone to believe what I'm about to say, it was to my shock that the ink she placed on my hands turned *blue*—a positive test for antimony on my right palm. I failed the GSR test. To this day, I do not have the slightest idea how gunpowder got on my hands or, alternatively, why that test came out a false positive. Hey, maybe they framed me like my fellow SoCal minority, O. J. Simpson.

"Looks like you shot a gun, Kenny."

"Maybe I lit a match," I said with a smirk, trying to keep my cool. Honestly, I couldn't really laugh this off—I was suddenly an odds-on favorite to get convicted for murder. You could see Tom Carney's eyes dilate—this guy was about to blow his load. He started sizing me up for the electric chair: I was stripped naked so they could test my clothes, had my blood drawn to see if it showed up at the crime scene, and had every millimeter of my nude body photographed in case a sign of a struggle was discovered.

For the next few hours, the coppers took a prolonged dump on me, using their limited acting ability and verbal talent to convince me of the hopelessness of my situation. It was variations of "You're going down for murder, Kenny!" delivered in tones that fluctuated wildly from straightforward statement of fact to heavily sighed pity to exultant bragging to finger-in-the-face screaming. Homicide cops get desperate and overstimulated when they think there's a possibility of a quick, case-closing, clearance-rate-boosting confession. I wasn't copping to shit, innocent or guilty, and I concentrated my attention on seeing how much I could piss them off. I'd answer every question with *another* question, the more ridiculous the better. I wanted them to think I didn't give a shit if they had me in the electric chair or not.

After a while, I got tired of this game and said, "Hey, I'm not under arrest, I don't have to put up with this." Announcing that I was hungry, tired, and bored, I invited the Two Toms to file charges or lick my ass as I walked out the door. A positive GSR test was damning but hardly conclusive enough to press capital murder charges against me. They let me go on the promise that I show up the next day at the sheriff's substation in Aliso Viejo for more questioning.

A free man once again, my mind returned to Clyde's murder. I had two missions in life now: to avoid going to jail for his murder and to avenge myself on the real murderers. Naturally, like O. J. Simpson a few years later, my first concern was to duck jail time; after all, I could never take care of Clyde's murderers if distracted by the full-time job of fending off prison rape.

The quickest way to secure my freedom from prosecution was to eliminate everyone even remotely connected to the crime. Even though I was innocent, I knew that with witnesses as untrustworthy as Frank, his basehead girlfriend, Teresa, Lalo, and Greg, there was no telling what crazy stories they would concoct to save *themselves* from jail time. On the other hand, if *no one* was available to testify at trial, *no one* could be proven guilty beyond reasonable doubt. Even if the cops went after Lalo or whoever really killed Clyde, I preferred to do the job myself to make sure it was done right.

This was the end of my patience with Frank. I had let him get away with a million screw-ups and betrayals, partially out of sentimental attachment and partially because the screwy little cokehead was a moneymaking maniac who rewarded forgiveness with bags of street cash. At that point in my life, I'd have been buddies with Joe Stalin if it made me a profit; hell, I was friends with Officer Jerry, and it didn't get much lower than him.

Unfortunately, there was no way I could trust that Sid and Nancy wouldn't conspire to save their own asses by framing Greg and me for the murder. Frank and Teresa had made the cops' job easy: by admitting that they were high at the crime scene and had suffered blackouts, they became the default suspects if they didn't offer up someone else to take the fall. They had already thrown Greg to the pigs, and, since not even Greg's family would think he was smart or enterprising enough to commit a well-executed gangland murder by himself, they were going to have to eventually toss me in along with him to tie up the case.

Thanks to Jerry's info, I knew that the Two Toms were leaning on Frank to give me up and save poor waifish Teresa from jail. Later, I saw the interrogation transcripts and confirmed it for myself. For the good of everyone, Frank and Teresa needed to disappear. I had saved Frank's life the night Clyde died; now I began to regret the decision.

The simple solution was to kill Frank; after that, Teresa would let her own mom go to the electric chair for Clyde's murder before she'd say anything about me. Once, I had paid Clyde to shoot up Frank's previous girlfriend's car to drive her out of the O.C. and out of my life. This time, it was Frank's turn, and Clyde wasn't around to do the job. While Frank was driving his truck down the 405 freeway by the Irvine Meadows outdoor amphitheater, a gentleman with black hair and a Mike Marvich–style gangster cap drove up next to him, whipped out a shotgun, and fired into his car.

Frank believed the attack was an ambush by Greg's homies from the Shotgun Crips in retaliation for ratting out Greg. Frank survived, but psychologically, my already-fragile pal lost his shit. Facing either first-degree murder charges or death if he ratted me out, he went on the lam.

A fugitive murder suspect with the cops and FBI on his tail, Frank fled to Chicago and then to his ancestral homeland, Serbia, where he became a barkeep in a pub on the Kosovo border. During the chaotic dismemberment of Yugoslavia and the vicious genocide that followed, Frank's pub catered to an exclusive clientele of Serbian Army grunts, Croat soldiers of fortune, and run-of-the-mill Balkan wino savages. His yappy bitch girlfriend, Teresa, naturally lost interest in testifying.

Since Greg was in custody and not clever enough to frame me or hold up to cross-examination in court, the only remaining witness to Clyde's last night was Lalo, the likely murderer. And I ran into him at the most appropriate possible venue: Clyde's funeral.

The remaining members of my crew were getting ready to carpool down to the cemetery when I received a phone call from Lalo. I was in shock when I heard his voice—I felt cold and numb. He told me he was back in town from his a.m. train ride in Mexico and really wanted to attend the funeral to honor Clyde's memory. As I gave him the details, I reflected that, even for a murderer, Lalo wasn't the sentimental type.

The funeral was the saddest thing I've ever experienced. The casket was closed since Clyde had a golf ball–size hole in his face, and the mortician wasn't given a George Lucas budget for special effects. Clyde's mother, whom we all knew and liked, was wailing and weeping in unimaginable misery.

As I tried to conceal my tears at my friend's funeral, Lalo was close by my side, looking like he was sleeping with his eyes open or calculating how much he could get for a kilo that week. Lalo's bored look stayed in my mind afterwards while I tried my emotionally retarded best to comfort Clyde's mother at the wake. Clyde's mom complained to me that Frank had bounced a check that he owed the family, which was typical of that short-money idiot. She then took me to Clyde's old room at home, which she confided to me had been left completely untouched since he first went to military school. It would stay untouched—unlike Lalo.

The funeral of one of my best friends was followed by the last night I would ever spend with the love of my life. Tara paged me during the funeral; I was already overloaded with conflicting emotions, and hearing from her made me delirious. My mind reeled with excitement, worry, and speculation. Though I had tried to reconnect with her the night of Clyde's death, she had been so disgusted by my lifestyle that she had listened only to make a show of how little chance I ever had with her. Now she was contacting me in the aftermath of yet another murder of one of my closest friends.

In the old days, speaking with Tara would make me feel fleetingly conventional, almost normal—I could be a positive contributor to society if only Tara discovered just the right way to love me. After Clyde's death, I felt nothing but sadness and contempt for everyone I met. On the street, I would be able to expend all that wickedness and hatred on sick fucks who deserved it, but as a suburban lawn-mowing Republican dad, I knew I'd be so bored and suppressed that one day I'd just snap and kill at random. Instead of murdering an evil creep like Lalo, my volcanic psychotic rupture would come at the price of an unsuspecting golf partner brained with a 5-iron, or a PTA president dispatched with a pencil through the eyeball.

Tara looked great when she came over to my place—tan, healthy, less girlish and more lean and womanly. It was awkward at first as we just sat and watched TV, green bottles of Mickey's malt liquor in our hands. Eventually, she mustered the courage to start talking, and when she got going she was as straightforward and brutal as Mike Marvich: I was a loser, a freak, an asshole, a criminal, and a profoundly fucked-up kid who was going to get myself killed.

"Joey first, now Clyde. Ken, you don't see a problem that *two* of your friends have been killed? You don't see anything wrong with that lifestyle?" Finally, after a thorough scolding, she told me that I had one last chance with her if I abandoned crime and all my friends. She said it almost grudgingly, cautiously, as if she expected to get her heart broken and was already wincing in preparation. I wondered if she was motivated by pity for me after Clyde's death, or if she hoped that Clyde's death had been enough to shock a smart kid like me away from crime. Was she sacrificing her feelings and self-respect trying to save me from Clyde and Joey's fate?

Regardless of her reasoning, Tara was a wonderful girl who loved me enough to open herself up to heartbreak one last time. In my entire life, I've never been as selfless and generous to another person as Tara was to me that night. She put my best interest ahead of her own safety, emotional health, and self-respect; she wanted to save my soul and save my life.

Looking into Tara's crying eyes and telling her for the final time that there was no hope for us remains the most heartbreaking and chilling moment of my life in which no one died. That day I had watched Clyde get buried; that night I buried Tara alive. Whatever delusions I retained about my moral standing were gone. It was one thing to exploit drug addicts and other criminals, but I had humiliated, abused, and betrayed the best person I'd ever known. This wasn't a crime; this was a sin, something that I felt was grievously wrong and *shameful*. I have never forgiven myself, and I have never forgotten Tara, even for one day.

The world would be a much more beautiful place if it was easy to murder depraved jackals like Lalo. If Lalo had been just a normal innocent civilian instead of a bloodthirsty sociopath, I could have killed him with ease and impunity. Lalo was immunized against murder thanks, ironically, to his professional standing as a murderer. Because he was suspected of killing people, the Two Toms had Lalo under surveillance at all times, making it nearly impossible to isolate and kill him. Likewise, Lalo's rare skill as a strong-arm guy and hit man ensured that he was an untouchable made guy in the Orange County underworld. Lalo did indispensable grunt work for Mike Marvich, Sal Avila, and just about every Colombian dealer I knew. It would be impossible to kill a useful problem-solver like Lalo without creating a nightmare for myself.

Since Lalo was one of Mike Marvich's boys, I needed Mike's blessing if I wanted to take out Lalo, which seemed about as likely as resurrecting Joey and Clyde to join Big Mike's new break-dancing crew. Nonetheless, I had to try.

I always felt like I was playing chess with Death when I walked through the doors of the home where Mike had killed his wife. This was the man who had Joey killed and bragged that he wouldn't have minded if I had died with him. I was powerless before an old paralegal who, with one phone call, could muster all the firepower of Pablo Escobar's cocaine empire. As long as I was in the California cocaine trade, every moment of my life was a gift granted by the mercy and self-interest of Mike Marvich. I could never be calm or confident in Mike's presence since the slightest slip-up would result in the effortless massacre of my entire crew.

I was already on shaky terms with Mike since I had only nominally honored my agreement to get my dope and my orders from Tommy Thornton. I used Tommy as my wholesale coke distributor once in a while, but just often enough to keep up the pretense that I was obeying Big Mike. Though I was relying on the incredible size of Mike's drug empire to distract him from my comparatively small-time operation, I still made a point to see Mike whenever I could to remind him that I was a likeable, crafty little con man.

I flattered Mike by asking for his expert advice on legal matters, which would prove to benefit me greatly in my career. Otherwise uncharitable with his time, Mike relished the opportunity to talk shop about criminal law. Mike introduced me to his counsel and running partner, the ancient attorney Roger, and used Roger's office to teach me how to perform legal research, file my own lawsuits, drown my enemies in time-consuming and expensive legal distractions, and pull search warrant affidavits at the courthouse that might reveal who was ratting against my crew.

Usually when Mike took me to Roger's office, he'd be carrying a garbage bag or grocery bag stuffed to the point of overflowing with rubber-banded cash. Other criminals try to be a little sneaky about dumping off garbage bags full of drug money, but, as I said, Mike just didn't give a shit. While dropping off the cash with Roger, I'd hear Mike talk about the boatyard, the homes, the planes, the construction companies, and the plots of land that he owned under various names and companies—all more or less just for the sake of owning them. In the process, Mike gave me a tip or two about how to play three-card monte with the IRS and the feds to conceal the illicit proceeds from my drug business.

Mike began to enjoy my company since I was one of the only criminals he could talk to as an intellectual equal, but our relationship never progressed to the point where I wasn't in mortal danger. Mike didn't really form friendships intimate enough to preclude murder—as shown by the fate of his wife.

Whenever I did talk with Mike, I made sure to approach him on my belly, groveling, and for a predator like me that manner of behavior was so bizarre and unfamiliar that I felt like I was hallucinating. Whenever I left Mike's house, I had to wake up from a nervous trance, run my hands through my hair to make sure I hadn't missed any bullet holes, and reassure myself that my meeting with Death had not proved fatal.

Regardless of the risk, I confronted Mike about Clyde's death and, as humbly and indirectly as I could, asked for permission to kill Lalo. Uncharacteristically for an underworld tyrant who reveled in bluntly saying anything on his mind, Mike was opaque when I brought up Clyde's death. When he didn't outright ignore my questions, he gave evasive and vague answers. The only thing that was clear to me was that Mike was deliberately being unclear. He didn't want me to know where he stood on the matters of Clyde's death or Lalo—probably just to fuck with me, a petty power trip for a power-hungry maniac.

Instead of telling me what I wanted to know about Clyde's murder, Mike took the opportunity to return to his subject: Sal needed to speed up his repayment of Joey's debt or more people would die. "They already lost one brother," he said, back to his signature straight-shooting Mike Marvich charm. "They must've fucked with the wrong guy. I guess they just don't learn." Mike smiled, shaking his head at the incompetence and stupidity of the Avila family.

As I was walking out after this dispiriting sendoff, Mike called after me. "Personally," he said, "I think Lalo is a suspect." That changed everything—after jerking me around for his amusement, Mike seemed to be giving me the tacit, plausibly deniable approval to kill Lalo. I hesitated to act on this assumption, but I had it confirmed a few days later when Tommy Thornton, Big Mike's lieutenant and Lalo's frequent accomplice, happened to run into me. He looked down at me with his spine-melting black eyes and, like Mike, made a completely unprovoked statement against Lalo. "That murder sounds like Lalo's MO," he said in his slow, rumbling volcano voice.

Tommy was a disciplined, no-bullshit guy; he would never have implicated his own partner in a murder unless he was following orders. While retaining plausible deniability, Big Mike wanted to let me know that he wouldn't be heartbroken if something happened to Lalo. For a murderous crime boss with a bottomless stable of fly-in, fly-out Colombian hit men, it was a good insurance policy for Big Mike to periodically thin his crew of its most bloodstained members to minimize the chance of a murder prosecution. The way was clear for me to kill Lalo and avenge Clyde's death.

I took Lalo out in Irvine and spiked his drink with an entire vial of LSD. I planned for him to OD in the passenger seat as I drove down Bonita Canyon Road so that I could dump his comatose body on the side of the road and blast him in the head. I was dumbfounded: like Rasputin, Lalo acted completely unfazed by the fatal dose of poison I had given him. I just kept driving around, acting like I was lost.

This gave me pause: maybe killing Lalo wasn't meant to be. Joey's death had taught me to incessantly question and game plan my every move in the underworld since the penalty for stupidity and carelessness was death. My intense suspicion of Big Mike's motivation made me hesitate: why would Mike Marvich allow me to kill one of his own mercenaries without any repercussions? Why would he let himself look so weak that a twenty-year-old could get away with clipping one of his top enforcers?

Mike wouldn't: if I took care of Mike's spring cleaning by killing Lalo, either Tommy Thornton would dispose of me "in retaliation," or Mike would use Lalo's death as a down payment on my ass for the rest of his life. Besides, the Two Toms were already closely watching us, and it's not like I especially needed to give them *another* murder investigation against me. There were ways to get rid of Lalo that wouldn't raise my profile with Mike Marvich or the Two Toms. It was time for the Officer Jerry Special.

Lalo delivered himself to me gift wrapped with ten kilos as the bow. Without warning, Lalo called and asked me to meet him at Woody's Wharf, a bar in Newport Beach. When I arrived, the greasy Mexican nonchalantly showed me ten kilos of coke in his trunk. Completely oblivious of my intention to destroy his life, Lalo asked if I could guard this stash for him while he went to take care of business in Mexico for a few days.

That question elicited the biggest smile to cross my face since Clyde's death: Lalo might as well have said "Here's ten kilos of cocaine on the house!" This dumb Mexican cocksucker was never going to get them back. While I was with Lalo discussing what he wanted me to do with his kilos, a trustworthy Peruvian dealer named Lolo from South Coast Plaza paged me and asked for a front of two kilos. Since I had Lalo's kilos, that would be no problem; Lalo was so excited at the quick score that he decided to be generous: "Kenny, I'll give you half!"

Yeah, you dumb bastard, we'll see how much I get. I dropped off Lolo's two kilos immediately, letting the Peruvian know that it was my coke and that he was to pay only me. Independent of my need to avenge Clyde's death, this was too much free cocaine to pass up under any circumstances: Lalo was done.

Babar and I visited Lolo to drop off another kilo and pick up the $70,000 he owed us for the two kilos I had already advanced him. I did not tell Lalo about the cash when he returned from Mexico, but I did tell him about an imaginary deal I had set up for him the next day involving two ounces of his coke, some acid, and a gun.

Lalo was ecstatic; this was more easy money for him. I had Babar call the Irvine PD and say that he would call again later to report the license plate of a car carrying a murderer en route to a major cocaine and weapons deal. The next day, I gave Lalo two ounces of cocaine (shitty cocaine, not the good stuff he gave me), fifty hits of acid in a vial that we bought at a Grateful Dead concert, and a crappy gun to ensure that there was a weapons charge to pile on the years. Blinded by the easy money, Lalo drove to the rendezvous with half the Irvine police force shadowing him in unmarked vehicles.

I positioned myself in the bleachers at a baseball diamond near the drop-off; I had a front-row seat when the Narcotics Task Force swarmed a screaming, cursing, frothing-at-the-mouth Lalo. To this day, the memory of Lalo squealing as the cops wrenched his arms behind his back to be handcuffed makes me giggle.

Multiple drug and weapons charges took care of Lalo and gave the Two Toms one less reason to pay attention to my crew. Babar and I partied that night like we hadn't partied since before Clyde's death, hitting all of our old spots; with Lalo gone, it was finally safe for us to have fun like Joey Avila taught us. In the morning, I woke up hung over to discover thirty-two messages from Lalo on my answering machine. In celebration of his downfall, I bought myself a Rolex President wristwatch, which I still own and is now worth more than most new cars.

For the next few years, the only person who would speak about Lalo was Mike Marvich: he made a point to show me the ass-kissing sentimental birthday cards Lalo sent him from jail each year. Big Mike was so scary that macho killers like Lalo and Tommy Thornton went out of their way to shamelessly lick his ass.

To complete my sudden turnaround in luck, Clyde's murder case disappeared. With Frank on the lam, Teresa intimidated out of testifying, and the interrogation of Kenny Gallo, the prime suspect, proving nothing except my skill as a comedian, the Two Toms charged Greg with the murder in an attempt to get him to implicate me in return for a reduced sentence.

The case against Greg was chickenshit bordering on preposterous. There was no way a competent jury could have said that Greg was the murderer beyond a reasonable doubt: Frank had left town to avoid prosecution; they found unexplained gunpowder residue on my hands and none on Greg's hands; they had no murder weapon because forensics disqualified the fully loaded, unfired pistol he carried that night; they had no witnesses to the crime; a footprint found on Clyde's chest did not match Greg's shoes; and there was no conceivable motive for Greg to commit the crime that didn't involve an un-charged third party.

The best evidence the Two Toms had against Greg was that he was a big, scary black guy who had been at the scene of the crime that night—in the company of three other violent felons. I told Greg just to relax and look forward to being the first gangbanger to get acquitted in a California murder case in decades.

Thanks to a lifetime of racist treatment at the hands of the judicial system, Greg had no faith in an Orange County jury, regardless of the evidence. He had been continuously guilty of felonies since childhood to the point that he acted like a guilty man even when he was completely clean. Apparently, this air of defeatism and hopelessness infected his already lethargic legal team, and the entire case was botched beyond belief. Somehow, Greg ended up in jail for the murder of Lee Matthew Clyde, though he was unapologetically euphoric over his luck at getting nailed for the comparatively minor charge of Involuntary Manslaughter.

I was euphoric for much better reasons: there was no way the Two Toms could build a case against me for Clyde's murder with a Shotgun Crip already in jail for the crime. I was free.

But I was also alone. With Joey, Clyde, Tara, Frank, and Greg all gone from my life, I had lost everyone that engaged my human side, everyone who was capable of momentarily arousing love, empathy, or guilt from the venomous pit of my psyche. I felt as if the umbilical cord connecting me to mankind had been cut, leaving me free to become an animal. I had completed the long gradual descent from what seemed like my idyllic days of reckless teenage mischief into a "life" that was little more than one long, uninterrupted, grim, methodically calculated, hedonistic crime spree. The purpose of my existence was to hunt for money, adrenaline highs, and the petty satisfaction I derived from the violent domination of the weak.

I shared the despair I was suffering from the loss of my childhood, my mentor, my best friends, and the love of my life with the entire world—one violent felony at a time. As a great man once said: he who makes himself a beast takes away the pain of being a man.

> *"When Kenji's your friend, he's the best ally imaginable. When he's your enemy, he's a nightmare you can't wake up from. He was on a constant rampage: lighting people's cars on fire, blowing cars up, having his guys shoot up people's houses. He is a tough cat; I've seen him wreck dudes. I've never seen Kenny lose a fight."*
>
> Chuck Browntooth

After spending my formative years studying how Joey Avila, Griselda Blanco, and Mike Marvich did business, I discovered, much to my surprise, that suburban California could be an inhospitable environment for career narcoterrorists. The police and the press are sensitive to car bombs and drive-by shootings in the suburbs. Knowing that the Two Toms were already outraged by my escape from prosecution, I should have spent a few months doing business in a faraway city until they were distracted. Instead, I waged literal war with a group of Orange County kids in as public a manner as possible.

The beef in question was a year or two old: I was still pursing my vendetta against the remnants of the punk gang that had jumped me outside of a house party while Babar held my pistol and did nothing. Although I had succeeded in humbling most of the jerkoffs, there were still a couple guys who apparently could not process the concept that I would respond to their existence in the same area code as me with massive physical and psychological punishment. They were like kids who never learn that touching fire equals pain. Under a relentless barrage of threats, beatings, near-miss shootings, fire-bombings, and car-bombings, these coke-fortified punks kept coming like the little mushroom dudes in Super Mario Brothers.

In one month in the summer of '89, I must have committed half a dozen serious felonies against Jimmy P. and his associates. At least three of these attacks made the front page of the *Orange County Register:*

> *"A car was set on fire early Wednesday, and Irvine police said they are trying to determine whether it was started by the same person who torched another vehicle earlier this month."*
>
> July 20, 1989

> *"An Irvine man awoke Friday to find a firebomb on top of his car. John Hart, 22, called police shortly after 5:30 a.m. from his home on Ash Tree Lane in the University Park neighborhood, asking them to defuse the device, a 32-ounce bottle containing gasoline linked to a 4-inch pipe bomb."*
>
> August 19, 1989

> *"A childhood feud that began with pranks such as throwing raw eggs appears to have escalated into a war in which the cars of three University High School graduates have been targeted by an arsonist, a victim of one of the attacks said Saturday. In the past two months, two cars have been firebombed and an explosive device was discovered on a third."*
>
> August 20, 1989

The press that my guerilla campaign earned me also exhausted whatever patience the Two Toms had left. Mirroring my campaign to drive the punk gang insane or out of Orange County, the Two Toms resolved to finish me off. To impede my cash flow, they hassled and threatened my associates, making sure that word got around that doing business with Kenji guaranteed police attention. Wherever I went, the police stopped me, toyed with me, interrogated me, and threatened me. They engineered the type of smothering surveillance effort that drives paranoid coke dealers into spectacular Kenny DiMartini–style breakdowns.

It got to the point where I forgot what it felt like to walk out of a house without a police van conspicuously parked nearby, or to drive around town without a convoy of unmarked cars tailing me. I was so nervous about getting busted that some of my friends were convinced I was becoming a typical self-destructing paranoid coke dealer, the type who suspects that the cashier at Dunkin Donuts is an undercover agent and that black helicopters are shadowing his every move.

At the peak of my paranoia, I received a tip from a friend whose relative worked for the CIA: there was a phone number that CIA agents could call to see if their phone was tapped. If you called the CIA number and the machine repeated your number back to you, then your line was clean. When I called the number, there was silence; my phone was tapped. Jerry thought I was crazy for believing that the number was for real; years later its existence became public knowledge. It was shut down after being compromised by cocaine traffickers like me.

Though my instincts were to abandon the coke business and change zip codes, at that point I was simply having too much fun. Being a coke dealer was like being a celebrity without all the paparazzi and autograph hounds.

I remember one night when my friend and fellow dealer Black Dave took me to dinner. Black Dave was a tall, muscular, unbelievably fly black dude who dressed only in the finest suits and carried himself like a black Sinatra. I never saw Black Dave spend a cent of his own money. Everything from his wardrobe to his Corvette to his cocaine was paid for by his "bitches," the girls who would do anything to persuade Black Dave to grace them with his company. Black Dave's game was so tight that it seemed like there was nowhere in California where he didn't know the bouncer, the maître d', the manager, the busboys, the hostess, or the boss. His coke paved the way.

So Black Dave took my stripper girlfriend and me out to a fancy Italian joint in his Corvette, but we got to the restaurant late, well after 10 p.m. The maître d' told us that the restaurant was closing, but Black Dave coolly ignored him and requested to see the owner. It took only a special handshake and a word in the owner's ear for us to be escorted to the best table in the place. The customers who were finishing their meals at this fashionable yuppie restaurant all seemed to be my clients, and I could hear "Kenji" being whispered from table to table like I was a star. All the waiters fluttered around us, kissing our asses, hurrying wine and bread and settings to our table.

While this production was happening, superstar Los Angeles Dodgers pitcher Orel Hershiser was sitting at the bar with his high-powered agent—watching us, pissed off because they had just been refused a table. This sports star could not believe that a Japanese kid, a black dude, and a stripper were being treated like the Beatles while he was denied even a basket of breadsticks. Orel walked up to our table with a smirk, extended his hand, and told me, "Kid, I don't know what it is, but I guess you have what it takes to get served in a place like this."

In retrospect, I should have invited Orel and his agent to sit with us; they might have introduced us to their friends and made me the official cocaine dealer of the Los Angeles Dodgers. Instead, I just smiled and nodded, acting like hot shit as Orel turned around and left, hungry and embarrassed.

I wasn't ready to abandon that lifestyle yet, but I needed a new business model that would allow me to continue trafficking while insulating me from police surveillance and the attention of Mike Marvich. The first step was obvious: get the fuck out of Orange County. My old neighborhood and hangouts had been imbued with so many heartbreaking memories of Tara, Joey, and Clyde that it was impairing not only the enjoyment but also the execution of my crimes. I could be a merciless cannibal much more easily in a neighborhood that wasn't littered with reminders of my former life as an emotionally engaged friend and lover.

Since I still intended to maintain some of my Orange County business obligations, I couldn't move too far, so I chose nearby Palm Springs. The ritzy desert resort town was in adjacent Riverside County, freeing me from the Two Toms and Big Mike's immediate orbit. For my new home base, I conscientiously chose the most criminally inconspicuous neighborhood I could find: a heavily guarded, gated community on a golf course. I paid in cash and took out a lease under an assumed name; my neighbors, primarily retired Jewish doctors and wealthy L.A. yuppies, took little notice of the new well-spoken, well-dressed Asian kid on the block.

I quickly came to love Palm Springs. The local cops

had no idea who I was and never bothered me. Doing business was easy. In addition to the surrounding desert's usefulness as an all-purpose gangland firing range, burial ground, meeting place, and explosives testing site, it also provided me with countless hours of recreational pleasure through off-road racing. Sometimes I had too much fun in the desert: after taking a friend shooting with the Tommy Gun and rifle that Frank had bought me with his bounced checks, I tossed my guns in the trunk and drove my pickup truck at top speed on the way home, using the sand dunes as launch ramps. Either a lucky hiker happened upon a surprise or there is still a Tommy Gun and a rifle lying somewhere in the desert around Palm Springs.

The next step in my criminal makeover was to obtain legitimate business interests. Luckily for me, I simultaneously found two inherently sleazy and semi-criminal ways to go legitimate: becoming a porn producer and a club owner. Before I discuss my much more lucrative and protracted foray into the world of pornography, I will concentrate on my shorter but inestimably more violent time as the owner of Genesis, a dance club and sushi bar.

I had known Genesis' owner Safar for years as one of Frank's regular cocaine customers. Safar was a fat sleazy Turkish car dealer in Newport Beach who also owned a fried chicken place. Apparently, he thought he would be better served in these business pursuits by renaming himself Antonio and pretending to be a mafioso. The similarities between Antonio and me ended at "Asian-American who adopts Italian pseudonym."

This lazy, pot-bellied, swarthy pig had a big mouth, a tough guy self-image, and a penchant for compensating for his slovenly appearance by making a big deal of driving around in flashy Lamborghinis and Ferraris. Antonio was so eager to be in business with a legit criminal that he offered to let me buy half of the club for a first installment of $35,000—the price of a kilo of pure cocaine on the streets.

Are you fucking kidding me? A club for a kilo? I had kilos to spare! I laundered $35,000 using Mike Marvich's favorite techniques and had our lawyer prepare the documents. I owned a club months before I was able to drink alcohol legally. I couldn't get over how funny it was that Antonio honestly believed I would keep my word and continue making payments to him after he had given me the keys to the club. Get real, Safar, you fucking amateur.

Regardless of how much I paid for it, the club was a priceless addition to my criminal portfolio. To survive as a professional criminal, I needed to own a legal cash business through which to launder my illicit drug profits. It would also legitimize my image as a conventional businessman so that I could own property without drawing IRS attention. Buying half of Genesis made me feel like I was making a long-term commitment to my criminal career and Southern California. After losing so much, I enjoyed the feeling of stability and purpose that came with owning a business.

Genesis was stylish for 1989: all black leather, bright colors, and neon lights. After walking through a fashionably long T-shaped entrance hall, a visitor to Genesis could choose the sushi restaurant with the gorgeous lake view to the right or, on the left, the dance floor with the hottest L.A. hip-hop and dance DJs spinning and scratching records in a corner. Unbeknownst to me, the club's décor and image was on the brink of cartoonish obsolescence, as that tacky '80s look would become toxically out-of-fashion within a couple years, but at the time the venue seemed unimpeachably classy and hip.

My idea for promoting the club was to stock it like a game farm with tits and ass. I bought off strippers from a nearby strip club called Captain Cream's (which specialized in "hot cream wrestling") by arranging for them to receive free cocaine and booze, in addition to "special" perks for participating in regular wet T-shirt contests. These girls were incredible, just filthy porn-fantasy slutzillas with huge '80s hair. They emulated the Rodeo Drive groupies that Mötley Crüe and Poison music videos made famous. I made so much money, thanks to those strippers in short denim skirts and DayGlo sneakers shaking their asses at my customers. I saw legit players and crooks literally drool as they watched these coked-out strippers do their day-job for free on the dance floor.

Since no dealing was allowed on the premises to prevent the club from being confiscated in a drug raid, I needed the girls to attract the steady flow of rich playboys that would keep the club supplied with communal cocaine and champagne. I had Keith work the door, which was hilarious to our circle because Keith was the most prolific bar brawler in Orange County. Hiring a violent, alcoholic maniac like Keith as a bouncer was like hiring Griselda Blanco as a marriage counselor. Keith's job was basically to finish the fights our own crew started, steal money from the till, and help lure dozens of girls to our party house in Irvine, where we'd take turns fucking them on my pool table.

In addition to playing the year's big dance hits like Young MC's "Bust a Move," I occasionally tried to attract crowds with live bands. The most memorable act I ever booked was the hardcore band led by my two buddies from high school, Zack and Tim. Zack had been good friends with my steroid-smuggling buddy Chuck, whom Zack had taught to play guitar. I kicked Zack's ass in his high school at a party when he made the mistake of hitting on a girl my enforcer Phil was screwing; afterwards, I compounded the humiliation by stealing his cooler of beer. Though unknown nationally, Zack managed to draw over 300 paying customers to our tiny dance floor on the basis of his previous local bands. It was an incredible, unheard-of turnout; the crowd was packed more tightly than a Tokyo subway car at rush hour. The room was so cramped that one partier moshing in the center of the room pressed dozens of others against the walls along the perimeter. For months I had been trying every promotional tactic I could think of to sell the cases of Michelob Light I had sitting in storage; one announcement over the PA system of "$1 beers" to this hot, thirsty crowd of punks sold out the entire stockpile in minutes. After a few songs, the fire marshal arrived to stop the show for being a safety hazard. I ran over and assuaged him by ushering a token fraction of the audience into the back parking lot to give everyone some breathing room. When the fire trucks drove off, I opened the door and let the rest of the audience back in to enjoy the show. In a couple years, Zack and Tim's band would become famous as Rage Against the Machine.

The club's peak was New Year's Eve 1989, when I ran a special promotion where, for $25 a person, our patrons received all the shitty bar food and shittier champagne they could stomach. We got the swill cheap—stolen-cheap—and made a preposterous profit from the partiers who came for the bargain and got so drunk on the bottled ass-sweat we served them that they started splurging on Dom Pérignon to show off. I was no longer drinking, but I was drunk on the tens of thousands of dollars in my pocket as I left for my Irvine party house with Babar and some girls. I scarcely imagined that the night would end with me attempting to murder an old acquaintance, nearly shooting an innocent bystander, and almost killing a woman.

I was about as sophisticated and morally evolved as a rabid pit bull at this time of my life. I was impulsive, sadistic, and completely remorseless especially if I felt like I was being challenged. My behavior depended wholly on what course of action had the highest likelihood of spiking my adrenaline, filling my wallet, or satisfying my libido. Partially due to the enormous amounts of testosterone I was swallowing and injecting, at every single waking moment I felt like I was on the verge of losing control and murdering someone, anyone, everyone. After Joey's and Clyde's deaths, it felt safer to be the aggressor in almost every situation.

As my Corvette pulled up to the house in Irvine after our New Year's celebration at the club, another car suddenly sped away from the curb. "That was Sid Johnson!" Babar yelled—Sid Johnson, the degenerate who had stolen a stash of cocaine and nearly half a million dollars of counterfeit money from me. Since he had never paid restitution and all my previous attempts to kill him had misfired, I still owed him dearly. I nearly stomped the gas pedal through the undercarriage, my eyes flaring.

When I finally boxed Sid Johnson's car somewhere in the Turtle Rock neighborhood of Irvine, I rushed out and pulled Sid by his hair onto the street; I was going to have to be physically restrained from beating him to death. As I was unloading on him with wild haymakers, Sid was stupid enough to reach for a heavy aircraft-aluminum Maglite flashlight in his car. The poor sonofabitch was too slow, and I intercepted the Maglite, lifted it high above my head, and crushed his skull with such force that the flashlight ricocheted over my head and all the way back to my Corvette.

Sid wasn't exactly moving, but my mind was consumed by this orgiastic ecstasy of violence. I couldn't stop; as far as I could tell, I didn't want to stop. I wanted to crack open his skull and just rip out his brain. I was delirious, covered in blood.

Suddenly I was stunned, stumbling, teetering on having a blackout. Something had hit me *very* hard on the back of the head. Barely conscious, I roared around and nearly decapitated my assailant with a lightning crack punch. It was Sid's girlfriend, bravely attempting to save Sid's life. Babar was supposed to be holding her back, but Babar was busy chasing my Corvette as it rolled downhill. I had forgotten to put the car in park. Now the poor party girl was unconscious on the asphalt; I wondered if I had killed her.

I wasn't too distressed about her fate, as I nonchalantly recommenced my homicidal beatdown of Sid Johnson. I barely got another kick in to his ribs before the situation progressed even further into chaos and absurdity: a screaming middle-age suburban dad was running across his lawn toward me brandishing a hammer. This aspiring hero was also determined to save poor, innocent Sid Johnson's life—at least until I whipped out my .45 caliber hand-cannon. That was the end of his civic heroism; Orange County's vigilante lawman sprinted back to his house with a prolonged high-pitch shriek.

At this point, the pleas of the party girl who had been tagging along with us and the dawning realization that the cops would be joining us within moments convinced me to flee. Sid Johnson lived; his survival is a testament to the sturdy design of the human body.

My excessive cruelty toward Sid Johnson was uncharacteristic only in that it was unpremeditated. Usually, I took my time to micromanage and savor revenge. I had no compunction about killing people, even longtime friends and associates; after all, if I was not opposed to blasting a shotgun into Frank's car at high speeds, how much could any human life (including my own) really mean to me?

One premeditated murder was set into motion when my house was mysteriously robbed. I later heard on the street that the Irvine Police Department had illegally raided my apartment to obtain and suppress evidence against Officer Jerry who was in danger of losing his badge and bringing down the Irvine PD brass with him.

Though I could not at the time identify the culprit, *someone* had to die in retaliation to deter future attacks on my livelihood. It was a matter of survival: I had too much money, cocaine, and guns to survive for very long as a gangster who could be robbed with impunity. In short order, I settled on a lackey I'll call "Liu Kang," a sneaky little thief from high school and my front guy for various purchases and apartments, as the most likely suspect and my scapegoat. Liu would die.

As a black joke, I decided to kill Liu on his birthday. Promising him a special birthday surprise if he came to my party house in Irvine, I lovingly furnished the bathroom for a murder with plastic tarp and paint drop cloths. With Babar at my side, we ambushed Liu as he walked through the front door, smacking him on the head and binding his arms and legs with duct tape. Like two paramedics rushing a gurney into the ER, Babar and I hauled this duct-tape-wrapped mummy into the bathroom and tossed him on the floor. While I turned on the bathtub faucet and arranged my tools so that we could bleed Liu out, Babar must have lost his concentration pondering the mysteries of the universe because the stunned, bound Liu Kang somehow bunny-hopped right past Babar and clear out the door!

By the time I caught up with him, Liu was on the front lawn. Don't ask me how he opened the front door; I wish I could find him and ask how he pulled off that Indiana Jones shit. Though Liu was moving at the speed of mortal terror, my unencumbered limbs made running him down pretty easy. With a touch of wicked amusement at the slapstick farce of Liu's last moments, I dropped him with a pistol butt to the back of his head. As I was dragging his supine taped-up body back into the house, I suddenly realized that some of my neighbors were standing on their front lawn in jaw-hanging terror.

"Don't worry about it, we're just pretending! It's like a class project or movie or something!" I said, smiling, as I escorted my unconscious friend back inside. With multiple witnesses who could identify me, I had no choice but to grant Liu a reprieve. When he came to, I told crying, incoherent Liu it was a big birthday prank. I noticed that his pants were soaked with piss.

Happy birthday, Liu! Needless to say, I gave the dumb son of a bitch both the worst and best birthday present of his life.

The only man in California luckier than Liu Kang was Kenny Gallo. My behavior was so reckless and aggressive in every direction that I was practically begging to be killed on a daily basis from 1989 to 1991. Though I remember having an incredible time, in retrospect I may have been in such a deep depression over everything I had lost that I was subconsciously courting death. There even came a time when I had to rely on Mike Marvich, the Grim Reaper himself, to save my life.

> *"A large cache of dynamite and ammunition was found Monday by Baldwin Park police at the home of Collin Quick, 22. . . . Stored in a garage were 17,000 rounds of ammunition for an 8-mm German-made Mauser; 150 sticks of dynamite, U.S. Army rifle barrels, three hand grenades, and a number of foreign-made guns and rifles."*
>
> Los Angeles Times
> December 4, 1960

I got a tip on the location of the stash house of a heavyweight Colombian dealer named Rubin, so I did my duty as a gangster and tore his shit up. It was nothing personal, just a quick and painless business transaction. When I was called in shortly afterwards to see Emperor Mike, I took Babar with me to Marvich's now familiar home in the suburbs so he could see what a freak this guy was. Mike was in his easy chair as usual, looking out the giant heavily tinted living room window. Babar and I were instructed to sit on an antique couch with our backs to the window and our faces to Mike in his recliner.

Big Mike had a serene smirk on his face. In a tone that was almost humorous, he informed us that "Rubin knows it was you who stole his shit." Big Mike could assume an almost seductive tone when he was on one of his power trips. You could tell he *really* got off on your reaction.

"Rubin's very angry and promised me that he would hunt you down and shoot you on sight. He said that even if you're in a crowd, he'll shoot twenty people to make sure he gets you. Rubin doesn't give a fuck," said Mike with a raise of his eyebrows and a nod. If an authority on not-giving-a-fuck like Mike Marvich said so, then I was convinced that Rubin truly did not have a fuck to give.

This was my first indication that Rubin was one of Mike's guys and that Rubin had an idea that I was responsible for the burglary. I became uneasy as I recalled Rubin's reputation as a stone-cold killer, the even scarier reputation of Rubin's knife-scarred enforcer, and the solid-gold endorsement of Rubin's homicidal tendencies just delivered by Big Mike. I was scared shitless.

My fear was instantaneously multiplied when this gigantic, tattooed goon in overalls stomped down the stairs and into the living room as Mike talked. The choreography of this intimidation routine was impeccable. The colossus walked right up to the couch and stood over us with a look that nearly made me faint. "Kenji," Marvich said as he gestured to the giant, "this is CQ. He is into some *heavy* shit." I could only imagine the atrocities this CQ must've committed to be distinguished as *heavy* in Mike Marvich's mind. As I shook one of the huge calloused hands of this dude, I honestly felt like I was going to die.

I did not know then that CQ, at the age of 22, had been indicted as one of the most prolific arms and explosive traffickers in the United States, or that he had succeeded in a James Bond–style escape from San Quentin Prison by clinging to the undercarriage of a moving garbage truck, or that he was supposedly Mike Marvich's top gun drug-smuggling pilot known for his ability to evade DEA planes and radar. All I knew was that CQ was into some heavy shit.

"About the Rubin thing," Marvich continued, adjusting himself in his seat as if CQ's unexpected arrival had caused him to lose track of his thoughts. "Don't worry about it, Kenji. Just ride it out, and it'll be fine. I'll take care of it." Mike settled his stare on me for a few moments longer than I would have preferred, transmitting to me in body language what he would never say out loud.

I thanked him profusely and played the only card I had available: I reminded Mike that I was his exclusive source for inside police info, thus hopefully giving him a reason not to kill me. Though Mike tried not to react, I could tell he was surprised when I told him that my source (Officer Jerry, of course) had informed me that the DEA was going through his trash, possibly to obtain evidence for IRS prosecution. To further remind Mike that I was worth keeping alive, the next day I dropped off something like $5,000 or $10,000 to Mike's house to ensure that things were smoothed over.

I'm sure the only compensation the Colombians received for their lost kilos was the knowledge that, if they behaved, Mike Marvich would choose not to have them killed. The beef was squashed.

Unfortunately, some of my enemies were not as forgiving as Mike Marvich. I began to notice that a brightly painted red Chevrolet Suburban and assorted vans were more or less permanently parked around Genesis. It didn't take a genius to see what was going on: the never subtle Two Toms had found me. When I waved to the coppers in their van, I got brought in for questioning. "Did Officer Jerry tip you off?" they asked, one of the many occasions where "good cops" tried to nail my rogue ally.

"Nope, you told me. How could I miss a big red Suburban? You guys just happen to suck at your job."

"On 1-20-90 the Orange County Fire Department investigated a possible arson at the nightclub Genises. . . . During the investigation, a

confidential informant (C/I) came forward. . . .
The C/I told me that . . . [Kenji was] involved in
the sales of cocaine. The C/I further stated that
[Kenji's] share of the money to buy Genises had
come from cocaine sales, and that there is a cur-
rent 'rift' between [Gallo] . . . vs. [Antonio] over
ownership and money debts. . . .

"[Gallo] had sold a great deal of cocaine during
1989. . . . During this time, they formed a 'semi-
organized crime' outfit and were distributing
cocaine with amounts as much as 'kilo quantity.'"
Orange County Sheriff's Report from 1990

My inability to resist busting the Two Toms' four balls
transformed the nightclub into far more trouble than it
was worth. In retaliation, the cops were so ostentatious
in their surveillance that it scared away a lot of Genesis'
best paranoid coke-snorting customers. Once, they arrested me in front of everyone because a doorman was
tricked by a fake ID, which was a chickenshit move they
could pull at any bar or club in California on any given
night. The club became a major liability, as being a sta-
tionary target was certainly not the best way for me to
evade the Two Toms' surveillance.

The heat became so bad that Jerry, who was also
under constant investigation, became reluctant to help
me. The risks began to outweigh the profits of being my
buddy, so Jerry gradually stopped taking my calls. Having known his character all along, I felt stupid for feeling
betrayed or ever thinking that he was my real friend. One
of the last things Jerry told me was that the Newport
PD's investigation was very close to producing an indictment, so I needed to get out of Genesis immediately.

The club's co-owner, Antonio-the-Turkish-wannabe-gangster, also wanted me to move on—desperately. The two of us had been feuding ever since he realized I wasn't ever going to hand over any more installments of the agreed-upon price. When, in an attempt to pressure me into paying him, Antonio closed the club's accounts to me and rerouted all the revenue streams, I circumvented him by ordering my guys to rob the registers and collect a cover charge at all the entrances. I also contacted the payroll company that advanced Antonio the cash to pay the staff on time, and I had $50,000 of "wages" advanced to Kenny Gallo and his friends.

Being an inept wannabe jackoff, Antonio retaliated by hiring another wannabe to intimidate me—this time an Iranian whom he had found at the Commerce Casino in Los Angeles. That didn't work out too well for Antonio or Mr. Khomeini: my crew cornered the Iranian in the back office, beat him senseless, stole his Walther PPK pistol, and sent him running. I let the Iranian off the hook (his only sin was being bad at his job), but not his Turkish boss; Antonio had betrayed our partnership in a manner that was too stupid to receive my mercy. I mean, c'mon: hire some guy you met at a casino to take on my entire crew? I felt like Mike Marvich again; I felt like I needed to punish Antonio on *principle* for being such an embarrassment as a criminal.

Antonio's stupidity extended to placing Genesis' insurance policy in the name of a convicted gangster, one who he just blindly tried to screw over: me. Antonio should not have given me a half-million-dollar incentive to destroy his fucking club. I called in an Italian kid I knew in Brooklyn named Johnny, the son of a slain Colombo wiseguy. While I established my alibi by making a point not to lose my police tail on the way home for an early night's rest, Johnny broke into Genesis, set one of the couches on fire, and cranked on the gas.

To my disbelief, I woke up the next morning to find that the club was still there: the cooks had left the kitchen hood on which sucked up the gas fumes in the air and stopped the fire from spreading. Instead of a half-million-dollar insurance payday, I received a burnt-up couch I would have to replace and a police arson investigation that hung around for years.

Disheartened by our mutual failures and sick to death of dealing with each other, Antonio and I came to an agreement. Antonio offered to buy me out of the club for the $35,000 I had originally put into the club, a deal that I was happy to accept. I needed to cut my ties with Genesis before I ended up in handcuffs.

Too late: when I went to Antonio's house to pick up an installment of the money he owed me for the club, the shifty fucker tried to give me a paper-trail-establishing personal check. This was *not* how business was done; Antonio already smelled like a sewer rat and now he was acting like one. Within seconds I was swarmed by police officers. I was under arrest for extorting Antonio, and the cops claimed to have audiotape of me making the threats against him. I was furious; for the second straight time, I was under arrest for one of the few serious crimes that I did not commit.

In the process of framing me for extortion, Antonio had unintentionally framed me for *treason*. I had recently pulled off a $26,000 insurance scam with my exiled friend Frank's mother, and, because Antonio had a mole at a local bank, I let him cash the check for me. When Antonio began cooperating with the police, he made a point to rat out the insurance scam so that he could deflect the police's attention and give himself enough cover to keep the money from the score. Unfortunately, the Turkish asshole didn't know the difference between Serbians and Russians because he claimed the woman I got the check from was a Russian. Thanks to a coincidence that Antonio could not have fathomed, this slipup would have gotten me sent to Guantánamo Bay if it had occurred in 2001 instead of 1991.

The police had investigated me years earlier for accidentally meeting a supposed KGB spy with Frank before he split. On our way to our favorite clubs, Frank stopped at the airport to pick up a stranger, a quiet Russian girl, whom he had promised his mom he would give a ride. We dropped the Russian girl off at the Century City commercial district before heading out to party. Little did we know that we were being followed by the FBI or that the unassuming Russian girl would meet another suspected Eastern European spy in Century City. When Antonio accidentally claimed that I had been paid $26,000 by a Russian woman, he confused the feds into thinking he was talking about the suspected spy. The feds became convinced I was in the pay of the KGB.

To my surprise, after my chickenshit extortion arrest, the local cops treated me like Pablo Escobar. I was shackled and heavily guarded on the way to Newport Beach and detained without bail over the weekend. On Monday, when the cops transported me to the "high power" wing of Orange County Jail—where only the craziest bikers, crack-slinging gangbangers, Mexican Mafia hombres, and Colombian psychopaths were detained—I began to wonder if Antonio was secretly the illegitimate son of our dear ally the Emir of Kuwait. It was one of the great shocks of my life when FBI agent Betsy Cordova confronted me and announced that she was from the Counter-Espionage Squad. At first, I thought she was joking. Her take-no-shit, bullying attitude dispelled any doubt I had about her sincerity. I desperately needed an attorney and told her so.

I used my one phone call to tell Babar to go to Mike Marvich, who would make sure Roger was on the case. Of course, Babar was too busy doing blow and hitting on chicks to answer the phone. Left to my own devices, I consulted a public defender. She was no help; she said she had heard "the tape" of me threatening Antonio and that it was such damning evidence that I had no hope of winning the case. She advised me to cooperate with the FBI about my ties to the Soviets and let her negotiate a plea deal for the extortion charge that would send me away for six years. I told her to fuck off. Unlike Greg, I was never going to agree to do a day in jail unless I was convicted—even if I was guilty, and especially for one of the few crimes in California I didn't commit!

I was taken into court the next day for my arraignment; I was terrified that Babar hadn't gotten my message and that no attorney would show up. I sat nervously in the steel cage against the courtroom wall, chained by the wrist and ankle to the most serious, hardcore convicts from the jail population—scarred and tatted-up Mexican hombres, giant black dudes, mountainously muscled skinheads, bikers with eye patches and inappropriate forehead tattoos. They were looking down at me like I was a straight bitch, the first course on that night's prison-rape menu. One of the guys who faced the judge before me pled out for a nine-year sentence with a pissy attitude like it was a slight workplace inconvenience. I was not liking my odds as the lone Asian-American guy in this prison population.

Finally, a healthy, stylishly dressed old man of medium build walked into the courtroom. It was my attorney, Roger, Big Mike's courtroom enforcer. With Roger on my side, I began to feel a little more secure; he was a great attorney, good enough to impress legendary paralegal Mike Marvich at least. Roger's slow, laidback, midwestern style of speaking disarmed judges and juries alike, inspiring trust through its casualness and simplicity. I felt confident that Roger's motion to have bail set for my release would be granted.

The district attorney strenuously disagreed. In the most condemnatory language imaginable, the DA informed the courtroom that I was a suspected murderer, a potential traitor under FBI investigation as a domestic spy, and a major organized crime figure and international drug trafficker. This lady made me out to be Genghis Khan; I still laugh when I think about how the body language of the criminals I was chained to changed from contempt to wary respect as they listened to my Charles Manson rap sheet. One of those convicts gave this unforgettable look to the guy sitting next to him that seemed to say "What the *fuck* is *this* kid's problem?" Another one of the guys smiled and nodded at me; apparently my contempt for humanity had earned his respect.

Roger earned his exorbitant salary: I was set free on $40,000 bail. Though I was almost immediately cleared on the espionage suspicion, Roger was very worried about the extortion charge. The DA told the judge and Roger so many times that I was caught "dead to rights" on audiotape that I began to doubt my innocence myself; every time I saw Roger, he would ask me to be honest and come clean with him. Finally, at a pre-trial motion we got to hear the lynchpin of the prosecution's case: it was a tape of *Babar* threatening Antonio over money he was owed. Roger challenged the DA to authenticate the voice on the recording as mine, and soon the state dropped the charges with prejudice.

My face-to-face encounter with life behind bars as a violent offender convinced me that I needed to make serious changes in my career to avoid jail time. If there has been one unifying principle to my life in the underworld, it may be that I've never met anything or anyone worth going to jail over. I have never understood people like the mobsters in Brooklyn who are released from jail and continue with their old lifestyle even though they know damn well that if they go back to their old hangouts and old friends and old rackets they will be arrested and sent back to jail for even longer sentences. Even if you still want to be a criminal, it's not like crime only exists in *that* neighborhood.

I've always figured that guys who keep going away for the same crimes must enjoy prison; maybe they're too insecure to deal with freedom. Not me: I love my freedom, and I wasn't going to give it up for Antonio, Genesis, Mike Marvich, or anything else.

Being chained to those hardened convicts at my arraignment sapped me of all my enthusiasm for the nightclub, for revenge against Antonio, or for the drug business as a whole. I wanted a new life. I was existentially tired of the Two Toms, of the police surveillance, of the worries that my toehold in the cocaine business would lead to Mike Marvich or some Colombian smuggler or some Mexican stickup kid killing me. I felt like my freedom or my life would end very soon if I went back to the cocaine trade full-time.

The cocaine business was no longer as profitable and fun as it had been; by 1991 the market had long been saturated, prices had collapsed, the ghetto crack wars had robbed cocaine of its style and glamour, violent street gangs like the Crips and the Bloods and the Mexican Mafia were increasingly prevalent players, and too many of my friends and acquaintances had died. The profit margin on selling an uncut kilo to a dealer to whack up had fallen to as low as $400, down from as high as $6,000 in California or $35,000 in Hawaii when I started. The difference in my profit margin left me feeling pissed off at inanimate packages of powder after every deal, as if cocaine had personally betrayed me.

More importantly, it takes a lot to keep a hyperactive guy like me interested, and cocaine and cokeheads with their endless rambling, bragging, and bullshit had simply become boring. It was one thing when I was high on coke—but I had been sober for a couple years, and a sober coke dealer is usually a miserable motherfucker permanently stuck in long, boring conversations that he desperately wants to escape. I had been dealing with cokeheads since I was fourteen; I needed a break.

Besides, the sexy cocaine social scene of the 1980s that Joey Avila and Jerry had introduced me to had disappeared, replaced by the depressing and lame grunge culture of the '90s and the new fashionable drug, heroin. You can trace heroin's rise through pop culture as the cokehead influence of the late '80s—colorful fashions, hyper dance music, swaggering and sleazy hair-metal music—was slowly replaced by the junkie squalor of the '90s: slumming denim and plaid clothes, *E.T.*-puppet Kate Moss as a sex symbol, grimy and tortured grunge music. I didn't fit in with this scene, and I certainly wasn't ever going to become a heroin dealer, which seemed about as much fun as performing assisted suicides.

I decided to move on from the cocaine trade and lifestyle; it wasn't worth going to jail over. Nothing ever is. To tie up loose ends and pay Roger what I owed him in exchange for my freedom, I needed some money. Since I had built up a nearly decade-long track record as a reliable wholesale cocaine dealer, making that cash would be easy: I'd simply screw some guys on a multi-kilo deal whom I had never scammed before. They would never expect it, and I didn't care if I burned any bridges or made any mortal enemies. I just wanted some cash.

The Alley Boys were a Mexican street gang that Babar and I helped to put in business in Santa Ana, selling them bulk quantities of cocaine and guns in the 1980s. Though in recent years they've been making news by dropping bodies left and right, at the time the Alley Boys were small-time Chicano gangbangers. By 1991, however, they were growing in stature and territory; sometimes, I'd call *them* to buy kilos in case I was short on a deal, even though their product was usually diesel-based, yellow ghetto cocaine that my yuppie clientele would have to be real desperate to buy. Their leader, Big Joe, sometimes did business out of his mom's shoe store, and I remember once camping out all day at this Mexican shoe store waiting for them to come up with the money they owed me on a deal. If I didn't get my cash, then Big Joe's mama wasn't going to have much of a store left.

I called Big Joe and told him I had a huge quantity of "primo shit" that I desperately wanted to unload. I arranged a meeting with the Alley Boys' leadership to provide them with a sample of the coke to prove its quality. They were impressed with the taste I gave them (which, I made sure, was legitimately primo shit) and asked for five kilos. That was just perfect; they would never expect to get screwed by a dealer with my reputation on a deal for only five kilos.

After the meet, I drove to the grocery store and purchased eleven pounds of flour and a ream of tan packing tape. I mixed iodine crystals from my bombmaking supplies and a little water into the flour to give it the hospital smell that's indicative of good uncut cocaine. I then molded a couple pounds of this iodine/flour mixture into slabs, covered it with foil and red plastic, and bound it with the tan tape. In case the Alley Boys wanted to check the kilos, I cut L-shaped easy-access "windows" into each package around which I stuffed a little real cocaine in case the cholos performed a sniff or taste test. Since I had real kilos of cocaine at home to compare the fake ones to, I made sure they were identical in smell and appearance.

For the finishing touch, I told my undead buddy Liu Kang to give me his Toyota MR2 sports car for the weekend since he still owed me money. I drove to Santa Ana in the MR2 with Babar shadowing me in my Corvette. We met at Big Joe's place and hung out with the cholos for a little while to make them comfortable; we passed around some joints, told some stories, cracked some jokes, invited them to Babar's fictitious birthday party the next day. When they asked where the kilos were, I told them I needed the cash upfront. Without hesitation, Big Joe produced around $60,000 in cash.

Only when the cash was safely in the car with Babar—in case the deal went wrong in a split-second— did I tell the cholos that I would drive with them in their van to my stash car in Irvine for the kilos. You never kept the money and the cocaine in the same place; it made the cops' job too easy. The Mexicans were reassured of my honesty because I was leaving Liu's MR2 at their place as proof of my integrity.

It was practically a joyride; there was no tension whatsoever because this was just a day at the office for the Alley Boys and me. With Babar following the van in my Corvette, my only concern was whether he could keep his cool, since he had a history of cracking under pressure. When we arrived at my stash car, I took out the five kilos of iodized flour and handed it to the smoked-out, bleary-eyed Mexicans. My name was so good with them that they didn't even check to see if the kilos were legit. The Alley Boys threw the coke into their van, and we told them we'd follow them back to their place in the Corvette to pick up the MR2. Instead, when the cholos turned right, I just kept going straight.

We floored it to Roger's office to pay him what I owed in gangbanger cocaine cash—which was hardly the first time that had happened in his career as a criminal defense attorney. I then called up Liu Kang and told him to say goodbye to his Toyota MR2; he could report it stolen, and I would call his debts even. For my own amusement, I then called the police to report Liu's stolen car at the Alley Boys hangout, leading the police to a banged-up Toyota MR2 surrounded by the entire bat-wielding lineup of Santa Ana's most vicious Chicano street gang.

I drove Babar and myself straight from Roger's office to John Wayne Airport with nothing but the neon beach shorts and tank tops we were wearing and around $50,000 cash as luggage. After a score like that, it was time for hookers, gambling, and partying; it was time for a couple weeks off in Las Vegas.

I remember thinking that there were some perks of the drug-dealer lifestyle that I was going to miss.

"'I don't go prowling around,' [Mike Marvich] said, pulling up his pant leg and sticking a mottled white calf in the air. 'At that particular time I had blood clots in my leg. I was spending most of my

*time in bed.' Now, Marvich said, the government
is using anti-drug laws to steal his house. But police and prosecutors say Marvich is no infirm retiree, taken advantage of by a drug-dealing house
guest. They say he is a sharp-witted ex-con with a
prison record dating back to 1934 and more than
a casual knowledge of the drug trade."*

January 31, 1993

*"A 1990 police search that led to the conviction
of [sic] 78-year-old man on drug charges and
the forfeiture of his Costa Home [sic] home was
illegal, a state appeals panel has ruled. The 2–1
decision by the Fourth District Court of Appeals
reversed the conviction of Michael Patrick Marvich, who is now 82 and living in a trailer park
in Stanton. 'I'm glad I'm finally getting some justice,' Marvich said Tuesday. 'I'm not the criminal.
The police are the criminals for violating my civil
rights.' [. . .]*

*"To avoid prison, Marvich says, he pleaded guilty
to possession of narcotics for sale. . . . But Marvich, a retired paralegal who boasts of helping
to defend the late '60s LSD guru Timothy Leary,
wasn't done. He challenged the search of his home
on Fourth Amendment grounds, accusing police
of lacking sufficient cause to conduct a 'protective sweep' of the home that subsequently turned
up the drugs. . . . Marvich said he'll begin seeking
reimbursement for his house, now worth about
$400,000."*

Orange County Register
October 3, 1997

Before I shift my focus from the cocaine trade to the Mafia and porn industry, I should provide a "where are they now?" accounting of the characters that made my adolescence so gruesome and exciting.

Though Joey Avila died in 1987, a genetic copy of him lives on in Orange County. Sal Avila is a pretty compelling case against the efficacy of human cloning; though I love the man and consider him my good friend, Sal could never fill his identical brother's shoes. After paying off Mike Marvich in full, I assume, Sal retired *completely* from the underworld and enjoys a life of semi-leisure that comprises surfing, overseeing the still successful El Ranchito chain, compulsively marrying younger women, and crusading on behalf of Jesus Christ in as lazy a manner as possible.

A few years ago, Sal contacted me in a state of panic; one of his beautiful teenage daughters had been missing for two weeks. She was hooked on crystal meth and ran away from home to live with this deadbeat dealer. Sal asked if I could rescue his daughter without jeopardizing his place in heaven by spilling more blood; I assured him I could secure the return of his daughter without shooting a gun or throwing a punch. In fact, I assured Sal I could save her from the comfort of my home.

"Hello?" answered the meth dealer when he picked up the phone.

"Hey, do you have Sal Avila's daughter?" I asked in a pleasant voice. "You need to send her back home."

"Who the fuck are you?" the meth dealer replied in his best gorilla-tough-guy voice.

"I'm just the guy that's going to kill you," I responded in the tone of a happy preschool teacher.

"Uh," the dealer began, unsure how to respond.

"Yeah . . . whatever, dude, fuck you. If you want her, you'll have to come and get—"

"You *really* don't get it," I said with a friendly laugh. "I really *am* going to come over to your house and kill you. Just like *that*. You are talking to the guy who is going to kill you in cold blood without a second thought and never get caught. I'm going to laugh about it. I'm already excited. I can't wait."

"Oh, really, asshole?" the crank dealer stuttered, trying to go on the offensive. Puffing himself up, he started reciting a list of minor-league Orange County bouncers, part-time dealers, and thugs who would vouch for his credentials as a serious tough guy. Among the names he dropped were some of the guys who worked the door at Sutra, a connected club in Orange County that I knew well. This was very convenient; now I had a job reference!

"You know the guys at Sutra?" I asked as if he had just mentioned my best buddies in the world. "That's *great*. Call them up, tell them that 'A guy named Kenji says he's going to kill me' and then call me back and tell me what they say about me." I hung up and looked at the clock.

Less than five minutes later, my phone rang. "Um, I'm very sorry," the dealer whimpered. "I had no idea that you were . . . who you are. She'll be on my front lawn with all of her stuff in five minutes to be picked up."

"No-o, stupid," I said, unable to hide the pleasure I was taking at this idiot's humiliation. "You'll be buying her a cab ride home. If I have to go through the trouble of driving to your dump to pick her up, I might as well walk the extra few feet and just shoot you in the fucking head for wasting my time."

Sal's daughter was returned home within the hour

and has since cleaned up. She is now a beautiful, sober, and intelligent woman who Sal hopes will take a more direct route to mature Christian piety than he did. Some of Sal's former accomplices are also still in the neighborhood, despite the laundry list of crimes and atrocities they've committed in Orange County through the years. As recently as a few years ago, Tommy Thornton was living in the area with his best buddy, Lalo. These two bloodsuckers were as thick as thieves can be until Lalo allegedly shorted Tommy on a deal and disappeared off the face of the earth. No one has heard from Lalo since. Tommy is still around, spending his days in the local grind-joint casinos, drinking nonstop and losing his money to Vietnamese card sharks one-third his size. He still smiles whenever he sees me.

Officer Jerry, Irvine Police Department's Most Wanted, is still wearing his badge to the dismay and disbelief of cops and crooks alike throughout California. Despite innumerable attempts by police investigators and the district attorney's office to send the most transparently crooked police officer in California to jail, sufficient proof has never been mustered to bring Jerry up on charges—allegedly thanks to the Irvine PD's own efforts to suppress the evidence. The rapidly aging Jerry is maintaining a desperate claw-hold on a desk job so he can keep his full health benefits and salary as his body breaks down from a lifetime of abuse and debauchery.

Griselda "The Black Widow" Blanco is another unlikely survivor of the 1970s and '80s cocaine wars that she began. In what has to rank as one of the most spectacularly botched criminal investigations and prosecutions in American history, the feds were unable to convict Griselda of any of the 200-odd murders she committed or ordered. Sent to jail on comparatively inconsequential drug charges after the DEA arrested her in Irvine in 1985, America's most prolific mass-murderer was paroled in 2004 and returned to Colombia a free woman. Her sons did not inherit her magical luck; three of them, including Osvaldo, my tormentor at Setoya, were whacked. I am told that the youngest son, Michael Corleone Blanco, runs a Hispanic gangsta-rap label out of Miami.

While The Black Widow managed to get off light with only nineteen years in jail for her reign of terror, The Black Widower, Mike Marvich, suffered absolutely no repercussions for his crimes. If Griselda Blanco's escape from justice was a combination of massacring all her accomplices, law enforcement's stupidity, and pure dumb luck, the way Big Mike reversed the laws of karma was an act of criminal genius. Mike's entire criminal career is a masterpiece of underworld performance art; he robbed, betrayed, and slaughtered with virtuoso skill. There was no such thing as luck when it came to Big Mike, only calculation. Marvich was a cerebral predator; his greatest weapon was his brain.

Big Mike not only thrived during the most dangerous era in the history of the drug trade; he did so as a feeble old paralegal. Mike scammed his way into the inner circle of the Medellín Cartel when it was the most powerful criminal organization in history; he embezzled tens of millions of dollars as the cartel's proconsul in California; and he emerged unscathed when most of the cartel's hierarchy was murdered in the late '80s and early '90s. While his legendary bosses, Rodriguez Gacha and Pablo Escobar, were gunned down like vermin, no one even had the balls to talk mean to Big Mike. When all his lieutenants and competitors were imprisoned, Mike continued his peaceful life as a retired civilian family-man undisturbed. Mike's entire world collapsed around him, but he just brushed himself off and went about his business. Mike simply won at life.

And Mike had a secret. Shortly after Joey's death, Mark Ruiz, the heavyweight smuggler that Big Mike brought to his last meeting with Joey, was ambushed by the feds during a deal and sent away for years. The Orange County underworld was abuzz when news leaked that the feds apparently had Ruiz under close surveillance for some time, which meant that more indictments and busts were likely forthcoming. Everyone consequently expected Big Mike to go down with him, but the feds never so much as knocked on Mike's door. This made me suspicious: how could the feds have Mark Ruiz dead to rights while never coming across his overlapping business interests with Mike Marvich?

A couple years later, the police went after Marvich's roommate and bodyguard Collin "CQ" Quick. In the process, they searched the modest Marvich residence in Costa Mesa, found thirty pounds of pot along with some meth and explosives, and arrested seventy-seven-year-old Mike, CQ, and Mike's hot new twenty-eight-year-old girlfriend. Although the drugs were found at Marvich's home, he once again evaded jail time while his accomplices went down. Mike even managed to successfully challenge the search and seizure of his home in court, tying up the state in litigation to this day regarding whether the Marvich estate is owed full restitution for the lost property. With a record dating back to 1931 and a reputation throughout the California underworld as a mass-murdering kingpin, Big Mike certainly seemed to get off easy.

In one of my last meetings with Marvich, who at his advanced age looked and acted more than ever like Emperor Palpatine from *Star Wars*, I tried to get Mike to confirm my suspicions. I brought up the imprisoned Mark Ruiz, just to see what Mike would say. His face lit up with that devious, sadistic smile that usually came out only when his wife or Joey Avila was brought up in conversation. "I guess Mark just fucked the wrong guy on a deal and got what he deserved."

I felt stupid for never figuring out Mike Marvich's secret to invincibility: he was a rat! It was so obvious: Mike was smart, so *of course* he was a rat! Why wouldn't a savvy operator like Mike volunteer for the get-out-of-jail-free cards that the federal government hands out willy-nilly to anyone with underworld credentials?

Big Mike, one of the most experienced criminal paralegals in America, had ample connections within the DEA and FBI. As one of the only white Americans with access to the highest echelons of the Medellín Cartel, Big Mike should have had no trouble securing federal protection for himself in return for elite insider information on high-profile international fugitives like Griselda (who I bet he set up), Escobar, and Rodriguez Gacha. While Mike Marvich killed Joey Avila, his wife, her ex-husband, random civilians, and basically whomever else he wanted, certain elements in the United States government looked the other way and did their backroom, under-the-table best to dissuade law enforcement from pursuing him. This was confirmed to me by a police source who admitted that the feds interceded off-the-record on Mike's behalf when he was arrested in 1990.

Big Mike was hardly alone; his mass-murdering contemporaries, James "Whitey" Bulger of Boston's Winter Hill Gang and Gregory "The Grim Reaper" Scarpa of the Colombo Family, both killed with impunity thanks to their position as prized FBI informants. At the same time, I was a protected and highly paid informant for Jerry at the Irvine PD and the FBI while I was blowing up cars and ordering drive-by shootings. The Game Is Rigged.

Once his status as informant was obvious, I could appreciate the towering criminal genius of Mike Marvich in full. Big Mike was universally duplicitous and dishonest; he never acted in good faith for a single moment in his entire life. As far as I know, Big Mike never did business with a single criminal, civilian, or law enforcement agency that he did not comprehensively double-cross, nor do I know of a single instance where Mike suffered meaningful retribution for any of these betrayals. Mike was a full-time con man who enjoyed a 100 percent success rate in the last few decades of his life. He lied every second of every day and was never punished. To this day I marvel at his ingenuity and skill.

Big Mike began as an old-school crook but violated the street's code by leaving the Life to become a civilian who worked with law enforcement. As a paralegal, he obtained the trust of the Medellín Cartel, which he then proceeded to exploit, rob, and rat on until its demise. With Rodriguez Gacha and Escobar's support, Mike then betrayed the confidentiality of his other criminal clients by re-entering the underworld and using his inside information to outmaneuver and defeat them. Among the ex-clients Mike stabbed in the back was Joey Avila, whom Mike most likely framed for stealing millions of dollars' worth of cocaine and then had killed. Anyone who supported or aided Mike likewise faced destruction: Mike killed his wife, handed Mark Ruiz to the feds after taking him to the meeting with Joey to give himself an alibi, offered Lalo up to me as a human sacrifice, and, in one final tour de force, threw his most trusted enforcer, CQ, and his girlfriend under the bus when they were all finally arrested together.

Most importantly, of course, Mike made a deal with the American government to be an informant and then abused his protection by killing at will throughout the late '70s and into the '80s. Of course he did—any smart crook will want to work for the strongest crime syndicate around, and the strongest organized crime family in the world is the U.S. government. There's a reason why the only players to make it through the heyday of the Orange County cocaine trade without paying a price were Mike Marvich, Officer Jerry, and me: we were all rats that played for Team USA! We understood the central lesson of the 21st-century underworld: The Game Is Rigged, so Play For The House.

"You know, Bomp, we put too much emphasis on clipping guys and not enough on fucking broads."

Jimmy "The Weasel" Fratianno
Advising fellow L.A. Mafia capo
Frank Bompensiero in the 1950s.

Top Ten Porn Titles Directed or Produced by Kenji
10. *Girlfriends: Strap-on Asshole Buddies* (1995)
 9. *Down and Dirty: The Grunge Girls Chronicles* (1995)
 8. *Rosie the Neighborhood Slut* (1994)
 7. *In Search of the Brown Eye* (1995)
 6. *Buck Soup* (1995)
 5. *Fuck Soup* (1995)
 4. *Adventures of Big Schlong & Little Dong* (2000)
 3. *National Poontang's Sex Vacation* (1990)
 2. *Dr. Finger's House of Lesbians* (1995)
 1. *Slammin' Granny in the Fanny* (1995)

One of the immutable rules about women I learned from Joey and Officer Jerry was that a well-dressed man with money and cocaine can always get laid. There is an exception to every rule, and, ironically, the exception to this rule had a nine-inch dick.

Al Brown was the Reverse Pickup Artist. Al was one of my best customers, a hardcore Canadian cokehead who, at first sight, you would expect to be an irresistible chick magnet. Al had it all: tall, tan, muscular, fastidiously well-dressed, and graced with immaculate soap opera–star hair and an ivory fortress of perfect white teeth.

None of it mattered. Even with help from my cocaine supply, Al was hopeless.

Although Al's mere presence seduced women, he rapidly managed to repel them by actually talking. Girls would drool as he approached and retch as he left. Al's melting nerves, stuttering come-ons, and painful self-consciousness could creep out any woman. They looked at him and figured he had to have something epically wrong with him to be alone. They were right.

Babar and I laughed for hours watching the General Custer of the Orange County dating scene; we were always speculating about the possible source of his social disorder. Our curiosity was deepened by the fact that Al—despite slurping cocaine by the gram into his skull—only acted like a cokehead around women. Al shoveled coke up his nose yet still floated around in a pleasant haze like a wake-and-bake pothead; a case of permanent sluggishness that he claimed was due to severe insomnia. I was convinced Al's insomnia and neurotic issues with women sprung from a common source: the gorgeous gym rat with the obsessively color-coordinated wardrobe was a suppressed, self-loathing homosexual.

I was right. You can go into the gay section of any porn store and buy a DVD of Al chewing on a pair of sweaty white briefs while a super-size dick anally devastates him. Depending on the store's inventory, you can also buy 1,000 to 2,000 DVDs of Al anally punishing some of the most beautiful women in the world.

Al Brown is better known as porn legend Peter North, one of the most virile babe-hunting studs in heterosexual America. Most actors in straight porn are just bipedal dildos, jacked-up props who are paid pennies to stay hard, come on command, and draw absolutely no attention to themselves. Not Peter North; he's a legit *star*, a product-mover, a bankable name brand. Peter North is a rarity in the porn business: a male porn star whose name alone can sell straight videos to straight men. To a special subculture in America, Al Brown as Peter North is a larger-than-life celebrity, a hero, a super-hero—Sperm Man.

Peter's appeal to straight men is based upon the freakish nature and dimensions of his ejaculations. When Peter climaxes, his female co-stars are doused with round after round of pearl fluid. Peter's load is measured by the barrel; he jizzes like his dick is hooked up to a fire hydrant. For reasons beyond my comprehension, this freakshow stunt makes Peter North a star attraction and something of a hero to millions of straight men.

America is so sexually dysfunctional and insecure that the volume of a man's ejaculation has become a measure of his manhood, and, by that ridiculous stan-dard, stuttering punk Al Brown was crowned the hunkiest stud in the porn world. There are millionaire software programmers who will stop Peter North at the mall and start crying because they're meeting their idol. There are lawyers who will wait in line for an hour, pay $25 for Peter's autograph, and babble at him about how great an inspiration he's been in their lives.

In fact, I found out about Al's secret career because my crewmember Phil was awestruck when I unwittingly introduced him to his porno hero Peter North. Until Phil clued me in, I had no idea about Al's dubious brand of fame; to me, he was just some dude who claimed to work at the phone company. I only let a dork like him hang around me in the first place because he hooked us up with new cocaine customers in Hawaii. I was shocked to see that a normal guy like Phil honestly looked up to some gigolo as a *celebrity*—which is one brand of culture shock that I would never outgrow in the porn industry.

When Phil broke his cover, Al immediately became one of my favorite people because I saw how easy it would be to fuck with him. Since Al was so ashamed of his porn career, I loved to enthusiastically introduce him to everyone we met as "PORN STAR PETER NORTH!" I disliked Al, but I began to like Peter; I always like people I can drive completely crazy at will.

The gay porn angle was another source of comedy to me: any guy who is willing to surrender his asshole to enormous jackhammering penises for a couple hundred dollars, yet claims to be 100 percent straight, is a study in hilarity. I could give a shit whether a guy is gay or straight or bisexual; it's the hypocrisy and denial that amuses me. Whenever I broached the subject of his homosexual behavior, wrinkles would spread over Peter's leathery face and his skin would begin to sweat and glow red. He looked like he was about to have a stroke. Peter is still touchy about his gay porn career to this day; ask him about it if you see him. No, seriously, please ask him and then e-mail me about it. I always get a kick out of those stories.

Peter put up with my bullshit because he needed someone to bankroll his ambitions of becoming a director. Though I had little faith in Peter's cinematic or entrepreneurial skills, I agreed to finance his films since I'd make money regardless of the outcome: either Peter's directorial debut would be a success or I'd get a funny story and a debt I could milk for the rest of his career. That's the great thing about being a gangster investor—you never accept losses. Someone else always pays the price.

Besides, I was always happy to diversify into a new, easy-money cash business. My attorney Roger had introduced me to porn producer Jim Haskins, who liked to have coke dealers on set because porn stars love cocaine. When I talked with Jim, he made it clear that even a total idiot like Peter could make money in porn. "Shit, Kenji, some directors just point a single camera at two people fucking without any other sound equipment or crew, play elevator music over the film so no one realizes it's silent, and sell it the next day. The demand outstrips the supply. A retard can make a profit at porn."

Apparently, Peter and my lieutenant, Babar, were dumber than "retards." In retrospect, our first film was doomed the second I handed a supervising role to Babar, who never made money without me as his criminal babysitter. That flunky was a half-ass crook, but he was a stone-cold killer when it came to women, so I figured he might do a bang-up job working in porn. Despite his Stanford Law School credentials, Babar would trade a spot on the Supreme Court for the opportunity to construct a career and lifestyle centered on easy access to easy women.

"Bro, I'm totally going to be Derrick Ramrod, porn mogul and superstar," Babar told me with his usual flailing hand gestures and cokehead sniffling. "Dude just wait, I'm gonna make you crazy money, bro, *cray-zee* money," he promised with serious, squinting eyes before going back to his full-time job chugging beers and chopping out lines. You could tell he was already stage-managing gangbangs in his head. Since Babar was a big fan, he rented out genius comedian Sam Kinison's home for a weekend and planned to stage his porn-film debut there.

With Sam Kinison on my mind since we were going to use his home for our first film shoot, I decided to head out to Las Vegas to see Sam in person at Bally's. My crew was a mess: tooled up with guns and knives, coked up, raging on steroids, and just mind-fucked into a different dimension by the most potent LSD we had ever encountered. I was so high that every time I blinked, my head was kicked across the galaxy into an immeasurably distant black hole, only for it to be spat out and sent crashing back into place on my shoulders by the time my eyes reopened.

My crew bribed our way to a table right up front between Guns N' Roses (I was their drummer's dealer) and porn icons Ron Jeremy and Seka. Ronnie was famous among porn fans for being fat, ugly, Jewish, and so well-hung that he could suck his own dick. Ronnie the Hedgehog was his normal, gregarious, glad-handing self, so we went over to network with him.

While we were standing up and chatting with The Hedgehog, we apparently infuriated crusty old L.A. sleazeball Bill Gazzarri, who was sitting at the next table. Gazzarri was a local rock legend for running a Sunset Boulevard club that started the careers of the Doors, Van Halen, and a couple dozen other big bands. Though Gazzarri dressed like Al Capone and fancied himself a wiseguy, he was just some fucknut club promoter to me. Thinking that I was an Asian kid whom he could look tough bullying, the skeletal Gazzarri wheezed and then hissed at me to "Sit the fuck down, kid!"

"Oh, shut the fuck up, old man," I snarled, for once failing to muster my smiling, placid, Zen brand of aggression. I was so high that I didn't even give the old buzzard a chance to respond before I reached for my piece.

"Get the fuck out of here!" Gazzarri barked in his worst tough-guy impersonation. I turned around to see that Gazzarri had some big, beefy bodyguards at his side; no wonder he was acting tough. I decided that moment to shoot him in the fucking head. Luckily for Bill, Ronnie hated confrontation and hopped between us like Super Mario; he saved that old shithead's life and rescued me from twenty-five-to-life. Instead, I sentenced myself to the punishment of watching Kinison on acid, which felt as if my brain was being stretched, tweaked, and twisted by a master torturer. He was just too intense, a gust of sulfurous fumes right through my eyes and into my brain.

Back in California, the ragtag duo of the Mexican wannabe lawyer and the closeted Canadian insomniac cokehead proved to be an ill-advised choice to produce a movie at Kinison's house. Without a boss, Peter slept in and repeatedly missed his scheduled scenes, while the coke-happy Babar exploited the star's absence by diligently fucking all the actresses off camera. When Babar had the good sense to occasionally turn on a camera, he of course proved incapable of maintaining an erection and committed to film some tragic softy-slamming "sex" that resembled a sweaty Mexican assaulting a bored woman with a wiggly cocktail frank.

It was a debacle; watching the video later, I began to admire the patience of the actress, who diligently persisted in moaning for what seemed like hours as this sweaty Latino weasel suffered a prolonged, booze-fueled emotional breakdown and desperately slapped his sad slippery noodle all over her exhausted body. Even Babar was traumatized by the experience: he paid a quack headshrinker to hypnotize his penis into becoming erect on demand—an experiment in penile psychotherapy that failed. Eventually, far behind schedule, a rump cut of something too pathetic and pathos-laden to even be called a jackoff flick was handed to the editor, Jim Talmadge.

Scared of my temper, Babar and Peter blamed the long-delayed release of the film on Talmadge "just sitting on the goddamn thing," which of course dictated that my gun and I visit Jim Talmadge immediately. I was used to making quick, easy money, and "production delay" was nothing more than a euphemism for "incompetence," "laziness," or possibly "robbery" in my coke-dealer mind-set. I told debuting director Peter North to escort his executive producer to the editor's office and mediate.

When I walked into Talmadge's office, I remember thinking that this guy looked exactly like I had expected. Jim was a pornographer if I've ever seen one: a bald, morbidly obese, disheveled schlub with a sly twinkle in his bloodshot eyes. Jim was such a stereotypical perv that a couple years later a porn studio cast him as "Uncle Roy," the girl-diddling MC of the Uncle Roy's Amateurs porn series.

Well-read and professional to the core, Jim took about fifteen seconds to convince me that the delays were caused entirely by Babar's and Peter's complete ignorance of pornographic filmmaking. Impressed by Jim's intelligence and mastery of the porn game, I told him that I wanted to back him in the porn business in order to redeem my investment. I promised that, from now on, I would personally assure that he received everything he needed in exchange for his promise to salvage Peter North's movie, make some new ones for me, and give me on-set lessons. Jim extended his hand; I shook it. I was no longer an investor; I was now a full-blown porn producer.

The most important decision up to that point in my career was an accident, a fluke in my otherwise carefully calculated criminal portfolio. I became a porn investor because Peter North seemed like an easy mark to leech money from, and I became a porn producer for no better reason than I could not stand to let Babar and

Peter's incompetence cost me money. As a hot-shit club owner and coke smuggler, I would have been appalled to learn that my work in the sleazy porn biz would one day come to define my criminal career, and I cannot imagine how humiliated I would have been had I known that some of the crooks I would meet in the sex rackets would prove exponentially smarter, more skillful, and cooler than I was.

There was only one problem with my new career choice: I didn't know anything at all about porn, and what I initially found out I hated. I didn't watch porn; I didn't care about porn; I hadn't even looked at porn since I learned how to catch some of Joey Avila's and Jerry's pussy shrapnel. Consequently, I didn't know how porn worked, let alone how to make a film. When I first talked to Jim Talmadge about our movies, I knew so little about porn, its conventions, and its terminology that I had no idea what he was saying. All I knew was that Jim sounded much more convincing and trustworthy than Peter North and Babar when he spoke.

Though I got laid regularly from the age of fourteen, I honestly wasn't too comfortable with the *idea* of the sex rackets. While "coke dealer" in the '80s was a glamorous job in my circle, "porn peddler" just seemed sleazy—a sordid gig for an educated suburban kid like me. Helping shut-ins jerk off was a step down from helping celebrities and millionaires party. Even though I screwed around with strippers every night, the idea of grown women fucking for money in the middle of a workday genuinely made me feel uncomfortable and disgusted. It was so mechanical and cheap. This was the era before the "barely legal" porn fad, so most of the women were much older than me, which gave it a weird "watching your mom fuck" vibe.

I had been uncomfortable at porn sets ever since my first visit to one of Jim Haskins' movies, two years before my first Peter North production. Within seconds of my arrival at Jim's set, I ran into porn superstar Christy Canyon, a stunning woman with beautiful long brown hair, caramel skin, and the largest natural breasts I had ever seen. Did I mention that shapely Christy was topless, casually introducing herself to teenage me with her Olympian thirty-six DD breasts swaying majestically in my face?

Christy laughed at how flustered I was, like it was the cutest thing she had ever seen. "Don't worry, Ken!" she said like some warm, nurturing, big-tittied earth goddess. "You can look at them, Ken. Come on, feel them! It's no big deal!" I nearly fell over. Christy was rolling her eyes, apparently having never encountered such outlandish propriety at a porn set.

Despite a year or two of intervening experience, my first day on set as a porn producer was, if anything, less auspicious. I arrived early at the avocado farm that Babar and Peter had rented. The door to the actress's trailer opened and out sashayed Lois Ayres, a skinny degenerate with a mangled blond punk-rock haircut and a cute face clown-blasted with whore makeup. She marched over to me with laser-like focus, her boobs showing through the thin robe she wore. Before I could introduce myself, she asked, "Do you think I need a boob job?" and whipped out her gorgeous tits for me to inspect.

Despite Christy Canyon's attempt to accustom me to titty ambushes, I was unprepared. I self-destructed like Peter North trying to pick up a girl who wasn't specifically hired to fuck him; I was spazzing out, incapable of keeping eye contact, completing a sentence, or stopping myself from blushing. I had no idea: Where should I look? Could I look at those tits? I thought back to my seduction messiah and asked W.W.J.D.: What Would Jerry Do?

Before the little Officer Jerry devil on my shoulder had time to offer advice, Lois began to tease me with a schoolyard bully tone in her voice. "Come on, what's your problem?" Lois was *this close* to saying "What's your problem, *fag*?"

"Come on, do my tits look okay or not?" she asked as if the fact that her job was to show her tits on film was not sufficient proof that they were generally satisfactory to mankind. I wanted to say, "Back off, bitch, I'm twenty! Of course your tits look fine to me!" but I was dumb-struck.

My inability to speak worked Lois into a cackle. "Hey, Samantha," Lois screamed, "come see the virgin!"

Samantha Strong, the film's torpedo-chested blond bombshell, did the streetwalker stroll over to us with a smirk on her face and one of her large, dark, expressive eyebrows raised with mischief. When she reached us, she too brandished her bare breasts. A moment later, my right hand was involuntarily dragged onto one of Sa-mantha's breasts and my left hand to one of Lois' more humble pair.

"How do you like *that*, virgin?" teased Samantha, a short and shapely smartass who I dug immediately.

"Come on, give 'em a squeeze, virgin!" laughed Lois.

"Which one do you like better? Real or fake?" Sa-mantha asked with deadly professional seriousness. I was still speechless, hopeless, just like with Christy Can-yon. The scoreboard read Porn Titties 2, Kenji 0.

I stumbled over to Jim's director chair with a shoe-box full of coke cash and told him it was for the crew's salary. "Don't give it to me, Ken," Jim said with a smirk.

"*You're* the boss here. Pay the talent yourself; get a feel on how to handle them."

With my humiliation at the hands and breasts of Lois and Samantha still fresh in my mind, I was not too excited about this job. It got worse: sleepy-time Peter North ignored his alarm clock for five hours, giving me all the time in the world to make small talk with the cast and crew. I was not in the mood to be patronized by prostitutes again, but I had little else to do but talk to the girls while we waited for Peter. Jerry had trained me to hold women in contempt, so it was extremely disconcerting and displeasing to relate to women in situations where I was at a clear disadvantage. They held the power.

By the time Captain Heterosexuality Peter North begrudgingly arrived at his job fucking gorgeous women, I had relearned how to speak and figured out my answer to Samantha's question. Though real tits were always a pleasure, I had to admit I was partial to a pair of giant, science-fiction fake tits.

When the filming started, I was in for another shock: now that I knew Lois and Samantha, watching them fuck was even more unpleasant than listening to them talk. The girls had become humanized to me, so it was excruciating to see them get brutalized by a bunch of jacked-up apes. It was like when my Southern relatives made me watch farm animals get slaughtered—I knew that was the reason the animals were there, but that didn't mean I wanted to witness the moment when they were gruesomely reduced from living creatures to cuts of meat.

Still jarred by their abrupt shift from normal women into degraded sex pigs, I wondered how the girls could act like nothing at all had transpired after the scene was finished. They would just amble over, all sweaty and sticky, and make chitchat like normal women, as if they had not just lowered themselves to the status of livestock. It blew my mind how many of these girls would flirt with me right after a shoot, as if I were not going to mind that they were covered in Peter's jizz.

The greatest culture shock of all were the delusions of grandeur that some of the girls entertained. Some of these prostitutes fancied themselves A-list celebrities who deserved to have their asses kissed at all times. These are the cocksucking clowns who will deliver a tearful, deadly serious acceptance speech thanking their Lord and Savior Jesus Christ, Mommy and Daddy, and their method-acting coach when they are handed the Adult Video News Awards trophy for Best Gangbang Scene. As a criminal with plenty of experience with segregated lives, I was intrigued by the heightened psychological compartmentalization of the porn women: how could they perform the most debasing acts imaginable in front of dozens of strangers on the set and then, when the scene wrapped, still act with the undiminished hauteur of a movie superstar? I just wanted to scream, "Bitch, drop the attitude. You suck dick for a living. Should I be impressed?"

My first day as a porn producer was an interminable binge at an all-you-can-swallow buffet of shame and social discomfort. Pimp may have been Babar's dream job, but it certainly was not mine; I was on the verge of puking the entire time. I would have never come back to the set if not for my reluctant realization that the business fundamentals of the porn racket were almost too good to be true. Babar's fantasy was to fuck easy girls, but mine was to make millions in dirty money and never get caught.

Everything in porn in the late '80s and early '90s was done with *cash* and with a minimum of paperwork; it was the perfect money-laundering scheme. I could pay everyone in drug money, sell the movie to a distributor, and receive a valid, taxable check in return! If I made a deal where I received some of my movies in wholesale bulk, I could sell them twice: once on the black market and once more on paper at a ridiculously inflated price to allow me to launder even more money with a completely authentic, verifiable paper trail.

Suddenly, I could own property *legally;* my drug money became as clean as whatever Babar could make as a lawyer. I transformed my drug money into porn films that I sold legally and at a profit, all the while enjoying the collateral sexual benefits of working with the hottest and easiest women in California. A porn studio was that rare front business that actually might add to my drug profits while laundering them. Even if I quit my other criminal pursuits, that just meant I could pay my talent in *other* gangsters' illicit money, taking a fee from them for laundering their cash and keeping all the film profits for myself.

The legitimate business of making porn delivered nearly criminal profits on its own. Everyone was making money at porn in those days; even idiots like Peter North eventually became millionaires. The VHS and VCR revolution of the 1980s had exponentially increased the customer base and revenue streams of the porn studios; but, thanks to porn's disreputable image, its convoluted legal standing in Reagan/Bush America, and the innate incompetence of most pornographers, the porn companies had yet to capitalize by becoming professionally run corporations. Though the studios were making ten to twenty times the profits of a decade earlier, the underlying businesses were still mom-and-pop operations run in an amateurish, haphazard manner. There were no megastudios, no multinational conglomerates. These

inefficient, incompetent, and undercapitalized companies could not churn out smut quickly enough to meet
the enormous demand for new VHS and film titles. This
imbalance in supply and demand meant that, as long as
you could point a steady camera at sex, you could find a
buyer for your film.

Despite my initial distaste with the porn business, I
had to follow the money; I was a crook, after all. What is
a criminal if not a capitalist without a moral gag reflex?

Part of my apprenticeship under Jim involved learning how to convince distributors to buy my films. Jim
explained that the quality of the porn itself mattered
far less than the producer's ability to relate to the old
boys' network of wiseguys and wannabe mafiosi who
controlled the distribution channels. As late as Bill Clinton's first term as president, porn was still largely a Mafia
racket.

The root of the Mafia's power was the fundamentally
illicit nature of the adult entertainment business. The
Mob expanded its control over the porn business during
the first two thirds of the 20th century, when the production and distribution of pornography was explicitly illegal. In those days, smut peddlers were unable to appeal
for police protection since they were crooks themselves,
so the Mob had no trouble muscling into their businesses.
Over a period of decades, the Mafia methodically co-
opted the black market film processing plants and distribution networks and extorted protection money and
ownership points from adult bookstores and theaters.
The peak of the Mafia's porn empire came in the 1970s,
when Mob money financed the *Deep Throat/Behind the
Green Door/Debbie Does Dallas* pornography boom that
made it briefly normal for respectable couples to publicly
attend porn films on dates.

The Mafia's influence waned in the late '70s and early '80s; advances in easy-to-reproduce VHS technology made it impossible to monopolize and police the porn distribution networks. Nonetheless, when I started in porn, the Los Angeles Family and all of New York's Five Families had heavyweight capos and made men embedded within the industry. These mafiosi were not archaic gangland leftovers from porn's outlaw days hanging on for dear life in a reformed, mainstream industry. The Mafia was present throughout the porn industry because porn was still a criminal industry.

Outside of certain illegal content (pissing, shitting, fisting, rape fantasy, snuff, child porn, and so forth), the act of making pornographic content itself was generally no longer illegal, but the business practices of adult-film studios to produce pornographic content certainly were. Though the industry made billions of dollars annually, the producers remained penny-pinching, corner-cutting crooks. All industry regulations were ignored: no filming permits, no safety permits, no commercial zoning for the sets, no legally mandated policemen and firemen on set, no paperwork for the stars. Since the vice squad would raid the shoots and seize the masters and equipment, most sets had guards posted outside with walkie-talkies.

Porn producers were still committing crimes, so they were wary of law enforcement and therefore still vulnerable to organized crime families. The result was wiseguys playing "Hollywood tycoon" in spacious corner offices in at least a dozen porn studios and distributors across the San Fernando Valley. The presence of hardened criminals in positions of power throughout the porn industry was a fantastic advantage for me. As a criminal with a good street rep and a bad rap sheet, I could speak to them in their own language.

When it came to doing business with the Mob, I had a unique mind-set: I didn't respect them. At that time, I had hardly paid attention to John Gotti, *The Godfather*, or any of that bullshit; it was just pop-culture white noise. It was about as real as *The A-Team* and *Magnum, P.I.* to me. It was only through cultural osmosis that I knew the basics of the Mafia—that non-Italians could make money with the families but only Italians could become "made men"; that the neighborhood bosses were called *capos*; that the top of the leadership pyramid consisted of a boss, an underboss as his right-hand man, and a *consigliere* as the family's top advisor; that the punishment for violating the code of secrecy or any other Mafia rule was supposedly death. It all seemed very pretentious, artificial, and insecure to me, like the fat unemployed crackers who dub themselves Imperial Grand Wizards when they put on their white bedsheets and meet with their Ku Klux Klan buddies. A crook is a crook; if he's good, he doesn't need to rely on a puffed-up title or mystical secret organization to get what he wants.

My few Italian criminal friends—my buddy from Brooklyn who failed to torch Genesis and my dipshit goombah mentor Kenny DiMartini—did not fill me with awe for the Mafia brand name. When I saw how much respect Mafia guys received at Setoya or other clubs around Orange County, I thought it was fucking silly. In my blood-and-guts, street-criminal calculus, if the local mafiosi were not exactly known for dropping bodies, why should I respect them? With murder off the table, what could a "made man" use to threaten me that a bullet to his head wouldn't solve? Jump me, beat me up, you can even break my legs; I'll just wheel myself right back at you like Elroy and shoot you to death. Please.

Mike Marvich: *that* was a scary man; he had a

bottomless supply of stupid Colombian and Mexican cavemen who, at his word, would slaughter you, your mother, your wife, your priest, and your newborn daughter. *That* was power on the streets—not some fruity title.

The Mafia never fucked with Marvich; Big Mike never paid a cent in street-tax for dealing and dropping bodies all over the Los Angeles Family's territory. The most feared mafiosi in California when I came of age were Anthony "The Animal" Fiato and Michael "Mike Rizzi" Rizzitello, and they hardly seemed impressive to me at the time: Anthony turned rat, and Rizzi, who knew Joey's circle and never dared to demand tribute, went to jail for personally firing three bullets into the head of titty-bar owner Bill Carroll—who lived. I was no Mob boss, but I knew I had people to do my dirty work for me and, in an emergency, I could kill anyone given an opportunity to fire my gun three times directly into their head.

As far as I was concerned, the Mafia was a joke. This arrogance turned out to be an advantage: Mafia guys who were not otherwise likely to take an Asian-American "kid" seriously were impressed with me precisely because I was clearly unimpressed with them.

With twenty time-coded copies of our first movies in hand, I went out to woo porn distributors and meet some mafiosi. First on my list was Visual Images, the home of Bonanno and Gambino Mafia Family associate Tommy Sinopoli and alleged Los Angeles Mafia made man Michael "Batman" Esposito. "Batman" Esposito was so dubbed because he was a short little dork who looked like cereal mascot Count Chocula.

Batman's father, Sal Esposito, worked as a driver and gopher for Anthony "Tony Ducks" Corallo, the legendary Lucchese Family godfather whose gangland credibility dwarfed John Gotti's at its peak. Coming of age in Italian Harlem during Tony Ducks' reign, Batman himself was apparently connected enough to be caught on a FBI bug meeting with Anthony "Fat Tony" Salerno, boss of the Genovese Family. Batman told me that, after U.S. Attorney Rudy Giuliani sent him to prison for refusing to testify in front of a grand jury against Salerno, he moved out West to escape the heat and ended up buying a Mob-owned porn company previously called TGA with Tommy Sinopoli, another wiseguy. TGA's previous owner, Teddy Gaswrith, was the prototype for the sorry schmucks who passed for "wiseguys" in California in that he looked like Larry from *The Three Stooges,* carried himself like Mike Tyson, and ran in a panic to "call New York" the second a threat was made.

I drove out to the Visual Images headquarters, which like most porn studios in those days was just a big, nondescript, unlisted warehouse. People in the industry called the building Esposito's Batcave. Inside, I found my first real-life porno mobsters: Batman and his butt-buddy Tommy, in the flesh.

I expected to encounter the cliché in-your-face, crotch-grabbing, guido tough-guy routine you see in the movies, but Esposito and Sinopoli were classy and extremely likeable gentlemen. Tommy was a well-dressed, chill character with slicked-back steel-gray hair and a wrinkly face that was half Al Pacino, half scrotum. He made no attempt to hide his street background: on the wall of his office was a caricature drawing of his face behind jail bars and a poster of Pacino as Michael Corleone from *The Godfather.* The effect was accentuated by Sinopoli's North End Boston accent, which had a nice gravelly edge. You could tell Tommy was a wiseguy, but unlike so many others I would meet in the future, he realized that he would look insecure if he stressed his underworld credentials.

Batman Esposito was a lot less low-key but equally likeable. Mike was just a jolly little guido with a smile on his fat face and a line of bullshit ceaselessly spilling from his mouth. I was treated to five or six wiseguy tall tales and ball-busting stories before I even had a chance to sit down; Batman was one of those easygoing bullshitters who love nothing more than to perform their wiseguy routine for strangers. Almost all of the mafiosi in California, real or otherwise, have forgotten about the "secret criminal society" facet of the Mafia—which is sort of the whole point, if you ask me. It's more of a Halloween costume for them.

Since I had been vouched for as legit by a mutual acquaintance, Batman Esposito was especially loose-lipped in his attempts to let me in on the "secret" that he was a crook as well. We got along so well that I thought for sure that Batman and Tommy would buy my movies, but my hopes were quickly disappointed. Our straightforward, formulaic "Peter North fucks big-tittied bombshells" movies did not fit within Batman and Tommy's porn portfolio. They operated along the margins, distributing low-budget fetish pornos that serviced niche audiences neglected by the big studios. Fat chicks, midgets, female ejaculations, footjobs: this is the type of smut that paid their bills. Though Batman and Tommy were not interested in the Peter North films, they told me to drop by anytime, especially if I had some real lowdown, sleazy shit to sell. I promised them that I could do lowdown and sleazy; I would be back.

To give you an idea how mobbed up the porn industry remained in the early '90s, I only had to walk right across the street to meet with three more wiseguys:

Colombo Family soldiers Anthony "Big Tony" Peraino and his sons Joseph and Louis. Louis, the brains of the family, was known as "Butchie." The Perainos were a stereotypical Brooklyn hillbilly clan in the grand tradition of the Persicos and the Garofalos: an extensive family tree full of backstabbing wiseguys who hate and occasionally kill one another. Big Tony was the son, brother, father, and uncle of mafiosi. Big Tony's father, Giuseppe, was a whacked Colombo soldier, and when Tony and his brother Joseph "Joe the Whale" Peraino came of age, they formed a Colombo crew that eventually integrated the talents of Tony's sons along with The Whale's son, Joe Jr.

The Peraino family crew financed and produced 1972's *Deep Throat,* the highest-grossing porn film in history. Overnight, the Perainos were worth tens of millions of dollars. This was bad news; nothing worse can happen to hillbillies than striking it rich. Look at Elvis or Britney Spears.

Neanderthals like the Perainos weren't any more equipped to handle being millionaires than the medieval villagers in Medellín, Colombia, when the cocaine cash tsunami hit. Even with a fortune worthy of the Saudi royal family to divvy up, there was not enough to satisfy the previously blue-collar Perainos. According to Colombo Family rats, Big Tony was jealous that his own flesh and blood was sharing in the *Deep Throat* windfall, so he accused Joe the Whale of pocketing tribute owed to bloodthirsty Colombo boss Carmine Persico. The Persicos only have one way of arbitrating disputes: killing the weaker party and robbing their graves. Joe the Whale and his son Joe Jr. were chased by a bullet-spraying Persico hit-team throughout Gravesend, Brooklyn.

Though Joe the Whale was hit *nine times,* he

survived due to his enormous obesity; his thick arctic coat of protective lard absorbed the bullets before they could pierce his organs. However, Joe Jr. and an innocent bystander—an ex-nun at that—both perished from gunshot wounds. It was a classic Persico hit: sloppy and indiscriminate. The critically wounded Whale and his deceased son had their share of the family business summarily requisitioned by Big Tony, who banished his injured brother from the rackets and distributed his dead nephew's interests among his own children. This cannibal was the first made Colombo soldier I ever met, and I guess it says a lot about me that I later consented to work with that inbred clan of vampires.

That said, my first impression of Big Tony was actually favorable. He seemed to be a likeable, respectable old hood. Though Peraino had earned his "Big" nickname by being a fat slob like "The Whale," in his old age Tony had become trim and fit, and he represented himself well in a shirt and tie, slacks, and polished shoes. Sometimes Big Tony would even whip out a dashing Bill Cosby sweater, a unique wardrobe choice in the torrid San Fernando Valley. Big Tony's Cosby sweaters were like a bowtie on a pit bull; his grizzled mug, cold black eyes, and cutthroat Brooklyn manner belied his grandfatherly wardrobe.

Which may be why I liked Big Tony within seconds of meeting him: he reminded me of Mike Marvich in that he was an old-school thug who was so secure in himself that he never needed to flaunt his toughness. Even when Big Tony told his wiseguy stories, he delivered them with winning nonchalance and understatement, without the usual dick-swinging braggadocio and implied tough guy "this is what happens to guys who fuck with me" threats.

Since members of his immediate family had been major players in the New York Mafia from the 1920s until the 1990s, Big Tony had access to some great stories. When I was getting to know him, I figured it was in my best interest to ask the man behind the most successful porno of all time if he had any tips on how to promote my movies. Big Tony shrugged. "Uh, I don't know, maybe slip Johnny Carson $50,000 to mention it in his monologue. That's what I did with *Deep Throat*."

I heard my favorite Big Tony story when he dropped in unannounced during a meeting I was conducting with Batman Esposito and Tommy Sinopoli. Like all wiseguys, Big Tony liked to shoot the shit about old gangland tales, and with Tommy and Batman right across the street, he was never too far away from a good wiseguy conversation.

"Back in the old days," Big Tony said, "I hired a guy named Red to run dis film-processing lab I had back in Brooklyn. One night, I dropped around to check in, you know, and I noticed this bulge in the lab's ceiling. So I get up on a chair," Big Tony says as he starts to smile. "And I'm pokin' at a tile to see why it was bulging when this big pile of money spills down from the ceiling right on top of my fucking head! That punk was robbing me and stashing the loot in *my* fuckin' ceiling at *my* fuckin' joint!" Big Tony said with a wheezy old man laugh and a slap on his knee.

"I wanted to hurt dat fucking mutt, but he was good at his job, so I let it slide. I mean fuck it, good help's hard to find," Tony muttered with palms upturned and a weak shrug.

As much as I liked Tony, his fucknut son "Butchie" tested my patience. And unfortunately for me, it was Butchie who had to okay my films for distribution through the Perainos' porn empire. I walked into Butchie's office, with its gaudy fish tank, overflowing

ashtrays, and porn tapes piled in every corner, and I concentrated on holding my breath. Butchie was the type of
meathead wiseguy cliché I had been expecting to meet: a
short, sloppy, Brooklyn-accented weightlifter with a permanent five o'clock shadow and gold chains spilling into
the triangle of hairy chest painstakingly exposed by his
unbuttoned shirt. When I pitched my movies to Butchie,
the asshole barely paid attention and just rambled in his
loud, gruff wannabe's way about how tough he was and
how he liked to "hurt people." I guess he'd heard about
my reputation and felt insecure. I could tell by the dismis-
sive look in his eyes that I was just "some chink" to him.

So while I wouldn't be working with the Perainos—
yet—I did find a home with yet another wiseguy studio.
Batman Esposito referred me to Ed Deroo, who was
known for garish gonzo shit like *Girls Who Puke* and the
Lactamania breast-milk-fetish video series. A fat sleazebag with glasses and that authentic porn griminess about
him, Deroo was backed by Reuben Sturman, the world's
most powerful pornographer, John Gotti's puppet dictator of the adult entertainment industry.

Originally a protégé of Carlo Gambino himself, Sturman owned hundreds of adult stores and controlled the
largest pornography distribution network on earth. In the
same way that Lucky Luciano delegated the stewardship
of the Mafia's Las Vegas gambling empire to numbers-
savvy, boardroom-ready Jewish hoods like Meyer Lansky,
Moe Dalitz, and Bugsy Siegel, so too did the Gambinos
allow a brilliant Russian Jew from Shaker Heights, Ohio,
to manage gangland's most lucrative sex industry portfolio. While Sturman was building an international porn
distribution monopoly that extended to forty countries
and grossed a million dollars per day, the Gambinos were
happily skimming from his profits and settling his beefs

with other hoods for payments as high as $200,000 per phone call.

Since Deroo was backed by Sturman's billions, he didn't even need to watch our shitty films; he just bought them. Sturman's mammoth network always needed new product. With this sale in my pocket, I was not only a bona fide producer, but a producer who was plugged into the adult entertainment industry's elite distribution network. Overnight, I had industry cred to go with my street cred; I would never have trouble selling my movies again. I was in business.

> *"About ninety-five percent of porn girls do side work [prostitution]—ninety-five percent at least. Trust me, I know. It's so strange because there is this stigma attached to escort work, as if when you fuck a stranger for money, you're an actress if there's a camera there and a whore if it's in the privacy of a hotel room. I never understood that; if anything, you should be less ashamed for fucking some guy in privacy than on film where you'll have to live with it for the rest of your life. That's just the business. You just live with it."*
>
> Kendra Jade
> Ex–porn star

To understand my success in the adult entertainment industry, you must understand the grim reality of the racket. Porn is the business of procuring, packaging, and marketing acts of prostitution committed by professional prostitutes looking for publicity. A woman who sells her body on camera for the entire world to see is usually selling her body in private for much better pay. Anyone who tells you otherwise is a liar.

I know—for over a decade I was the pimp who cut the deals, the spokesman who told the lies, and the nurse-boyfriend-husband who tended to the psychological wounds. It is impossible to understand how dysfunctional the porn business is without realizing that its daily reality revolves around clandestine meetings with unattractive civilian johns in hotel rooms—not photo shoots, not sex scenes under hot film lights, and certainly not appearances on Howard Stern's radio shows.

You won't find Hollywood glamour in Porn Valley. Most porn girls film the first "scene" for free by fucking an overweight producer on the infamous casting couch in his office. Once cast, they make about $1,000 ($300 to $500 when I started out) in return for surrendering their bodies to an hour-long fuck-a-thon delivered with punishing indifference by a gauntlet of coke-snorting, steroid-injecting porn meatheads. The sets are dirty; the lights are hot and blinding; the action is heavily posed, unnatural, and punctuated by plenty of pauses for still-camera photos; the crewmembers are gawking sleaze-bags; the directors are often sadistic misogynists who see you as a punching-bag surrogate for their mother or the ex-girlfriend who broke their heart; herpes infections are epidemic; the orgasms are almost always fake; your costars are often supremely damaged and disturbed people.

Besides a pathological mania for "fame," why would a girl who *volunteers* for that career ever refuse to make $5,000 (500% her normal salary) to fuck a retired oil executive for seven minutes until he pops prematurely? Why would she have the image of her gaping, fucked-loose asshole committed to film for her great-grandkids to enjoy, yet turn down the opportunity to suck off a dude in private? The porn racket is so degrading that no one familiar with the working conditions could possibly imagine a girl who would be "above hooking" but somehow still enthusiastic for porn. Trust me: most porn stars much prefer to hook than withstand the blood-curdling barrage of indignities that comes with "acting."

Porn stars are hookers—I was around the business from 1988 to 2004, and I do not recall a *single* major female porn star who was not open to turning tricks at some point. Not one. So whenever you hear some "porn-positive" adult-film star talk about how the profession is mainstream, healthy, and normal, remind yourself that you are listening to someone whose body you can get delivered to your neighborhood Hilton with a phone call. Most porn "celebrities" are fucktoys that can be rented with your VISA or MasterCard.

The key to success as an agent, director, or producer in porn is to reduce a woman to the level of a fucktoy while deluding her into believing that you're elevating her to Hollywood stardom. Though occasionally some girl will debut in a depraved orgy, most women need to have their humanity and self-esteem methodically broken down in order for them to be rebuilt as a dead-eyed porn queen. The "regular" girl must be killed and reborn as a jaded, unthinking porno zombie.

I always thought the recruitment and brainwashing techniques porn uses to convince girls to do unthinkable things on camera paralleled the tactics the military uses to recruit and train people to do the unthinkable. The scam is the same: a talent scout zeroes in on a generally ill-educated civilian from a broken home; caters to their longing for stability and approval; blitzes them with a Hell Week of work to establish a brutal, unthinking routine; alienates them from reality by giving them a new identity and dissociates them from their gruesome work using jargon; and keeps them going with meaningless trophies and awards that glamorize the day-to-day reality of their profession.

Despite the supposed glamour of these celebrities' lifestyle, the porn industry pay scale is so hilariously meager that countless "superstars," "icons," and even "megastars" have to suck freelance dick just to pay their rent, let alone fund their mammoth Stevie Nicks–level cocaine habit. As most musicians barely make any money from their albums and instead use them as an advertisement for their live tours, so too do porn stars, out of necessity, use their on-camera prostitution as a vehicle to promote their "live appearances" at strip clubs and your local escort agency. This business model has become so ingrained that, if the market for actresses collapsed, most porn chicks would fuck on camera for free or even pay for the honor in order to protect their touring brand.

This rootless, lonely, gypsy lifestyle spent in strip clubs and anonymous hotel rooms is poison to women who, by virtue of being desperate enough to fuck for fame, are already predisposed to being insecure, desperate for stability, and starved for attention and approval. Often banished from their families and from their hometown social circle because of their line of work, they are alone in a mean and dangerous business. The majority of their interaction with the human race is conducted in situations where they are strictly classified as dehumanized and submissive sex fantasies. Consequently, sex becomes their only connection to other humans, their only way to express their feelings, and their only way to justify their own worth.

When I traveled with porn veterans, I never had to hit on them; even if they were complete strangers who found me unattractive and unpleasant, they'd end up volunteering to fuck me out of boredom. It was like making conversation: "Wow, there sure is nothing on TV. Wanna stick it in my ass?"

Sex was also the prescription for every ailment. "Aww, poor thing, I'm sorry your girlfriend dumped you. Would it make you feel better if I let you fuck me?"

"Yes."

"Oww, baby, that's one mean black eye. You think a blowjob would help it heal?"

"Definitely."

"God, your snoring is keeping me up! I'll let you titty-fuck me if you go sleep in the bathtub."

"No deal."

"How about anal?"

"Deal."

Brutally shallow porn producers naturally foster and exploit this desperate-to-please attitude. Believing that the easiest body to market weighs from 90 to 110 pounds and boasts gigantic plastic tits, the producers remind the girls of the surplus of newer, younger, and fresher models ready to literally suck dick for a chance to take their place if they don't measure up. The girls almost universally accept the producer's twisted body image as their own, developing eating disorders and burdening themselves with as much as $100,000 in debt to the plastic surgeons who gut them with what looks like an ice pick, stuff their chests with cancer-causing synthetic jelly, squirt botulism into their lips and foreheads, and paint their assholes with bleach.

It is a pathetic and self-destructive subculture, and, as such, it attracts pathetic and self-destructive recruits. Porn is a merciless business that warps psyches, breaks hearts, and devastates self-esteem; the people who consent to such a heavy toll are the few who are already psychologically warped, broken-hearted, and bankrupt of self-esteem. I'm a sex-positive guy who has no personal objection to prostitution or pornography in theory, but you have to be really naïve not to know, intuitively, that any girl who starves herself and undergoes round after round of painful, expensive cosmetic surgery just to be the semen-drenched star of *Cum Fart Cocktail 3* or *Dirtpipe Milkshakes* is most likely a psychological freak show.

If the image of the porn industry I'm painting seems too grim to believe, consider this: How corrupt, criminal, and exploitative must the adult entertainment racket be if it allowed me to become a successful, respected member of its business community? The Kenji who made his name in porn was the Kenji who was bombing cars, ordering drive-bys in the suburbs, attempting to kill his friend Liu Kang more or less on a whim, selling coke to inner-city Crips to be turned into crack, being investigated for murder and espionage—*that* Kenji was seen as one of the more normal, well-behaved, professional, and civilized members of the industry!

If anything, I'm grateful that the porn industry was such an insane asylum. I'm one of the few people in the world who can honestly say that deciding to work in porn was the healthiest, sanest career move he could have made. Having come of age in the '80s coke trade, the climate in the porn business was conventional and dignified by comparison—at least no one was getting orphaned or shot full of holes.

Though porn was a grimy and horrible business, I wasn't particularly employable. I was an immature, habitually violent predator and con man with expensive tastes, no conscience, and serious emotional detachment from everyone in the human race. I derived joy from screwing and hurting others and found it almost impossible to trust or love anyone after Tara left me. I was a disturbed little prick with a pistol under my waistband and a smirk on my face, permanently locked into that smartass, authority-flouting teenage persona. Besides, I was in my twenties without a college credit to my name or anything approaching a work history. The closest thing to credentials I had was my long rap sheet and my street degree from Medellín University.

There were very few trades, legal or otherwise, that the early-'90s version of Kenny Gallo could have entered, and of those, the sex rackets were by far the healthiest. The porn-prostitution game proved downright therapeutic. It was a laidback, nonviolent, half-legitimate business full of pussies who were too soft to kill me and too soft to push me hard enough to kill them.

Whatever I lacked in integrity I made up for in work ethic and competence. In an industry filled with flakes, pillheads, and outright dummies, I was a disciplined businessman who could be trusted to produce good work and deliver it on time and on budget. Of course, if you were a chump, I would defraud you, rob you, and use you, but a legitimate player could rest assured that I was more interested in a lasting business relationship than pulling some short-term, short-money scam.

I took porn as seriously as anything else in my life. For the same reason that I had taken gem-grading classes to bolster my burglary sideline, I began perfecting the art of smut-peddling as soon as I was in business. I was always taking classes in cinematography, still photography, editing, and film theory, supplementing my coursework with hands-on study. I shadowed the cameramen, learning all the angles and tricks; I quizzed the directors, got to know the girls, learned how to use the filming and editing equipment, and gradually figured out how to manage the talent. I mastered all the jargon—from the difference between DP ("double penetration," the simultaneous penetration of the vagina and anus) and the spit roast (simultaneous oral and vaginal or anal penetration) to DVDA (double vaginal, double anal penetration). I even learned the secret to Peter North's ability to shoot huge loads three or four times a day: the constant consumption of large volumes of milky protein shakes.

Porn turned out to be just as easy as I had originally suspected. I rented a soundstage once owned by *Highway to Heaven* TV-star Michael Landon. A month or two into the new sideline, one of my degenerate porn cameramen tried to shake me down for more cash. "There's no way you can find another cameraman on such short notice," he said. "You'll lose the money you spent renting the equipment and set. So you might as well pay—"

WHAM! Black Dave, who was watching the proceedings in his usual immaculate Nation of Islam suit and sunglasses, nearly slapped the cameraman's teeth out of his mouth for disrespecting me. I always traveled deep, shadowed by thugs and dealers who would chauffeur me around like Secret Service agents as long as I let them hang around the set. With my old crew decimated, my new posse was a grab bag of bikers, Crips, dealers, and Mob associates, all very violent and very into porn.

I told the dazed cameraman to fuck off and took over the filming myself. We were shooting on celluloid, 16-mm and 35-mm film stock, so the cameras were enormous Cecil B. DeMille monstrosities, each about as light and maneuverable as a couch. Nonetheless, I decided to give it a shot; how hard could the job possibly be if the cross-eyed junkies I employed as cameramen could do it?

I proved a natural, and from then on I often filmed

my own scenes. If I had a reliable cameraman in the studio, I'd double-up my profits and take still photographs of the scene to sell to magazines. Years later, after my experience working in a semi-legal Mafia porn business in Florida, I reinvested my profits into purchasing my own porn shop, where, thanks to stolen or pirated merchandise and creative accounting, I made more money than I ever made from cocaine. I never thought about a single purchase I made during my last decade on the streets, thanks to a tiny strip-mall porn shop: if I wanted a new apartment, car, computer, suit, vintage weapon, or pair of shoes, I just whipped out my roll and bought it with cash.

Clearly, porn was a disgusting racket, but I did not feel like the money I made from it was dirty. There is no dishonesty involved, no scam or intimidation, no victims. Porn victims are *voluntary* victims who are consenting adults that beg to be used up to feed their own vanity and insecurity. I felt as little guilt making money from porn as most readers do from masturbating to it.

In the end, I'm just a guy like any other, and the easy money, constant parties, and complete satisfaction of my every sexual fantasy with no effort on my part meant that I was a very, very happy man during my early years in porn. I was pussy-rich and morally bankrupt.

My professional life in porn would have been perfect from the start if not for my decision to partner with Al "Peter North" Brown. I felt like I had to tolerate Peter because I had been warned never to alienate one of the "old hands"—male porn actors with a proven track record for filming scene after scene. There's a reason why, from the 1970s until the advent of Viagra, you would see the same two-dozen porn actors providing the erections and cumshots for most of the porn scenes made in America. There are very few people born with that rare combination of penis size and complete mastery of their erections and orgasms. Before the advent of erection-in-a-pill medications, the skill set required to succeed as a male porn star was so rare that studios preferred not to alienate someone like Peter North, who was a pain in the ass but never fucked up a scene.

Of course, the best known and most reliable of the old hands is my buddy Ron Jeremy, the biggest male porn star of all, in both popularity and mass. Since Ronnie requested too much money for his scenes, I never booked him and only worked with him when he showed up at my sets and begged to be cast in order to bang some aspiring porn actress who wouldn't touch him off-camera. Though The Hedgehog was honestly doing me a favor whenever he asked to contribute his name to my film, I always pretended that I was dangerously overbooked and over budget in order to drive a hard bargain, which was easy—Ronnie is extremely cheap, extremely horny, and usually extremely hungry. The best deal I ever arranged was obtaining the worldwide rights to a Ron Jeremy threesome for $125: $100 for the girls, and $25 and a free plate of food at our catering table for Ronnie the buffet-busting bargain glutton.

With Ronnie priced out of my range, I was stuck with Peter—whom I hated. Whenever Peter looked at me with that simian bodybuilder's mug and those sleepy, hooded, uncomprehending eyes, I wanted to retire and join a monastery. The guy got under my skin like no one else. The prissy, vain gorilla with a black Wayne Newton pompadour thought I was being a merciless taskmaster when I told him it was unacceptable to show up five or six hours late for a shoot because he wanted to sleep in. He simply couldn't comprehend that it was unfair for me to have to rent equipment and pay the crew for an extra day just because his pinched, dark-circled eyes wanted to go nighty-night.

Once Mr. Sandman finally arrived on the set, it's not like he suddenly became helpful or accommodating, either. Peter would disappear for an hour or two to further perfect the hairspray sculpture on top of his head, or he would simply plop himself in a free chair, sigh, twiddle his fingers, and stare into space like Andy Griffith relaxing in the rocking chair on his porch. If I tapped my watch or mentioned that we should probably start filming, Peter scowled and huffed and puffed as if he deserved a pre-work break before we got to that bothersome sex scene. Once Princess Peter finally deigned to stick his dick in the girl, the entire scene would be derailed and have to start again if the girl accidentally touched his plastic hairdo, which would precipitate an epic, indignant hissy fit.

"I CAN'T CONCENTRATE IF YOU TOUCH MY HAIR!! UGH! No one has any respect for me!" Peter would exclaim in his exasperated *Napoleon Dynamite* voice as he stamped his little Canadian feet.

Finally, after a couple dozen films, my partnership with Peter North came to an end when I purchased *Matt Ramsey: The Man*, a title showcasing his gay porn alter ego's greatest gay hits. Peter sped across town and screeched to a halt at my place, fuming that I intended to widely distribute evidence that he was "once" a homosexually active adult.

"Listen, bro," I said with the enormous smile that involuntarily appeared on my face whenever I had an excuse to remind Peter that he sucked dick on camera. "I'm in the porn business to make money, not friends. If you didn't want that movie sold, you shouldn't have taken it in the ass in the first place."

"Kenji, seriously, man!" he squealed. Throbbing, roid-freak veins were popping up all over his throat and face. "People are going to think I'm gay! I'm not gay!"

"Hmm, let me think on that one," I said, barely containing myself as I rubbed my chin and screwed up my eyes as if I were in deep thought. "You've got a good point—I now own pretty incontrovertible evidence that you enjoy anal sex with men, so I think I can make a pretty strong case that you're a fag, Al. And I'll be happy to make money reminding people of that."

"But Kenji . . ."

"Fuck off, dude, just fuckin' deal with it and stop living in denial."

After that frank and honest exchange of views, I was pretty sure that my long and consistently annoying affiliation with Peter North was finished. I was relieved, and I was also mistaken. In a few years, Peter North would call in the Mafia to teach me a lesson.

EIGHT
The Jujutsu Gangster

> *"To live outside the law, you must be honest."*
> Robert "Bob Dylan" Zimmerman

Everything I ever learned about the art of the con I learned from two men named Jerry. As befitting master scam artists, the Two Jerrys were the opposite of what they seemed: Officer Jerry, the charming, handsome cop, was in reality the most vindictive and vicious prick imaginable, and Jerry Zimmerman, the disreputable Jewish shyster and wiseguy, was one of the most trustworthy friends I have ever had. Besides their name and criminal association with me, the only thing the Two Jerrys had in common was their trade: deceit.

"Suckers are the same, man or woman," Officer Jerry used to tell me in between sharing footlong lines of cocaine with my teenage crew at Pompeii. "Whether you want to get a girl who will suck your dick, or a big-money sucker who you can take for a ride, it's the same strategy. It's called 'planting the greed seed,' Kenji.

"You never go to the suckers. You make them come to you," Jerry continued, his bloodshot, coke-vampire eyes scanning the dancers and drinkers with glowing red contempt. Jerry thought the human race comprised two distinct subspecies: Officer Jerry and total fucking idiots.

"You don't need them—they need you. You never chase. You're hot shit. You're a superstar. You gotta make them envious; make them so jealous that they will do anything to get a piece of the action you got going. You just plant that greed seed and let it grow until it's ready to be harvested. You don't search for greedy idiots to scam; you let greedy idiots come to you and beg and plead to be scammed. It is their honor to be your victim. Never forget that you're doing them a favor—the greedy bastards think you're going to make them rich!"

In practice, Jerry's "greed seed" play meant acting like you were living in a big-budget rap music video. You would walk into a fashionable nightclub dressed like a *GQ* cover, tip everyone with $100 bills, buy the most expensive champagne, treat the bar to rounds on the house and free key-bumps of coke, flash your polished jewelry and drug-dealer beeper, and generally ignore everyone because everyone is beneath your attention. Within seconds, this would attract easy girls, and the girls would help attract suckers—civilians, wannabes, even legit crooks—that you could rob blind. After they saw how you were living, they would beg to be cut in on your schemes so they could enjoy a taste of that high life.

Anyone who wants to do business—especially illegal business—with a stranger has already proven himself to be dangerously rash, gullible, and insecure. By being patient and letting the suckers come to him, the con man assures that his target audience consists exclusively of "live ones," marks so greedy and desperate that they will agree to be put in extremely vulnerable positions for a piece of the action. It's almost impossible to fail with a target audience like that; it was about as hard as trying to get a no-strings-attached blowjob at a porn set.

With a mark identified, Jerry had little trouble stealing the person's money thanks to his badge. That was the ultimate con job: I can only imagine the comprehensive tour de force of lies, bribery, and evasion that was required for Jerry to maintain his job as a police officer.

Whatever Jerry had to do to keep his badge, it was worth it on the streets; as soon as Jerry identified a target with cash, he "busted" them and kept part of the loot. Jerry never developed his criminal skills past that one-two combination: identify the target and use the badge as a license to steal.

When I applied Jerry's techniques in my own career, a bit more ingenuity and finesse was required. In my circle, the best partner available was Babar. Handsome, stylish, sleazy, Latino, and always pursued by hot girls, Babar looked the part of a high-rolling VIP drug dealer without being an intimidating felon. Babar was also a compulsive braggart and tall-tale artist, which in this one instance worked to our benefit. Anyone who spent five minutes with that Mexican dildo would figure that, if I could make that dummy rich, then I could make him or her rich as well. Babar would be my buffer, running interference and wasting the time of would-be players for weeks on end as they desperately tried to get my undivided attention. By the time I finally graced them with direct eye contact, they were so honored and impatient that they would agree to absolutely any opportunity I offered them on any terms.

Our favorite mark was an ex-stockbroker we called Blinky because his lazy eye would blink uncontrollably whenever he used cocaine. Blinky quit his Wall Street job to be a full-time degenerate drunk and cokehead, a progressive lifestyle he financed by periodically buying two kilos of coke from me and selling it at a huge markup to his millionaire yuppie friends. Blinky followed us around in a desperate ploy to be seen with two known criminals and thereby increase his street cred. That was fine with Babar and me; the more civilians Blinky conned, the more coke we could sell him.

But Blinky was greedy; he didn't just want to con the squares, he wanted to con us—the *real* cons. Blinky bombarded us with hilariously transparent, cocaine-inflated lies about how tough and dangerous he was. This both exasperated and amused me, since while I suffered I could also enjoy watching Babar, my own tiresome flunky braggart, get tortured by an even more tiresome flunky braggart.

Blinky was too stupid and insecure to be satisfied with life as a groupie, a scabies mite feeding off our hard-earned reputations; he wanted to be a player, our partner. Instead, we decided to turn the tables on our parasite. Babar and I began to enjoy torturing Blinky, flaunting as much cash, coke, and women as we could in front of his envious eyes. We didn't just plant the greed seed; we shoved it down the fucker's throat. I devoted my considerable talents to giving Blinky the world's worst case of criminal blue balls; I wanted Blinky to be just *aching* to do business with us. By the time our trap was set, Blinky was in a state of permanent agitation because he felt that he was *this* close to being a kingpin, which he wanted so badly.

Finally, the moment came to call Blinky up to the big leagues and play ball, and the only person more relieved than Blinky was me. That's the secret of the con artist: in the long, dreary process of setting up a scam, the scammer becomes so bored with tolerating his target that he begins to loathe him and believe that he *deserves* what he gets. I had cultivated such contempt for Blinky that I was impatient to destroy his life and be done with him. The opportunity came when Blinky begged to be let in on a big, multi-kilo cocaine deal. Frustrated with being rejected again and again, Blinky finally lost his self-control and threw his trump card on the table.

"If you guys are worried, I got collateral. I got the cash to finance anything you want. I got a safe full of cash in my bedroom." Jackpot.

The first step in taking down Blinky's safe was to befriend Thor, the gigantic Rottweiler that guarded his house in Mission Viejo. Whenever we saw Blinky out on the town, we snuck over to his house with raw hamburger and fed our new canine buddy. When we were sure that we'd compromised Thor's loyalty, we took Blinky to the Red Onion in Orange County and destroyed him with free cocaine and drinks. We dumped his completely skull-fucked and comatose body at my apartment, grabbed his keys, and immediately headed to his house.

Our plan worked perfectly; Thor was as happy as shit to see us and courteously escorted us inside with a wagging tail. I tossed him some meat like I was tipping my favorite doorman and headed to Blinky's bedroom. I intended to lug the safe out to my car and dismantle it at my place, but my experience as a safecracker paid unexpected dividends.

Most civilians keep the dial to their safe only a few spots away from the last number in the combination because they are too lazy to enter the whole sequence every time they open the safe. When I checked Blinky's dial, the pointer was only two or three notches from a spot that was clearly worn. I spun the dial over to that worn number and the door popped open; I saw $36,000 in cash and two little white envelopes.

I laughed and laughed; Blinky was such an idiot. I was so happy that I decided to share my good fortune by tossing some more meat to Thor, who responded by jumping up and down on Blinky's bed with glee. A moment later, I felt like joining him: I opened up the two envelopes and poured a rockslide of 1.3- and 1.4-carat diamonds into my hands. The diamonds were flawless to the human eye. Later, using my trusty magnifying glass and the expertise I had picked up in a gem-grading course I took to bolster my burglary side-business, I graded them a near-elite VVS1 on the GIA diamond grading scale. Those diamonds were worth about $25,000 on the black market, $100,000 on the legitimate market. Put together, Babar and I made over $60,000 in one hour.

After putting up with Blinky for so long, the cash was almost just a bonus; I already had plenty of money, but the thrill from ruining that little shit's life was a rare delight. I really savored his pain.

"Kenny, they robbed my place! The pricks robbed my vault!" Blinky screamed over the phone the next day. "Worst of all, they ruined all of my furniture and decor!" This caught my attention since we had not trashed anything during the burglary.

"How did those assholes ruin your stuff, Blinky?"

"They locked the dog inside! Thor had horrible, rotten diarrhea all over the house!"

That $3 of raw red meat was the best value purchase I've ever made. In exchange for $3 of meat, I obtained $36,000 in cash, $25,000 in diamonds, and the priceless satisfaction of ruining Blinky's life. I thought I was a master con man and that Officer Jerry was a genius.

It would take a very different Jerry to teach me that a true master con man operates without sadism, without violence, and—if possible—without his crimes even being noticed by his mark.

"I never trusted Jerry [Zimmerman], and suspected him of pocketing payoffs and ripping me off for petty sums in countless ways. Regardless,

the big Jewish man was a world-class con artist
whose crazy schemes were wildly amusing."

Michael Franzese
Former Colombo Mafia Family capo
in *Quitting the Mob*

"Jerry Zimmerman was a fun-loving producer.
Because of his clandestine lifestyle, I never knew
which films he produced, backed, or whatever,
but what I do know is that he was a fun-loving
guy with a great family, and, being fellow Jews,
he always brought great delicatessen. He didn't so
much care about my performances, he just wanted
to make sure I didn't go hungry. Whenever he'd
see me, he'd go 'Hey Ronnie!' and then tell one of
his guys to go to Jerry's Deli to take care of me."

Ron Jeremy

My life in the Mafia began when one Jewish movie
producer introduced me to another Jewish movie producer in the San Fernando Valley.

Porn producer Frank Rubin was a hairy little meatball
with a past as a bookie and the crooked head of the Hollywood projectionist union. I was always hanging around
Frank because, like my childhood friend Frank, he was
the type of hard-luck crook that always amuses me. We
were such good friends that I might have formed a porn
studio with Frank if not for his business partner Perry
Ross, whom I loathed. Befitting a guy whose crowning
achievement in life was playing a meathead in a Steven
Seagal B movie, Perry was just another porn industry
"tough guy" like Butchie Peraino who confused a bodybuilder's physique and a lot of bragging with street credibility. It was not surprising when wannabe Perry pushed

his luck on a trip to Holland to collect a debt and was killed with what appeared to be a "hot shot" of heroin.

Much more to my liking was Frank Rubin's next-door neighbor in wiseguy-friendly Chatsworth. One day when I was visiting Frank, we ran into this bumbling, disheveled, 6'5", 300-pound schlub with an enormous smile on his fleshy red face. He looked like Rodney Dangerfield and a grizzly bear's love child.

"Kenji, this is my buddy Jerry," Frank said, as he introduced him with what I could tell was sincere pleasure in his voice. I craned my neck to try to make eye contact with this Hebrew Shrek and instead got a good look at the garden of gray hair growing from his nostrils. Jerry slapped me on the shoulder, gobbled up one of my comparatively tiny hands in a vigorous politician's handshake, and leaned forward with that big smile. Jerry was one of those goofy, ungainly, smiling hucksters you immediately like.

"Jerry's a good guy, he's with that guy Sonny, y'know," Frank continued, with the inflection of his voice being that "Sonny" was a mixture of the Pope and Mike Marvich. I had never heard of any "Sonny," so I figured it was just another bullshit old Mob guy.

I was wrong; John "Sonny" Franzese is certainly a mafioso, but he is anything but bullshit. Wiseguys talk about Sonny like Republicans talk about Ronald Reagan—he is the embodiment of everything they believe in and admire. In an era defined by rats and declining standards, Sonny is just about the only mobster in New York City who lives up to the standard of propriety, loyalty, and toughness set during the Mob's golden age.

On the street, they call Sonny "The Rock" because the old sonofabitch has done decades of jail time and never rats, never complains, never changes, never challenges the family leadership, and never hesitates to violate his parole within minutes of being released. If ninety-two-year-old Sonny was told tomorrow by Colombo Family boss Carmine Persico to whack the president of New York's Hells Angels chapter, he would walk right into their clubhouse, ask one of the 300-pound bikers who the top guy was, and blast him away.

Sonny had been in line to succeed Joe Colombo as family boss as far back as the early 1960s, when he was a short Neanderthal-ugly hood with a reputation as a prolific hit man. Though his chance at becoming godfather was derailed by a false conviction on a trumped-up burglary charge, Sonny persisted and is currently the underboss of the Colombo Family and its street boss whenever he is (briefly) out on parole. Short of being "with" Genovese Family boss Vincent "The Chin" Gigante or Chicago's Anthony "Joe Batters" Accardo, an endorsement from Sonny Franzese was the highest praise a modern mobster could receive.

Jerry Zimmerman's sitdown with destiny occurred at his car dealership in Long Island in the 1960s. Jerry was the picture-perfect stereotype of a crooked used car dealer, swaggering around his place in search of a customer to charm with hokey jokes and bewilder with fast-paced sales talk. One of the visitors to this dealership was a hairy little Italian named Sonny Franzese; Jerry unwittingly greeted the most feared and powerful young wiseguy in the Colombo Family with "Hey, Spaghetti, what's doin', man?"

Just as Sonny was about to rip Jerry's balls off, a concerned onlooker informed Jerry of Sonny's identity. Since Jerry, despite his size, was absolutely useless with his fists, his only self-defense was charm. In mortal terror, he overwhelmed the coldhearted mobster with vaudeville facial theatrics, flouncing slapstick body language, rapid-fire apologies, self-deprecating humor, off-topic tall tales, and racial jokes. To the shock of both men, Sonny found himself laughing, and Jerry found himself a lifelong sponsor in the American Mafia.

Something of an underworld talent scout, Sonny Franzese saw great potential in the shyster car salesman. While the wimpy Jew could never become a made man or a street hood, Jerry, with his gift of gab, shameless salesmanship, and innate likeability, was clearly a blue-chip prospect as a con man and racketeer. It was impossible not to love and trust a big endearing goof like Jerry, which made him extremely dangerous as a scam artist.

Jerry was so charismatic that he even won over the hard-ass killers in the Colombo Family, who hold Jews and wimps in contempt. A mutual friend in the Colombo Family told me the story: word was being sent out all across Brooklyn that the collectors for a feared loan shark were looking for Jerry. Naturally, the gentle giant was terrified, but he figured he couldn't hide forever. One day the collectors showed up at the car dealership where Sonny was hanging out with some other wiseguys; Jerry mustered his courage.

Sneaking out back and jumping into a giant Lincoln sedan, Jerry slammed on the gas and drove straight at the collectors like a maniac. The tough guys dove out of the way as the Lincoln screeched to a stop. The driver's door swung open and out stepped the angriest, toughest-looking giant anyone had ever seen. "I'm Jerry *fuckin'* Zimmerman!" screamed the mad-eyed, fuming, hyper-ventilating beast. "Who the *fuck* is looking for *me*?"

The collectors took one look at the savage Hebrew Goliath and hauled ass. As soon as they were gone, Jerry's chest deflated, his shoulders slumped, his fists unclenched, and his eyes began darting left and right, like a kid waiting to see if he's going to get away with his mischief or if he's going to get spanked. Sonny and the rest of the guys were crying with laughter.

I always wondered if Jerry ingratiated himself with the Italians by playing up his Jewishness to cartoonish levels. Jerry acted like the classic stereotype of a New York Jewish racketeer: the charmer who peppers every sentence with Yiddish, gets a tension headache whenever he has to pay for *anything*, considers it an epic triumph whenever he scams his way into free merchandise or services—and, of course, dies of old age an exponentially richer and freer man than his imprisoned Italian "bosses." A no-frills, no-drama, no-risk moneymaker, Jerry was a particularly indispensable addition to the Colombo Family, which has always been rich in brute power and impoverished in brain power.

During Sonny's interminable jail terms, his stepson, Colombo capo Michael Franzese, inherited Jerry. Michael was a well-educated, white-collar suburban kid with a passion for legitimate business and distaste for the "hard stuff" that made his father's name. Michael and Jerry were perfect partners: two reputable, charming, nonviolent racketeers who relied on Sonny Franzese's badass reputation and their own guile instead of muscle. In Michael's memoir *Quitting the Mob,* he described Jerry as his "court jester" and "love slave," the lothario he sent to seduce a homely, fat, scarred-up witness who had testified against Sonny. Jerry's cocksmanship worked wonders, and the witness reversed her testimony. Even Michael was surprised when Jerry ("275 pounds of indiscriminate manliness") admitted that he enjoyed fulfilling this grotesque assignment.

In 1979, Michael deputized Jerry to oversee his

automobile distribution business in California and his interests in Hollywood and Las Vegas. Convinced that their skills as white-collar criminals were easily transferable to legitimate pursuits, Jerry and Michael decided to go into business together as moviemakers. The success of the Perainos, who went legitimate after *Deep Throat*'s success with movies like *The Texas Chainsaw Massacre*, inspired the far more intelligent Jerry and Michael to dream of Spielbergian levels of success. To their surprise, the brainy wiseguys lacked Butchie Peraino's cinematic instincts: their hard work produced a shitburger horror movie costarring Adam West and a feature-film musical centered on break-dancing.

Counterintuitively, Jerry and Michael would not only prove to be less successful legitimate businessmen than the savage Perainos, but also infinitely more successful gangsters. Together, Michael and Jerry could get their ass kicked by Siegfried and Roy, but that didn't stop them from becoming one of the greatest duos in Mafia history. In the '80s, the Franzese gang minted more money than any other Mafia crew in existence. By orchestrating a complex black market distribution network for tax-free gasoline from Canada, Michael and his con artist mentor Jerry grossed hundreds of millions of dollars in only a few years.

It may have seemed impossible to top the most lucrative scam in Mafia history—and the greatest robbery of the U.S. government to that point—but Jerry's brilliant student, Michael, had an even greater con in mind. When the feds inevitably came calling with indictments about their fraud, Michael flipped without hesitation and avoided serious jail time. The real genius of Michael's play was that, when he turned rat, he never handed over any of his illicit gains, something his cooperation agreement stipulated he must do, and claimed that just about every single cent of the hundreds of millions of dollars had just disappeared. It was a calculated bet: if the IRS or FBI found where Michael had stashed his dirty fortune, the feds would void the deal and send him to jail. On the other hand, if the money lay undiscovered until the statute of limitations for perjury and fraud expired, Michael would become a legitimate centimillionaire.

Guess what? The coppers never found the money. The opulent Michael Franzese currently operates a thriving tax-free evangelical Christian ministry. His new calling makes perfect sense: I think every crook should worship at Michael's altar. I also have to give it up to Jerry: not since Aristotle tutored Alexander the Great has a gifted teacher produced a pupil who so spectacularly exceeded all expectations.

With Michael disgracing the Franzese name by living as a peaceful, law-abiding citizen, there was an opening in Sonny Franzese's West Coast crew for a brilliant young con man with a pleasant, professional façade whom Jerry Zimmerman could tutor.

Of course, when I first met Jerry outside Frank Rubin's office, I didn't even know his last name, let alone the history of the Franzese crew. I just knew that I was hitting it off talking to this old crook about our shared culture shock as two newcomers to the porn industry. Like me, Jerry picked up on the incredible potential for financial fraud and money laundering, but he was too old and scatterbrained to go about methodically developing contacts and business relationships across the San Fernando Valley, as I had.

Nonetheless, Jerry had an incredibly quick and sharp mind, so he recognized my value as a young crook on

Me and my buddy Phil in a Tijuana meeting with Mexican drug traffickers. This was around 1983, when I was a fifteen-year-old cocaine smuggler. (*Photo from Kenny Gallo's collection*)

Partying with my drug-dealing crew in the mid-'80s. *From L-R:* Babar, Frank (beard), Phil, me, and Officer Jerry of the Irvine Police Department. (*Photo from Kenny Gallo's collection*)

My crew circa 1989–1990. *From L-R, top row:* Liu Kang (whom I attempted to murder), me, Peter North, Phil. *Bottom row:* Keith and Babar. (*Photo from Kenny Gallo's collection*)

Griselda "The Black Widow" Blanco.

Joey Avila. (*Photo from Kenny Gallo's collection*)

Lee Matthew Clyde in military school. (*Photo from Kenny Gallo's collection*)

My room as a teenager, complete with loaded Uzi and kilo of cocaine in the background. (*Photo from Kenny Gallo's collection*)

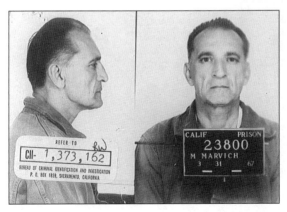

"Big" Mike Marvich in 1967.

My L.A. Mafia Family capo Jimmy Caci and me. (*Photo from Kenny Gallo's collection*)

Ori Spado, Colombo Family associate and rat. (*Photo from Kenny Gallo's collection*)

"Wild Bill" Cutolo. (*Photo from Kenny Gallo's collection*)

Michael Franzese.

Anthony "The Animal" Fiato. (*Photo from Kenny Gallo's collection*)

Stevie "The Whale" Cino.

Anthony "Fat Tony" Peraino.

Domenico "Danny" Cutaia.

Carmine Baudanza.

My ex-wife Tabitha Stevens and me. (*Photo from Kenny Gallo's collection*)

Tabitha with Gary Dell'Abate, *Howard Stern Show* producer. (*Photo from Kenny Gallo's collection*)

Colombo enforcer "Jackie di Padova," Tabitha, and me. (*Photo from Kenny Gallo's collection*)

Tabitha and Jimmy Caci. (*Photo from Kenny Gallo's collection*)

Dayton, Michelle, porn legend Ron Jeremy, and Tabitha. (*Photo from Kenny Gallo's collection*)

Porn superstar Jenna Jameson and me in the infamous "Cash Ho" photograph. (*Photo from Kenny Gallo's collection*)

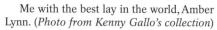

Porn icon Janine Lindemulder and me. (*Photo from Kenny Gallo's collection*)

Me with the best lay in the world, Amber Lynn. (*Photo from Kenny Gallo's collection*)

MY TROPHY WALL

Left to right:

Michelle "Nici" Braun, the most successful American madam of the modern era, whose empire collapsed thanks to me.

Theodore "Teddy" Persico, Jr., the Colombo Family heir apparent whom I sent to jail. Teddy trusted me enough to deputize me as his wingman on the attempted mob hit of Craig Marino.

Craig Marino, the tiny Colombo Family–made guy who Teddy Persico wanted me to help whack. Instead, I helped send Craig to jail.

Left: John "Kool" Baudanza, the youngest capo in the Lucchese Family, with his crush Dayton Raines, my roommate and call girl extraordinaire. (*Photo from Kenny Gallo's collection*)

Right: Eddie Garofalo, Jr., who was also nearly killed by Teddy Persico before being indicted.

the make with the knowledge, contacts, and hustle that he lacked in the porn game. In the same way that Sonny Franzese spotted a born racketeer in a barrel-chested Jewish car salesman in Long Island, Jerry Zimmerman immediately recognized that an anonymous twenty-one-year-old Japanese-American porn producer was a blue-chip criminal prospect. Don't forget: Jerry was just as ignorant of my past as I was of his, so he deserves credit for seeing through my straitlaced exterior.

"So, Ken, bubeleh, I think I maybe got sumthin' for ya," Jerry began in his thick, phlegmy New York accent, his hyperactive hands dancing along with the rhythm of his speech. "You see, I conned some chinamen for two chink container loads of blank VHS tapes fresh off the fucking boat. I know a guy here or there who may be interested, but I got major bulk, man, tens of thousands of the little shits, just two big chink container loads of these things. I need someone with the connections to schlep these tapes around Porn Valley and hustle up orders for a thousand tapes here, five thousand tapes there, for like pennies on the dollar, y'know, a great deal you're giving these people. I'd cut you in on the deal, and it'd be a couple thou, good score for bullshit work, y'know?"

Almost twenty years later, I would hear the full story of the "chink container loads" of VHS from a porn-star friend of mine. This gentleman was asked to attend a "family barbecue" at Jerry's place; when he arrived at a beautiful house in the suburbs, he saw kids running and laughing all over the lawn, dogs playing fetch, friends gathered around picnic tables, and Jerry Zimmerman supervising the grill. As he introduced himself to everyone at this idyllic scene, he noticed something out of place: a table of five or six formally dressed Chinese business-men, sweating in the heat and socially discomforted by the raucous displays of American family life. When the porn star introduced himself to the Chinese guests, the businessmen were clearly starstruck; they swore that they were his biggest fans in Asia.

The next day, the porn star came over to Jerry's house to drop something off that he forgot to give him at the barbecue and found the beautiful home in the suburbs abandoned, empty. There was a dirty "For Sale" sign on the yard that certainly did not appear to be new. Feeling like he had lost his mind, the porn star called around to ask what happened to Jerry and received a shocking answer: the entire barbecue had been a setup.

The home did not belong to Jerry, and many of the attendees were anything but the blood relations they were playing. Even the pets were extras from the pound. Jerry had broken into a home for sale in the suburbs and furnished it to look like his own house so that it could act as the set to the fake "family picnic" he was throwing in honor of the Chinese businessmen. After meeting Jerry's entire family and being accepted into his home, the Chinese felt so comfortable with him that they had no qualms about advancing him a few thousand VHS tapes. The fact that Jerry had invited the businessmen's favorite American porn star certainly bolstered his credibility, as well.

I sold a couple thousand of Jerry's tapes within the week and made around $3,000 in easy cash—earning goodwill from the porn studios for "doing them a favor" by letting them in on the great deal. In the process of picking up and distributing the tapes, Jerry very quickly earned my respect and admiration. You did not have to spend a long time around Jerry to realize that he was one of the cleverest, quickest, and savviest criminal minds in the world. He was working every moment of every day;

within seconds he could size up, charm, and leverage a stranger for profit.

Jerry would brainstorm aloud about potential schemes, and it was humbling entertainment: he could rattle off twenty solid-gold winners in a row at auctioneer speed while only half paying attention. I have no doubt that these performances were meant to subtly establish his credibility and persuade me that it was in my best interest to work with him. He succeeded—I would be Jerry's eager student and devoted friend until the day of his death.

One day I was answering the phone at Jerry's office, surrounded by the framed posters of his two movies and any other movie that coincidentally sported the name of any other Jerry Zimmerman, when I received a phone call from federal prison. "Hey, it's Sonny. Who's this?" came the whistling death rattle over the line.

Like a good student of Jerry, I immediately switched to worker-mode and started charming the bored, desperate-for-conversation, octogenarian New York Mafia legend. During the conversation, it came out that we both knew Batman Esposito's father, Sal, so I gave Batman's phone number to Sonny, who now had a new Mob contact to compulsively collect-call to kill the time. Batman was furious with me—the FBI would be up his ass like Peter North once they caught Sonny Franzese calling him—but it established my bona fides with my new first-name-basis pen pal, Sonny.

I was now an associate in one of the most prestigious and powerful crews in the Colombo Mafia Family.

"You gotta have a couple of people that, if you are in a jam, you know to go to. You see, if you ain't got that, you got trouble, you get it? The shit

*that you do, to me, is worth eight million dollars.
You never say 'blablabla,' you say here [take what
I have if you need it]—well that's the way we do
things. . . . See what I tell Ori [Spado, mafioso], I
say this kid [Kenji] is a winner, y'know?"*

Jerry Zimmerman
From a recorded conversation with Kenji

There has always been a direct correlation between
my martial arts studies and my behavior as a criminal.
As a teenager, I studied Bruce Lee's Jeet Kune Do system in tandem with boxing and kickboxing, and from my
sparring experience I derived the lesson that the most
reliable way of winning any confrontation is to strike
first with overwhelming force and persist without mercy
until you annihilate your target. This kamikaze style of
self-defense was perfectly suited to the "cocaine cowboys" era of Orange County, when gun-shy crooks like
Joey Avila died and mass murderers like Big Mike and
Griselda thrived.

As I've aged, however, I've specialized in jujutsu,
the Japanese and Brazilian martial art that focuses on
grappling and submission holds. Jujutsu means "the
way of softness" or "the gentle art" in Japanese, which
may seem contradictory at first. "The gentle art" is so
named because, unlike strike-based martial arts systems,
jujutsu teaches a fighter to neutralize an opponent with a
minimal outlay of energy, force, and risk. A jujutsu prac-
titioner shuns high-risk, high-impact fistfights, in which
anything can happen and even the winner earns a trip to
the hospital with broken knuckles. Instead, he gradually
reduces his opponent to helplessness using low-risk and
low-impact trips, takedowns, grappling holds, joint locks,
and chokes. Jujutsu teaches a fighter the ability to win

while doing the absolute minimal damage to himself and, if he wishes, his opponent.

That is why the art is gentle. Of the few martial arts that have real-world use, jujutsu is the discipline that most focuses on minimizing unnecessary damage, pain, and risk.

Though Jerry Zimmerman never won a fight in his life, he was the greatest jujutsu teacher I've ever known. Jerry was the Jujutsu Gangster: his governing principle was to make his money in as gentle, easy, safe, nonviolent, subtle, and merciful a manner as possible.

In Jerry's mind, why should a crook risk his life, his freedom, and his humanity to be a violent street criminal when he can make twice as much money painlessly defrauding impersonal institutions like casinos, banks, insurance companies, and financial markets? Why expose yourself to dangerous drug dealers, junkies, and hit men when you can safely do business with movie producers, car dealers, and stockbrokers? Why ruin a mark's life and earn his eternal hatred when you can just as easily deceive him, stay his friend, and leave the door open for future swindles?

Jerry taught me a simple yet profound truth: the wise criminal concentrates on simultaneously maximizing his profits and his own security. Jerry patiently tutored me until I understood that the over-the-top gangster theatrics that I specialized in did not make me a badass; it made me a suicidal idiot. The underworld did not operate according to the rules of a videogame—no multiple lives to expend, no bonus points for kicking ass and wreaking havoc—so why was I living as if Kenny Gallo were a disembodied videogame character whose life I could throw away?

"Ken, the guys who have to use muscle don't got

nuthin' up here," Jerry might say as he tapped his head. "You gotta ask yourself: are you in it for the money or are you in it to make your schlong feel big? You got somethin' to prove? All you're provin' is you're a schmuck who likes to make enemies and catch the cops' attention.

"I've known a lot of real tough guys, and most of them are dead or in the clink. Look at Sonny. No one tougher, and no one been away longer. Fuck that cowboy shit. It don't lead to no life worth livin'. I'm not talkin' about just jail or getting whacked for being a cowboy, bubeleh," Jerry said and lowered his voice almost to a whisper. "Between you and me, why live like a fuckin' animal? Why be a lowdown, no-good, heartless schmuck, when if you got a fuckin' brain and a little chutzpah you can be an all right guy and still make money? Being bad for bad's sake don't make no one happy, and more important it don't make no one money.

"Lemme tell you a secret, Ken, and maybe it'll get through your head. You don't need violence. Ever. All you need is the ability to talk. You can drop me anywhere in the world, but as long as I have enough pocket change to pick up a payphone and start dialing I can scam my way into a fortune. That's all I need: a phone. Why fuck around with guns when you can get rich talking on the phone?"

Jerry only spoke this forcefully when he was riled up from watching one of his friends or partners suffer the repercussions of being a "meathead." In general, happy-go-lucky Jerry preferred nonconfrontational methods of persuasion. With decades of experience trying to reason with stubborn and egotistical street thugs, Jerry knew that violent, hectoring rhetoric would rarely persuade a crook to admit fault. The most effective way to change a gangster's mind was to make him think he had come to the conclusion himself.

Here's an example. One day I stomped into his office furious over a porno business deal. "Jerry, this prick distributor thinks I'm a pussy. The rich bastard doesn't want to honor our deal and keeps trying to pay me in merchandise. He's about to learn that I'm not fuckin' around when I bust his fucking head."

"Aww, Kenji," Jerry sighed, "wait a second, why don't you, before you get yourself locked up. Let me wrap my head around dis here deal. So, this is just some porn guy, right?"

"Yeah, another wannabe tough guy," I said with disgust at the idea that some smut peddler thought he could muscle me around.

"And, for argument's sake, let's say you smack him around, ya get me? What are the chances the tough guy ain't that tough and goes to the cops?"

"He's a porn guy, so of course there's a chance."

"So is this go-to-jail money? I mean, are we talkin' a fortune, you see what I mean?"

"Nah, just a few thousand. But it's the principle; I'm not letting anyone rip me off."

"Who's saying that? Not me! Hold on, we're just talkin' here," Jerry would say, waving his hand as if he were just shooting the shit. "Besides, I'm a Jew, I'm not into that 'turning the other cheek' bullshit, you get me? I'm just tryin' to figure out this here deal. So, this guy signed a deal to buy your film and wants to pay you in his product, right?"

"Yeah," I said, slowly beginning to doubt myself because Jerry had that glimmer in his eye that told me he had analyzed this deal many steps ahead of me and spotted an angle to exploit.

"So this schlemiel wants to pay you in product. Did he ask you to sign anything? Did he specify exactly how many of whatever you'd be getting?"

"No, of course not. It's porno; he's winging it."

"Okay, so how would you get this product?"

"He wants me to come over to his warehouse and pick out tapes from his inventory to resell."

"So this dummy is going to take you to his warehouse, open up the doors, and let you loose?"

I nodded, a smile creeping across my face.

"And, for hypothetical sake," Jerry said, "let's say you were to walk in there and take ten times, or twenty times, what you're owed from his product, do you see? Would this guy be able to stop you?"

"Fuck no, are you kidding? He ain't touching me."

"And would this sleazy pornographer have any recourse to police assistance?"

"Nah, what is he going to do? Bring the cops to his warehouse full of porn that he shot without permits and paid for illegally? Say that I violated a vague verbal agreement after he defaulted on his payments for the porn film that we shot illegally?"

"So!" Jerry paused to clear his throat. "For conversational purposes, you could rob this guy blind without any repercussions whatsoever, and, in the process, teach him and everyone who hears the story a good lesson about honoring agreements with Kenji, right?"

"Right! I think I might have an idea how to handle this."

"Of course you do, Ken, you're a smart kid figurin' all this out on your own," Jerry said with a wink. "It just goes to show you what can happen when you settle down and think things through, don't you see?"

Another lesson Jerry taught me was that, while there

was no such thing as a victimless crime, a great scam artist can create the illusion of victimless crimes and, in certain instances, commit crimes that are microscopically close to victimless. Crimes without evident victims are very slowly noticed and almost never solved.

For example, who was the victim when Jerry defrauded the crooked managers of the Sands Casino in Las Vegas of $100,000 in casino credit, hotel suites, lavish dinners, front-row tickets, and spa treatments by convincing them that his flunky was a Mafia godfather who could be bribed into investing in the casino? The perks cost the hotel nothing, and the owners would have "skimmed" the credit off the top of the casino's massive profits anyway.

And good luck finding the victim when Jerry, in his words, spun "the Wheel." The Wheel was Jerry's term for check kiting, the complex one-man Ponzi scheme which Jerry utilized to finance his entire criminal career. A criminal skilled at check kiting never needed to commit any other crime; he could write himself a daily paycheck out of thin air. Check kiting exploited the long delay between banks making funds available and the transfer of those funds; Jerry artificially lengthened this delay by scratching the magnetic ink off the bottom of the checks so that they could not be read by computers and required manual handling. This created a limbo period, sometimes a couple weeks, between the time Jerry cashed a bad check and that bad check bouncing. In that span, the valueless check was effectively "good," allowing Jerry to practically mint cash at will.

The Wheel would start spinning with one bad, often forged check from some out-of-state mark. That one bad check would initiate a never-ending cycle of bad checks financing new bad checks financing newer bad checks that acted as collateral for no-interest-in-the-first-year lines of credit that covered the old bad checks and allowed the cycle to start all over again and metastasize in every direction. Each spin of the Wheel would blow more hot air into what quickly became an enormous economic bubble.

From one bad check, Jerry could create a financial empire with dozens of bank accounts, shell companies, lines of credit, bank loans, and investments that were all worth a lot less than nothing when factoring in the interest owed. All of these valueless accounts and investments could nonetheless transform into real cash if Jerry moved quickly. With careful number juggling, the Wheel could keep spinning for years and years before all the accounts went bust, and by that time the web of transactions would be so convoluted that no one could trace it back to that first bad check—which certainly didn't come from anyone that could be tied to Jerry.

Jerry and I would spin and spin the Wheel and land on sums in excess of $50,000 before we'd cash in by purchasing thousands of untraceable porn VHS tapes. We'd then ship the tapes to Jackie di Padova, a member of Sonny's crew in Florida, who would sell them at 100 percent profit while the banks and porn distributors got stuck with the bill when all the checks bounced. Jerry was right: it was possible to make drug-dealer money without exposing yourself to drug-dealer danger. It was thanks to Jerry that I finally let my narcotics obligations gradually lapse into oblivion.

Since I no longer dealt with cutthroat drug dealers, Jerry painstakingly recalibrated my moral compass. "You don't got to be like that, bubeleh," was his admonition whenever I thought with my primitive, ultraviolent mind-set. His point was not just that violence was counterproductive but also that it was morally and spiritually damaging to me.

Jerry was one of those old-time carny crooks who could con himself into living by a convoluted, arbitrary code of honor. It was not the Mafia's traditional us-against-the-world "honor among thieves," but something even stranger. The code of honor among old-school carnies, grifters, scammers, confidence men, and bunko artists was that, while it was kosher to "work" a mark out of his money, a real con should refrain from stealing his dignity.

It was incredible to see how many of Jerry's victims—including gangsters like Michael Franzese and me, whom Jerry shorted as a matter of course—could not help but love the guy. He had that Clintonian rascal charisma where the knowledge that he's pimping you out somehow makes him even more lovable. Many of Jerry's victims would catch him stealing their money, confront him, and finish the meeting by freely investing more money and trust in him than ever before.

An extreme case of this phenomenon was Jerry's good friend Mel, a tiny, frail, terminally ill retiree who looked like Hans Moleman from *The Simpsons*. Since Mel was insensibly infatuated with gangsters and porn, Jerry planted the greed seed and harvested a six-figure "investment" in a porn movie from Mel. Of course, Jerry just pocketed the money, but unlike what I would have done, he didn't abandon Mel after liquidating the old man's retirement nest egg. In return for believing in his con, Jerry practically adopted Mel.

In Mel's dying months, Jerry made sure the wannabe producer spent every waking moment seated in the big chair behind the desk at Jerry's office. I've rarely given anyone the joy that Mel got when Jerry spun these incredible up-and-down tales of the hardships he went through every day to produce Mel's imaginary movie or manage Mel's imaginary distribution business (or any of the other fraudulent businesses financed by Mel's long-spent money). Even when Mel didn't have a cent left to give, Jerry spent dozens of hours every week charming and working him, convincing Mel that he was a hot-shit, connected player in the porn game. We took harmless, withered old Mel everywhere we went, making him in effect my weirdest criminal partner. We were quite a crew: a giant New York Jew mafioso, an ancient little brown dude, and a jacked-up twentysomething Japanese-American gangster.

Mel died a happy man, and Jerry attended his funeral, where it was evident that he was Mel's best friend in the world. Jerry even took his own daughter to pay her respects to Uncle Mel.

When I asked Jerry why he went through so much trouble over Mel, he winced. "Ah, bubeleh, nuthin' in the world is for free. Mel wanted to be around guys like us, so we provided him that service. That's what that money was for. Mel didn't care about no movie; he just wanted to feel like he mattered and belonged with guys like us. It was a thrill to him, like, y'know, an experience that was priceless, and we got paid for our time."

"And our friendship," I said.

"Nah, Ken, that was real. I took Mel's money, but I was there for Mel. Long after his money was gone, I made sure he was happy. That was my duty; I took him for a ride, so I owed him to be his chauffeur to his last stop, money or no money, you get what I'm saying, bubeleh?

"Nothing in life is free. You can't take and give nothin' in return. That's what all those Italians back east do, and that's why they have rats fallin' over each other to put them away. Mel? He would've gone to jail for me. The way I treated him, he was more loyal to me as my mark than Sonny Franzese's two wiseguy sons are to him as their father and capo. That's because I gave as good as I took. Mel had no reason ever to want harm done to me.

"Mel woulda done for me in the same way I would do for you, and in the same way I know you would do for me. Nothing in life is free. It's give-and-take. My hands are clean."

Con artists are almost always their own biggest marks. The more street smart they are, the easier time they have scamming themselves into believing whatever feels best. When it came to payrolls and checkbooks, Jerry was the master at cooking the books, and you could tell he used the same talent for making the valueless appear valuable to convince himself that his life's moral ledger was somehow balanced. Jerry thought he could spin the Wheel and write himself a karmic blank check.

If you believe in divine retribution, the case of Jerry Zimmerman makes a wonderful parable. The terminal ailment that made Mel so careless with his money was chronic kidney failure; we used to tease the poor guy all the time about Jerry and me having to schedule our day around his dialysis treatments. Within a few years of Mel's death, Jerry himself would be slowly and miserably killed by kidney failure while I teased him about his dialysis treatments.

Very early in our friendship, long before I would become tamed as his full-time apprentice, Jerry approached me with a scheme that would go down as one of our most spectacular swindles. Our tour de force would go down in adult entertainment business folklore as the Porn-A-Thon.

It all began with a Samoan porn star who was always sucking up to Jerry and the Samoan's brother-in-law, the owner of one of the world's greatest porn distribution empires. You could see Jerry's eyes glaze over with con man fantasies as he listened to the Samoan's descriptions of his brother-in-law's gigantic VHS production and distribution operation. It was one of the few times I ever saw Jerry speechless—massive cash-based operations are the Holy Grail for all financial con men.

Jerry stuffed a fist up his Samoan puppet's ass and had him regurgitate a proposal to his multimillionaire brother-in-law. The play was simple: since the tycoon's unrivaled mass-production capabilities made him chronically undersupplied with content, Jerry and the Samoan offered to produce as many films as the distributor could use, all at once, for a single huge, easily embezzled lump payment. "Great, I need 100 within a month," was supposedly the brother-in-law's answer.

So who do you think produced all those quickie porn movies for Jerry? "Bubeleh, you know me, I don't know a camera from a cumshot, but with you to handle all that I can concentrate on, y'know, cutting all those corners. You know I was a real producer, not smut shit, but Hollywood features—I'm a pro, an old hand at *this* racket. Help me out and I'll take care of you on the back end. I'm going to Jew the shit out of these motherfuckers."

Jerry wasn't joking. He made 100 porn movies without spending a dime on anything legitimate. A large part of his gargantuan budget was earmarked for renting multiple sets for the month-long marathon shoot; instead, Jerry simply broke into an abandoned YMCA building that was condemned due to severe earthquake damage and stuffed it full of old furniture. We scrounged together cameras and equipment through borrowing, extortion, and various bartering deals, and since Jerry did not want to "waste" money on paying people to fuck, he paid all the talent with bad checks.

For thirty days, a rotating crew of other directors and cameramen supervised by the Samoan, Jerry, and I shot nonstop—one plot-free gonzo fuck scene after another. My circle of hardcore criminals were all crashing at the YMCA building to watch the festivities, which contributed to the mood of utter degenerate abandon. Porn stars were passed out, fucking in dark corners away from the cameras, trying to suck and fuck for coke, and introducing us to their pimps or "agents" who tried to shake us down for more money. It was every horror story you've ever heard about the porn industry dramatized in an interactive museum of sleaze. After we were done shooting each day, Jerry and I would stash all the masters so that we could make prints to resell on the black market later.

At the end of the thirty days, Jerry was generous with those of us who were in on the scheme: I received a brand-new white Toyota 4 x 4, and the Samoan received the Porsche of his dreams. Jerry, of course, saved the best gift for himself: the hundreds of thousands of dollars of leftover profit.

The Samoan, unaware that he had been given the shiny Porsche to distract him from the inestimably larger reward Jerry was keeping for himself, was delighted with his loot and begged to work with Jerry again on whatever his next grand scheme was. Outside of porn, the Samoan was useless except as a patsy; luckily, Jerry always had use for a patsy.

Utilizing a network of investors of various shades of shady, Jerry convinced the historic Great Circus Bim Bom from the Soviet Union that he was financing a two-year tour of the United States. The prestigious Soviet circus, which had roots dating back to the reign of the last czar, was greedy for American money and thus extremely gullible. Jerry even convinced a Kuwaiti sheik to invest a tidy sum in the tour, which he of course kept for himself.

All told, 125 Russian clowns, carnies, strongmen, trapeze artists, bearded ladies, contortionists, and freak-show acts crossed the Atlantic with their Marxist menagerie of dancing bears and marching elephants. Almost immediately, the enterprise went bankrupt in Marietta, Georgia, of all places, where the entire circus was stranded at a dreary motel for over a month. Penniless, the carnies relied on the kindness of strangers and gawkers to survive. It was a classic Jerry Zimmerman scheme: underwrite a cash business with bad checks for just long enough to steal every movable asset and collect whatever money you can from investors, advertisers, and anyone else with an interest. Meanwhile, the dancing bears were seized by creditors, which I can imagine was one hell of a memorable day for that collection agency.

Who do you think was dumb enough to take the heat for this atrocity? That's right, the Samoan—who was positively delighted when Jerry appointed him press spokesman for the defunct circus. Jerry rightly figured that a loudmouth porn gigolo desperate to step in the national spotlight would distract journalists and investigators from paying too much attention to the camera-shy, multiple-time felon and Mafia scam artist skulking around in the shadows. Jerry probably gave the porn star a stolen Jet Ski or something equally shiny in return for providing cover for yet another million-dollar scam.

Most of Jerry's schemes, of course, were not as ambitious and complex as the Porn-A-Thon or Bim Bom con.

If anything, Jerry enjoyed living up to Jewish stereotypes; he was always proud that he was not above clipping coupons or grinding out his illicit profits in $5 to $10 increments. "I can hear a penny drop from a mile away!" he might say with unmistakable pride.

"A hustle's a hustle, bubeleh. Don't be ashamed to reach down and pick up a nickel here and there. If you only go for jackpots you'll end up in the jackpot, get what I mean?"

It was one such small-time hustle that would cost Jerry and other members of the Mafia untold millions of dollars and years in jail. Ironically, this penny-ante scam began with the heaviest gangster in the Colombo Family.

"Hey! Kid! Is that you? It's Sonny."

"Yes, Sonny, it's Ken. It's wonderful to speak to you!" I said in my best eager-to-please underling voice as I fiddled around at Jerry's desk.

"How's everything going, buddy? How are things out there in the sun?"

"Everything's great, Sonny."

"Okay, kid, is Jerry there?" For once, Sonny wasn't in the mood for small talk.

"Nope, I'm the only person here."

"All right, all right. Do you have a pencil? I got sumthin' I need you to write down," Sonny whispered in a comically conspiratorial tone. Old-school gangsters came of age when FBI surveillance equipment was outrageously poor, so they all take the precaution of whispering on the phone and turning up any nearby TV or stereo. This always made me laugh, since I knew from working with Officer Jerry that the FBI's modern phone taps are so sensitive that they can listen to the digestive cycle of a tapeworm in Sonny's colon.

"All right, this guy is with me. He's a great guy. He

hustles. He'll be coming around. Write down this name. O-R-L-A-N-D-O S-P-A-D-O. Goes by Ori, O-R-I. Got that?"

"Ori Spado. Yes, Sonny, I have it," I said, underlining the name on Jerry's calendar blotter.

"Tell Jerry. He's good people. He's wit' me. You sure you got that name? He's got the hookup with that informational stuff, the telephone TV-shopping people. He's got a hookup there; he's got hustle. You got the name? Ori?"

When I told Jerry about Sonny's message, Jerry looked like he was going to puke. "Oh, Jesus, not another deadbeat! Kenji, you go see; I don't wanna touch this."

If I knew then what I know now, I would have stabbed Ori in the nutsack the moment he introduced himself. As soon as I saw Ori, I knew he was a sad motherfucking excuse for a gangster. He looked exactly like what he was: a crooked insurance salesman from Rome, New York, with a Moe *Three Stooges* haircut. Ori was a wannabe waddling about in pressed jeans, a white polo shirt showcasing his man-titties, and a ratty blue jacket. This fat, bug-eyed, diabetic, chain-smoking old guido introduced himself and began trading on Sonny's name like it was a blue-chip NASDAQ stock.

I wanted to punch him directly in the face just for being so square, so lame, and so fake. Within seconds of opening his ashtray mouth, Ori explained that he was tougher than Rambo and was doing everything but butt-fucking his good buddy, best friend, confidant, and blood brother Sonny Franzese. I was rolling my eyes, but he was Sonny's guy, so I had to play along.

Ori's big score was that he had a connection at the QVC shopping network and could obtain truckloads of Jack LaLanne–brand fruit-juicers for $8 to $12 apiece instead of the normal three-payments-of-$19.95. What a heavy-duty gangster: Ori's street racket was haggling for good prices on Jack LaLanne juicers. Why would the Mafia need labor unions and casinos and the drug trade when it had super-gangsters like Ori Spado and his monopoly on the cheap, piece-of-shit, made-for-TV fruit-squeezer racket?

Jerry could not believe that Sonny had risked his chance at parole to set up a transcontinental Jack La-Lanne juicer deal over a supervised prison phone. "Sonny must be getting old," he said, "but we gotta indulge this schlemiel. For fuck sake, I'm gonna feel like a crackhead schlepping these pieces of shit around town."

"Imagine how I feel. I went from moving kilos to moving juicers," I said.

Jerry cooked up some fake letters of credit and "bought" a few truckloads of juicers. Every office, apartment, home, and car that we owned between us was stuffed to the ceiling with these contraptions. I drove around with a trunk full of juicers and just hocked them in the direction of absolutely anyone who looked like a big enough hippie or health nut to buy an infomercial fruit juicer out of the trunk of my car. Finally, I met an Israeli at a swap meet who would eagerly pay $15 apiece for as many juicers as I could get him—so Jerry and I ground out a couple thousand dollars. More than anything, we were just relieved to no longer have to see Jack LaLanne's ancient mug anymore.

"I know that they're going to take a shot at me. It could be today, tomorrow, or ten years from now, but it'll come. . . . I'm not going to make it easy for them. They're never going to be able to call me into a room, or take me for a ride, and put

*a bullet in the back of my head. If they're lucky
enough to catch me on a street corner or in a restaurant, so be it."*

Michael Franzese
Quitting the Mob

The 1992 book *Quitting the Mob*, the memoir of
Michael Franzese, the son of Sonny Franzese and the
former capo of my crew in the Colombo Family, was
worth its weight in cocaine to me. *Quitting the Mob* was
underworld currency, a gold-plated resume: fact-checked,
hardcover evidence that I was hanging with the most
financially successful crew in the history of the modern
American Mafia.

In 1991, only a few people knew who Sonny and
Jerry were, but in 1992 their names suddenly became
tradable commodities. A namedrop of Sonny or an introduction to Jerry was suddenly enough to plant the greed
seed in a mark and convince him to start handing over
his money. Ask anyone who has lived the Life: you never
get more business than when you're publicly named as a
gangster.

Quitting the Mob was also priceless as a historical
document, a comprehensive personal and career history
of my colleagues from a proven expert who worked
with them for decades. I now had the advantage of
comprehending my new friends and business partners in
the context of their lives, while to them I was mostly a
mystery.

Best of all, I could tease the shit out of Jerry and his
crew with all the gossip that Michael had made public
knowledge. As a practical joke, I bought a dozen copies
of *Quitting the Mob* on its release date and handed them
out to everyone as a gift. I expected to see revulsion on

their faces; after all, there was nothing a mafioso supposedly loathed more than a rat.

I was disappointed; Jerry's guys devoured the book with barely concealed enthusiasm. Despite their best interests, most mobsters love seeing their name in print, and if there was any resentment against Michael it was very faint indeed. Even Jerry, who was revealed to have pimped out his sexual services to a witness on Michael's behalf, was unmoved by the apparent betrayal of his protégé.

"Bubeleh, it is what it is," Jerry sighed without any apparent rancor. "It's how the business is, these days."

"Oh, come on," I tried to egg Jerry on, "I know you would give a couple thou to know where that rat was."

"Oh, please, Ken. Shit, the guy is right across town, here in L.A. Everyone knows where he's at." Jerry laughed as an idea occurred to him. "Kid, come here, let me show you sumthin'." Jerry took me behind his desk and pulled out a framed picture. There in the photograph was Jerry, surrounded by at least a million dollars in banded cash—with a dedication from Michael Franzese.

"Nothing is simple as it seems, Ken. Nothing is for free. Revenge ain't worth the heat, and more importantly revenge don't make money."

I felt my opinion of Jerry concurrently rise and fall in different categories: I was impressed by his maturity and self-control as a man but disappointed in his lack of ruthlessness as a gangster. Wasn't the whole point of being a gangster to never have to take shit from anyone? What was the underworld coming to when the American Mafia was gun-shy about taking out known, open informants?

Shortly after the book came out, I spoke with Sonny by phone in Jerry's office. As we were making small talk, I kept wondering how enraged Sonny must have been that the stepson he had raised as his own had betrayed him, profited from that betrayal, raised Sonny's profile as a ranking mafioso, and consequently raised the likelihood of more jail time. Soft-touch Jerry was one thing, but surely "The Rock" of the Colombo Family, the upholder of the Mafia's old-school values, had not gone soft. Just as I was thinking about what I could do to Michael to earn Sonny's gratitude, Sonny mentioned something about talking to "his grandchildren in California. They're just doing wonderful." I was astounded; Sonny not only knew where Michael was, he was still in contact with him!

Whatever lingering misconception I may have had about the strength and fearsomeness of the American Mafia was dispelled. You could not only rat on the Mafia and get away with it; you could *rat on your own father*, publish a book about it, appear on TV and radio promoting the book, and then not even go through the trouble of hiding. You couldn't get away with doing that to Sal and Joey Avila, let alone any of the truly scary narcotraffickers I worked with for years. What good were "friends of ours" like these in a bind?

I was given a chance to find out—thanks to detectives Tom Dove and Tom Carney.

When the market for cocaine collapsed simultaneously with my loss of Genesis, porn became my base income, which I supplemented with whatever scams Jerry and I put together. Though I enjoyed working in porn and the scams racket, it was just a day-to-day gig, another way to grind out some dollars. It wasn't a love affair like coke smuggling had been. White-collar crime didn't provide me with the existential release and ecstasy that violent crime did. The only way I had learned to relieve the pressure in my brain and untie the knots in my muscles was to expose myself to violence and danger on the streets. Quite literally, street crime had become my fix: it fixed me like nothing else could.

I was addicted, so I could not help but get my fix meddling in drugs and robberies even though I was making great money in porn and with Jerry. I was violating the one ironclad rule that I had learned through much heartbreaking experience: never dabble. For the first and only time in my career, I was half-a-gangster, a dabbler in violent crime. Like Joey Avila, I took quick, invigorating dips in the cocaine bloodbath as a break from my normal, staid life. Like Joey, I would pay for it.

Dissatisfied that I had gotten away once again, Detective Tom Dove called in the DEA as soon as he heard that I was still dealing here and there. Some snitches referred an undercover narcotics agent to me who was posing as a dealer looking to buy kilos at an above-market price. I met the guy and immediately got a bad vibe off him; to see if he was a narc, I told him that we could do business only if he met me in Mexico to conclude the deal or if he paid me upfront with a machine gun fixed with a silencer—two conditions that an undercover agent could never meet.

While I was waiting for the DEA agent to get back to me about completing the deal, I was tipped off about his true identity. I knew I was fucked; just talking to the agent about a drug deal was a conspiracy charge. I was in a panic and called the only person who might be able to help, my old friend Officer Jerry.

"Hello?"

"Hey, Jerry, it's Kenji. What's up?"

"You," Jerry grunted. Dial tone. Jerry always was a selfish asshole.

The DEA agent gave the Two Toms what they needed

to obtain a warrant for my arrest for conspiracy to traffic narcotics, but Tom Dove's work was so characteristically sloppy that it was only after the warrant was issued that he realized he had no valid address on me. The Two Toms had no way of taking me into custody—until I made the mistake of pissing off a stripper I was sleeping with who called the cops in a demented coke rage and told them where I lived. The police never showed up that night. With my location pinpointed and surveillance established, the cops waited for the right moment to take me down—for good, they hoped.

I was at a stash house preparing for a burglary when a historic event occurred: the Two Toms actually failed to botch a case against me! For the first and last time, they had me dead to rights. While the cops were surrounding my apartment, I was methodically disassembling sawed-off shotguns, a Smith & Wesson 9-mm automatic, and a couple AK-47s and loading them into backpacks by the door. As always, before doing dirty work I took a shower, which was the precise moment the safety-conscious cops chose to knock on my door. I immediately knew I was going to jail; this was a stash house unknown to anyone but me, so the only people who would drop by for a visit were the cops.

I knew I was going to be led away in handcuffs, but I wanted to ensure that the Two Toms derived as little pleasure as possible from the experience. My boy Keith had reinforced the stash house door with a Keith Special: thick steel bolts that ran through the door and locked into place within the metal frame of the building. Since the cops could not kick the door in, I decided to make them sweat while I enjoyed my shower. After all, I thought, it might be the last relaxing, private shower I would take for a while.

As the cops screamed and threatened and thrashed against the door like apes, I took my time drying off and getting dressed so that I would look sharp for Tom Dove. When I finally let the cops in, they were so agitated from their dislocated shoulders and aching feet that I was tackled and smashed face-first into the floor. I was dumped in jail and spent the long, four-day Fourth of July weekend there.

It was the usual routine: Tom Dove promising me that I would be going away until the 21st century, Internal Affairs begging me to rat out Officer Jerry, Customs bargaining with me to sell out Joey and Sal's *federale* uncle, the FBI sniffing around for leads on the Colombians. Customs even asked me to go undercover to Colombia to verify that Mike Marvich's protector, Rodriguez Gacha, was actually dead. As always, the only person the police did not ask me about was Mike Marvich himself—why compromise such a valuable federal informant?

I dismissed all of their offers; I never negotiate with a weak hand. Instead, I had my Marvich-approved attorneys make an ultimatum: either the district attorney slaps me on the wrist, or we give him the most drawn-out, expensive, appeals-ridden, wearying legal dogfight imaginable. Since the district attorney knew I was an ID-collecting drug smuggler who had partnered with an international fugitive (Frank) and had been investigated for espionage, I was considered not a flight risk but a flight certainty. They were right; I would be one fake-passport-stamping motherfucker if the DA tried to send me to some dungeon where illiterate, racist prison guards would hold absolute power over every facet of my life. I was no Greg Benjamin; if I were looking at jail time, a U.S. Customs agent would be looking at my back as I strolled across the border into Tijuana.

The DA caved, and the Two Toms' world caved in with him. I received no jail time in return for my plea to an assortment of lesser charges—with the proviso that I be straitjacketed with hardcore probation. The tiniest breach of my probation guidelines would send me to jail for years, and I was assured that the Two Toms would be so far up my ass that Peter North would be jealous. It appeared that, outside of filming pornos without permits, my criminal career would have to go on hiatus unless I intended to chill with Greg and Lalo behind bars.

"Bubeleh, don't worry about it." Jerry laughed and waved his hand when I shared my distress. "That's what you get for bein' a fuckin' cowboy. What, do you not listen? Your eyes, don't they work? I've been telling you for years; you'd think it'd get through that fuckin' head of yours," Jerry said with a sigh and a slightly too dramatic shake of his head. I could tell he really didn't mind too deeply; he was used to being the only sane person in the room.

"But, luckily, you have friends like me who are used to cleaning up hotheads' messes," he continued with a reassuring smile. "I made a career out of it. Here's a little secret: you know what happens when the heat gets too hot for me? I fuckin' move away from the fire! You think those dickhead cops are going to follow you around the world? Just move. Don't be like these dummies in Brooklyn who think that if they move out of their neighborhood they die. What are you goin' to miss, all these California strip malls? Fuck it. We have friends! All over the place!"

"But I'm stuck here because of my probation agreement," I responded, annoyed at Jerry for falsely raising my hopes. "There's no way a judge will let me leave the state."

"As I said, we have friends! Actually, we've already been talking about this. You know our friend Jackie di Padova in Florida? He's got that porn warehouse in Fort Lauderdale that he has no idea what to do with, and he wants to get more into the business. Why don't you go down there to Florida, run the shop for him, teach him how to get the movies for free, get him a little taste here and there of the backend of the porn rackets. He'll set you up with some jobs, a nice place to live, some good places to film, introduce you to the half of the Mob that lives in Florida these days. It'll be good for you."

"Shit, Jerry, that sounds great," I said with an edge of sarcasm in my voice. "But, as I said, they won't let me leave the state. I'm not going on the lam."

"Aw, bubeleh, let me finish. Jackie has friends. Jackie has *very good* friends, including a couple Broward County sheriffs who would be happy to write a judge a few letters vouching for your honest, upstanding intentions in their neck of the woods. The judge will sign off without a second thought."

"And you already talked to Jackie?"

"Jackie is expecting you, bubeleh. I'd miss your company if I didn't know how much help you'd be to our good friend. You'll have fun—Jackie's a fucking character!"

"Jackie di Padova" is not his real name. He joins "Babar" as a former partner whose identity I've purposely hidden. Like Jerry, Jackie was my constant and loyal friend on the streets, and unlike Jerry, Jackie is still alive, still very much active, and still very much annoyed at Michael Franzese for mentioning his name.

It was farewell to California for me, and most importantly farewell to the Two Toms. I was not sorry to leave my home state: too much law enforcement pressure,

too many bad memories, and too many stone-cold killers with long memories. If I were ever going to have a
chance at establishing a new, nonviolent, even-tempered
identity for myself as a person and as a Jerry Zimmerman–style criminal, I would need a change of scenery—
and a lot of help.

Before I left California, I met a Colombo Family associate who had worked with Jackie for years. He was
an ugly, short, ill-educated hood with a bulbous nose, a
crooked smile, and a comical Bensonhurst-by-way-of-
Hollywood accent. He moseyed into Jerry's office as if
his balls were so huge that they obstructed his ability to
walk and looked at me like I must be the Chinese take-
out delivery boy. He seemed familiar to me, but I didn't
know from where. "Hey, Jerry, how you doin', brother?"

"Great, great, how can I help you?"

"Yeah, it's Junior, Jerry, Junior, you know I use-ta be
with Jackie and Sonny and 'dem. One of 'dem shoulda
called. I need to get some money . . . eh, uh, hmm—" He
stopped short, looking at me with suspicion. Dismissing
the need to be polite, the guido gestured at me with his
thumb and twisted his head as if he were saying "Not
in front of the dog-eater, capiche?" I stepped outside so
Jerry could handle this fucking meatball.

When shit-for-brains left, I asked Jerry why he looked
so familiar. "Oh, Junior? He does a lil' bit of actin' like
Jackie. Bit parts and such. He was in that *Goodfellas,*
some other shitty movies."

"He must not be much of an actor if he's collecting
debts out here."

"Nah, he ain't much of an actor, and he ain't much
a thinker either. He went down with Jackie back in the
day as one of Sonny's muscle guys—y'know, collecting
for shylocks and sticking people up. He used to beat guys

with bats. Tough dude, but he's dumb as a fucking rock and has been kissing ass since the '60s without getting nowheres."

Within a decade, Tony "Junior" Sirico would become famous as the barely fictionalized "Paulie Walnuts" on *The Sopranos*, and we would live in the same apartment building in Brooklyn. Even as a mainstream celebrity, Junior Sirico still found plenty of time in his schedule to kiss the ass of every illiterate thug in the Colombo Family and look at me like a Chinese delivery boy whenever we ran into each other.

> *"I had no idea about Kenji's past, but then I go to Florida with him to film some movies, and he tells me we're going out to dinner with some friends of his. I walk in, and it's like something out of* The Godfather, *just thirty of the most obvious, straight-out-of-the-movies wiseguys you've ever seen. I was like, 'Whoa, this is pretty ridiculous.'"*
> Chuck "Philmore Butts" Martino

I fulfilled what Robert De Niro's character in *Heat* suggests is a requirement for any gangster: if necessary, I could abandon everything in my life within thirty seconds and skip town.

When I was planning my move to Florida, I considered moving all of my belongings—furniture, guns, vehicles—cross-country, but it suddenly occurred to me that I honestly did not care about any of it. Ever since the loss of Joey, Clyde, and Tara, I found myself unable to feel lasting affection for any person, possession, or location. I had always made money, so I never had to worry about replacing anything.

I packed only the essentials—$20,000 and a .22

pistol hidden in the trunk, a cooler of healthy food in the front seat so I wouldn't have to eat at truck-stop diners—and hit the freeway. On my way through the Arizona desert, I happened upon a dead hitchhiker on the side of a desolate road and pulled over. It was 110 degrees in the sun, and his rotting body was wet, bloated, and gamey like ham gone bad. He looked like a greasy pimple ready to pop. A couple ravens were pulling at his cheeks. I was so pissed that I didn't have a camera! I would have loved to take a photo of me smiling next to a raven that was eating a hobo's corpse to use as my Christmas card for 1992 and the author photo of this book.

After a short stop in New Orleans to visit some cousins and eat fried okra, I spent the last leg of my trip slogging through the heaviest torrential storms I have ever seen. There were stretches where I couldn't go more than ten miles an hour due to the complete lack of visibility. As if in a movie, the storms broke and a rainbow poured down from the sky the moment I entered the Fort Lauderdale city limits. The sunshine was warm and bright when I arrived at the plush beachside hotel where Jackie di Padova had reserved a room for me.

Though I had spoken often with Jackie on the phone, I met him in person for the first time in Fort Lauderdale. I was impressed: though Jackie was a big guy at six feet one inch and a solid 240 pounds, he dressed immaculately in a colorful suit with matching polished Italian loafers. About forty-five years old at the time, Jackie still had black hair, which he wore slicked back, and his round tan face was handsome in that charismatic chubby way Mob guys can sometimes pull off. You could tell by his slow, smooth, confident stroll that he had once been a bruiser and definitely had been the tougher fighter in his strong-arm partnership with Junior Sirico.

"Kenji, you'll be staying in this hotel for as long as you want," Jackie said, gesturing to the gorgeous, colorfully painted, *Miami Vice*–style beachside hotel. Young, wealthy college girls were fluttering around us in their bikinis; the sunset was breathtaking. "I got—well, an arrangement with the place. Don't worry about it. You could stay here for however long you want until you get comfortable." Jackie snapped at a bellboy he knew, palmed him $20, and said, "Take it to his room. We've got partying to do. Let's go get some *pigs.*"

Jackie was all style, the first and last Mafia guy in my experience to ever wield the sort of silky cool that you always see in mobster movies. In addition to his pimp's wardrobe—Jackie had an entire closet exclusively for polished candy-bright Italian designer shoes—the secret to Jackie's cool was his voice and its deep, rich tone. Jackie's voice was literally one of his most valuable assets: Sizzler would later hire him as its TV announcer and in-house appearance spokesman. One of the Colombo Family's toughest enforcers was paid to memorize Sizzler PR copy and travel to chain restaurants throughout Middle America in a chef's uniform as "The Sizzler Chef" and charm the customers. It actually turned out to be great, easy money for Jackie, who especially loved all the free food.

Jackie liked the Hollywood lifestyle so much that, like his buddy Junior Sirico, he started auditioning for bit parts in movies. Naturally, like Junior, he was often cast as the default mafioso, which he didn't mind except for one role that hit way too close to home. When Jackie showed up on set to play the Mob boss in a made-for-TV documentary, he was handed a script that almost turned his hair gray. In this reenactment, Jackie would be inducting an actor playing Michael Franzese into the Colombo

Family! Jackie briefly considered leaving, but he realized that the story would be too good to pass up, especially since he knew that Michael would get a shock when he saw his father's old enforcer intruding on his moment in the spotlight. "That should serve that little fuck," Jackie told me with a wry smile.

Though Jackie shared Junior Sirico's hobby of chasing film roles, unlike Junior he was anything but a small-time suck-up as a hood. Jackie had superlative credentials: he was crafty enough to be the main partner in Jerry Zimmerman's cons, tough enough to be Sonny Franzese's driver, bodyguard, and enforcer on the streets of Brooklyn, and lucky enough to avoid a long jail sentence even though he was a multimillion-dollar player within Michael Franzese's gas scam.

Even Jackie's enemies were members of the underworld A-list. Jackie nearly lost his life when Sonny handed him a casino in Port-au-Prince, Haiti, to supervise while he was in jail, which Jackie did ably by befriending mass-murdering Haitian dictator Francois "Papa Doc" Duvalier. Papa Doc wasn't the problem—he loved Jackie; the problem was the jealousy of Anthony "Tumac" Accetturo, the boss of the New Jersey wing of the Lucchese Family. Tumac coveted the casino in Port-au-Prince, and, with Sonny in jail, he assumed that he could pressure the far-outranked Jackie to buckle and hand it over. Tumac was not a great judge of character: after the Luccheses shot up Jackie's house as a warning, two New Jersey Lucchese associates were allegedly whacked and dumped in a ditch. Who knows if the two incidents were related, but Jackie subsequently earned the reputation of a tough negotiator.

A sitdown was set up by the leaders of the New York Mafia to prevent an international street war, but Sonny's representative, Michael Franzese, was too busy financing his break-dance musical to attend. Tumac won the rights to the casino by default, and Papa Doc lost one of his favorite dining buddies. Though Jackie could not take revenge on Michael as long he was in the Colombo Family under Sonny, he might have sought Michael after he flipped, had the way not been blocked by an even tougher wiseguy: Jackie's little sister.

Whatever ingredients are in the di Padova genetic stew, they sure make for great gangsters. Jackie's little sister, whom I'll call Sofia di Padova, is the all-time wiseguy dream-girl: an old-school Brooklyn chick with the body of a swimsuit model, the mind of a seasoned ex-con, and the loyalty of a pit bull. When I first met the dirty-blond Sofia, she was in her forties, but her face was stuck in her early thirties and her body never aged past her teens. Men worshipped Sofia, and just about every New York and Florida wiseguy of note had been after her since the Kennedy administration. Unfortunately for them, Sofia was always taken: first by berserk Irish hit man Vinnie Lynch and then by Sonny Franzese. Sofia only fucked stone-cold killers.

Vinnie Lynch was a very bad guy even by New York standards—a Grim Reaper for hire. An alleged burglar, kidnapper, and shooter, Vinnie was known and feared throughout the New York underworld as a freelancer with no fear and no margin of error when it came to getting his man. Vinnie made a good living getting his hands dirty for the trigger-happy Harlem drug cartel known as the Pleasant Avenue Connection, which eventually produced Mafia dons for all Five Families. One of them was Matthew Madonna, who, in addition to his services to the Lucchese Family, served as the godfather to Sofia and Vinnie's kid. An even closer friend was Jimmy Coonan, boss of the fearsome Hell's Kitchen gang known as the Westies, whose wife, Edna, carpooled with Sofia to visit their husbands in jail.

Vinnie and Sofia were a dangerous couple to know: two hothead partiers with crazy, don't-give-a-fuck tempers and a social circle comprising heroin smugglers, Mob bosses, and coked-out Irish hit men. One of the couples they liked to party with was hard-luck wiseguy Angelo Bertolotti and his wife, Sharon Murphy. Angelo had dated Sofia for a second back in the good old days and secretly never recovered. One day when Vinnie and Sofia were relaxing together at the Galt Ocean Mile beach in Fort Lauderdale, Angelo walked up to Vinnie without knowing that Sofia had just ratted him out for still pining after her. Without hesitation, Vinnie pulled out his gun in broad daylight and supposedly capped Angelo in the leg. "Talk to [Sofia] again, and it'll be your head next time, fuckface."

That was the very public end of that relationship. I'm sure the di Padovas in retrospect regret that incident, because Angelo's daughter, actress Brittany Murphy, would have been a great Hollywood connection for Jackie in his burgeoning acting career.

Shooting Brittany Murphy's dad was hardly Vinnie's only brush with Hollywood royalty. Pulp novelist Elmore Leonard, whose books have been adapted into such movies as *Get Shorty, Jackie Brown,* and *Out of Sight,* supposedly drew upon the personality and exploits of Vinnie and his partner Jimbo for a few books. When Sofia wrote him a scathing letter, Leonard, obviously aware of Lynch's reputation, penned Sofia a cringingly polite letter and Christmas card assuring her that all of his characters were fictional—and "coincidentally" never used those characters again.

Vinnie and Sofia's love affair came to an end when

some convict stabbed the Irishman directly in the eyeball
in prison. According to Sofia, the prison authorities intentionally withheld proper medical treatment, leading to
his slow and miserable death.

The grieving Sofia wasted little time in finding a re-
placement: Sonny Franzese, the toughest Italian in New
York. She exchanged one constantly imprisoned gangster
for another; Sofia liked the danger, perks, independence,
and connections that came with dating A-list imprisoned
mobsters.

Sofia's connections were incredibly deep—she was
friends with everyone from ancient 1970s Genovese
Family boss Frank "Funzi" Tieri to Colombo boss Carmine "The Snake" Persico, whom Sofia claimed to have
witnessed murdering people on two separate occasions
in their younger days. Of course, Sofia barely blinked
and never talked when The Snake came around with his
trench coat and shotgun, which is one of many reasons
why you won't find many people more popular in the
New York underworld than her.

Sofia's success at seducing the entire wiseguy social
scene was the key to Jackie's underworld success. Jackie
was just a neighborhood knockaround guy when Sofia
set him up first with Vinnie's heroin dealer friends and
then with Sonny's crew. The price for Sofia utilizing her
influence and feminine wiles to further Jackie's career
was that Sofia demanded and received a full partnership
in her big brother's rackets. This essentially meant that I
was the partner not only of Jackie di Padova but also his
foxy, yet no less formidable, sister—which was fine by
me. Between Phil's mom and my cocaine hookups Gladis
and Marta, I had been working with female crooks for
my entire criminal life, so I had ample experience charming them. Female crooks love me because I'm intelligent,

well spoken, and not the usual meathead who is threatened or feverishly aroused just because they have tits. I treat them with the respect and honesty I would give to a male crook *and* the sweetness that I use on women I am trying to charm.

Working for brother and sister may have been my happiest time in the Mafia; if I had not been forced to leave Florida, I might never have ratted on or left the underworld. Jackie and Sofia still make huge money without breaking a sweat or ever seeing the face of any cop they don't already own. Since I was Jerry's boy, they took incredible care of me, and in return I made them enormous profits.

Within a month of my arrival, Jackie moved me into a luxury beachside condo in a gated community that his local crew had reserved for their extramarital liaisons. I began my routine every morning by looking out of my window and watching the sun rise over the Gulf of Mexico. Rarely a day ended without Jackie escorting me to a night on the town at Fort Lauderdale's and Miami's best restaurants, lounges, and parties.

Mafiosi tend not to be needlessly generous: Jackie and Sofia doted on me because I made them cash like no one else could. I was a priceless addition to their fledgling porn operation. I reported to work each day at the di Padova family's wholesale porn warehouse, where they marketed and sold videos to porn shops across the Southeast. My porn industry connections, stash of porno movie masters, and skill as a con artist gave the di Padovas unparalleled access to stolen, extorted, or hugely discounted merchandise. Thanks to me, Jackie and Sofia's distribution business could offer tapes at under-the-table black market prices, which led to their porn shop clientele doubling and then tripling in a matter of months.

I also filmed and sold a great deal of my own porn in Florida through their company. Before I sent the masters to the porn distributors in the San Fernando Valley, I would mass-produce a couple thousand copies using Jackie's equipment and blank tapes from Jerry Zimmerman. Since the distributors paid for the filming and the tapes were obtained using bad checks, every VHS we sold was pure profit.

From 8 to 11 a.m. every morning, I would oversee operations at the wholesale porn warehouse and dial up business for the di Padovas. I would also act as their liaison to the underworld early risers; Sonny Franzese, Jerry Zimmerman, Jimmy Coonan, and Brooklyn racketeer Frank "Boobie" DeAngelo were all my frequent phone buddies.

At around 10 a.m., my shift as warehouse boss came to an end and Sofia's began. Called "The Prez" by all of the employees, Sofia was hardworking, competent, and a hit with shop owners and distributors alike, who would buy anything for the chance to flirt with her over the phone. Between my winning, sunny charm and Sofia's sultry way with words, the di Padovas' porn warehouse consistently racked up orders throughout the morning.

At 11 a.m., my porn responsibilities ended when Jackie picked me up at the warehouse and drove me to the headquarters of his telemarketing scam empire. Jackie rented huge expanses of office space in various cities and states to house "phone rooms" full of minimum-wage slaves who called up strangers and tried to sell them cruise trips, vacations, timeshares, golf clubs, and whatever else anyone paid us to sell. The telemarketers conducted some wholly legitimate and legal transactions; the only catch was that the products they sold were shoddy.

Jackie sold people trips on the skankiest cruise ships imaginable, timeshares at a Fort Lauderdale hotel that would not have looked out of place in war-torn Baghdad, and merchandise made by the finest craftsmen in China's child-labor pool. Of course, Jackie also indulged in the occasional Jerry Zimmerman–style scam, like eliciting donations to fake charities. To avoid federal mail fraud charges, he had the donations picked up by local couriers to avoid crossing state lines.

Within minutes of our arrival at the telemarketing business every day, I'd observe Jackie as his twin weaknesses of boredom and hunger slowly short-circuited him. We rarely lasted more than an hour at the office before Jackie announced that it was time for a long, expensive lunch. Restaurants are almost always the preferred venue of conducting business with New York mobsters, who tend to be the most gluttonous and gastronomically snobby of all mafiosi. If you want to know what working in the New York Mafia is like, spend four or five hours a day in the type of Italian restaurant that caters to fat old guido loudmouths who only stop eating to bitch about the local sports team or tell dirty jokes as they choke and wheeze with sweaty laughter. That's the Mob. Jackie was better than most because at least he was intelligent and funny, but he still had the table manners and appetite of a tyrannosaurus.

After our long lunch, we returned to the telemarketing office, and I collected all of the day's credit slips. This was before it became easy to conduct and verify credit card transactions electronically, so a large part of my day was spent manually collecting these little slips, running the data, and finding a bank that would accept our business. Since both our volume and the proportion of cancelled charges were so high, every bank in

Florida and California gradually turned away our business. Eventually I had to call my old crewmember Phil and convince his Mexican gangster mom to escort us to Guadalajara and introduce us to a carnet bank there that would handle our business.

Guadalajara operated according to rules Jackie and I understood: you needed to bribe everyone to do anything. The soldiers at the Guadalajara airport even refused to let us leave the terminal without paying "airport tax."

By 3 p.m., the hardworking Jackie had usually lost all interest in pretending to be a legitimate businessman. With barely concealed impatience, Jackie roamed the building until he found me and could shout his beloved catchphrase: "LET'S GO FIND SOME PIGS!" "Pigs," of course, was Jackie's pet term for women.

I'm not sure whether Jackie appreciated my abilities more as a criminal or as a wingman. Trained by Joey Avila and Officer Jerry, I was the first criminal partner Jackie had ever found who could keep up with him as he stalked the posh yuppie wine bars, cocktail lounges, and restaurants where he hunted his "wild pigs." Hunting for women with me presented Jackie with a serious strategic advantage: the wealthy, middle-aged divorcées and trophy wives that Jackie preferred usually traveled with friends who loved the prospect of a dangerous one-night stand with a young, muscular, ethnically exotic criminal. Jackie fed me a steady diet of older, doting women who tried to buy my monogamy with their checkbooks. This was helpful since I needed money to buy drinks for the college girls across the street at the beachside Howard Johnson hotel.

One of Jackie's buddies we liked to party with was Joey Castellano, the grandson of Paul Castellano, the Gambino Family boss whom John Gotti assassinated and replaced. Joey C. was a spoiled rich kid who claimed to own commercial strip malls, restaurants, and clubs all over Fort Lauderdale. I befriended Joey and was regularly invited to his wiseguy poker nights. I would have accepted more frequently if not for Peter "Petey Bop" Sabatino, the 240-pound gnat that always followed him around.

You could not spend a minute in the same room as Petey Bop without him telling you that he was carrying around a black leather satchel stuffed with a pistol and his "shylock" (loan shark) cash, as if it were kindergarten show-and-tell. Petey Bop smelled like a rat to me, so I never liked being in the same room as him and his little black purse.

The only thing I liked about Petey Bop was his mental-case son James, who scammed his way around the world by claiming to be a powerful hip-hop record executive. The recently incarcerated James Sabatino pulled one of my all-time favorite pranks when, in 2008, he convinced the *Los Angeles Times* to publish his patently false story that rapper P. Diddy had involved him in the plot to assassinate rival Tupac Shakur back when James was still a teenager. James supported his story by typing up fake FBI documents on his prison typewriter in which he refers to himself as a feared Mafia heavyweight, which is true only in that the kid is Italian and must weigh 300 pounds.

I did not have a particularly oppressive work schedule in Florida, so I had plenty of time to enjoy myself in a new state where no one knew who I was, and I had friends in the police department. It was incredibly liberating to be an easygoing, anonymous crook again after so many years of being stalked by the police.

With the new low-key tricks that Jerry Zimmerman

had taught me, making money was ridiculously easy, safe, and stress-free. All I ever had to do was open a bank account using one of my countless fake California IDs, keep it open long enough for the restrictions to expire, and then write a flurry of bad checks. I could score a few thousand dollars each weekend by renting a moving truck, taking orders from the local wiseguys for big-ticket merchandise like furniture, and then buying the quick-to-load floor models at stores throughout Florida using the bad checks. After I resold all of the merchandise to Jackie and Joey Castellano's friends from the back of my moving truck, I'd leave the checkbook in some sleazy part of town for a bum or gangbanger to find, use, and get arrested with. That way, the case would be closed, and no one would ever look for me.

In retrospect, my life would have been as close to ideal as humanly possible had I stayed in Florida with Jackie and Sofia. The girls were hot; the climate was perfect; the lifestyle was laidback; the social scene was great; the crime was easy; the cops were crooked; the FBI wasn't interested in our crew; and Jackie and Sofia were generous, capable, and trustworthy partners. Jackie even offered to hook me up with a Subway restaurant franchise as a front business and long-term investment in the Broward County area. Between Fort Lauderdale and nearby Miami, I had ample opportunity to continue to advance both in the American Mafia or, if I changed my mind, in the international drug trade.

More importantly, I had found unprecedented peace of mind in Florida. The four years I spent in California at the foot of my Zen criminal master, Jerry Zimmerman, had finally paid off, far away from all the cocaine temptations and long-standing violent feuds that had obstructed my progress there.

Everything in my new environment inclined me toward heeding Jerry's advice and behaving myself: the mellowing side-effects of aging, my probation and the accompanying threat of jail, the absence of any serious physical threat to me on the streets, my older and comparatively bourgeois social circle, and the fact that, if I were arrested, I would be responsible for dumping a world of shit onto my friends Jackie and Sofia. Besides, acting like a batshit 1980s-style cocaine cowboy in 1994 in a Spring Break party-town like Fort Lauderdale made no sense socially or professionally. With every incentive to become a "good" crook, I finally retired my coke-dealer way of life and became a full-fledged disciple of Jerry Zimmerman's white-collar criminal jujutsu. I serviced my demon by sparring for a couple hours every morning at the local boxing gym and spent the rest of the day as a smiling, relaxed, happy-go-lucky, pot-smoking hood.

But you would not be reading my story if I could have maintained this lifestyle. I should have heard Fate cracking its knuckles when the Florida probation officials took one look at my record and refused to accept my transfer from California's system. This would turn out to be the beginning of an apocalyptic decline in my luck.

The Florida justice system's refusal to babysit me meant that I had to fly back to Orange County every month to check in with my parole officer. I didn't mind since it let me drive up to Porno Valley and cut deals. However, after two years of contentious negotiations with the Florida officials, someone pissed off my parole officer and caused her to lose her patience. Without any warning, she called me up and ordered me to return home immediately or prepare to go to jail. I was devastated.

So was California. My arrival home during the

early morning hours of January 17, 1994, induced an immediate and severe allergic reaction: California was instantaneously wracked with a pants-shittingly violent earthquake. Even for a seasoned SoCal native, the Northridge Earthquake of 1994 was terrifying because it emerged from absolute stillness as a full-force, paint-mixer-severe earthquake without any buildup whatsoever. The destruction was immense, with $20 billion worth of damage centered on Porno Valley. America's smut industry was well and truly assfucked: tens of millions of dollars worth of uninsured, untaxed, off-the-books inventory and illegal sets were biblically scourged from the face of the planet. A train was swept clean off the tracks behind Batman Esposito and Tommy Sinopoli's warehouse and barely missed blasting through their offices like a giant flaming dong.

They were lucky: the giant flaming dong of fate was headed my way instead. Jackie and I had being doing our business at the bank in Guadalajara for a while, which took quite a bit of bribery; they nearly shut us down on the very first day when they received suspicious transfers totaling nearly $100,000. We painted everyone's palm green every time we visited and even hired the bank manager's wife to a no-show job, but the Mexicans were shortsighted, short-money people. On my next trip to Mexico, I was short on cash and failed to make an unexpected bribe, and that was that. I was detained, escorted by the army to the airport, and compelled to take the next plane to the United States. Our bank account was seized, and there went my $86,000 nest egg from Florida. The only good news is that, despite having been banned from leaving the United States by my probation agreement, I got deported from Mexico without American law enforcement noticing.

The next dong was delivered via telephone: the news that Phil's tiny Mayan gangster mom had just dropped dead without warning. I always loved that crooked little Oompa-Loompa; she was yet another of my formative influences to die or disappear. Of my old friends and mentors, everyone was dead, imprisoned, on the lam, addicted to drugs, brain-fried, violently opposed to ever speaking to me again, or Mike Marvich. The only person from my circle who had become a conventional success was Babar—which tells you all you need to know about the black humor of a life in the underworld.

"There are lots of stereotypes about porn that are false, but one that is absolutely true is that all the girls are fucking nuts. There are some nice girls; there are some smart girls. But almost all of them are nuts. They all have daddy issues. Seriously. I've filmed a couple thousand scenes with them. I know these women. NUTS."

Chuck "Philmore Butts" Martino

Top Porn Star Lays, Ranked by Kenji
5. Tabitha Stevens
4. Savannah
3. Crystal Gold
2. Jill Kelly
1. Amber Lynn

I was twenty-five when I returned to Porno Valley; though I had matured in my two years away, I can't say I noticed any change from anyone else in the business. With my newfound mellowness and respectable way of conducting myself, I felt so superior to the garish freaks in Pornoland that I no longer had my old wariness and unease around my porn colleagues. Without that fear to keep me away, porn industry people gradually became my new social circle—and there stopped my progress towards maturity.

One day shortly after my return, I was on set watching the camera monitor with a production assistant and some friends as porn icon Chuck Martino was fucking a girl bent over a couch. The cameraman was crouching behind Chuck, capturing the between-the-legs "ball-sack cam" angle that's customary in doggy-style scenes. As we watched on the monitor, we started to notice that fine white crumbs were falling from between their legs. "Oh, my god, are those toilet-paper dingleberries?" I asked in disgust.

The cameraman panned up to reveal a foot-long sub sandwich that Chuck was happily gnawing on while he fucked the actress. He must have stashed it on the set in case he got hungry in the middle of the shoot.

"Chuck, what the fuck are you doing?"

Chuck took a second to swallow and lick his lips before answering. "What?! I'm hungry. You guys don't need my face for doggy-style. Can you tell my mouth is full when I moan?"

"Dumbfuck, you're dropping crumbs all over."

"Oh, shit, I'll be more careful," Chuck said as he took a very dainty bite of the sandwich. The actress was pretty offended that her pussy wasn't good enough to distract Chuck from his hunger, but he didn't notice.

"How's the sandwich, Chuck?"

"Oh, it's fucking good. Wanna bite?" Chuck mumbled with a full mouth as he extended the sandwich to the camera and continued his mindless, no-hands thrusts. Chuck was the same way with his women. Every time I happened to walk in or be around when he was having off-camera sex, he'd take a break from the festivities and check to see if I "wanted some," as if he were a consummate host asking a guest if he wanted to sample the cheese platter.

That was Chuck Martino, the most chilled-out porn star in the world and the ideal successor to Peter North as my male anchor. A tan Chippendale's dancer with a goatee, the usual enamel fortress of bright white teeth, and a Kirk Douglas jawline, Chuck was always up for work, always ready to party, and always in a cooperative mood. Chuck could fuck whoever, whenever, wherever, keeping a hard-on for hours while filing his nails, eating lunch, doing his taxes, or talking on the phone. He was practically a prop—just a big hard dick that was on call twenty-four hours a day—which made him the perfect male porn star.

With Chuck, I could film ten scenes in the time it took me to film one scene with Peter. Unlike Peter, Chuck was also a likeable person and a great partier. As a chick-magnet and my unofficial casting agent, he scouted and seduced girls at strip clubs and bars, in which we would film improvised, spur-of-the-moment scenes.

One of the girls Chuck met we outright adopted and transformed into a full-fledged porn star: a stacked blonde named Joy Marquart, whom Chuck renamed "Farrah." We met Farrah at a Tampa strip club during a visit to Florida to film a few flicks and discuss business with Jackie di Padova and his crew. Within moments of looking at Chuck, Farrah was begging to film a scene, so we took her to a nearby multilevel parking garage and filmed the two of them fucking on the stairwell. Chuck apparently did good work because Farrah quit her stripping job that moment and insisted on driving with us, in her stripper gear, to Miami for our meeting with Jackie. Farrah fucked Chuck in the passenger seat of my car the entire drive down the Florida Turnpike. Then she sashayed her sweaty and sex-stinking body all around the exclusive Italian restaurant that hosted our private dinner with Jackie di Padova, Joey Castellano, Petey Bop, and numerous other wiseguys.

Farrah went on to have a pretty successful porn

career over the next five years, though she eventually aged herself out of stardom. With her diminished earning potential, Farrah picked up on some of the tricks and connections she had made hanging around me and became a financial scam artist. She went to jail for ripping off banks using forged documents, which, considering she was about as intelligent as a pineapple, should tell you that she had plenty of help.

That is one of the great structural evils of the porn business: girls who get used to making money and getting everything they want thanks to their looks become obsolete by the age of thirty. With no other professional skills, they turn to full-time prostitution and ultra-degrading gangbang and pseudo-snuff films to make their cash. Those revenue streams rely on novelty and run dry quickly, usually leaving the porn girls spoiled, deeply in credit-card debt, too surgically altered to mix with normal society, and progressively reliant on alcohol and narcotics to cope. Some, like my fuck-buddy Savannah, commit suicide.

A busty blonde with long bangs and a bright smile on her round, cheeky, girl-next-door face, Savannah first met me on the set of one of Chuck's movies. She was about twenty years old, a plump little sex bomb who was sitting in hot pink lingerie while an older woman curled her hair into little-girl ringlets. Though Savannah had a bitchy attitude with everyone on set because she was one of the biggest stars in porn, I disarmed her with my blasé contempt for her "celebrity."

To impress me, Savannah started bragging about how she had been the underage girlfriend of rock star Gregg Allman, and how she had matured into the adult lover of goofball comedian Pauly Shore and Slash and Axl Rose from Guns N' Roses. Toward the end of our conversation,

Savannah handed me her number and introduced me to her mom—the woman styling her hair into the Shirley Temple 'do.

Growing up in a family that dysfunctional, I thought, should have made Savannah a sex demon. When I took her home, I was disappointed; she was about as active as a crash-test dummy in bed. I only learned later that severe bouts of depression and drug abuse rendered her periodically unable to summon the energy to fuck on- or off-camera. We feuded or fucked depending on the fluctuations of her mental state over the next couple years. In 1994, an allegedly shit-faced Savannah crashed her car into a fence, busting her nose and slicing up her face. Terrified that she would be worthless without her good looks, Savannah hurried home and shot herself in the head. She was twenty-three.

Almost a year after Savannah's suicide came another pathetic case, the death of Alex Jordan. Alex was a porn star in her mid-thirties with a wild lion's mane of 1980s hair and a tight, muscular body. Though she did not possess a porn headliner's face or youth, Alex was still a bankable supporting act thanks to her rabid sexuality and niche appeal as an athletic, all-natural fitness model. Alex came across like a woman hysterically searching for the remedy to her nervous, manic unhappiness; she attacked everything in life with the reckless energy of a terminally ill woman who will try anything in the hope of finding a cure.

This sadness manifested itself in an obsession with exercise, a feverish-bordering-on-desperate appetite for sex, and drug abuse. But Alex was also unique among porn girls for her naked honesty and great sense of humor. We had a lot of fun making jokes and pranking each other on a naughty-nurse porno I made. Shortly afterwards, her beloved pet parrot died at a bad time in her mental cycle, and she hanged herself from a clothing rod in her closet one morning.

When mutual friends told me that she had killed herself out of despair for her lost pet parrot (she had addressed her suicide note to the parrot), I remember thinking how sad it was that I wasn't even surprised to hear a story that fucking crazy.

> *"Buck Adams was a strong performer, but hung like a rabbit. He always kept in great shape, though. In the peak of his career, he didn't have one inch of fat on his body. The time he spent at the gym, I spent at the buffet table."*
>
> Ron Jeremy

> *"I don't even want female actresses anymore. Dress up men in the parts. No women . . . want to go back to the days of Shakespeare where men played women's parts. If someone has a problem with that, give them an extra $100. Women are way too much trouble. That's it. Call me when they're off the set. I no longer want to be around women. . . . Fag hags! . . . Everyone has one. Even those men who aren't gay have fag hags these days. . . . Fuck women hookers. Hours late on fucking heroin, on crack, on every kind of glue there is. They can all kiss my fucking ass. And when my crew people stick up for those fucking people or for somebody's girlfriend, then fuck them too. The fucking show is over."*
>
> Buck Adams
> Being cracked out and crazy,
> as usual (as quoted by Luke Ford)

"The problem with Cal Jammer was that he was always threatening to kill himself and blow people away. He was my buddy, and after a while you can't take him seriously anymore. No one took Cal seriously because he literally threatened to kill himself just about every day. Well, he proved us wrong there."

Chuck Martino

Take for instance my longtime friend Cal Jammer, who set out to claim the head of porn icon Jill Kelly and instead had to accept the consolation prize of putting a bullet in his own. I first met Cal in the 1980s when he was considered a rising blue-chip porn prospect on his way to "regular" status. Cal was like Peter North without the gay porn past, another "too handsome for porn" guy with a spokesmodel smile, athletic body, immaculate porn mullet, and a capable dick.

Behind the good looks and usual frat-boy swagger, Cal was a weak man with the emotional maturity of a catty teenage girl. His dumb roguish grin and brash attitude were covering up the usual toxic dump of envy, insecurity, and bitterness. He was the sort of porn bimbo who would walk up to you and ask if his dick was big enough, if his biceps were toned enough; did you like the color of his mullet, should he dye it?

The cause of Cal's Chernobyl was a skinny, tan, blond tomboy I met in the lobby of porn studio Video Exclusives. I was waiting for a meeting when this flat-chested girl with a backpack purse slung over her sundress cautiously stepped inside and tiptoed around with the barely concealed curiosity and excitement of a novice. Though she lacked the curves of a typical headliner, I immediately knew she would be a star because her bright eyes and naughty, nervous, lip-biting smile filled my entire body with sexual tension. She had the rarest attribute of all among porn girls: a beautiful face that communicated. She didn't just look hot; between her evocative eyes and her smile, you could tell that she was smart, funny, and a real sweetheart.

She introduced herself to me as Jill Kelly, and I'll admit it was the first time in my porn career that I was actually smitten with an actress. To my surprise, my surreal suspicion that this girl was actually *smart* and *sane* and *funny* and *nice* turned out to be true; she even read books for pleasure! These attributes were so rare in porn that it bordered on supernatural; it would have been scarcely less believable if Jill had told me that she was my representative in Congress. Though Jill had the entire staff of Video Exclusives bewitched in minutes, for whatever reason she focused on me and gave me her address in Apple Valley. "Come visit, and we'll have fun."

Apple Valley was, by California standards, on the other side of the earth, but I drove to Jill's house through a "hell freezes over" snowstorm like a man possessed.

Jill greeted me at the door with the most disarming, relaxed casualness, as if I were her old high-school boyfriend. For a paranoid freak who hated sleeping anywhere but in the security of his fortified apartment, I felt completely safe and at home in Jill's apartment. I spent the next few days at her place, sleeping in her bed; we didn't fuck—not yet—we just flirted, drank, and had fun. The high point of the weekend was when Jill sat me down in her living room and gave me the most spectacular, hypnotizing lap dance of my life to prove that her braggadocio about her skills as an exotic dancer was justified.

After that weekend, I was positive that Jill would

become one of the biggest stars in the history of porn; her Hollywood-ready face possessed so much raw charisma that it was palpable even after being shellacked with the porn clown makeup and flattened into two-dimensional photos and films. After Jill bought some nice fake tits, nothing could stop her from becoming a mainstream adult-entertainment brand name.

There was one problem: Jill's husband was aspiring porn superstar Cal Jammer. Cal had seduced Jill using the age-old "I'll get you into the business" line, only he had no intention of pimping out his new love; much to his consternation, his ambitious stripper girlfriend went behind his back and broke into porn anyway. As soon as Cal realized that Jill was becoming a superstar, envy killed his ability to get an erection on set; he lost his manhood, his career, and eventually Jill.

While Jill became one of the most recognizable faces in America that no one will admit to recognizing, Cal languished as an envious porn also-ran and Jill's venomously jealous and possessive husband. He quickly transformed from an amiable jock into a wife-beating creep consumed with resentment of Jill's success. After Jill fled their home, Cal lost his mind completely. I should know; for some reason, he chose to hang around my sets, where he even managed to creep out the Hells Angels and the Crips. He was constantly ranting about Jill and later Chuck Martino, who was fucking Jill. Not only was Jill no longer his woman now that he couldn't get it up, but she was with a certifiable porn stud like Chuck who, in contrast, was some kind of erectile Jedi.

One day in January 1995, I was at Buck Adams's office when Jill called and said that Cal was threatening to kill her on the telephone. Even though I dug Jill, I did not get involved. There are two immutable rules to having fun in the porn business: never get involved in other porn relationships, and never try to be Captain Save-A-Ho.

I knew better than to try to mediate between the feuding lovers, but Buck felt he had to back up Chuck Martino when Chuck called him and said he was going to Jill's house to ensure her safety. On the way to Jill's house, Buck spoke with Cal on the phone and told him that, if he wanted to hurt someone so bad, he should just hurt himself. Buck then called Jill and told her to hide. Under no circumstance was she to answer the door.

When Cal started pounding on Jill's door, Jill was hiding in a locked bathroom. The desperate banging on the door stopped after a few minutes with the crack of a gunshot. Cal, with his limp dick, was dead in her driveway. They found a birthday card and $500 for Jill in his pocket. In the adult entertainment press, it was reported that Jill occasionally took Cal's urn to the set for "inspiration." As far as I am concerned, that story is about as plausible as saying I gave Joey Avila's skull a good-luck rub before every crime I committed.

Our porn circle would suffer one last casualty in the '90s, and this time it was a legitimate surprise. Israel Gonzalez was my prop guy and production assistant who specialized in making prosthetic dicks that ejaculated the piña colada mix that we used when actors couldn't produce satisfactory cumshots. I figured Israel was a normal guy since he didn't work on-camera and seemed like your average chilled-out Mexican pothead. I was wrong: without warning, Israel snapped and held his girlfriend hostage. When he fled and a cop found him hiding at a porn studio, Israel shot the cop in cold blood. After a literal Mexican standoff with police surrounding the porn studio, Israel chose suicide over a death sentence for killing a cop.

The fact that life in porn had transformed even the agreeable little Mexican dude who makes prosthetic dongs into a psychopathic cop-killer only made me feel increasingly well adjusted and psychologically healthy. After all, while everyone was suffering meltdowns, I was actually mellowing out. I seemed to be the only person who stayed cool in the hothouse of dysfunction. For the first time in my adult life, I began to feel *normal*—and then I married Tabitha Stevens.

"Holy shit, this fucking family ain't for real."

Jimmy "The Weasel" Fratianno
Former Acting Boss of the L.A. Family
in *The Last Mafioso*

When I returned from Florida in 1994 to my old cocaine territory in California, I decided I needed a tough, no-bullshit partner like Jackie di Padova to keep me in line and away from the temptations of the drug trade. Jerry Zimmerman was good for moneymaking scams, but I already knew from experience that working with him did not provide adequate rush and gangland prestige to keep me occupied. Ironically, I needed a real gangster to keep me honest.

There was no other candidate besides Vincent "Jimmy" Caci, the Los Angeles Mafia Family's capo in Palm Springs and an old acquaintance of mine from my time living there in the late '80s and early '90s. Like Jimmy and innumerable other criminals, I had moved to Palm Springs for the boutique town's reputation as one of the least policed, least nosy, and most tolerant communities in America. Within days of my arrival, I started sniffing around to see who was the heaviest crook in town so I could start making money, which in short order led to a brokered introduction with Jimmy.

Since I was smart, well-dressed, and had the good sense to be polite and use clean language, Jimmy took a shine to me; I was very different from the Andrew Dice Clay–style wannabe goombahs who usually approached Mafia legends. Jimmy was imprisoned almost right after our meeting, leaving me to pursue my Mafia career with Jerry Zimmerman and Jackie di Padova instead; Jimmy let me know that, whenever he got out, I was free to join up with him. When I returned to California in 1994, Jimmy was out of jail, and I began to work in his crew.

Born to a poor family in the Italian ghettoes of Buffalo in the Roaring Twenties, Jimmy was a Depression-era street urchin and petty criminal. Nicknamed "Torch" or "Torchy" by his friend and mentor Willie Sutton and some of his buddies from the legendary Purple Gang, Jimmy first made his name as an armed robber and safecracker who was a master with a blowtorch. In his twenties, Jimmy branched out in the rough stuff—shootings, bombings, kidnappings—and regularly sold his services to warring gangs and strikebreakers. Later, Caci was nicknamed "Horse," which derived from his gambling habit or the then-current nickname for heroin.

Jimmy was an old-school, James Cagney–style outlaw, a reckless tough who bragged about getting busted sometime in the Truman administration for sticking up a brothel with a machine gun. I've seen Jimmy's police file: it's thicker than a dictionary, a year-by-year record of a life spent doggedly pursuing blue-collar, meat-and-potatoes violent crime. By middle age, Jimmy looked like a central-casting Hollywood hood: a hard-staring guido with a prison-honed physique, a square-headed crew cut, and stubbly, rugged good looks.

Arrested with Mafia godfathers Russell Bufalino of the Scranton Family and Frank Valenti of the Rochester Family on more than one occasion, Jimmy told me that he had opportunities to join either of those two families in addition to his hometown Buffalo Family. Though clearly in demand, Jimmy declined to become a made man, claiming that he was already far too familiar with the frigid prison cells of Upstate New York and Pennsylvania to invite increased police attention. Had Jimmy accepted any of those three crime families' offers, I am certain he would have died a godfather.

Instead, Jimmy fled west with his crew of wizened Buffalo felons with the hope that a change of location might make them harder to catch. Wary of straitlaced Protestant towns, Jimmy decided on the cosmopolitan resort town of Palm Springs, California, which was a well-known safe haven and "open territory" for Italian mobsters. Within a few years, Jimmy had established lucrative rackets in bookmaking, gambling, loan sharking, and burglaries in his Palm Springs territory, sometimes partnering with the Los Angeles Family.

When the offer to get made in the L.A. Family was extended, Jimmy hesitated. "I had a good crew of my own guys, good money, no headaches. I didn't need nobody," Jimmy told me twenty-five years later. For reasons that he could not verbalize, Jimmy joined the Milano Family and was quickly promoted to capo of what remained his mostly autonomous Palm Springs crew.

Jimmy was always the outcast of the L.A. Family, an auto mechanic with dirty fingernails trying to fit in at the country club. Los Angeles Family boss Pete Milano and his top capo Louie Gelfuso were suburban, bourgeois West Coast criminals who became queasy at the sight of blood and strove to avoid the company of blue-collar street thugs. They lead a small (ten to fifteen "made" members, another ten to fifteen serious associates), nonviolent, and cautious criminal outfit that has little muscle, no "turf," and no exclusive rackets. You could rape Pete Milano's wife and set his kid on fire, and the likely response would be a criminal complaint filed by his attorney.

Compared to the Colombo Family, which takes pride in beating people up on a daily basis and killing someone every once in a while, the L.A. Family is positively allergic to violence and the police attention it attracts. Anthony Fiato accurately captured the style and attitude of Milano's crew when he dubbed it The Members Only Mob because all of the schlubby, suburban wiseguys wore cheap Members Only jackets in impersonation of Pete. There was no style, no swagger, no balls.

Since Jimmy, despite his advanced age and wealthy Palm Springs surroundings, still clearly thought, acted, and talked like a New York blue-collar street thug, the L.A. Family leadership didn't understand him or trust his abilities. He was white trash to them, an Italian redneck who could be expected to jeopardize family interests through reckless threats and violence. There was an unbridgeable gulf between the gangland authenticity of Jimmy, a man built by the prison system and the Italian ghettoes of Buffalo, and the suburban pseudo-gangsters of California. One was a domesticated, neutered lap-kitty, and the other was a fucking tiger.

To illustrate the unique cultural and criminal niche that Jimmy Caci to this day occupies, I will now transcribe a phone message that I received from him on one of the anonymous cell phones I carried on the streets. Jimmy got the number when I used the phone to call his lawyer and ask when he was expected for a court date. I made the mistake of not leaving my name. The report of this anonymous phone call convinced Jimmy that someone was claiming to be with him who wasn't, and one week later, the following tirade was spit onto my telephone:

"You cocksucker you! You understand? You don't hang around with Jimmy Caci, you fucking asshole, whoever you are! You understand? Come out in the open, you motherfucker. You understand me? You're a motherfucker! You understand? Come out in the open, whoever the fuck you are. You want to be a wise cocksucker, huh? That is, that's what you want to be, you fucking asshole? Huh, you want to hang out with Jimmy Caci, you motherfucker? That's what everybody wants to hang out with, Jimmy Caci. That's why I'm in trouble, you fucking assholes, all you fucking piece of rat motherfuckers, all of yas. You understand? Now why don't you reveal yourself, you motherfucker, and I'll meet you somewheres, the cocksucker that you are! You are a motherfucker!"

This incredible argument with silence was not an impression of Hollywood gangster movies; it was the type of vintage guido viciousness that *inspired* Hollywood gangster movies. This was Jimmy Caci at his most unfiltered and honest, the product of a 1940s bank-robber mind-set. Jimmy Caci, like Sonny Franzese, was an adult New York mafioso when Lucky Luciano was still a boss. He was authentic, a relic from the Mafia's golden age bumbling around 1990s Palm Springs without a clue of what to make of his surroundings. Working with him was like *Back to the Future*.

That's why the Milano wing of the L.A. crew had trouble relating to Jimmy. They were products of the Mob in its degraded Hollywood form, which was as out-of-place as a hockey league in the Congo. Unlike them, Jimmy was a product of a family, a neighborhood, a culture, and an era where the Mafia was the dominating and defining influence. It was like the divide between an

Orthodox Jew who grows up in a kibbutz in Israel and my secular Jewish high-school buddies in Orange County. Jimmy was defined by the Mafia, programmed by his surroundings to treat the Mafia and its tradition with the reverence and possessive cultural pride that old Italian women reserve for the Pope.

In his own mind, Jimmy *was* the oath he swore when he got made—the way a Catholic priest's identity is determined by his marriage to the Church. That's how the old-school guys back East were: When they burned the saint's card in their hand during the initiation ceremony, they replaced their devout Catholicism with an equally fervent sect of Mafiaism.

With his simple, straightforward, Old World–peasant outlook, Jimmy lived as if the only commandment he would be judged on was "Thou Shalt Obey the Rules of the Mafia." A reckless outlaw in all other respects, Jimmy was a neurotic stickler for the rules and rituals of the Mafia and would suffer conniptions when he saw them disregarded. The rituals, the mysticism, the rules mattered to Jimmy; organized crime was the only organization in a life that was otherwise lived in total, primal chaos.

Jimmy could rob and murder, but as long as he did so according to proper Mafia procedure he would die "a stand-up guy" and "a man of honor." It was a simple moral code that facilitated criminal behavior by suppressing a mafioso's conscience in all respects other than his relationship with his crime family. As bizarre as Jimmy's righteous way of thinking about crime was to me, I envied his delusions. He was a natural. Jimmy went about his business with less second-guessing and more deadly focus than any other criminal I had met since Mike Marvich.

Though Jimmy never wasted time thinking, he

instinctually understood the gangster lifestyle far better than his boss, Pete Milano, ever would. Pete lived in fear of the consequences of the Mafia life; Jimmy embraced the Life fearlessly and reveled in it. While Pete conducted himself like an upstanding citizen to lower the chances of getting arrested, Jimmy lived moment to moment without any constraint, reflection, or worry. Jimmy knew the entire point of being a gangster is to enjoy your freedom from society's values and do absolutely whatever the fuck you want without any concern for the consequences or what people think.

If someone disrespects you, punch him in the face; if you want something, take it; if a girl is sexy, fuck her. What's the point of such a dangerous, self-destructive lifestyle if you still have to act like a polite, well-behaved square?

"This isn't just some club, Ken," Jimmy used to tell me, indirectly letting off steam about Pete Milano and his strictly nonviolent way of doing business. "You know, we're not just a bunch of guys who get together and talk and have funny names for each other. We're not the Elks. I'm not a Boy Scout. We're supposed to be gangsters over here, that's what this thing used to be and is supposed to be.

"Lemme tell you somethin', kid. Nothing can replace a good asskicking. You understand? There's a time to talk, there's a time to wait, and there's a time to kick fucking ass. I ain't got time to worry about the repercussions; I'll kick ass and worry later. Fuck anyone who expects me to take shit and smile, you understand? Jimmy Caci don't eat shit, and Jimmy Caci don't take shit. That's who Jimmy Caci is. I'm no tax-paying, country club motherfucker."

Though Jimmy claimed not to be a country club

motherfucker, he nonetheless fancied himself as something more refined and upright than a common, shameless crook. Befitting his New York immigrant upbringing,
Jimmy liked to picture himself as the very picture of a
traditional Sicilian mafioso, the knightly "man of honor"
who is defined equally by his integrity and his asskicking prowess. As uneducated and uncultured as Jimmy
was, he conducted himself conscientiously to prove on a
minute-by-minute basis that he was a gentleman who just
happened to live by a code of conduct that sanctioned all
manner of predatory and illegal behavior.

Jimmy was a gangster, but he was also the former
altar boy who performed the sign of the cross whenever he passed a Church; the charmer who pulled out
a woman's chair at the dinner table and never cursed or
spoke harshly in her presence; the self-made man who
refused to accept gifts, charity, or handouts from anyone;
the unfailingly polite and gracious customer who never
called a waiter or a cashier anything besides "Sir" or
"Ma'am"; the blue-collar striver who took pride that his
hair was always neatly barbered, his cheeks and throat
cleanly shaved, and his daily outfit—a sports coat and
slacks—always pressed and coordinated. If no one else
took Jimmy seriously, that only meant Jimmy had to take
himself seriously enough for everyone.

Though Jimmy never regretted committing crimes or
acts of violence in the course of his job, he always felt
intensely self-conscious whenever he committed crimes
against etiquette. Jimmy deluded himself into believing
that his temper tantrums might "expose" the lack of
social polish that he did not suspect was obvious to everyone he met. Jimmy might rob some woman's husband
of their life savings, but saying "ass" in front of her was
out of the question. Jimmy would beat a man bloody,

threaten to kill the next guy, shake down a few degenerate gamblers, and then call *me* a dirtbag for wearing a T-shirt in public.

Jimmy's traditionalism applied just as incoherently to drugs, which were proscribed by Mafia rules in theory but almost never in practice. When the Los Angeles Family leadership convened at a house in Westlake to conduct the initiation ceremonies for Orange County gangster and minor-league drug dealer Robert "Fat Bobby" Paduano and others, Jimmy claimed that he and his brother, lounge singer Bobby Milano, left in a huff the moment they saw Fat Bobby. "I don't want nuthin' to do with dope," Jimmy explained to the scandalized L.A. Family leadership. "Bobby better clean up his house if he wants to be around Jimmy Caci. I don't associate with that shit."

Jimmy's absurd self-righteousness reached its peak with restaurants. Somewhere in his criminal travels, some idiot convinced Jimmy that any restaurant that wasn't fitted with wall-to-wall carpet on the floors was beneath serving a man of class like Jimmy Caci. Jimmy drove other gangsters crazy by demanding that meetings planned for restaurants without carpet be moved to "some place that isn't such a dump." If the other participants at a sitdown were too powerful to be inconvenienced, then Jimmy would scowl and fidget uncomfortably in the restaurant booth like he was being held hostage at a gay-porn shoot.

Once Jimmy was securely seated in a restaurant blanketed with carpet, a new neurosis took over: a paralyzing fear of anyone paying for any part of his meal. Jimmy acted as if he would become known as a welfare queen if he let someone buy him a scotch on the rocks or cover the tip; he would stab a guy with a fork before letting him pick up a check. Jimmy even refused to let us take him to dinner when Tabitha and I picked him up from a long stay in jail that left him malnourished and starving. Since Jimmy had no money in his wallet, he insisted that he wasn't hungry even though he was obviously on the verge of passing out.

I knew what I had to do: I had Tabitha say that she was hungry, took them to a restaurant, and ordered extra dishes despite Jimmy's firm stance that he wasn't hungry. After fifteen minutes of asking if Tabitha was sure she couldn't finish the enormous portions, Jimmy's animal instincts finally burst free of his self-control, and he lunged at the cold food as if ambushing prey that might escape.

Tabitha, like all women who knew Jimmy, thought of him as a sweetheart, everyone's honorary grandpa. She fell in love with Jimmy because he would draw *Looney Toons* and Disney characters on paper napkins at restaurants and give them to little kids at nearby tables. Jimmy even included his cartoon sketches with his letters from prison. Tabitha would melt whenever I received one of Jimmy's sketches in his sad letters from jail.

Of course, Tabitha could never believe that the uptight, painstakingly polite gentleman we always had lunch with was the same mad dog who bombed cars and almost shot two FBI agents. Years before I met Jimmy, he was approached by two undercover agents who gave him cash to "launder"; Jimmy, of course, just kept the cash and told them to fuck off. Since Jimmy had not technically committed any crime, the feds tried to trick Jimmy into threatening them, spreading the rumor around town that they were preparing to take revenge. Instead of returning threats, Jimmy, like any smart crook, kept his mouth shut and got ready to strike back with fatal force. Jimmy set up a meeting in a hotel room "to make things right," obtained a hot pistol and went up to the room fully planning to murder the two "no-good cocksucking rats" for talking about his business in public.

Jimmy was saved from the death penalty by his own neurosis: "Kenny, just as I was taking out my gun to blow these two jackoffs away, I get this overwhelming feeling that the television set is watching me. I know this sounds crazy, but I was just positive the people in that TV were watching me. So I just left. Thank Jesus, Mary, and Joseph!"

That was Jimmy, man of honor: a man who refused to curse in front of women but was ready to cap two FBI agents for gossiping behind his back.

In the same way that I cross-trained in every martial art I could find instead of studying one style, I also methodically sought new partners in the underworld who could expand my knowledge, challenge my preconceptions, and hone my criminal abilities. I have a completist's curiosity; I want to know everything. I never stayed too long with any one organization, racket, or partner because, as soon as I learned everything there was to learn, I became bored and seconds later became unhappy.

In Jimmy, I found a new gangland mentor with a unique skill set to teach. Jimmy's craft was what I like to call Grind Fu: the classic wiseguy art of grinding out a living one dollar at a time. Under Jimmy, I would perfect the arts of loan sharking, bookmaking, protection rackets, and other meat-and-potatoes wiseguy crimes.

In Mafia convention, a made man is never "given" a racket to oversee; he is given nothing besides an order to pay tribute and go out into the world to steal cash any way he can. The Life comes with no time off, no sick days, no pension, no vacation, no recourse to the police or courts, no second chances, and no excuses—you are

on your own, one fuckup away from a bullet in the head
or one bad month away from complete bankruptcy. The
pressure can be crushing, suffocating.

Without any leads or any help, the mafioso is just
a self-employed grunt desperately searching for angles,
marks, and lucky breaks; his day is a twenty-four-hour
hobo hustle for anything that might be of value. Before
the days of credit cards or computers, the gangster's tools
were just his hands, his bat, his name, his words, and
a pencil and pad of paper. Jimmy thrived under these
primitive conditions, hustling every cent he earned in
person, face-to-face, with no buffer and no safety net. If
all Jerry Zimmerman needed to make a living was a telephone, then Jimmy could make a living anywhere in the
world with nothing more than his fists and his language-
transcending style of intimidation.

"This thing is just shoe leather, elbow grease, and a
little asskicking," Jimmy might say as we tirelessly sped
through our list of appointments. If Jerry Zimmerman
was the criminal version of an online stock trader who
traffics in millions of dollars from the comfort of his
bed, then Jimmy was gangland's door-to-door vacuum
cleaner salesman. Whether it be extortion, bookmaking,
shylocking, gambling, fencing stolen goods, or simple
robbery, Jimmy reveled in getting his hands dirty. There's
nothing sexy or glamorous about this type of crime, but
it provided me with "an honest day's work" satisfaction
akin to a bricklayer's pride in watching one of his buildings rise.

Unlike Jackie di Padova, who lived a truly charmed
life for a gangster, Jimmy showed me that the Mob lifestyle for the average wiseguy was as far as possible from
the Hollywood depictions of leisurely days wasted in
bullshitting sessions at social clubs and long nights spent

partying and whoremongering. The margin of error is too slim and the behind-the-scenes politics too cutthroat. Unless he is the son of a don or has a connection in the drug business, your average made man is more likely to be caught shaking down hotdog vendors and taking $20 bets on a Yankees game than he is owning strip clubs and pissing away $20,000 on a weekend in Atlantic City.

The Life is shitty, mundane, working-class—a dying way of life, like the Midwest steelworker and the New England family fisherman. Working with Jimmy was fascinating from a historical standpoint to me, like I was riding with Sitting Bull and one of the last bands of outlaw Sioux warriors.

The physical embodiment of the Life to me will always be the racetrack, the only place in civilian society where you can see the decay, pettiness, shabbiness, and all-round dreariness of the wiseguy social scene. Seemingly alone among everyday Americans, old wiseguys and their civilian demographical counterparts love to watch and bet on the ponies, which made Hollywood Park racetrack our informal headquarters. Jimmy loved Hollywood Park for the symbiotic reasons that he was both a small-time degenerate gambler himself and a skilled predator who preyed on other small-time degenerate gamblers. Jimmy could get his fix while ripping off the other junkies, servicing their addictions with shylock loans and sports-book bets.

Like a lot of track fanatics, Jimmy had encyclopedic knowledge and fantastic instincts that he neutralized by over-thinking every race. I always bet on Jimmy's first instinct, and he always bet on his seventh revision of that instinct; I always won, and Jimmy always lost. Though I enjoyed hanging out with Jimmy and listening to his war stories, the racetrack was my least favorite venue for doing business: the place smelled like sun-baked horse-shit, and the air was stagnant and heavy with pervasive, existential failure. I felt like a loser for being there, and it became tiring listening to Jimmy share bad-beat tall tales with other gamblers, broken old men with nicotine-stained mustaches, ratty shawl-like gray sports coats, and raw, deadened eyes.

Much more to my liking was Las Vegas, which we visited frequently for business and for pleasure. Though the Mafia had been booted from control of the casinos and local unions during the '70s and '80s, the Los Angeles Family, along with many others, maintained a foothold in street-level rackets like loan-sharking, bookmaking, fraud, extortion, counterfeiting, and gambling scams. Jimmy frequently visited Vegas for more personal reasons: his brother Charles was an also-ran, Vegas lounge singer who went by the stage name of Bobby Milano.

Though Bobby was a made man in the Los Angeles Family, his heart and what passed for his talent was in the music business. Bobby's mainstream music career began and ended in 1958 with "Life Begins at Four O'clock," a minor rockabilly hit single. Stuck as his brother's criminal flunky for the next two decades, Bobby hit the jackpot when he managed to win the heart of jazz legend Keely Smith, Louis Prima's ex-wife and duet partner.

With her exotic part-Cherokee looks and black Betty Boop hairstyle, Keely was something like a 1950s jazz version of Cher, a talented singer who was more famous for her deadpan comedic appearances alongside her spastic Italian husband on variety TV shows. Though Keely's onstage persona was that of a long-suffering square, the rumor around the L.A. and Vegas underworld was that she was just as kinky as the infamously perverse Prima. In addition to marrying a Mafia soldier,

Keely was known in her day as a "sex degenerate," with the most often-repeated example being the story of a Vegas casino dealer whose extramarital sex with Keely was interrupted when Louis Prima snuck into the room and, without warning, started licking his balls.

Keely and Bobby Milano's marriage was a perfect professional fit: Bobby married into a singing career, and Keely married a Louis Prima substitute who could step into their routine without challenging her headliner spot. Jimmy also appreciated Keely since she gave him frequent, legitimate excuses for the visits to Las Vegas that he inevitably would have to explain to cops and juries.

A Bobby and Keely show at the Desert Inn was the pretext for our first trip to Las Vegas together. Jimmy and I were in the midst of a marathon door-to-door fund-raising campaign to pay an elite attorney to handle Jimmy's appeal of a recent conviction. We visited everyone from porn producers to Arab telemarketers, collecting a few thousand dollars apiece in what was part charitable donation, part Mob tribute, and part barely disguised extortion. Ori Spado, eager to suck up to a second Mob legend, took a break from selling Jack LaLanne juicers to organize a benefit dinner complete with raffle tickets. Though driving over the state line to Las Vegas was a violation of Jimmy's bail, we headed over anyway with raffle tickets to sell, mobsters to meet, and a Bobby Milano concert at the Desert Inn to subject ourselves to.

To be honest, I really enjoyed Bobby Milano's lounge act. Keely, with her dyed black hepcat hairstyle, was still entertaining, despite being old enough to pass for a Trail of Tears survivor, and what Bobby lacked in talent he made up for in voluptuousness. Watching Jimmy Caci's fat little brother sing jazz standards while bouncing around the stage like a Jell-O Pac-Man was surreal. "Now that's good, wholesome entertainment. You can't argue with talent like that!" Jimmy told me as the show ended.

Out of respect for Jimmy, many of the local wiseguys came to Bobby's show. The Buffalo Family delegation was always led by Vegas rackets boss Robert "Bobby" Panaro, a trusted family member of the Buffalo godfather Joe Todaro, who is worth hundreds of millions of dollars thanks to his La Nova Pizzeria restaurant chain. John Gotti's buddy John "John Mash" Mascia, a fat and gray old guido who at that point may have already been dying of cancer, offered the Gambino Family's regards and may have been down for a few bucks of raffle tickets.

We were joined after the show by Steve "The Whale" Cino, a Buffalo-bred made guy in Jimmy's crew who worked Vegas. The Whale had to meet us after the show because he was not allowed in the Desert Inn—or any casino for that matter. Stevie had attained the highest honor for a Las Vegas criminal: an exclusive spot in the Nevada "Black Book." To this day, Steve Cino is banned from stepping foot in any casino in Nevada due to his criminal prowess, and any casino that takes his business can have its license revoked. Only Milano's Vegas rackets boss John Vaccaro had a more impressive record: both he *and* his wife Sandra were in the Black Book for orchestrating a multimillion-dollar scheme to rig slot machines. Sandra Vaccaro is the first and only woman ever to make the list.

The Whale, like Joe "The Whale" Peraino, lived up to his nickname: he was five-feet-six-inches tall and five-feet-nine-inches wide, a beast suffocating in blubber. When he was told of his nomination for the Black Book, The Whale quipped, "You just ruined my lunch!" He was the prototype member of Jimmy's crew: a blue-collar, prison-tested, hard-luck career criminal from Buffalo who worked hard to be pleasant and charming unless the situation demanded otherwise. Despite looking like a head and two feet stuck on either end of a giant titty, The Whale never acted like he had anything to prove.

"Stevie, this kid is good people," Jimmy said as he kissed The Whale on the cheek and slapped his shoulder. "He's with me. If he ever needs anything, take care of him." From that moment, The Whale was as reliable a friend and partner as Jimmy.

While the three of us were talking, another old prison friend joined the party: Vincent "Vince Lupo" Arcuri, an East Coast hood who did time at Attica Prison with Jimmy years before both men moved out West. After hearing that I was interested in working regularly in Las Vegas, Vince told me to see him the next day at the Rio Casino so he could introduce me to the local hoods.

After kissing Keely's ass a little bit, Jimmy took me to visit restaurateur Nicky Blair at his Vegas location. Sitting down in a booth with us, Nicky encouraged his old friend to tell me one of the definitive Jimmy the Elderly Gangster stories: how a sitdown with Genovese Family capo Joe Dente had given Jimmy gout. The story began with Jimmy borrowing $10,000 from Los Angeles–based Gambino soldier Joe Isgro, a record producer who for decades managed the payola rackets that kept Mafia-owned entertainers on the radio. Since Isgro was more a moneyman and Hollywood cocktail fixture than a feared criminal, Jimmy was planning to blow off the debt until Isgro, suspecting Jimmy's intent, sold the debt instead to Joe Pesci's Mob rabbi, capo Joe Dente from Arthur Avenue in the Bronx.

Since he had already retired his debt in his mind, Jimmy reacted to the news that Joe Dente expected him to fork over $10,000 as if Dente was trying to extort him. Finding out that Dente held court in Los Angeles at his friend Nicky Blair's restaurant, an outraged Jimmy sent word that either they arranged a sitdown at the restaurant to talk—or Jimmy would come unannounced without any intention of saying a word. Accompanied by two associates, Jimmy sped over to Nicky Blair's as if he had a blood vendetta to settle, stomped out of his car, and slammed the car door so hard that it dislodged the .38-caliber pistol tucked under his waistband. The pistol fell and bounced off Jimmy's big toe, smashing it and causing a case of gout that lingered for years.

Now enraged beyond all reason, Jimmy hopped into Nicky Blair's on one foot and started a shouting match with Dente that I'm sure was punctuated with frequent reiterations of "cocksucker," "motherfucker," and third-person warnings about "Jimmy Caci" and what he did and didn't do. To ensure Dente's comprehension of his message that he didn't want him operating in his friend's restaurant or in his family's territory anymore, I assume that Jimmy also repeatedly asked "Ya understand? Ya understand?" Dente, who was known as a physically abusive john in the porn world, understood Jimmy's intentions but not his motivation; where did this Palm Springs nobody get off talking shit to a Genovese Family capo? They parted on the worst of terms, each making reciprocal promises about how the other wiseguy "would see."

When Dente called New York to ask who the fuck Jimmy Caci was, the authority he asked was another former cellmate of Jimmy's in Attica. With a mutual wiseguy acquaintance identified, now Jimmy Caci and Joe Dente could be introduced to each other as "a friend of ours," fellow made men and capos, which meant they had to make an effort to get along. The second sitdown between the two equals went amicably: Joe Dente invested

$100,000 in a crooked card room Jimmy was running, with Jimmy's share of the profits going to pay off Joe Isgro. Both men also apologized to Nicky Blair, who, as Jimmy finished telling me the story in Las Vegas, admitted that he was ecstatic to have the Jimmy Caci–Joe Dente showdown to add to the Mob lore of his restaurants.

The next day, I visited Vince Lupo at the Rio and was escorted to the local Mafia social club. As soon as I saw this "social club," I realized how far the Mafia had fallen in Las Vegas. The Mob's top Vegas hangout was this anonymous nook in some out-of-the-way strip mall. The dump was owned and operated by "Fat" Tony Angioletti, a tub-of-shit gambler who gave real criminals free drinks and homemade Italian food if they consented to ornament his clubhouse.

Even in a subculture stuffed like a truck-stop toilet with "Fat Tonys," Angioletti was noteworthy for being a truly stupendous fat fuck; he was unsurprisingly cooking when Vince introduced us. I could barely maintain eye contact with this fat fucking mess with his thick Coke-bottle glasses and dirty barbershop-floor haircut for fear that I would laugh in his face. He was like the nerd who opens up his tree house to all the cool kids in the hope that he will become one of them. Fat Tony had failed; I fit in with wiseguys far better than he did.

As Fat Tony and Vince Lupo were dragging me around to each of the fold-out tables where two-bit locals were playing cards under the big Italian flag, in walked a hood who at least looked the part. Giovanni "John Branco" Brancato was a muscular older guido with a black helmet of shellacked John Gotti hair, a gold "GB" ring on his finger, and gold chains around his neck. I thought he was going to be someone important, but as soon as he introduced himself I knew not to be excited.

John Branco had a long-standing reputation as a tough guy with his fists who lacked the brains, the balls, and the killer instinct to make it big in the underworld. Jimmy had an especially low opinion of Branco as a "talker," someone who could beat a debt out of a civilian but grew a pussy when a real man talked to him. When Branco heard that I would be working with Steve Cino in Vegas, he tried to interest me in a fake casino chip scam he was running, but trying to steal money from casinos with hundred-million-dollar security budgets seemed like a guaranteed-to-fail crime to me.

When I returned to Los Angeles, I figured that since I had helped Jimmy call in his old debts to pay for his lawyer, he could help me out with one of mine. In 1996, I produced a Buck Adams action-porn extravaganza based on *Blade Runner* called *Blade,* which we filmed at an abandoned train yard using a jerry-rigged "hover car" and homeless people as actors. I sold the worldwide rights to David Sturman, the son of Reuben Sturman, the deceased Gambino Family porn-distribution kingpin. Without giving me a reason, David never paid.

Since I had heard that Jimmy, Jerry Zimmerman, and Ori Spado had recently shaken down Sturman for a few thousand dollars he owed one of their friends, I asked Jimmy to accompany me to a meeting with Sturman. To me, it was a meeting; to Sturman, it was an ambush. I had Black Dave keep an eye on the headquarters of Sin City, Sturman's production company, so I was tipped off when Sturman came into town for a visit. As he walked into the door of his company, Jimmy Caci and I followed a few steps behind.

"Where's my money for *Blade,* David?" I asked. Sturman looked at me like I was insane.

"What the fuck do you think you're doing? Get the fuck out of here! You don't know who you're pissing off!" he said, another guy who thought being "with" someone would stop me from getting my money. How was "having friends" going to protect him from someone like me, who always kept a ski mask, a clean blade, a clean gun, and a container of flammable liquids in an undisclosed location "just in case" I needed to wait outside his house and ambush him for real? Were his friends in New York going to teleport across the country to stop me?

"I want my money for the worldwide rights for *Blade*, David." Jimmy was even-tempered at my side, relaxed since he knew from his previous experience that David would buckle.

"It's not your money. I cut a deal with Buck for the film," Sturman said with a conviction that clued me in that he actually believed what he was saying.

Buck, *really*? That's where all of this is coming from? Dude, Buck is just some retard. He has no say in this. It's my movie."

"Kenji, you have no leg to stand on. It's Buck's movie, and he sold it. Let's get him in here."

"Dude, Buck's like retarded, seriously, and I don't give a shit what he has to say. If he actually sold anything to you, he screwed you because it isn't his. I have the checks paid from my account, the copyright on the scripts, the cash statements, everything. Buck didn't have any cash or any accounts. It's my movie, and I want the cash, now."

"Listen, I don't have to take this shit . . ."

"Dude, shut the fuck up and just give me my fucking money," I said as I began to lose my temper.

"Hey, don't talk to him like that," interjected Mickey Blank, another porn producer who happened to be in the lobby and decided this was prime opportunity to suck up to Sturman.

"Mickey," I replied, "one more word, and I'm going to kick your teeth in."

"Oh, so that's how it is?" Sturman asked as he started to nod with crazy eyes and a fool's confidence. I knew what was coming. "Y'know, Kenji, I have *friends*." Before I had a chance to pull Sturman's bitch card like I did Peter North's, the hitherto dormant Jimmy Caci suddenly erupted like Mount Etna. As an actual Mafia capo, nothing made Jimmy more livid than civilians who tried to play as if they were one phone call away from launching a Mob war.

"*Listen here,* you bubblegum-chewing motherfucker you," Jimmy hissed through clenched teeth, his eyes so intense they looked like they were about to pop. Jimmy picked up the phone at the reception desk and slammed it in front of the startled pornographer. "Call whoever the fuck you gotta call. We don't give a shit."

I was choking with giggles over the "bubblegum-chewing motherfucker" line, which is still my favorite wiseguy insult. That line by itself guaranteed I would never testify against Jimmy. I collected myself and broke the silence with an amiable offer to fight Sturman outside with the money he owed me as the purse.

"Listen, you guys," Sturman said, "I really do know people!" It was verging on a desperate plea, as if Jimmy and I didn't know about his ties to the Gambinos. We just didn't give a shit.

"Listen, I ain't stopping you from calling anybody, you motherfucker you," Jimmy said as he lifted his hands toward the telephone like a Vegas card dealer in a "hands-off" gesture. "Call absolutely anyone you fucking want and tell them to come talk to Jimmy. Ya understand? I don't give a fuck who you call—call the fucking Pope for all the shit I give!—but you're paying my friend here in the meantime or I'm going to rip your asshole out. Ya understand?" David understood; David paid.

The drawback of working with a gangster like Jimmy who has a reputation a half-century in the making is that you lose any pretense of anonymity. The FBI is national, and they'll spend millions of dollars to follow a name crook *everywhere* until he *dies*. Jimmy had a connection at the Claremont Auto Center who was hooking up Ori, Vince Lupo, and Jimmy's crew with cars at a fraction of the list price. All they had to do was pay the first three lease payments, and after that the Auto Center was no longer liable for the bad lease. Jimmy offered to get me a new car, but Jerry Zimmerman and Jackie di Padova, both veterans of Michael Franzese's car dealership scams, advised against it since automotive fraud was easy to trace and easy to prove. I declined Jimmy's offer after a courtesy visit to the Auto Center.

Three weeks later, my parole officer called me and told me to come to her office immediately. On her desk were surveillance photos of Jimmy and me at the Claremont Auto Center, which was pretty conclusive evidence that I had violated the terms of my probation by consorting with a known felon. Of course, in the previous few years, I had done almost nothing besides consort with known felons, but none of them had been as known or as felonious as Jimmy. Luckily, the photos were blurry enough that I could claim they were of someone else, and I dumped the clothes I was wearing in them to thwart the police search of my apartment that I rightly predicted would soon follow.

At the time, the lesson I took away from this close

call was to avoid meeting Jimmy at high-visibility locations or at the site of rackets that might interest the cops. I was stupid. I had missed the obvious lesson that two automobile crime experts had explicitly told me: stay away from car scams at all costs, because you will get caught.

"[Los Angeles underboss Dominic Brooklier] comes in with Pete Milano and introduces him as a made guy. So Brooklier says, 'Pete's a capo now,' and I look at this piece of shit and I want to laugh in his face. It's a fucking disgrace."

Johnny Roselli
As quoted by Jimmy Fratianno in *The Last Mafioso*

Sometimes, working in the Los Angeles Family felt like being a kid caught between two mismatched parents: a spoiled, prissy suburban shrew named Peter Milano and an insensitive, temperamental, blue-collar roughneck named Jimmy Caci. Unfortunately for us children, both Peter and Jimmy were Italian Catholics, so divorce was not an option. Jimmy maintained absolute loyalty to the oath he took to support and obey the family leadership, and out of necessity Pete Milano stood by his capo Jimmy despite the biannual, highly publicized indictments and trials. Pete did not have the muscle to put Jimmy "on the shelf" or survive on the streets without his crew as a deterrent. They were stuck with each other.

Pete Milano was an interesting criminal: he was either the worst or best mafioso in California. Pete was always soft, but as a second-generation wiseguy he skirted past the usual process of proving himself thanks to nepotism. His rackets were the usual Los Angeles mix of smalltime suburban bullshit: bookmaking, loan-sharking, and gambling rooms with magnetized roulette wheels, weighted dice, and rigged slot machines. In his entire half-century criminal career, I don't think Pete ever collected a single debt or extorted a single cent using anything but his last name or hired muscle.

Pete was soft, but he was also dangerously intelligent. He doesn't get the credit he deserves: as the only 1970s Mafia boss to maintain his freedom and his position until the present day, Pete is probably closer to a master criminal strategist than yuppie wannabe with soft hands and bitch tits. His family has survived the great downfall of the past thirty years with its (low) numbers intact, his rule unchallenged, and his rackets mostly unaffected. Milano's cautious, low-key, and nonviolent-bordering-on-polite way of conducting business has merited only the most cursory law enforcement attention. When he dies, the elderly "Shakes" Milano will become one of the very few major godfathers of any generation to die in the comfort of his own home as a wealthy and happy family man.

In an organization of halfwits he was always sly, clever, and a vicious intriguer. Pete was cagey enough to play to his strengths. Like a devious court eunuch, Pete advertised his lack of balls as a reason for the bosses to trust and confide in him. Once he had access, Pete focused his skills as a gossip, flatterer, and liar to manipulate his bosses and sabotage his opponents. Since Pete came from a stand-up family and had no street muscle, L.A.'s old-school bosses felt comfortable in promoting him since he would neither rat nor try to take their spot by force.

They were right: Pete bided his time, and eventually all the old-timers, tough guys, and real gangsters were killed, flipped by the government, or locked up. Suddenly Pete Milano, the bookmaker who looked and dressed like movie director Peter Bogdanovich (the male psychiatrist on *The Sopranos*), was the Mafia godfather of America's second largest city.

As boss, Pete quickly abandoned hope of running Los Angeles like a typical Mafia territory. He didn't have the street credibility to be a boss who rules through terror and intimidation. Pete learned the hard way that prison-tested tough guys cannot rationalize doing jail time for a pussy boss. All of the big-name Mob "hitters" that worked with Pete backstabbed him. Jimmy "The Weasel" Fratianno and Anthony "The Animal" Fiato both turned rat rather than put up with the bullshit and later filmed a TV talk-show pilot where they made fun of lame L.A. gangsters like Pete. Frank "Bump" Bompensiero turned rat and was killed, and Mike Rizzi refused to recognize a "half-a-fag" like Pete as boss and briefly created his own rival family in Los Angeles. If this was how real gangsters performed, Pete was satisfied to be a half-ass wannabe surrounded by other half-ass wannabes.

"I've been through so goddamn much," a long-suffering Pete confided in Fiato when he was still undercover, "that when you see people that go out and cowboy, you say to yourself, 'these guys, if they only knew how it really is.'" To Pete, none of the tough-guy stuff was worth it; you collected more money in the short-term but guaranteed yourself long, miserable, and completely unprofitable jail sentences. Pete tolerated Jimmy Caci because he wanted to have *some* muscle on his side in case times got rough, but Jimmy was kept at a distance so Pete wouldn't be caught in the crossfire.

Instead of the old predatory way of doing business, Pete Milano transferred the Los Angeles Mafia Family into a concern that I would classify as a service industry. The Mob in Los Angeles did not predate but instead politely *offered services:* a nice card game, a high-interest loan, the opportunity to bet on sports locally, small quantities of coke and pot, and the prestige of working with a Mafia family. Pete himself ran something of a wiseguy escort agency. Instead of extorting his way into businesses, he would let his name and title attract scumbag Hollywood businessmen who happily paid to bask in his glory so they could claim to be connected.

Everyone in California wants to have a gangster's name to drop—I actually used to get paid to visit Hollywood producers' homes as a dinner-party ornament and conversation piece. As "godfather," Pete safely and legally traded his name and friendship for shares in countless legitimate businesses. Today, Pete oversees an untouchable network of lucrative investments, including a vending machine company, a coffee distributorship, a bottled water company, and a few pizza parlors.

With his personal multimillion-dollar empire to protect, elderly Pete had every reason to be cautious. He had everything he could ever want, so what could be important enough to risk a jail sentence and the government confiscating his property? That's why Pete put Jimmy on a short leash, forswore violent crime, and promoted only limp dicks made in his image. The Los Angeles Family was trapped in a cycle of decline: insecure bosses bent on self-preservation favored the weak, who eventually attained power and favored the even weaker, leading to what Jimmy called an ever "faggier" family.

Instead of recruiting tough and capable street soldiers, Pete systematically surrounded himself with decoys: he appointed three capos and an underboss, meaning that somewhere between a third and a half of the family was nominal "management" that the feds could charge with masterminding operations instead of Pete. This policy led to travesties like "Mafia capo" Louie Caruso who, despite his title, had no crew, no muscle, no rackets, no balls, no street rep, and no idea about Mafia history and tradition. Louie Caruso was just another patsy to deliver Pete's messages, pick up his money, and attract all the heat from the cops. Pete especially liked Caruso because he understood him: just like Pete, Caruso's career plan was to be a loyal suck-up and lackey until, through attrition, he inherited more meaningless yet lucrative titles.

The problem with Pete's "promote complete fucking idiots" policy was that, outside of his presence, the idiots occasionally tried to live up to their titles and almost destroyed the family in the process. Louie Caruso, for instance, nearly triggered a civil war with Jimmy and then tried to induct an FBI rat into the family. You can't blame the poor guy—someone chose to give him more responsibility than he could handle.

Caruso's showdown with Jimmy and Jimmy's old running buddy, Death, came out of an argument at a Las Vegas strip club. We should have noticed the warning signs when Louie, a short Tony Danza–like Italian in his forties, started driving around in a brand-new Corvette, partying with young mistresses, and lifting weights. Caruso was clearly entering a midlife crisis and was thus primed to create trouble in some desperate bid to reassure himself of his virility. Caruso was smart enough to pick on John Branco, who bought into the Mob mystique and therefore wouldn't fight back. If Louie had fucked with a biker or a Crip, I might have been drafted to be a pallbearer; everyone else in the Members Only Mafia was old, fat, or infirm.

Louie created an excuse to berate Branco in the middle of a crowded Las Vegas strip club. Though John Branco wasn't a killer, he certainly was big and tough enough to knock out Tiny Louie, who was a classic L.A.

gangster: useless with his fists, knives, or guns, but a B-52 bomber when it came to dropping names and wiseguy movie-talk. Out of some vestigial fear of fucking with a made guy, Branco kept his hands in his pockets and instead argued with Louie.

Branco's refusal to back down at the strip club struck Louie's glass ego like a sledgehammer. Unable to punish Branco physically, Caruso, in fine L.A. tradition, struck back through gossip and diplomacy by ratting out Branco to Pete Milano. As always, Pete was reluctant to use force to settle "the beef." Instead of punishing the smalltime Las Vegas hood for disrespecting his family, Milano ordered that a sitdown be arranged through Jimmy in which the wayward John Branco could receive a "Tsk! Tsk!" lecture on the importance of refraining from sassing made men.

Jimmy deputized Steve Cino in Vegas to promise Branco that Jimmy would be his advocate at the sitdown if Branco agreed to come down to L.A. and settle matters peacefully. Branco, wary of poisoning his relationship with the one Mob family that took him seriously, consented and drove with The Whale to meet Jimmy and his lackey Ori Spado in L.A. Branco was promised that the beef would be "squashed" like gentlemen.

One of the timeless rules of the Mafia sitdown is that only family insiders and the parties involved can attend. When Louie Caruso and his second, Tommaso "Tommy" Gambino, arrived at the L.A. restaurant in matching sunglasses, designer black shirts, and belted slacks, they should have been alone. Instead, Bogey and Ryan, two gigantic bikers that Caruso knew through a weightlifting buddy, followed closely behind them into the restaurant. The two bikers had just walked through the door when Jimmy hopped out of the booth and started screaming.

"What the fuck are these assholes doing here? You know the rules, cocksucker!"

Needless to say, "the rules" are also pretty clear that one capo should not call another capo a "cocksucker" in a restaurant full of civilians, either, but Jimmy was incensed at what he considered blasphemy. He felt betrayed and insulted on multiple levels. Not only had Caruso shit on the holy Mafia rules; he had also insulted Jimmy's manhood by insinuating, with the bikers, that Caruso could muscle him, and he dishonored Jimmy by turning his promise to John Branco of a peaceful family sitdown into a lie. Jimmy was a product of an era when a mafioso who let disrespect go unpunished was usually eaten alive by his own friends, so he took this slight as a direct threat against his life.

Since Jimmy was following protocol and not carrying a gun, he started haranguing Louie and Tommy with his trademark barrage of obscenities, third-person invocations of "Jimmy Caci," and deployments of "Ya understand?" Tommy Gambino, who thought very highly of himself because of his infamous family, tried to interrupt but was brutally shut down by Jimmy.

"Fuck you, you designer motherfucker! Fuck all of you, you motherfuckers you, especially these two [the bikers], whatever the fuck you are! You other guys who are supposed to know better can meet me in a few minutes at Walter's [Deli, in Beverly Hills]. This thing here is off!"

Jimmy told John Branco to "hit the bricks," motioned for his guys to leave, and shouldered past the two bikers as if he were trying to give them an excuse to retaliate. They didn't.

"Ken, with God as my witness," Jimmy told me afterwards, his teeth digging into his lips between words and his nostrils flaring. "If I had been carrying a piece I would have blown those two bike-riding faggots away right in the restaurant. I was *steamed*. The balls on this guy! He's lucky I know the rules and didn't bring a piece to a family sitdown, because I woulda shot the lot of them for embarrassing me in front of a guy who I gave my word. I gave the guy my word. What a disgrace!"

According to the story that Jimmy and Ori Spado told afterwards, what ensued next was a dangerous scene. As Ori nervously shuffled, Jimmy ranted to himself and paced around behind Walter's Deli for fifteen minutes until Caruso and Gambino arrived. Once again, Caruso didn't have a chance to speak before Jimmy started ridiculing him for being an ignorant disgrace to a criminal tradition he barely understood. "What, you need fucking rednecks to act as your muscle at a meeting with your own family? You try to muscle your own guys with some leather-wearing faggot outsiders? What type of fucking pussy are you? There are old-timers spinning in their fucking graves over this shit!"

All the talk about tradition and old-timers excited Tommy Gambino's pride, since he was a relative of Mafia legend Carlo Gambino and the son of major Sicilian heroin smuggler Rosario "Sal" Gambino.

"Hey, calm down with that shit, I was *born* into this thing! My dad . . ." Jimmy took one look at the slender, fashionable second-generation European playboy and decided that he wasn't man enough to talk back to him. In one quick motion, Jimmy slapped the namedrop out of Tommy's mouth; he then waited a moment to see if Tommy had the balls to stand up to a seventy-year-old, which, like the bikers, he didn't. Jimmy signaled to Ori that they were leaving. "Next time I see you, Louie, if those two other guys are around . . ." Jimmy let Caruso's imagination fill in the rest.

This feud presented a diplomatic nightmare to the family: the only way for either side to save face was to pull a trigger or apologize, both impossibilities for various reasons. Like most problems that dysfunctional, codependent families cannot solve, the Caci-Caruso-Gambino-Branco feud was simply ignored until all the principals could pretend it had never happened.

A year or two later, Tabitha and I were eating with Jimmy and Ori at Tony's Pasta Mia in Palm Springs when Louie Caruso arrived in a shiny Corvette with some bimbo in the passenger seat. Caruso and his obnoxious chick were in-your-face friendly and talkative when they saw us, which made me suspect that Caruso, who was married, might have been enjoying narcotics along with his mistress. Louie's girl wouldn't shut up, so I asked Tabitha to sit with her at another table. Louie sat down with a conspiratorial smile as if he had an announcement that would change the California underworld forever.

"You know who I fucking love? That John Branco!" Jimmy, Ori, and I were dumbfounded; we had been given no indication that the former blood enemies had somehow become blood brothers. "He is just a tough guy, good with his hands, solid, dependable, trustworthy. You know, I've been really thinking about it, Jimmy, and I think I'm going to propose Branco [to become a made man in the family]." Though Jimmy, Ori, and I were very different people, at that moment all three of us were thinking identically: *Are you fucking kidding me?*

Short of molesting the godfather's kids or ratting out the entire family, there was no greater breach of Mafia protocol than one capo unilaterally bringing up the topic of who he plans to "propose" in the presence of unmade associates. It would be like an undercover CIA agent outing the identity of another CIA agent during a dinner party; Ori and I were technically not even supposed to know the Mafia existed!

Though Ori and I were future rats with no hope of getting made, we were outraged at the disrespect Caruso was showing to Jimmy. Caruso had just confirmed to two associates and a potential FBI bug that they were Los Angeles Mafia capos discussing the induction of someone into the family, which *by itself* was enough to bump up any future indictments to RICO charges for committing crimes in the course of an ongoing criminal conspiracy.

Needless to say, Jimmy began to shit lightning bolts within a second of Caruso's "propose" comment. Instructing Ori and me to "take a walk," Jimmy leaned over the table and stuck his boiling red face uncomfortably close to Louie's. With the most animated hand gestures I have ever seen out of a sober man, Jimmy lashed again and again and again into Louie as the entire restaurant watched, unable to hear what Jimmy was saying through his locked jaw but understanding every syllable of his body language. Fearful of getting slapped like Tommy Gambino, Louie patiently stared at his lap and stayed quiet as Jimmy exorcised a few decades' worth of frustration with the hopelessly fucked-up L.A. Family. By the end of his tirade, Jimmy looked less like an irate mobster than a disappointed and long-suffering dad trying to get through to a deadbeat son who *just . . . doesn't . . . get it.*

Caruso of course suffered no repercussions for making a mockery of the crime family; he was just doing his job! The reason Pete Milano put Caruso in a position of power in the first place was to install an incompetent prick who would make Pete look like Abraham Lincoln by comparison. Pete delegated any responsibility that rose above basic courier duty to "the other Louie," Luigi Gelfuso.

> "Lying low probably is the smartest thing the bungling Los Angeles bosses have done in years. 'They were always a weak sister,' says one ex-lawman. 'They never really had the organization and numbers other mob families had back East.' Frank Cullotta, one of the FBI's more celebrated mob witnesses, says the Los Angeles Mafia hasn't been well-regarded in the underworld, either. 'I don't think they're too bright,' says Cullotta, a childhood chum and witness against the late Chicago mob kingpin Anthony Spilotro."
>
> *Las Vegas Sun*
> July 15, 1997

Louie Gelfuso was basically Louie Caruso, only capable and older. He was a perfect fit for Pete Milano: a comically loyal, cowardly, well-behaved, energetic bookie and gambler who delivered cash without causing trouble or attracting attention. While Pete counted his money behind drawn blinds in an undisclosed location, Louie Gelfuso sped around California and Nevada like a hyperactive wedding planner trying to make sure everything was just to Pete's liking at all times.

Befitting the Los Angeles Family, Louie was more high-powered personal assistant than he was Mafia capo, but he was great at his job. As the on-call fixer for every family racket not personally run by Jimmy Caci or Las Vegas chieftain John Vaccaro, Louie "kept all the plates spinning" and made the family profitable. Despite Pete's nepotistic, power-hoarding appointment of his grubby brother Carmen to underboss, Louie Gelfuso was the number two in Los Angeles from the 1970s until his death.

Though Louie G. was a talented hustler and an effective multitasking middle manager, he was comically miscast as a gangster. Even when compared with fearsome presences like playboy Louie Caruso and elderly bridge-player Pete Milano, Louie Gelfuso lacked credibility. Short, thin, narrow-shouldered, and neatly dressed, he was a chain-smoking elf with a strong facial resemblance to film director and sex criminal Roman Polanski. Though charged with a murder in 1969 that I guarantee you he did not commit, in person Gelfuso had the physical presence of a yawning kitten.

Even the feds made fun of Louie for being a pussy. I wish I could have been in the surveillance van when the FBI wiretap of Gelfuso's apartment delivered stunning audio of Louie crying at a tender scene in his favorite soap opera. Louie also argued with the characters, telling one hussy who was claiming to be a virgin that "your cherry is so far up your ass, you can use it for a tailgate." From then on, the FBI's L.A. squad referred to Louie Gelfuso as "Louie the Couch" in honor of the ratty old couch from which Louie watched his beloved "stories."

The only thing more emasculating for traditional tough guys like Jimmy or Anthony Fiato than taking orders from Pete Milano was taking orders from Pete Milano through his miniature personal assistant, Louie the Couch. For Jimmy, Anthony, and the other old-school crooks, the insult was compounded by the open secret that Gelfuso was a degenerate cokehead. Despite the Mob rules forbidding drug abuse on pain of death, Louie felt so secure in Pete's protection that he not only used drugs but also dealt them using his own son Michael and, years earlier, Fiato's coke-snorting little brother Larry as proxies.

That just shows you how little street sense Louie had: he actually believed *Pete Milano* would deter a stone killer like Anthony Fiato from putting a bullet in his head. The only reason Louie even survived to meet me was that The Animal had already cut a deal with the FBI and thus couldn't blast Louie for selling coke to an addict in a made man's family.

Of course, what did I care if Louie Gelfuso sold a couple dime bags of cocaine? What did I care if Louie and his son snorted their own stash? The only thing that mattered to me was that Louie, after two decades as Pete Milano's eyes and ears on the street, was the most connected man in California. Overextended and undermanned, Louie always had collections that needed to be made, bookies that needed to be intimidated, marks that were waiting to be fleeced, and stolen goods that needed to be moved.

I wanted a piece of that action, and I also thought it wise to hedge my bets with Louie against the extremely high likelihood Jimmy and Sonny went away at the same time. To win Louie over, I added him to my Rent-a-Capo Program: $200 to $300 a week in tribute to Louie Gelfuso convinced him to delegate thousands of dollars of easy muscle work to me every month. Louie took a liking to me since I was the only other person in the family who could keep pace with his kinetic, quick-witted conversation and tireless schedule of meetings and sit-downs. Our relationship became a more casual, lower-stakes prelude to my very similar aide-de-camp job with Manny Garofalo in New York.

My favorite Louie Gelfuso story involves my least favorite porn star—Peter North. A couple years after our initial breach, Peter came back into my life by chance when a stripper I knew began to brag to me about how she was such a close friend of porn icon Peter North. "Oh, you mean *that* fag?" I asked.

"Kenny, Peter isn't gay!"

"The shit he isn't! Come over to my shop. I'll show you the fucking videos!"

Well, that was apparently the wrong move for me to make if I wanted to live my life unencumbered by the dopey presence of Peter North. I started receiving irate, threatening phone calls from Peter and some wannabe thug, telling me that I would "pay" if they ever heard that I was calling Peter—the man who is on camera sucking penises and being penetrated by other men—anything less than entirely masculine and heterosexual. You can guess my response: I started calling compulsively and reminded everyone I knew or met that Peter North was not only gay but a professional *bottom*.

Though I was amused by how much I had riled up Peter, I also gradually became enraged that a neurotic gigolo believed he could get away with threatening me. Finally, I told Peter over the phone to meet me at a nearby Black Angus steakhouse with whoever was pretending to be his muscle.

As soon as I hung up on Peter, I called over my buddy Speedy, a short, muscular, heavily tattooed Nazi drug dealer; Speedy was a straight-up prison thug with a Charlie Manson–style rap sheet. I picked Speedy as my backup for this meeting for two reasons: Peter's muscle sounded like a black guy over the phone, and Speedy was known throughout the prison system as a racist and a compulsive stabber, slicer, and sticker. I grabbed two of my favorite knives and told Speedy, "Speedy, we're going to cut up a porn star's face so he can never work again."

"Alright, boss," said Speedy with nonchalance that

bordered on boredom. Speedy was like the white Greg Benjamin: I could've told him we were on our way to castrate Tom Cruise, and his only concern would have been where I would take him drinking afterwards. To give you an idea just how crazy a criminal Speedy was, he once planned a burglary with my good friend and Ultimate Fighting Championship star Justin Levens using nothing more than a rusty hatchet as their weapon. During the writing of this book, Speedy's buddy Justin confided in me that he had murdered two drug dealers, which I didn't take seriously at first; a few weeks later Justin shot his wife and himself in a drug-fueled murder-suicide.

When Speedy and I walked into the Black Angus, I saw the always-fashionable Peter North sitting with some hardly imposing black thug. Speedy and I sat down with smiles on our faces. I asked North with a friendly tone, "So, what's the problem, buddy?"

"You're going all around California telling people I'm gay!" Peter spat out, sputtering with rage because I was acting like I had no idea what his problem was. "You're telling *girls* I'm gay!"

"Of course I am because it's true. You are Matt Ramsey, gay porn star! I have your gay videos at my porn shop! You want to come see yourself sucking dick?" The black guy with Peter was noticeably startled since he could tell from my voice and assertiveness that I was telling the truth. Most black gangbangers are homophobic, so he was suddenly put in a very uncomfortable situation. Obviously, I sought to exploit his discomfort. "Hey you, bro, lemme ask your opinion: if you've sucked a dick and taken it up the ass, does that make you gay or not?"

The black guy jumped up as if I was calling him gay, but Speedy calmed him down. "Chill out, *homes*," he said with a deadpan, mocking tone that let the homeboy know that here was a white supremacist who was always in the mood for stabbing a black guy.

"Now listen up, *Al*, I don't give a shit if you're a fag or not," I said as I leveled my hardest look at Peter. My temper, as it tends to do, had suddenly overwhelmed my amusement at this situation. "If you fuckin' bother me again, I'm going to stab you in the face so you can't get film work ever again, and then I'm going to kick you in the dick and stomp on your fucking nuts until they don't fucking work anymore either. Don't forget . . ." I cut off my sentence midway as rage short-circuited my brain, and I reached for my knife. Luckily, Speedy lurched over and stopped me from committing a stupid crime.

"Hey, you better watch it!" Peter said in a panic, his body language warped by spasms of fear. "I'm with people now! I'm connected! I've got people!" This misguided statement calmed me down in a second; I was not going to deprive myself of the hilarity of Peter North proving his Mafia bona fides just for the fleeting joy of stabbing him in the face.

"Okay, Al, you go get them, and I'll be waiting at my porn shop."

Peter showed up at my porn shop with this dumpy little mook nobody named Angelo, a minor-league associate of the Bonanno Family in New York. I knew Angelo from years back in Irvine when he was introduced to me and within two minutes of saying "Hello" asked for fifty pounds of high-grade marijuana. I remembered looking at that fucker like he was crazy and telling him I didn't know him or his people. "No, you don't get it, I'm connected. Ask anyone in Little Italy about me." I laughed in his face and reminded him we were in 1990s California, not 1920s New York, before walking out.

Angelo was unhappy to discover that the porn shop owner who Peter expected him to lean on was a well-known criminal who had already blown him off. Angelo was also clearly uneasy that I was sitting with Speedy and his brother Butch, a gigantic Hells Angels captain; wiseguys are terrified of bikers because bikers are violence-first animals who are never impressed by Mob mystique or "who you know"—the only two weapons most 21st-century wiseguys know how to wield.

"How may I help you gentlemen?" I asked.

"Uh, well, listen," Angelo began, trying to muster his best "dese-dem-dose" wiseguy routine even though he already knew it was going to fail. He had no other card to play. "Well, y'know, we got a problem between you and Peter. Well, y'know, this guy here, he's with me."

"And, if I may ask, who the *fuck* are you and why should I care?"

"Uh, I-I," Angelo stuttered, not scared so much as embarrassed that his tough guy persona was being pierced. "I'm with people. Y'know, back East, in New York."

"That's real cool," I said in my best impersonation of a stoned surfer. "But this is California, *bro*, and who you're with in New York don't mean dick."

"Well, I'm not just with people in New York," Angelo continued, clearly improvising to try to save face. "I'm friends with Pete Milano, y'know who he is?"

I certainly did. Needless to say, I was in a perfect position to call bullshit on Angelo's spur-of-the-moment lie. "Hold up!" I said, a new and cold seriousness to my voice. I raised my hand and put it over Angelo's mouth. "Slow down, slow down. Okay, big man, do you know who my partner is?"

"Uhhhh." Angelo the Stutterer looked at the ground

as I watched all the color drain from his face. He knew he had fucked up. "I, I-I-I, I mean, no. No, I don't."

"You come into my business and want to act like a big guy. You want to drop names and lean on people. Well, we'll have to get to the bottom of this."

As soon as I touched my telephone, Angelo lurched forward and started rambling. You could tell Peter was panicking—his big-time muscle had been proven to be a bitch. Angelo was defenseless. "Come on, come on, come on, let's not make this a big deal. I ain't trying to make this a big deal or lean on nobody. I, I-I-I, I just wanted you to please lay off my buddy Peter and stop with the gay bullshit."

"Bullshit? Hey, Butch!" Butch, as rehearsed, handed me Peter North's gay videos. I tossed them on the counter in front of Angelo for him to consider as I dialed up Louie. "Hey, it's me, yeah, yeah. So there's this guy in my shop from Irvine by way of New York, Angelo, claims to be with some of those other guys over there. He's in my face, giving me a hard time, yakking that he's friends with *that* guy out here, y'know?" Louie had no trouble comprehending my meaning.

"Tell that guy," Louie said, an uncharacteristic smidge of anger in his voice, "to give you his info, and we'll come see him and get to the bottom of that."

"Okay, Angelo, my friend and I are going to come see you and get to the bottom of this. As for you, Al, there's no gray area: you suck dick or you don't suck dick, and the truth is that you suck dick. Get over it." Peter and Angelo slunk out of my shop as Butch laughed at them—Angelo humiliated and frightened, Peter even more confused than usual.

Working as Louie's deputy put me in direct daily contact with the entire breadth of the West Coast traditional organized crime network. In addition to his daily powwows with Pete Milano and Louie Caruso, Louie often visited just about every independent bookie in Southern California, all of the porno mobsters, Jerry Zimmerman's people, the New York and Chicago Families' California soldiers, various underworld starfuckers in Hollywood, and all of the scam artists and racketeers who were ignorant enough to pay a premium for L.A. Family "protection." A great perk of my job with Louie was that all of the bookies, porn studios, and fencers saw us together and cut me extremely generous deals as a gesture of respect to Louie.

Louie's connections were so deep that I even met a few mafiosi that the FBI didn't even know existed, such as Paulie, Louie's good buddy who happened to run the Denver Mafia Family, which everyone claimed was extinct. Paulie seemed pretty alive to me: his family was arguing with Pete over a piece of a hotel they owned. As always, Louie took care of his concerns and everyone left happy.

It didn't take long for me to realize that I had been unfair judging Louie more for what he wasn't—a tough gangster like Jimmy Caci—than for what he was. Louie was a racketeer, a crooked capitalist who thrived by conducting legitimate business through illegal means or illegal business using legitimate business practices. Louie wasn't a deceiver like Jerry Zimmerman; he was an on-the-level businessman operating in the black market and gray areas of the law.

If you needed a little coke, a short-notice loan, two tons of stolen pepperoni for your pizzeria, or someone to set up a poker tournament, then Louie Gelfuso would take care of you at a fair market price and with minimum stress. He was a wheeler-dealer, a handshake-and-smile smooth operator. Everyone liked him.

Louie didn't need crime at all. He had the charm, the skill, the reliability, and the professional appearance to be a success in a multitude of normal jobs. He was like me: a criminal by choice, a criminal for the thrills. He didn't have sociopathic tendencies or an outlaw lifestyle. After spending his day meeting with other "high-ranking" criminals and collecting street cash, Louie went home to his bachelor pad that reeked of cigarettes, watched his favorite TV shows while splayed on his couch, cried at the sentimental moments, and maybe did a little coke if he was bored. This routine was occasionally interrupted by prison sentences or visits to see his son, Michael, in jail for the crimes that Louie had taught him and later ordered him to commit.

One day when I was watching Louie at his charming best, I realized that Louie was pathetic for very different reasons than the ones everyone suggested. Louie was pathetic because he was a wonderfully talented and cool guy who had become a criminal for shallow reasons and ruined his chance at a normal, happy family life. I could tell Louie knew the truth: you could see the sadness and shame in his eyes every time his son got in trouble with drugs or the law. I remember the first time I thought to myself: *Why the fuck is a smart guy like Louie wasting his time with the Mob and all its bullshit?*

It hit me like a sucker punch. *How are you any different?* I forced that thought out of my mind; the idea that I was little better than Louie the Couch was too emasculating and shameful to ponder. I tried to move past it, forget it, but *then I was hit again: What makes you different from Joey Avila at this point?* I tried to dismiss that out of hand as an absurd thought: I was no dabbler, even if my Mob revenue didn't come close to the money I made from porn and my shop. But still, my doubts lingered.

Once I started thinking about my life of crime with a critical mind-set, it seemed like there were examples every day of just how *lame* and dreary it had become. There was the time Jimmy, the criminal legend, had to take time out of his petty racetrack gambling habit to visit a disturbed girl in the porn industry who was claiming to be Sonny Franzese's niece. It was a sad scene all-round: people were pissed at Sonny since the girl ripped them off, the girl was a mess, and Jimmy let himself down by losing his temper and cursing in front of a woman: "Honey, that shit won't fly."

Then there was the day Jimmy sent me to beat up R2-D2. I was told Deep "Deeps" Roy, a dwarf actor who played R2-D2 and an Ewok in some of the *Star Wars* movies, was threatening B-movie director Joe "Joe Smashy" Tonatore over an unpaid debt. Since Joe Smashy was one of Jimmy's degenerate buddies from the racetrack, he told me to do him a favor and teach Deep not to mess with him.

This was beyond parody: who needs to bring in Mob protection against a man the size of one of Amber Lynn's breasts? What type of tough guy smacks around one of the genuine Oompa Loompas from *Charlie and the Chocolate Factory*? I had no idea if this bullshit had any basis in reality, and I felt sick with myself for having to act on it. I called Deeps and threatened him, but to my relief the little creature, not surprisingly, proved skilled at hiding. I never found him and quietly let the matter drop.

The disquiet I was beginning to feel rarely presented in the form of coherent thoughts or a "nagging little voice" in my head. I had far too much practice suffocating unwanted or troubling thoughts for that. Instead, my moral growing pains were transmitted to me physically when I went on my rounds, through a tenderness in my chest or two hard thumbprints of pressure on my temples or a discomforting twist in my stomach or a pain in my neck as if a man the size of Deeps was hanging from it. It was like a bout of the flu that flared up again just when I thought I had it beat.

In an attempt to immunize myself from further outbreaks of self-awareness and shame, I started to make tiny, painless gestures of decency, as if a few nickels and dimes in my karmic piggy bank would pay off my debt.

One opportunity to do good came when Louie took me to see Jerry Zimmerman, whose kidneys were beginning to fail. Jerry was still as gregarious and full of shit as ever, but he was wasting away. He looked thin, dry, and raw, as if all the moisture was being slowly drained out of his deflating body. Jerry was so happy to see me that he gave me a few thousand baseball caps that he had in the office from two semi-trucks' worth of merchandise he had stolen.

While I was picking up my share of the loot, Jerry told me there were a couple boxes of blankets and other less profitable items that he was going to dump at fifty cents apiece. I asked for them instead, acting like I had a buyer in mind, and donated them to a Sioux Indian reservation that was begging in the newspaper. I felt relieved for a day or two afterwards, and I was excited when the Sioux Tribe promised to write a letter to my parole officer vouching for my benevolent nature.

I also tried to lift the weight off my conscience indirectly by convincing Jimmy to unburden himself of a regret that had been nagging him for years. Jimmy had been close with Joseph "The Whale" Peraino for decades, and it appalled him how The Whale's own brother and nephews set him up to be killed for no reason other than pure greed. When The Whale survived the botched hit, which killed his son and an innocent woman, Jimmy was one of the few wiseguys who ignored the Colombo Family ruling that "put The Whale on the shelf" and continued to acknowledge and care for his lonely, crippled, abandoned friend.

From what I heard, Jimmy was the only "stand-up guy" who actually stood by the blacklisted Joey Peraino. His own family pronounced him "dead" even though they had failed to kill him. Unless you've lived in the underworld, you cannot understand how much courage it takes to associate with the weak, broken losers of a bitter family turf war—Jimmy was very brave to stand by The Whale. He was daring the Persicos and Perainos, two families of killers, to take notice of his close ties to their enemy.

When The Whale's brother, Big Tony Peraino, finally died, Jimmy and I went to see his brash son Butchie, now the unchallenged king of the family porn empire. Without his dad's protection, Butchie mellowed out, either because he no longer had to prove to his dad how hard he was or because he knew he couldn't get away with being such an asshole without daddy's protection. As a sign of how drastically things had changed, Butchie introduced us to a writer he had just hired to pen his "memoirs," a violation of the Mafia code that might have motivated Big Tony to pick up his chainsaw and start removing the immediate branches of the Peraino family tree again.

After Jimmy worked Butchie into a good mood by talking about the old days, he brought up the reason we had visited. There was some unfinished business that Big Tony had left behind: his wheelchair-bound brother. Butchie, like everyone else, had refused to speak to his once beloved uncle.

Jimmy looked Butchie in the eyes: "Butchie, your

pops is gone. The Whale isn't. He's old, he's sick, and he's lonely. It's been long enough—talk to him before he goes, why don't ya? Leave that other stuff in the past. Don't take that poison to the grave."

Butchie looked down, flushed and clenching his jaw, his nostrils flaring. He pulled his face back up, cleared his throat, blinked, and shook his head. "I don't think so, Jimmy. I don't think that's going to happen." Jimmy was heartbroken; the "men of honor," if they ever existed, were no more.

Jimmy was shaking his head slowly left to right, left to right, as his old legs shuffled out of Butchie's office at as brisk a pace as he could manage. Jimmy couldn't be out of there quick enough. "These guys don't act right, Ken. If that's how you treat your *real* family . . ."

Butchie and The Whale both died of natural causes within a few years of our conversation. As far as Jimmy knew, they never spoke again. By the time The Whale finally stopped breathing, I was in Brooklyn with the same people who had shot him, his son, and an innocent woman over a dispute about the profits of a porn movie. I was putting them in jail—where they would inevitably join Jimmy.

ELEVEN

> *"I heard a lot of rumors about Kenny before I
> met him—that he was with Tabitha Stevens, that
> he was crazy, that he was in the Mob—but you
> always hear lots of gossip in porn. I never paid
> attention to anyone's bad reputation because,
> y'know, when you're in a business where you
> fuck ten strangers in a day, who are you to
> judge about anyone else on their reputation?"*
>
> Kendra Jade

When I met my ex-wife on the set of Buck Adams'
1996 action porn *Blade*, she was not the composite of
artificial plastic parts that would later become infamous
as "Tabitha Stevens." She was still Kelly at that point,
the sweet middle-class housewife from Long Island who,
in a fit of depression and boredom, abandoned her life
to become a porn star. At twenty-six years old and less
than a year into her porn career, she wasn't disfigured
yet; the porn character Tabitha Stevens had not completely cannibalized the real woman.

I was instantly attracted to Tabitha: she had dyed-
blond hair, a lean but healthy fitness-model body, very
little plastic surgery besides the customary breast implants, and a glowing, youthful face. She did not have
that indescribably *hard* physical and psychological shell
that even gorgeous porn girls usually develop within
months. She wasn't a walking human callus; she was still
soft, tender, kind, not yet paranoid and jaded.

Even with the freak-show boob job, Tabitha basically
looked less like a porno queen than a fresh-out-of-college

NYC trophy wife who spent her days pampering her skin and jogging. When she talked in her mousy voice and laughed with her too-toothy smile, she had a perky, pixie-ish, normal-girl charm completely absent from any other porn star I had ever met. Think talk-show host Kelly Ripa with implants.

Though I liked Tabitha's look on the set of *Blade*, it was just a mild attraction. I didn't feel compelled to approach her. I tried to stay away from porn girls ever since the SWAT team had to rescue me in my underwear from Amber Lynn. The novelty of all the easy and wild sex was wearing off *very* slowly, but it was wearing off nonetheless. And it was becoming harder for me not to feel disgusted with life after every visit to a porn set.

It was like my fascination with the Mafia: the Mob was exciting when I was hitting the clubs with Jackie di Padova, but gradually the countless trips to the racetrack with Jimmy revealed the lifestyle to be a grind that was just plain *boring* and dreary . . . a *job*, a working-class job. In porn, there were only so many times that I could watch a girl accidentally shit on a guy's penis during an anal scene, or watch a guy misfire during a gangbang and ejaculate on another man's chest, before it stopped being funny and just became sad. Was this really all that I could hope for in life?

I became so soured on porn that I refused to even show up on set at the movies I was financing or producing. I was bored with the entire culture. This distressed my partying buddy and house director, Chuck Martino, who always wanted another "ho wrangler" on set to keep things under control so he could party. Chuck especially wanted me to accompany him to Hawaii to film our beachside sex film *Maui Waui* since we had so much fun on our previous work vacations to Florida and Hawaii. To persuade me, Chuck brought me a list of available porn stars.

"Bro," he'd say, "pick the girl of your choice, and I'll book you two in a hotel room with one bed for the entire week. Easy as that." The "captive audience" strategy never failed; porn girls are so conditioned by the business that, even if they don't like you, they'll fuck you for the TV remote or room service. Unfortunately for Chuck, all the girls on his list were either old conquests or creatures I had no interest in bedding even out of morbid curiosity.

Chuck was persistent. He came back the next day with a fresh list of candidates. I looked at the list, saw Tabitha's name, and reluctantly decided to go. My marriage started on a high note: an impersonal hookup brokered by Chuck "Philmore Butts" Martino.

Chuck was a thoughtful matchmaker: he booked Tabitha and me into a beautiful suite overlooking the ocean. Chuck always went the extra inch to show you he actually gave a shit about people other than himself. Unfortunately, opposing Chuck's good intentions was the male star of the movie, Shawn Ricks, who was crushing on Tabitha and mounted a vigorous cock-blocking defense to keep me away from her.

I didn't take Shawn seriously as competition because he was widely mocked for having the funniest warm-up routine of any male porn star. Shawn was completely incapable of performing without following a set diet and routine: before every scene, Shawn had to smoke a joint, drink a cap of "date-rape drug" GHB, and listen to "I Got the Power" by Snap! and "Stranglehold" by Ted Nugent while shadow-boxing and psyching himself up, and then taking another hit of pot.

Only after that last hit would the Popeye theme song

start to play, and Ricks' penis would rise for duty. It was as if he had a combination lock on his erections that could only be released by spinning the knob to "Pot," then "GHB," then "Snap!," then "Nugent," then back to "Pot." How could I hope to compete for Tabitha's affection with a guy who was functionally impotent in any scenario where he couldn't listen to Ted Nugent or that "I got the POWAH!" song?

Besides, there were plenty of girls to go around. While waiting for Tabitha to notice me, I let her costars Farrah and Nico Treasures take care of my sexual entertainment. This turned out to be an unwittingly brilliant plan for seducing Tabitha; for insecure and viciously competitive porn women, no man is more irresistible than the man who shows a clear preference for other porn women. It was clear Tabitha didn't much like me at first, but that didn't stop her from fucking me on the beach and giving me a handjob on the flight back to California just to prove a point to herself. The stewardess caught us in the act the moment I popped into a barf bag.

Until that trip to Hawaii, the porn-industry maxim that sex can be just an impersonal business transaction always held true for me. I never developed feelings for any of the porn girls I screwed around with, even when I spent fifty hours a go with Amber Lynn, or when Jill Kelly invited me to her weekend sleepovers.

What I didn't understand was that my immunity to emotional attachment had nothing to do with porn's no-strings-attached, anything-goes subculture and everything to do with the damage done to me by the loss of Tara, Clyde, and what was left of my self-respect in 1989. I was too wounded emotionally to care for anyone but other criminals.

The slow spiritual and emotional thaw that began

with my time in the L.A. Mafia Family had an unexpected side effect: I was emotionally vulnerable for the
first time in years. As I fooled around with Tabitha, I fell
prey to brief spells of tenderness, empathy, and affection.
It had nothing to do with the sex itself, which was pretty
good by normal standards but resolutely average on the
Amber Lynn Memorial Scale of Wild Porn Sex. Unbelievably, I was the one man in Tabitha's life to fall for her for
any reason *besides* the sex.

Tabitha was a beautiful, sweet-natured, troubled girl
who was subconsciously *begging* for a man to nurture her
and make her feel loved, and in my increasingly guilty
state of mind, I was susceptible to the "I need a daddy!"
routine. In retrospect, I think I was so excited to begin
feeling human for the first time since the 1980s that I lost
my mind, leaving a vacuum in which my heart took over
the operational controls and promptly sent my life into a
nosedive.

My courtship of Tabitha was completed before I
knew it had begun: the first gentle, caring look I gave
her won over her desperate, starving heart. Before I had
time to blink, Tabitha's feelings for me went from total
indifference to thoughts of marriage. Her insane, head-
long rush to emotional attachment would normally have
set off my Crazy Bitch Alarm and provoked a screaming,
hands-in-the-air retreat. We were in a fever dream, and
it was just the sort of daredevil, manifestly stupid, and
self-destructive rush I have always dug.

When we returned from Hawaii, Tabitha invited me
to Las Vegas to meet her family, and I was able to inspect the source of her daddy issues firsthand. That air
of normalcy and social polish that distinguished Tabitha
from most of her hard-living, street-urchin colleagues
was not misleading. Tabitha was an orphan adopted by a

financially secure, healthy family in Long Island. Though she had been troubled by the usual worries that she was not as loved as her parents' biological children, the fatal psychic wound had been delivered not by sibling jealousy or parental neglect but by a burst blood vessel in her father's head.

When Tabitha was an insecure teenage daddy's girl, a catastrophic stroke ended her father's Wall Street career and Tabitha's suburban Long Island adolescence. Suddenly, her brilliant, in-control dad was a drooling zombie strapped into a wheelchair, and she was dragged cross-country to Las Vegas and its dry climate, which doctors suggested might help her father recover. Instead, he just died, leaving Tabitha a grieving, fatherless hot chick in a strange high school. It wouldn't have taken a psychic to guess where Tabitha would turn to fill the vacuum of affection, self-esteem, and stability left by the loss of her father and her secure life in Long Island.

For a few months, my relationship with Tabitha provided her with the security and emotional fulfillment she was lacking, or at least gave her the illusion that it was doing so. Consequently, when I fell for Tabitha she was briefly whole, briefly secure with herself, maybe even briefly sane. She was a bright, cute girlfriend who, like me, was happier having a nice dinner, seeing a movie, and hanging out at home than club-hopping and doing drugs. In fact, she seemed like the perfect wife for me: a lady on the streets, a whore in the bedroom, and a bona fide moneymaker with a lucrative career that guaranteed me the right to fuck whomever I wanted on the side. I didn't "love" her—I let her fuck other guys on camera!—but I didn't expect to love anyone after Tara anyway.

Momentarily reconstructed as a demure, middle-class

Long Island princess, Tabitha was the one porn girl I could take around to Jimmy Caci, Jerry Zimmerman, and Louie Gelfuso without feeling self-conscious or ashamed. Their response was all the same: "Are you kidding me? *This* girl is in porn?" Even Jackie di Padova had to admit, "That's one nice pig you got there!" As long as the illusion was there that I might be the cure for whatever ailed her, Tabitha was a perfectly average girlfriend—only much, much, much sexier.

Of course, I had reasons to be suspicious. Tabitha had a heavy pill habit, which didn't bother me since I was always a fan of taking a cap of GHB before bed. Also, her appetite for food befit a super-heavyweight, but, since she never gained weight due to her Kenyan-marathon-runner metabolism, I didn't mind. Unfortunately, my metabolism could not keep pace, so our diet of multicourse restaurant meals turned me into a fat guy for the first and only time in my life.

The most serious warning sign was that, besides me, nothing pleased Tabitha at all: food, clothes, cars, homes. She was never full after a meal, never satisfied with where we lived, never comfortable with her wardrobe. She would buy $500 in clothes, dump them in the back of her closet, and wear sweatpants for a month. If I had been paying attention, I would have realized that her wasteful, irrational, compulsive shopping was a sign that she was desperately trying to fill a gaping hole in her psyche, the only gaping hole that she would not get paid to fill on camera. At the time, I figured her lunatic shopping addiction was a symptom of being born female, since that's how the type of spoiled party girl I dated *usually* acted.

Before I even realized we were seriously dating, Tabitha suggested that we get married in Las Vegas in this flippant, "feel like renting a movie?" way. That should have raised a thousand or so red flags, but I was out of my mind and searching for something to fix me as well.

"What the fuck? Why not?" We had an open relationship anyway, so it was not like I would be missing anything in bed. The only difference between getting married and dating were the tax benefits. Even if we got divorced, none of my possessions or assets were legal and documented anyway, so I figured I had nothing to lose.

> *"One day right after they got together, I visited Kenny and Tabitha at their apartment with my newborn kid. Tabitha seemed totally normal and sweet. While I talked to Kenji, my kid was playing on the carpet with Tabitha, laughing and smiling; she was real good with babies. I never would have imagined what she would turn into. When my kid grows up, I'm going to get out some photos and a video of Tabitha today and be like, 'Dude, you played with that!'"*

Chuck Browntooth

Shortly before our wedding in late 1996, Babar, Attorney-At-Law, called me one day and asked if Tabitha and I would like to see the Vince Vaughn movie *Swingers* with him. Babar was giddy: the film was about a bunch of hard-drinking, hard-partying L.A. hipster degenerates who brag about how badass they are and spend all of their time trying to pick up women in clubs with cheesy pickup lines. In other words, it was *The Life of Babar*. It was a cultural milestone for him; the *Roots* for club-hopping L.A. douchebags. Since Tabitha and I were indiscriminate movie nuts, and girls tend to enjoy Babar's slapstick ladies' man act, I agreed.

Babar, Tabitha, and I found great seats in our favorite movie theater in Orange County. After the lights went down, two stragglers hustled into the theater and snooped around for seats in the dark. Though they were on the other side, and I could only intermittently get in a glance at them as the "Coming Soon" trailers flashed on and off the screen, the woman seemed familiar. I felt my heart stop beating and my lungs refuse to take in air: it was Tara.

I had not seen her for at least six years, and, if there had been any doubt, all it took was a glimpse of her blond hair and round-cheeked face to remind me that, yes, I was still devastatingly in love with her. Though nine out of ten men would have preferred a swimsuit model sexbomb like Tabitha, at that moment she meant nothing to me, even though I was less than a week away from marrying her.

"That girl . . ." I whispered to Babar, who was giddily awaiting the start of *Swingers*. "That girl . . . who just sat down. . . . I think that's Tara. Really, I think that's Tara." Babar scowled and rolled his eyes at me. Sitting with his baggy of ecstasy tablets in one pocket, his pot in another pocket, and crumpled-up bar napkins full of faintly remembered names and tirelessly won telephone numbers in his back pocket, Babar could not have been less understanding of my heartfelt attachment to some girl-next-door from high school.

"Bro, bro-o-o-o-o-o. Seriously! *Man*. . . . Dog, c'mon," Babar whispered back, interrupting his droning pothead slang to work through the rest of his arsenal of "Babar is very disappointed in you" body language: furrowed brow, a slow shake of the head back and forth, widened eyes and upturned palms, even a drawn-back skeptical look as if I had just gone crazy.

"*Dude*, you're getting married in a couple days, and still you're thinking of her! Man, it's been like a *decade*!" he said with "I rest my case!" finality. With that, *Swingers* started, and my old friend ceased to pay attention to my distress so he could fully immerse himself in homoerotic admiration of Vince Vaughn's fast-talking hepcat character.

My highly developed instinct for self-preservation sprung to my defense: *clearly*, this lady wasn't Tara. It couldn't be true because I couldn't handle it if it were true. I rushed to convince myself—what were the odds that Tara would be seeing a dopey movie like *Swingers* in the same theater in Orange County? Depending on the angle and my memory, the woman in the movie theater was either too ugly or too good-looking to be Tara, too youthful or too worn, too short or too tall, too voluptuous or too thin. By halfway through *Swingers*, I had myself fooled; it wasn't Tara.

With that settled, I started to pay attention to the movie—and discovered that the movie was about some shithead who couldn't get over his ex-girlfriend. Babar even turned to me once or twice to give me judgmental looks when the dialogue applied especially to lovelorn losers like me who needed to move on to new and better pussy.

After the movie ended, the three of us went to the theater restrooms. Babar and I finished first and killed time talking in the crowded lobby about the usual Babar subject matter: all the partying he'd done and how wild and crazy a guy he was. Tabitha emerged from the crowded ladies' room with fresh makeup; a step behind her was Tara. There was no room for doubt, or hope.

In order to survive on the streets, like most criminals I had to develop an alter-ego with none of my weaknesses, fears, morals, or doubts that I could substitute for the real me in dangerous situations. Like my soon-to-be wife Kelly and her whore alter ego Tabitha Stevens, eventually Kenny from Orange County became entirely subsumed by the merciless, unfeeling comic book villain Kenji Gallo. It was a necessity if I wanted to pursue a life in the underworld; without that mask of insane kamikaze aggression, normal Kenny from the suburbs would have been destroyed by people like Mike Marvich or Jimmy Caci, two men whose street identities ate them alive decades ago. I needed Kenji if I wanted to survive in the Mafia.

When Tara glanced up and recognized me, I felt Kenji dying: I was choking on air; my eyes blurred; my brain was dipped in and out of a pool of frying black static. I thought I was going to fall and slap the back of my head on the lobby floor, but finally air broke through to my lungs and my heart thumped back into rhythm. When my eyes refocused, I no longer saw through the eyes of a criminal; I saw through the eyes of the boy who once saw his entire reason for living in Tara's smile.

It wasn't an immediate, 180-degree Jekyll and Hyde transformation, but for the first time in almost a decade the operational controls of my brain were in the hands of Ken, not Kenji. After seven years of hibernation, I was awake again, though it would take another eight years before I would shed the dark, shadowy, Kenji side of my identity completely. He was mortally wounded, but it would take a very long time for such a beast to bleed out.

Tara was only a few feet away from me; she was smiling the uncomfortable, fake smile that polite girls adopt when they see a shitty ex-boyfriend to whom they don't want to give the pleasure of a bad response. Babar could see that I was shaking; he had no idea I wanted to run the fuck away bawling.

One look at Tara's beautiful face convinced me that, contrary to my pretensions, I was the stupidest motherfucker in the entire universe; I was a spectacular failure. I was born into a wealthy, supportive family who would have given me the money to do anything with my life, and as a teenager I stumbled upon a perfect woman who wanted to marry me. She would have put up with and adapted to anything besides the idea that I was a sociopathic coke smuggler; literally anything else would have probably been acceptable.

Instead of embracing that perfect life with Tara, I made decisions that resulted in the loss of my ability to love, the loss of my best friends, a long rap sheet, an engagement to a porn star, and a daily life spent filming gangbangs with Philmore Butts and collecting shylock debts at the racetrack with an elderly Italian who was pathologically afraid of uncarpeted floors. Most of these decisions had been made because the buzz of life on the streets was too fantastic for an adrenaline addict like me to pass up, but that excuse just made me a pathetic junkie. I had no excuse besides stupidity and weakness— the last two traits an arrogant, supposed tough guy like me would have ever wanted to define his character.

The agony of seeing Tara again was exponentially heightened by whom we were each with: Tara was hanging all over some handsome rich guy, and I was standing next to a porn star with giant fake tits and a sniffling cokehead jackass who hadn't changed at all since high school. Clearly, her 1989 suspicions about my inability to mature and lead a healthy life were proven. She stopped and gawked at the car wreck so that her boyfriend could fully understand how lucky she was that she had not strapped herself into the passenger's seat.

"Ken, oh my *God*, what's up?" she said with the sweet but flat voice that she once used with waiters and acquaintances in high school. I meant nothing to her.

"Oh, uh, nothing. Just seeing this . . . a . . . a, um, movie."

"Oh, great," Tara drawled as she turned to the man at her side. "*This* is my fiancé . . ." That word was devastating; "fiancé" was a word that guaranteed I would have to live with my mistakes for the rest of my life.

I'll omit the personal details of Tara's now-husband, but needless to say I had no choice but to respond by introducing Tabitha, who was fidgeting uncomfortably. At that moment, I realized that, although Tabitha looked like a normal girl to me, to an average woman her giant breasts still made her look like a freak. I could see Tara was not impressed. I winced when it came out that we were both getting married on the exact same day; now I knew for sure the exact day when my life would become an unsalvageable failure.

After we said our goodbyes a moment later, Tabitha was oblivious to the torment I was suffering. I wasn't doing a good job of hiding it, but this is Tabitha we're talking about, so I would've needed a blinking neon sign saying "Kenny's in pain!" for her to take notice. Babar knew, but Babar wasn't much of an empathizer or a therapist. Though I felt an intense, suffocating panic over how badly I had botched my life, I saw no way out. I had already sentenced myself to the *wrong* life; the only thing I could do was make the best of the time I had.

A week later, Tabitha and I were married in Las Vegas as scheduled. She looked very beautiful, very happy; I looked like a POW forcing my face to grin so as not to displease my captors. Before the ceremony, I met Steve "The Whale" Cino, high-powered entertainment lawyer and porn groupie Mark Mazie, and Babar at the Tropicana. We all threw down some shots and, for old times' sake, Babar and I snorted some lines of coke.

At the Excalibur Casino valet parking, I noticed a man standing next to a surveillance van taking photos of us using a camera with a telephoto lens. I wasn't surprised; it was, after all, a Mob wedding. The Whale, "Fat Tony" Angioletti, John Branco, Vince Lupo, and Jimmy Caci's girlfriend Gerri were all in attendance. Jimmy, naturally, was busy refusing to eat the prison cafeteria food because there was no carpet on the floors. Some douchebag dressed up as Merlin married us, which was pretty pathetic since I was thinking about what a beautiful, traditional wedding Tara was surely enjoying at the same time. Though I was depressed, no one could tell since I was flying on coke; I performed my vows with the energy of a black preacher and was hopping around afterwards like I would spontaneously combust at any moment.

My wedding had driven me to abuse hard drugs for the first time in years; I was very aware of how bad a sign that was. What could I do? I was beyond saving; I was *married* to a porn star.

Though I didn't know it at the time, my soon-to-be catastrophic marriage to Tabitha was not even my top problem. Two wired-up F.B.I. informants attended my wedding. I had chosen the wrong path in life, but at least I was a success: at twenty-eight years old I was receiving the highest accolades a gangster can receive. The United States government was paying informants to befriend me.

If my marriage to Tabitha had an upside, it was the discovery of a new and extraordinarily easy criminal racket: the extortion of madams and escort agencies.

Tabitha told me that most porn girls were making outrageous money doing "side work"—high-end prostitution and escorting. It wasn't uncommon for a star like Tabitha to make $10,000 to $15,000 in a weekend trip to New York City or Las Vegas for one of the big escort agencies or madams. If I had been a cartoon, Tabitha would have seen my pupils liquefy and take the shape of dollar signs.

I knew that there was no way that the madams and escort agencies who were trafficking in that type of cash had enough muscle to resist a visit from one of my mercenary terror squads of bikers or Crips.

I decided to test my theory on the owner of an L.A. escort agency who lived in an opulent mansion. I took my longtime buddy Keith along for the ride with two pistols in case the pimp gave us shit. I knocked on the pimp's door and politely introduced myself. He recognized me and knew my reputation. "I've decided that I'd like to be your partner," I told him with a look that conveyed my real meaning, "and would like some cash to seal the deal." Without hesitation, he walked inside, took $20,000 from his safe, and gave it to us to leave him alone. As soon as the door closed, Keith and I busted out laughing; it was the laughter of pure, impossible-to-verbalize joy.

I did this routine around Los Angeles and Las Vegas, and most madams and pimps saw the logic in delegating their collections to me so they could get something out of giving me my taste of the profits. Since I quickly became known as the Mob's go-to guy for the prostitution rackets in Vegas and Hollywood, Vince Lupo approached me with a problem. Some friends of his were having trouble with some disobedient prostitutes.

Arshak "Tony" Kazarian ran the city of Glendale, on the edge of Porno Valley. Glendale is home to the largest population of Armenian immigrants in America, around half the population, and at the time Tony Kazarian was the unchallenged dictator of that insular, 19th-century-style immigrant community. Tony's crew was making millions in extortion, prostitution, human trafficking, gambling, and rigged video-poker machines, which he put in bars, clubs, and restaurants all around town.

The problem Tony had taken to Vince Lupo concerned a racket involving the Sultan of Brunei, the richest man in the world. Tony's crew was providing hot young Armenian girls the opportunity to travel to the tiny Asian oil kingdom as "singers" or "personal assistants"—which in reality meant they would work as escorts and harem girls for the Sultan, crown princes, and multimillionaire oil-industry nobility. The longer the girls stayed, the higher their pay would become. Some are today worth millions thanks to the Sultan.

At the end of their stay in Brunei, the Sultan's chamberlain would hand the girls a visa and a bankcard for the Isle of Man, a small autonomous island off of Great Britain, where their cash was untraceably deposited. After the girls retrieved their cash, they were expected to pay twenty percent in tribute to Tony Kazarian for obtaining the jobs in the first place. Because they were stupid, two of these girls chose not to pay Tony and fled to Salt Lake City with his money.

Vince Lupo introduced me to Tony, who explained his problem in broken English. Though he knew where the women were in Salt Lake City, one of the girls lived with her father, a police officer. There was no way anyone in his crew of unintelligible, fresh-off-the-boat Armenian savages could negotiate a situation that complex without getting arrested. Tony offered $2,500 down and a percentage of whatever the girls paid in tribute if I would escort two of his goons to Salt Lake City, find the girls for them, and act as the negotiator and facilitator. He wanted the money returned peacefully, without drama and bloodshed. I was excited as hell to take on this *Grand Theft Auto*–style mission, as it was easily the most bizarre task I'd ever been given on the streets.

The two Armenians whom I chauffeured around Salt Lake City were real cavemen; most of the English words they knew were obscenities. Without me as their sherpa, they never would have found the girls. I can only imagine how their conversations with the cop father would have gone: "Your girl . . . fucking whore . . . need cash . . . now . . . or we not happy!"

Our arrival in Salt Lake City was underwhelming; the Armenians seemed disgusted by the putrid, disgusting stagnant pond they called a lake. Nonetheless, we settled in; this would not be a quick operation. The Armenians were distraught: as Soviet-style alcoholics, they found the lack of places to drink in Mormon Country completely inconceivable on both practical and spiritual levels. Why even go through the chore of living if you can't drink yourself to death? When they realized that they had no place to booze and party, the Armenians became psychotically impatient to get this job over with. Had I given them the word, they would have just knocked on the cop's door, put a bullet in his brain, dragged the girls by their hair to the car, and stuffed them into the trunk for the ride back to Glendale.

I chose to visit the girl without any law enforcement ties first as the easier target. I drove way out to the suburbs and told the Armenians to keep their mouths shut. The girl refused to open the door, but I gently talked to her from the front porch: no threats, no raised voice, nothing objectionable. I just calmly reminded her that she had made a business deal in good faith and had yet to fulfill her side of the bargain. I left my card and then drove across the state to another far-removed Mormon suburb to visit the cop's house. This was very dicey: I told the Armenians to disappear completely. I left my card with an older woman who answered the door and left.

Within a couple hours, I received a phone call from the cop and his daughter. The cop was adamant that his daughter should pay Mr. Kazarian the money she owed him for getting her the job as a "personal assistant." I was leery of a trap, so I repeated over and over that I was not collecting the money, that I did not know the details of the agreement, and that I was there only to say that they should wire whatever money they owed Tony to the offshore account they had been given. It wasn't a trap; the cop unwittingly compelled his daughter to pay her pimp. My cut of her tribute payment would be $4,500.

With that taken care of, we visited the first girl again, who screamed that she was calling the police as soon as I knocked. Who would have guessed that the girl *without* the police connections would be the hard case? I talked to Tony on the phone, and he told me to wait in Salt Lake City for a few more days to see if the girl changed her mind. This did not appeal to me, so instead I suggested that he pay me a couple thousand dollars in exchange for bombing the girl's car. Though he appreciated my enthusiasm and old-school gangster ethics, he was wary of getting into trouble with the Mormons and told me to just wait. After two more days of staring at the wall, Tony called us back to Glendale, gave me $7,000 in cash, and promised that he was sending someone else to take care of the holdout girl.

Considering that Tony's entire crew was wiped out a few months later when they tried to assassinate a Secret

Service agent, there's no limit to what may have happened to that girl in Utah. I never bothered to ask. I had prostitute difficulties of my own to worry about.

> *"There is always that one person who just drives you crazy, who you're just nuts about. I don't know about their private life, but from what I saw, Tabitha was the love of Kenny's life. He was just heads over heels, irrational, crazy for Tabitha. They made no sense as a couple—I told him all the time I just didn't get it—but that is just the way it is."*
>
> Jill Kelly

As a side effect of my marriage to Tabitha, I was effectively becoming a Las Vegas–based gangster. I traveled extensively, but Vegas was the most convenient base of operations since it was an international mecca for all of my most lucrative rackets: prostitution, loan sharking, sports betting, pornography, and financial scams. It was also "newer" and less predictable to me than Los Angeles, which made it less boring. The problem with Las Vegas was it was where the House Always Won, and, ever since my relationship with Officer Jerry ended, I was not playing for the House.

A day or two after our wedding, Tabitha realized that the ring on her finger had not resurrected her daddy from his grave or restored her self-esteem. She began to resent me for this. Thrown into a smothering depression, she refused to get out of bed until the afternoon, pilled herself into a staggering zombie the moment she woke up, and began throwing my money away like it carried communicable diseases. The only passion that remained in our relationship was her passion to tan, eat, and shop.

Since I honestly cared for Tabitha, I tried to be patient, but she was a teenage girl acting up for Daddy's attention and would not accept an even-tempered response. She wanted an eruption, so she began screaming at me, insulting me, doing anything she could to degrade me on a daily basis. I became pissed, but I was never so angry that I forgot that she was too fragile to take any pushback from me. After Alex Jordan and Savannah, I did not want another porno suicide on my head; besides, I saw how the porn industry had ostracized and blamed Jill Kelly for Cal Jammer's death, and I couldn't stand any interference with my income.

Desperate to elicit a reaction, Tabitha tried to fuck with my business: she went behind my back to the ill, elderly Louie Gelfuso with our relationship troubles. Like Jimmy, Louie was a sentimental idealist when it came to family, and it deeply disappointed him to hear from my wife that I was a shitty husband. "I just hate to see you two kids fighting!" he whined. "I'm still friends with my *ex*-wife! It's not worth it, Ken. Just do whatever she wants." I gave in, and Tabitha and I had breakfast with him to show him that everything was okay.

I tried to distract myself from my misbegotten marriage with my work on the street, but the catastrophic disintegration of my personal life coincided with the catastrophic disintegration of the L.A. Family. As everyone I knew started dropping, I should have followed Jerry's lessons and fled back to Florida, but instead I chose to stand still and wait patiently to get kicked in the nuts.

As always, the first soldier to fall in battle was Jimmy Caci, who could get sentenced to two-to-five years for failing to send his mail with sufficient postage. Fresh from a stint in jail, Jimmy set up a meeting at Frankie's on Melrose, a New York Italian restaurant that's a favorite

L.A. wiseguy hangout. Since Joe Isgro, Joe Dente, Joe Pesci, and made Bonanno soldier Vinny Faraci were regulars at Frankie's, Jimmy liked to conduct business there because you never knew what opportunities might come your way.

I was eating with Tabitha, Jimmy, and Mob groupie Ori "QVC Juicer" Spado, and I could immediately tell that the tubby shithead was hiding something. In addition to his usual bragging, Ori was broadcasting some of the sweatiest, most distressed body language I'd ever seen. He was fidgeting in his seat like he had a river otter stuck up his ass. Seeing that I was on to him, Ori went on the offensive. "Hey, big shot, I don't think you got the money to pay for our meals tonight," he sneered, insinuating that I was a lackey who had to throw down cash whenever he looked at me the wrong way.

"Why would I pay for dinner when your fat ass is paying for my dinner and I'm eating for free?" Safe in Jimmy's protection, Ori jumped up and made like he was going to come at me.

"Hey! Sit down and relax! Cut the shit!" Jimmy the referee made the save at the last second, just as Ori knew he would.

Ori was such an imposing tough guy that Tabitha, whose non-plastic parts weighed about seventy-five pounds, didn't even flinch when he lurched at us. I swear to you that I would have set Ori on fire the next day if I hadn't been conscientious about disrespecting Ori's protectors, Jimmy and Sonny.

After dinner, Jimmy drove home with Ori since he stayed in Ori's spare room when he was in Los Angeles. A couple minutes after Tabitha and I got home, we received a phone call from Ori, who sounded like he was going to cry.

"THEY GOT JIMMY!"

"Wait, wait, what?" I was panicked since Ori was so freaked out that I figured Jimmy had to have been shot. Surely, Jimmy Caci getting arrested for the thirty-seventh time would not merit such hysterics.

"The police! They got Jimmy! We were sitting watching TV, and suddenly there's this knock at the door. I go to open it and see who it is, and it's the coppers! They came in and got Jimmy. What are we gonna do?" I wanted to say, "Bury you alive in a cornfield, you rat fuck!" Instead, I asked Ori what the charges were, and he acted like he hadn't thought to ask.

I knew it was Ori; my suspicions about his behavior earlier were confirmed by this transparently bullshit story. Ori lived on the third floor in a heavily guarded apartment building with buzzers at the door; in that type of building, a Mafia capo and a longtime Mafia associate would know that a random knock at the door without any buzz over the intercom had to be the cops.

Ori was a rat, but he wasn't so stupid that he innocently bumbled his way into opening the door for the cops and letting them in without a search warrant. Like every other crook in the world, Ori knew that the first question upon seeing any cop is "What are the charges?" The only reason he wouldn't tell me what Jimmy was pinched for was if the crime might implicate him as the informant. Jimmy had been set up.

Right away I called Jimmy's brother, Bobby Milano, and our regular accomplice Vince Lupo to tell them what had happened. Without saying a word to them about my suspicions, they both independently fingered Ori for the setup. The word went out about Ori; he was a marked man if any of us saw him. Pete Milano was one thing, but Jimmy Caci and his crew from Buffalo were not above killing a rat.

A day later, Jimmy called me with venom in his voice. "Listen, Ken, that rat motherfucker opened the door for the cops, ya understand? He's a rat motherfucker! Twenty fucking minutes before he lets the cops in like old friends, that piece of shit went downstairs for some reason and came back up looking like he was going to shit himself. He was their fucking doorman, the shithead!

"I got something I need you to do, ya hear? This ain't no joke. Immediately, the second you get off this phone, you head over to that cocksucker Ori's place, get my car, and drive it down to Palm Springs. At my place, there's something I need you to get for me and take a look at. I was going through Ori's apartment, and I found it. It's a little tape. I didn't know what it was, and I didn't have anything to play it on, but I was suspicious so I kept it just in case. It gave me a weird feeling. It's hidden in a little cranny behind my trash compactor. Go get it and find out what the fuck is on it."

I took the mini-cassette tape from Jimmy's hiding spot and stuck it in my audio player:

"It's one o'clock on Saturday, July the sixth. This is a conversation I'm gonna be having with Scott Gariola, FBI agent based here in Los Angeles. . . ." It was Ori's voice. On the tape, Ori claimed that he was about to be inducted into the Los Angeles Family since "the little guys" loved him ("the little guys" usually referred to midget fashionistas Louie Caruso and Tommy Gambino). As a made man informant, Ori argued that he should get a deal without any jail time since, he explained, a prison guard relative of his had gotten "something close to tuberculosis" from working on the inside. You could practically hear the FBI agent's eyes roll. To make up for it, Ori ratted out Jimmy's location so the FBI could crawl further up his ass.

I had dinner with Bobby Milano in Palm Springs to tell him about the tape and get the story behind Jimmy's bust. Ori and Jimmy had been at Jerry Zimmerman's office when an acquaintance complained about some guy who owed him money. Ori, a compulsive braggart, insisted that they leave that moment so he could "personally collect the debt." Jimmy sat in the car and watched through the window as Ori walked into this guy's business and started screaming. Ori was putting on a show for Jimmy, though this very special episode of *Ori Spado: Badass Gangster* was interrupted when the guy behind the desk smashed Ori in the face with a tape dispenser. Jimmy ran inside just as the debtor was pulling his pistol; luckily, he knew Jimmy from the racetrack and made nice.

It was for being at the scene of *this* "crime" that Jimmy was being dragged back to jail. As you can imagine, everyone in Jimmy's circle was furious that the old man was going away for Ori's botched extortion attempt; nothing pisses criminals off more than the injustice of going to jail for the one crime they didn't commit.

Vince Lupo was even madder than Jimmy's brother. Lupo hated Ori more than I did and, but for Ori's connections, might have beaten Ori's ass on numerous occasions. Lupo called me up and reminded me about a meeting we had at his Culver City restaurant with Ori and Tabitha. At the time, we were both confused when sweaty-ass Ori wouldn't take off his jacket in the L.A. heat, and we made fun of him for lurching away when Tabitha tried to feel his "nice, soft, manicured hands." "Fucker was jumpy 'cause he was ratting!" Vince screamed. "What he did to the old man . . . if I see him, that's it."

I set up a meeting with Louie Gelfuso at Vince's

restaurant so he could hear the tape. Louie gave the tape to his son Michael to listen to in their car while he ate lunch; Michael, who was tougher than his dad, came back livid and begging to pop Ori. Vince Lupo then suggested that he call our buddy Tony Kazarian in Glendale and pay him to take care of it since it would never be traced back to us.

As I knew from previous experience, Louie's default response was to panic at any mention of violence, order everyone to calm down, and speed across town to Pete Milano's place. I received a phone call that night from Louie saying that Pete thanked me for the tape and ordered that Ori's punishment be a strict banishment from all L.A. Family rackets. In response to Ori ratting and sending our best capo to jail on a trumped-up charge, our "Mafia family" would retaliate by giving Ori the silent treatment.

Bullshit. I wasn't going along with that, especially after I learned from Jerry Zimmerman that Ori had framed him in a stolen merchandise sting. I loved Jimmy and Jerry like fathers, loved them far more than Tabitha if I'm being honest, and some douchebag had set *both* of them up to go to jail in their old age. I may have taken Jerry's advice to heart and abandoned my cocaine cowboy ways, but I felt like I wouldn't even be worthy of being called a man let alone a gangster if I let a little shit like Ori get away with hurting the two people closest to me in the entire world. Just as I was deciding how to get back at him, Ori called up Tabitha and threatened her for the things I was saying around town about him. Ori . . . threatened . . . *my* . . . wife.

I decided to kill Ori Spado, a man I hated from the moment I met him. Like Joey Avila, Ori was begging for it: he fucked with my money; he fucked with my two best friends; he threatened to hurt my wife; he was surely ratting on me to the feds for crimes that I never committed with him. Though I know better today, it still *feels* like Ori deserved to die, that killing him would have to be considered a *good deed* or at least a moral wash. However conflicted I feel about it as a reformed man, at the time I was never surer of anything in the world: I had to kill Ori Spado. There was no choice, and there was no shame in it. After months of feeling like I was growing out of the gangster trade, Ori reawakened crazy, homicidal Kenji overnight.

I was not going to get caught. I put on a disguise—a mullet wig, baseball cap, sunglasses, baggy clothes—and took a stolen car and a hot, untraceable pistol. I drove to Ori's building and waited in the underground parking lot near his space. The plan was simple: two bullets in the chest, control shot to the head to make sure, burn the car and disguise in an abandoned lot, toss the pistol in the ocean, and never say a word to anyone. I was sure I would get away with it, no doubts whatsoever.

I waited in Ori's garage for hours; he was a no-show. I came back the next night, and the night after that. I waited a week and then tried again. Nothing—he wasn't there. I finally realized my mistake; by spreading word of the tape, I'd tipped off Ori and the feds. What did Mike Marvich teach me: *Keep your mouth shut until you take care of business. Don't give your target warning.* I really was losing it.

After bungling the payback Ori deserved, I did my best to compensate according to the L.A. Family's guidelines. Within a couple days, everyone in the West Coast underworld had listened to one of my many copies of the tape. The response was always the same: "I shoulda known!"

Over the past few years, the police have caught Ori in everything from cocaine distribution to making threats to trafficking stolen merchandise, yet the walking marshmallow never did time. Everyone was too busy with their careers to notice how unlikely it was that a shitty criminal like Ori would get busted over and over and escape prosecution every time. Later, I even uploaded the Ori tape online and sent it to everyone I knew in the Mob, though it somehow didn't prevent Sonny Franzese and the acting boss of the Colombo Family, Thomas "Tommy Shots" Gioeli, from being indicted with Ori Spado in *late* 2008, over a decade after I personally tipped off Jerry and Jackie in Sonny's crew.

Once I started sending the tape all over, I received two very strange phone calls that should have revealed the identities of two more FBI rats. If I hadn't been distracted by my premature midlife crisis and nightmare with Tabitha, I would have saved one gangster's life and derailed a sting operation that sent twenty gangsters to jail and resulted in my cooperation agreement with the government. In the first phone call, Fat Tony Angioletti asked me about the price of a kilo of cocaine—which was so far above his criminal pay grade that he might as well have asked about purchasing a black market nuclear weapon. Shortly afterwards I got a call from John Branco, another guy who had neither the money to buy a kilo nor the customers to sell it to, asking me the same thing. How did these two-bit assholes I had never told about my long-extinct coke career know to ask me?

In retrospect, it's hard for me to accept how stupid I was for not immediately recognizing the truth. Sometimes, I think I was trying to get myself caught so I could have an excuse to leave the Life and start over. It still seems impossible to me: how did someone who got away with hundreds of cocaine deals, armed robberies, and aggravated batteries when he was a high, drunk, roid-raging *teenager* get nailed by idiots like John Branco, Fat Tony Angioletti, and Ori Spado?

My stupidity would cost Herbert "Fat Herbie" Blitzstein his life. Though the press portrayed Fat Herbie as a washed-up has-been, in reality he was still one of the biggest loan sharks in Las Vegas; Steve Cino told me he had well over a million dollars on the streets. Herbie had been Tony Spilotro's best friend when "The Ant" ran Las Vegas, and even after Tony was buried alive in a cornfield—a scene immortalized in Martin Scorsese's *Casino*—elite connections like the ones Herbie made with "The Ant" don't go bad.

Crooks such as Herbie, who are likeable, trustworthy, reliably profitable, and always sure to spread their cash around, *never* become washed up. Despite being in such poor health that he could barely walk or muster the lung capacity to talk, Herbie was still a moneymaker in 1997. All he had to do was listen, nod, write down numbers and directions, and hand the sheets to one of the younger knockaround guys in Vegas to do his bidding.

One of the thugs Herbie occasionally hired was John Branco, who desperately needed the money: he was mowing lawns for cash and living out of a trailer. On a collection for Herbie, Branco fucked up and got arrested. He took it personally, as if it were Herbie's fault and not a workplace hazard that comes with the job. Convinced Herbie should have used his ancient Jewish gangster superpowers to save him from justice, Branco nursed a vendetta against Fat Herbie that would have been homicidal if Branco had had the balls to pull a trigger.

Instead, I think Branco incited someone else to murder Fat Herbie. I was one of the tough guys he called.

Without telling me what we were meeting about, John Branco, Fat Tony, and this young thug named Tony Muso picked me up in front of the Rio Casino and drove me to Fat Herbie's condo. I asked what the fuck was going on, and Fat Tony handed me some newspaper clippings that supposedly indicated that Herbie was ratting. As I was looking them over, John Branco handed me a specially made business card that had Fat Herbie's face superimposed on a rat's body.

I burst into laughter; these busters were complete jokes. They were like teenage girls passing notes in class about the popular cheerleader. This was too ridiculous to be an FBI sting, I thought. Maybe *Candid Camera* was back on TV?

"John, what the fuck is all of this supposed to be?"

"The Milanos, they want Fat Herbie dead so they can take over his rackets. Carmen told me." If John had a brain in his head, he would have translated the look I was shooting at him as "*Dago, please!*" Carmen Milano, the underboss of the L.A. Family, was not visiting an irrelevant dipshit in Las Vegas and asking him to kill someone. Not only were Pete and Carmen Milano far too savvy to kill *anyone*, they were certainly too smart to believe that killing Herbie Blitzstein would somehow lead to them inheriting his loan shark business intact.

That was what John Branco was too stupid to understand: you could not win a gangster's rackets via murder in 1997. You couldn't kill a loan shark so high profile that he was a character in a fucking Scorsese movie and then take over his loan shark business without anyone noticing. The cops would be everywhere. I especially wanted to ask Branco about the logistics of it: did he plan to walk up to Blitzstein's former clients and explain to them that, as Fat Herbie's murderer, he would be taking over his loans? How would he even *know* who owed what, and when? Did he think Fat Herbie would leave detailed, easy-to-understand records?

There was another question I had on my mind for Branco and Fat Tony: Hey, don't you two penny-ante assholes owe Fat Herbie money? Besides jealousy, isn't that what all of this is about?

Of course, I kept my many questions to myself because tipping off such a devious idiot wasn't in my self-interest. I let him keep talking, knitting the rope I would use to hang him. Besides, we were headed to see Steve Cino, and I figured, as a made guy and the imprisoned Jimmy's acting capo, he would be better qualified to tell these guys that they were assholes. As I expected, when we met The Whale at the Blueberry Hill restaurant, Branco started babbling about Herbie being a rat and how they should arrange for him to be killed. Steve's eyes bugged out, and he looked at me to see if they were joking.

"NO . . . WAY!" The Whale said slowly, as if to a mentally handicapped kid. "I like Fat Herbie. He's no rat. He did hard fucking time with Jimmy, Bobby, and me a thousand years ago. He's our friend. Next time someone brings that up, tell them he's with Fat Stevie. I *make money* with Fat Herbie. That's stupid."

Branco was lucky he made his presumptuous, against-the-rules, outlandish suggestion to the most low-key, patient, and soft-spoken guy in Jimmy's crew. If an unmade, fringe associate like John Branco had approached Jimmy Caci and said aloud for any nearby bug to hear that they should kill someone, Jimmy would have bitten off his nose and spat it back in his face.

To both The Whale's and my surprise, Branco followed his first preposterous, get-us-all-arrested suggestion with a second: how about we "hurt and rob" Teddy Binion, the heir to the Horseshoe Casino fortune? "You know, I was mowing his lawn, and Tony [Muso] over here worked for him too. The guy's a real prick . . ."

The Whale cut Branco off right there; he decided that a made guy should not be encouraging an unemployed lawnmower to think he could use the L.A. Mafia Family as a personal army to settle his petty grudges. "You guys, just chill out with this bullshit. Let's eat."

Afterwards, The Whale pulled me aside in the parking lot. "From now on, stay as far the fuck away from these idiots as humanly possible. Stay away from their crackpot schemes. Don't touch them with a nine-foot pole. These guys are nuts."

"Don't worry, Stevie. I don't trust them. They're idiots."

"Good."

A few weeks later, "Fat Herbie" Blitzstein was found in his townhome with three short-range gunshot wounds in his head. Every mafioso in Las Vegas and California, regardless of their family, was sickened by the news. Herbie was an old timer, a stand-up guy, and an all-round mensch; he was so likeable and trustworthy that, alone among Tony Spilotro's 1980s crew, he was the one insider who got a reprieve from the blanket death sentence handed down in Chicago. He did his time and kept his mouth shut even after all of his friends were killed. Since he did business the right way, he deserved to die naturally, which, with his bad heart and wheezing lungs, was imminently expected. Why kill a terminally ill loan shark?

The Whale and I asked each other if it was actually possible that John Branco had arranged to have Fat Herbie killed. Surely, even our very own Paulie Walnuts wasn't that reckless and petty, and, even if he were, he would have had neither the balls to kill on his own nor the leadership skills to convince anyone else to do it for him.

To our horror, it quickly became apparent through leaks to the press, buzz on the street, and the increased surveillance around us that Steve Cino was the top suspect in Fat Herbie's murder. The idea was so ridiculous that no one even knew what to say. When one of the real murderers confessed months later, the cops arrested a grab-bag of local know-nothing petty crooks and mercenary hit men with no connection to the L.A. Mafia Family—in addition to Steve Cino, Louie Caruso, and Buffalo wiseguy Bobby Panaro. The feds claimed that Cino and Panaro had authorized the hit on behalf of their respective families to take over Blitzstein's business, which Caruso supposedly wanted for himself.

What I'm about to say is going to be controversial and will likely get me in a lot of trouble with the FBI, but it's the truth so I have to say it. Blitzstein's murder on January 7, 1997, was portrayed by the FBI and the press as the Los Angeles Mafia Family making an example of Herbie in order to steal his rackets and make a statement on the streets that they were back in town. If you've read this far, you should be able to tell that this story is unutterably preposterous.

First of all, the killing of a loan shark to steal his business in 1997 is a crime that only an extremely stupid and inexperienced criminal could ever commit. Regardless of their other faults, the L.A. Family was full of wizened, seen-it-all veterans who would never be so naïve. Furthermore, the only man in the family who could have authorized a hit, Pete Milano, would never authorize killing *anyone,* let alone an elderly bookmaker in good standing with the family. Pete Milano would have shied away from killing Osama bin Laden if Jimmy Caci had a clear headshot. The L.A. soldier who supposedly okayed the hit, Steve Cino, had no power to do so, was too much of a traditionalist to pretend that he did, and had no reason to kill his friend and business partner. Stevie is a guy who has done over a decade in jail to avoid breaking the Mafia code of honor, so the idea that he would flout every rule and disrespect Jimmy to get at Fat Herbie is absurd.

If the L.A. Family *were* to kill someone, they would also never subcontract the planning and execution of the murder to a half-dozen wannabe crooks that none of them trusted enough even for gopher work.

Despite the absurdity of the indictment against Fat Stevie and his counterpart in Buffalo, Bobby Panaro, the outlook for them was hardly optimistic. The FBI never loses Mob cases. The government boasts an outrageously high conviction rate (eighty-nine percent according to one study) in cases based on the testimony of cooperating informants subsequently put in the Witness Protection Program. If you narrowed that field down to cases against the Mafia in high-profile Mob cities like Las Vegas, where the juries are predisposed to believe anything the government says about the Mafia, that percentage would approach ninety-nine percent. Despite this track record and the cooperation of John Branco, Fat Tony Angioletti, and four members of the actual conspiracy to kill Fat Herbie, the accusations against Bobby Panaro and Steve Cino were so ridiculous that they were both eventually acquitted.

From my experience and what I have discussed with other people involved in the case, I can only conclude that—in my opinion—John Branco and Tony Angioletti directly precipitated the murder of Fat Herbie Blitzstein during the commission of their work as FBI informants. The Mafia had nothing to do with it, and this is coming from an FBI informant who worked with state and federal law enforcement to fight organized crime on a daily basis. The Mob regularly commits horrible crimes and occasionally does commit murders, but the murder of Herbert Blitzstein was not their work.

John Branco and Tony Angioletti were Mob associates in the strictest meaning of the word—they "associated" with some legitimate mafiosi, but they were not involved in any of the family's major rackets or criminal operations. There's a reason John Branco mowed lawns for a living and lived in a trailer, and Fat Tony spent his days cooking free food for real crooks. Unfortunately for Fat Herbie, the FBI saw fit to pay for the testimony and cooperation of these two guys who, at best, could tape-record some wiseguy social functions and idle-bullshit chats with minor-league Mob names like Louie Caruso. In the best-case scenario, someone would be short on muscle and hire Branco to beat up a debtor or welcher. This type of information was hardly worth a pardon in federal court and a slot in the expensive Witness Protection Program.

Faced with their failure as informants, I watched in disbelief as John Branco and Fat Tony apparently attempted to incite someone to murder Fat Herbie. I believe this was done partly to get out of paying Herbie the money they both owed him, partly to service Branco's asinine grudge, and partly to entrap their Mob acquaintances in a high-profile crime that would secure their worth to the FBI forevermore. Their plan seemingly worked, but if the murder was their doing, the only people dumb enough to buy into their sales pitch were the fringe slackers around Fat Tony's social club who knew so little about the Mob that they thought a murder would impress Pete Milano. In other words, I honestly believe that two FBI informants were rewarded with get-out-of-jail-free cards and hundreds of thousands of dollars for successfully conspiring to kill a rival on the street and just as successfully deflecting the blame onto completely innocent, higher-profile criminals.

In fact, if you ask me, I think John Branco and Fat Tony were guilty of conspiracy to commit *another* high-profile Las Vegas murder. I heard those two goons encourage Steve Cino to kill and rob casino heir Ted Binion using information they got from ex–Binion employee Tony Muso, and a year later Binion was murdered and his underground treasure vault burglarized.

Binion's mistress and her alleged boyfriend were convicted of the murder on extremely weak circumstantial evidence, only to later have their convictions overturned—years after I informed their attorneys that the FBI had not shared evidence that two of their paid witnesses had been conspiring to kill and rob Binion. Unsurprisingly, when confronted, the FBI claimed to have lost the tapes to the conversation between John Branco, Fat Tony, Steve Cino, Tony Muso, and me at Blueberry Hill. If those tapes had been made public, it would have been impossible to prove the guilt of the two defendants, and after their wrongful conviction, the agency would have been liable for hundreds of millions of dollars for suppressing evidence, obstructing justice, and defaming the two defendants.

Years after John Branco's disappearance from the streets, a highly laudatory story on his work as an informant came out in the *Guardian* newspaper and revealed that Branco formed a close friendship with his undercover FBI handler while investigating Blitzstein and the

Mob, which likely explains why they both emerged "heroes" from the fatally botched investigation. Today, the agent is a pensioned FBI retiree who does anti-terrorism work, and John Branco lives somewhere under a new identity, suffering no repercussions for his suspected role in the killing of Fat Herbie and the prosecution of Steve Cino and Bobby Panaro on false pretenses.

Of course, in early 1997, I knew nothing of John Branco and Fat Tony's relationship with the government or the upcoming, then-inconceivable prosecution of my buddy The Whale for the murder. All I knew was that Jimmy Caci was heartbroken. "That's a goddamn shame. Why would anyone do that? Herbie kicked up two brand-new cars to Bobby and me. He made money with us; he did good time with us. He's a good guy. What the fuck is wrong with people these days?"

Though Jimmy's crew suspected third-rate crook John Branco had something to do with the death, we couldn't prove it. Had we nailed down their guilt, Branco and Angioletti would have been the recipients of an off-the-record spray of bullets from one of Jimmy's guys—I would have happily volunteered, as would have Steve Cino. This is darkly hilarious in light of what actually transpired.

To the eternal discredit of the FBI, John Branco and Fat Tony stayed on the street after the killing of Fat Herbie, likely in the hope of salvaging the handful of weak cases the two of them made against guys like Louie Caruso, Carmen Milano . . . and me.

The crime was stupid, a little scam that Tabitha nagged me into doing against my best judgment. I met The Whale at a Marie Callender's restaurant to get permission to go after Fat Tony Angioletti since he owed me $400. Cino told me that he would handle it, but that I might have better luck getting my money back from a scam Branco and Fat Tony were running: they would pay wiseguys for cars they wanted to write off as stolen, then untraceably ship the cars overseas. I said I might know some people who would be interested in the service, but I decided to keep away since I had promised Jackie and Jerry that I would steer clear of car scams after I was caught with Jimmy at his crooked car dealership.

I made the mistake of telling Tabitha—who *of course* was tired of her immaculate, good-as-new BMW. Minutes after we started dating, Tabitha had (illegally, I assume) dumped her brand-new Nissan 300z Turbo sports car, so this was one crime she already felt entitled to commit at will. She nagged and nagged until my already worn-to-threads patience broke. I was so stressed out, depressed, and just bored with all the drama from every direction that I no longer had the patience to think. "Fuck it, the payments on the damn car are too high anyway."

I was stupid, and luckily for me I was *done*.

So I met Fat Tony and John Branco at the Sportsmen's Lodge Hotel on Ventura Boulevard, a gorgeous luxury hotel that had served as a regular sitdown spot for the Los Angeles underworld for decades. It was quick, no bullshit: some guy they called "Steve" gave me $4,000 and told me to wait until Monday to report the car stolen. I left the car at the Lodge and took my $4,000 over to Jill Kelly's place for dinner, where Tabitha spent most of it buying all of Jill Kelly's old stripper costumes. A few days later, I reported the car stolen. I was barely paying attention through any of this; it was the sixth or seventh most important scam on my mind that week. As far as the $4,000, it was just throwaway cash, toilet paper for Tabitha's g-stringed ass. I don't think she wore any of Jill Kelly's stripper costumes more than once.

I had just destroyed my life. In exchange for one

night's spending money for Tabitha, I had committed insurance fraud, mail fraud, false reporting to the police, and—depending on how aggressive the FBI chose to be—perjury, tax fraud, and a number of other auxiliary crimes. I was automatically going to jail just for ignoring the terms of my probation, and there was no way I would win at trial. All of my street rackets would disintegrate into nothing the moment I went away, and the feds would sue for my assets. I was losing everything; I was fucked.

Thanks to the Three Stooge Pigeons (Moe Spado, Curly Angioletti, and Larry Branco), most of my friends and allies were caught on tape and thus just as fucked: Jimmy Caci, Jerry Zimmerman, Bobby Milano, Fat Stevie, Vince Lupo, and probably even Louie Gelfuso and Tabitha. For a few years at least, it was all over, for *everyone*. For me, it was over forever—there was no way I was going to let John Branco give me jail time. With no one I respected or gave a shit about left to implicate, I saw no reason not to rat.

As I stewed over how shabby, underhanded, and pathetic it was for John Branco and Fat Tony to arrange the third-hand murder of a legitimate gangster like Fat Herbie, a searing throb appeared in my brain. For the last time in my criminal career, I had the desire to kill.

I told myself it was a case of self-defense. I knew they would never come after me man-to-man, but what was to stop them from calling me a rat behind my back and trying to incite some ignorant Las Vegas underworld yokel to kill me like they did Fat Herbie?

Joey Avila fell for not striking first at Mike Marvich; I certainly wasn't going to go down for hesitating to take out a little bag of shit like Tony. I put on my wig, glasses, baseball cap, and gloves; I took out a Gatorade bottle, filled it with gasoline, and plugged it with a cannon fuse.

In a different car, I drove over to Fat Tony's house—only to see that a wooden street sign had been thrown like a spear through the windshield of his Lincoln. Though I appreciated the sentiment, it meant that someone had already gotten to Tony that night and drawn the attention of law enforcement. I drove away without stopping. The next night, I visited the house again—and everything was gone: the car, the furniture, even the trash cans. Someone had scrubbed away Tony's existence.

"John Branco, too. Disappeared," The Whale told me the next day when I broke the news. Steve Cino looked fatter, older, and paler than ever; the flesh of his face melted toward the amorphous blob of lard that formed his torso. The Whale sighed and rolled his eyes up to heaven in that "Santa Maria! Off to jail again!" look that I had learned to recognize from Jimmy. He was going to take it like a man. Within minutes he was joking again, jolly as ever.

I drove to Palm Springs to visit Jimmy, who had recently been released from jail and was recuperating from hernia surgery. The surgery and yet another trip to prison had taken its toll on Jimmy, who was more Crypt Keeper than the ruggedly handsome hood he had once been. I wondered how long he had to live; surely he couldn't keep going on like this, spending years in prison cafeterias without the carpets that allowed him to absorb nutrition.

We met Philip "Fat Philly" Dioguardi, another made guy from New York in Jimmy's crew, in a bagel shop to discuss the case. Tough, fat, and nonchalant about prison, Philly lived up to his elite Brooklyn Mob pedigree. As a young 300-pound goombah from Bensonhurst, he had served godfather Joe Colombo as a bodyguard and supervised the youth division of Colombo's Italian-American Civil Rights League. Philly also managed Don Giuseppe's summer camp for local kids, telling the *New York Times* in 1971 that he even planned to accept "blacks, Jews, Protestants . . ."

When the Persico family and its allies supplanted Colombo in a public assassination attempt at a Civil Rights League event that "vegetabled" Joe, Philly threw in his lot with Jimmy Caci and stuck loyally by his side until his death.

Philly told me not to worry about jail. It was just "poppin' my cherry," something to "get out of the way." For a brief moment, I liked Philly's logic: a year or two to unwind, exercise away my Tabitha weight, and detoxify my poisoned psyche might be salutary.

Jimmy and Philly offered little sympathy over my upcoming bust. Prison was nothing to these guys; it was their home away from home. They would have been more sympathetic if I had blue balls or the shits. They were unbreakable, true men of honor even if their code was twisted and immoral. I did not admire their delusions about the sanctity and morality of mafioso life, but I did respect the incredible discipline, fortitude, and raw toughness they displayed in going to jail over and over again without complaining or wavering in their devotion to uphold their word.

I was troubled when I left Jimmy and Philly to go on the road with Tabitha on one of her stripping tours. I knew that I would be indicted soon—between Ori, Fat Tony, and John Branco, there was a multitude of cases, fraudulent or otherwise, that the FBI could make against me to obtain a conviction. The feds were not the Two Toms; they would hunt me down. I knew from years of observation and my previous work with the FBI through Officer Jerry that the feds take resistance personally. I knew I would be going to jail.

To be honest, there was never any chance of that happening; I would never go to jail to avoid ratting. I've always been too smart for the whole "never snitch under any circumstances" underworld commandment, largely because *anyone* who believes in honor among thieves is dumber than a box of shit. The whole point of being a criminal was to be completely free of all rules and restraints, to relish the excitement that came with living in perfect liberty. If I were going to follow another man's judgment on how I should live, why would I choose to venerate the wisdom of misfits, lunatics, and junkies like the Persicos, the Milanos, or the Avilas above everyone else who ever lived?

Think about the "don't snitch" rule for a second: it's completely acceptable for me to scam, rob, abuse, beat, cripple, ambush, sabotage, and even kill a fellow criminal on the street, but it's a moral atrocity if I tell a cop where the criminal is hiding his guns? Does that make any sense? Ever since meeting Officer Jerry, I never feel any worse ratting out someone on the street as opposed to planting a bomb in his car or jumping him with a baseball bat. Either way is sneaky, and there's no guarantee they wouldn't do it to me first. You're still a bad person either way.

I didn't care about fucking crooks like me who deserved whatever they got. I had robbed, set up, and beat up bookmakers, dealers, gamblers, madams, pornographers, and loan sharks my entire life—why would I go to jail to avoid fucking over guys I fucked over as a matter of course? I would have had to change my behavior and abandon my values *not* to rat.

Just as silly is the idea that working with the Mafia comes with some added responsibility or incentive to maintain secrecy. First of all, for a supposed racial inferior like me, Mafia rules don't apply: I'm not considered human enough to be formally inducted and take the Oath of Omerta in the first place. I was there for the Mafia to exploit and abandon or dispose of when convenient; if I went to jail, no one would send money or protect my interests or even respect my property. Non-Italian associate Frank Smith actually *killed* for the Colombo Family, but, when he was falsely imprisoned instead of a guilty Italian for a crime, the Colombos left him to rot while they robbed his defenseless family. When Smith finally flipped after keeping his mouth shut for over a decade, overnight he became a "rat piece of shit."

The "Mafia code of honor" is an oxymoron, a fairytale that may have contained a molecule of truth back in 19th-century Sicily but certainly has no correlation to reality today. Being "stand-up" for the sake of being stand-up in this era is for suckers and brainwashed old-timers who don't have anything else to live for.

Even more hilarious is the idea that mafiosi should be too paralyzed with fear to ever cross the families. Those days are over. The code of secrecy has been broken; the power to systematically corrupt juries, politicians, and law enforcement is long gone; the stakes are tiny in comparison to just twenty years ago. Mafia rats like Michael Franzese, Chris Paciello, Ori Spado, and, yes, Kenny Gallo live openly and without fear. I'm unique in that there has been more than one supposed attempt to kill me, and after you read what I have to say about Teddy Persico, you'll understand why there will be more. Nonetheless, I'm obviously still here. Today's Mob is too incompetent and weak to successfully kill anyone unless the victim hangs out in just the right goombah neighborhood or willingly gets in a car with a wiseguy.

The only rational or moral argument against snitching

has nothing to do with the act of snitching itself. The argument is simple: do not betray those who have earned your trust, loyalty, and respect. I've committed just about every other sin in the world, but the idea of doing harm to true friends like Joey Avila, Jerry Zimmerman, or Jimmy Caci makes me ill. That's what my next mentor, Anthony "The Animal" Fiato, always says: when you rat against a friend, you feel it *physically*, the most awful chills and nausea arising from a stomach-turning repulsion at your own behavior. It's as if nature programmed your body to self-destruct rather than commit that unforgivable taboo.

When I finally received the phone call in a Nashville strip club that the FBI was looking for me, that was my only concern: did I have to hurt Jerry or Jimmy? If not, I realized that I would honestly be relieved to flip. I was ready for adolescence to end and adulthood to begin. The violence, the power trips, and the danger were the meaning of life to me for fifteen years, but they seemed like a petty buzz or a key bump of cheap biker speed when I looked into Tara's eyes again and realized how lonely, shallow, and frivolous an existence I had chosen.

After that encounter with Tara, I felt about as respectable and mature as I did kicking around with the trailer park skinhead gang from Santa Ana as a teenager. I suddenly realized that I was a sleazy guy living a dead-end, depressing life—on my way to being just as damaged and desperate as crazy Tabitha, just as disposable and ultimately pathetic as Fat Herbie. I had become a criminal in an era when it was a feral, reckless, psychotic rush, and now it was just a grind. Life as a gangster had become *boring*—I hadn't thought that was possible. If I was going to have to put up with a shitty job, I certainly wasn't willing to go to jail over it.

I sat Tabitha down and told her what had happened and what I would have to do. Midway through my announcement I could tell she was mapping her route out of the door, but the words that came out of her mouth were, "I'll stick with you no matter what." She didn't think to apologize for insisting on dumping that perfectly good BMW, but I was past caring.

I called the FBI and let them know I was willing to talk. They told me "Great!" and then just told me to be patient, and they'd get in touch again. What the fuck? Weeks passed, we traveled from state to state, and still nothing from the feds; I started losing my mind, thinking I was going to be busted at every airport, every strip club. I thought they had decided against using me or were going to bust me first to stake out a better negotiating position, so I began to consider fleeing the country. Finally, after what seemed like months, I received the phone call: meet them in the morning at Kaplan's Deli in Costa Mesa, which just happened to be one of the places I used to pick up cocaine shipments as a teenager.

I left my watch and my money at home; I wore clothes that did not need a belt. In case we could not come to an agreement, I was prepared to go to jail. I did not tell Tabitha where I was going; I didn't need the drama, especially since I knew they would indict her if I didn't play along since it was her car. As far as I was concerned, she was acceptable collateral damage if I had to go down. I wanted a way out, but I was not going to testify against Jerry or Jimmy and his crew.

I walked into Kaplan's Deli, and there was the FBI's Los Angeles Mafia Squad leader, Stan Ornellas, waving me over. He was a huge guy, a typical Bureau jock: tall, broad-shouldered, solid offensive-lineman body, tightly trimmed gray hair. He escorted me to a booth and pointed out four or five other agents sitting nearby.

I was just a spectator: I knew the terms I would agree to and those I wouldn't, so everything was basically out of my hands. I projected my normal easygoing chill.

"Kenny, do you know why you're here?" This was the typical dumbass cop question. When I was a teenager, I'd have answered with something like, "To fuck your wife?" or "To take cooking lessons?"

"I don't know. I guess so you guys can arrest me?"

"That's up to you."

"Well, what do you want?"

"You're done," Stan said with the dramatic emphasis that I recognized from the Two Toms, only, unlike them, I could see in his eyes that Stan wasn't bluffing. "You understand? You're done, whether you help us or not. The question is: do you wanna work?"

"Depends." Wary of alienating the FBI too quickly, I hinted about Jerry Zimmerman or Jimmy Caci.

Ornellas blinked rapidly, as if he were trying to suppress laughter. It was as if I had asked if they wanted me to take down Walther Matthau and Jack Lemmon. Jimmy and Jerry were not priorities.

"We don't care about L.A. We have that covered. This is what we're interested in. You travel with your wife and some of those other porn girls all the time. You're all over the place, and, between the girls and your street connections, you have the credibility and the arm candy to meet all types of criminals across America. We picture you as a roving undercover informant, an asset who can penetrate into various organizations and crime families across America."

Like Kenny DiMartini and Officer Jerry a dozen years earlier, the FBI saw in me the perfect cipher, a cagy operator with the trustworthy demeanor, unsuspicious demographical profile, and raw street smarts to fit in anywhere.

"I mean, what the fuck?" I said with the biggest smile I may have ever smiled. "You guys got a deal."

As soon as the words left my mouth, my heart pumped a stiff shot of adrenaline through my body, and it felt as if a sponge soaked in cooling endorphins was wrung out over my brain. The twisted mess of my psyche felt like one of those intricate knots that can be instantly undone by tugging on a single thread. I took the most satisfying, deep-penetrating breath, and expelled a gust of tension, stress, and guilt as I exhaled. All of my muscles unclenched and hung loosely from my bones like pajamas from a laundry line.

Though I had not realized it, I had been leaning over the deli table, my ass hardly touching the seat, my entire body tense and poised, my stomach pressed to the table with my arms and legs arranged like a puzzle piece fitted around it. Now, my ass sank into the booth, and as I exhaled it felt as if I were blowing my body further and further into the cushions. I was slouching, practically reclining within moments. I started laughing.

It was a "born again" moment; hope instantaneously evaporating everything fucked up in my life. It was more delusion than salvation, a mirage of existential relief—by any standard I was still immensely fucked, but for a second I could foresee a new, healthy, and beautiful life for myself.

Just as importantly, in the meantime, my new role as an undercover agent restored to my dreary life everything that had once attracted me to the underworld: excitement, danger, and the thrill of outwitting other crooks and infiltrating far-flung secret societies that should never, ever give me access. I was an adventurer once again, and after this last high-stakes gamble, there would be a chance at a real life for me—without jail, without repercussions, and without conditions.

I would execute the greatest swindle of all: going from outlaw to respectable citizen by repaying my debt to society through—get this—committing more crimes and screwing more criminals. I reimbursed the world for my crimes with more crime.

This was change I could believe in. I have never regretted my decision to rat for a moment. Kenji was replaced by undercover agent BREAKSHOT, who fought crime by committing crimes.

TWELVE
In on the Scores, Out on the Beefs

*"It feels like, see, guys like us want to go
through this life getting everything for nothing
and never paying the tab. . . . And it seems like
I had a great banquet, these many years . . .
and I finally get hit with the tab all at
once. . . . Then seeing the so-called loyal trust
you imagined this Mafia has . . . which vanishes
immediately when there's a little trouble. You
know, in on the scores, and out on the beefs.
That's what it really comes down to."*

Anthony "The Animal" Fiato
getting busted for the final time,
in *The Animal in Hollywood*

I did not fear wearing a wire in the least. In the same
way that nations with nuclear weapons can assert themselves on the world stage without worrying about being
overrun, my arsenal of street knowledge made me fearless. Between military school, my martial arts studies,
and Officer Jerry, I have professional training to fire
guns, wield knives, rig explosives, make "hot shots" of
drugs, prepare fatal poisons, defend myself unarmed, and
recognize legitimate threats to my life. This array of skills
left me with nothing to worry about; if my cover were
blown, then I'd take care of business like I always had.

Besides, there is no chance of being caught wearing
a wire in the 21st century. Though I can't divulge the
details, take my word that the FBI's nanotechnology is so
advanced that the most thorough frisk and cavity search
would not have revealed a thing. Besides, the whole

"frisk a guy before a meeting" thing is a Hollywood invention I *never* saw on the streets. Most real gangsters would bust you in the face the second you even hinted at grabbing their nuts and implying that they were rats.

I'll give the underworld some free advice. You will never beat FBI bugs. The only theoretical chance a targeted crime boss has is if every conversation he participates in is conducted in a randomized location while completely in the nude or dressed in nothing more than a fresh pair of hospital scrubs and slippers. Even if the boss is thus protected from bugs by this antiseptic routine, his underlings will still operate in the real world, get busted, and rat on him.

Another urban legend about wearing a wire is that the FBI detaches a team of agents to sit in a van and listen all day long to your bullshit conversations in case trouble arises. That's a joke; my recordings were automatically transmitted to headquarters, where I'd be lucky if my handlers listened to them within a week. That lag reveals the one way that being an FBI informant actually did materially endanger me: since I was recorded at all times and bound by a cooperation agreement to be nonviolent, if my life suddenly was in danger I was fucked under every scenario. If I struck first to protect myself, I'd break my agreement and commit permanent evidence of my crime to the FBI's digital archives. If I didn't defend myself, I'd either be killed or exposed as a gun-shy informant. That potential catch-22 was my only worry about becoming an informant.

Though I was arrogant about how easily I would become the greatest rat in Mafia history, the FBI was too familiar with my history of violence to feel confident. They insisted I speak to someone who could help me change from violent criminal to strictly nonviolent confidential informant. For my Assholes Anonymous sponsor, they chose the last L.A. gangster with a history of homicidal violence: Anthony "The Animal" Fiato.

I had almost met Fiato a couple years earlier when I moved into his neighborhood in Newport Beach and started chatting with Tanya Brown, the little sister of O. J.'s murder victim Nicole Brown Simpson. Soon afterwards, I received a visit from the Newport cops informing me that Fiato was fucking Tanya's other sister, tabloid darling Denise Brown. They figured I was using Tanya to locate Fiato so that his old enemy Jimmy Caci and I could take him out. After the cops unwittingly informed me of Fiato's whereabouts, I researched my new neighbor in depth for the first time and came away impressed.

Fiato had a reputation as not only the most feared hit man and bone-breaker of his generation but also a smart-ass who took shit from no one and drove the guys in Los Angeles nuts. As a protégé of renegade L.A. crew boss Mike Rizzi, Gambino Family underboss Aniello "Neil" Dellacroce, and countless old-time wiseguys in his home-town of Boston, Fiato had the connections and muscle to destroy Pete Milano and rule L.A. in the 1980s. He was even a Hollywood favorite: James Caan begged him to take out Joe Pesci over a debt to Caan's friend Dodi Fayed, who would become famous years later as the stain on the road next to the late Princess Diana.

Unfortunately for Fiato's burgeoning underworld career, his younger brother Larry became a degenerate cokehead and ratted him out. The Animal was cornered: he could either break up his family and spend the rest of his life in jail—or screw over the guys in L.A. and Boston. Fiato was no martyr: he flipped, became a tabloid fixture when he testified at the O. J. Simpson trial, began dating Denise Brown, and released a best-selling memoir, *The Animal in Hollywood*.

Though I loved Fiato's book for the quality ball-busting I got out of it when I gave free copies to Jimmy, Louie, and even Pete Milano, I'll admit I was jealous that Animal made so much money from the O. J. trial. It was a missed opportunity for me: during O. J.'s low-speed SUV chase with the cops, that white Bronco puttered right past me on the freeway, and I considered ramming him off the road. In retrospect, I should have done it and secured my immortal fame.

I owe my current freedom to countless cell phone conversations, text message exchanges, and AOL Instant Messenger chats with Anthony "The Animal" Fiato. After the cops made the introduction, Fiato, with his deep voice, no-bullshit attitude, and North End Boston slang, quickly became my favorite advisor. Fiato was street brilliant: he talked like a bar brawler and thought like a cagy political strategist. Fiato did what the FBI wanted from him: by leveling with me, one ass-kicker to another, he gave me the insight I needed to control my temper in situations that, for my entire adult life, otherwise resulted in violence. He knew all of the excuses and all the rationalizations used by crooks to justify breaking the rules, and he never let me get away with a single violation of my agreement with the FBI.

TabithaStevens.com
List of Tabitha's plastic surgeries
- 6 boob jobs
- 3 nose jobs
- 2 cheek surgeries
- 1 under the nose implant surgery
- 1 chin implant surgery

- 1 nose implant surgery
- 1 fat transfer from my right leg to my entire face
- 1 cutting the fat deposit bands behind my thighs
- Botox every 4 to 6 months
- Restylane injections to my lips every 6 months
- Restylane injections to my smile lines every 6 months
- Anal bleaching

Fiato and I shared one weakness: "crazy broads" as he would say. He was no help with Tabitha, and to be honest at that point nothing short of a deal with the devil would have saved our relationship. Within three weeks of my deal with the F.B.I., Tabitha was done: I came home to an apartment that was completely empty outside of a tiny note explaining that she was too nuts for our relationship and needed professional help.

She was right. When Tabitha slammed the door to our apartment for the last time, she opened the rusty gate to the holding pen of demons, goblins, and nightmares in her psyche. In my absence, Tabitha proceeded to mutilate herself at the speed of a hummingbird. Scarcely a week passed without another round of plastic surgery, a new tattoo, or a new psychedelic hair and makeup color scheme. My beautiful and borderline all-natural wife soon resembled some species of insectoid alien.

Her psychosis was exacerbated when she replaced my good friend Kendra Jade as Howard Stern's featured porn-star sideshow. Obtaining the acceptance of Stern's ten million radio listeners became the existential focus of Tabitha's life; Howard became the source of paternal love that Tabitha so dearly needed. Her pursuit of airtime and audience acceptance became a mania; she was the Renfield to Stern's Dracula. It was an appropriate coincidence that her plastic surgery addiction made her look progressively like Gollum from *Lord of the Rings* with a hair weave and Astrodome fake tits.

Like the Evel Knievel of sexual debasement, Tabitha secured fame with a series of dignity-defying stunts to get on the almighty air. In order to earn Howard's approval, Tabitha agreed to have sex with countless freakshow Stern listeners, including a mentally retarded giant, a brother-and-sister incest combo, and a dog-shit eater. She also offered her services to Eric the Actor, a wheelchair-confined virgin dwarf, but he publicly told her that he preferred to die a virgin than live with the knowledge that he had so debased himself. Tabitha even consented to have sex with a dead man or live with a family of bears in a zoo cage for a week in return for some precious, unpaid airtime. The only thing Tabitha ever refused to do was have sex with a black guy.

I was in a very bad mood when I was called into the luxuriously appointed corner-office-with-a-view of Tabitha's high-powered divorce attorney. I had been receiving increasingly condescending messages from this asshole attorney telling me that I needed to fill out the financial forms that would give him the knowledge to steal my assets for Tabitha. Naturally, I was reluctant to help him mug me, but he insisted that I cooperate or else, so I went to his office to deliver my plea of "Or else."

I have always reserved a special loathing for attorneys, who all act as if their law degree grants them immunity from the asskickings that normally go along with being an aggressive, demeaning, threatening asshole to innocent people. They live within a subculture where being *verbally* tough, without anything but a lawsuit to back it up, is all that is ever required to be considered a badass. I like to see the look in their eyes when their "fuck you, I'll eat you for lunch" act dissolves into mortal terror at the realization that my rebuttal will be to shoot their children on the way to school.

I sat in one of the luxurious leather chairs in this aging, doughy, goateed lawyer's office and listened patiently as he told me that he would ruin my life and take every penny from me if I fought Tabitha in court.

"So you're going to take every penny I own?" I asked with a yawn.

"You'll wake up one morning with nothing after I'm done with you," the lawyer responded, extending a sausage finger in my direction from his ham-hock fist.

"Well, shit, if I have nothing, I'll have nothing to lose, and I'll just wait outside of this nice office in a mask and shoot you in the fucking head." I paused for a moment to let the meaning of what I said sink in; with my deadpan delivery, it usually takes people a second to process. "You see, I can do research too, and I found out where you live, where your son lives, where your entire fucking family lives, and I'll just kill them one by one before I let a fat pussy like you think you can threaten me and get away with it."

I then regurgitated the home addresses of everyone in his family, which, as a matter of due diligence, I had memorized earlier.

"Now, you fat fuck, look at me in my eyes and tell me if I'm joking." I gave him a chance to respond, but the lawyer looked hollowed out, a puppet robbed of its hand. Judging by his face, no one had ever called his bullshit at any point in his entire life. "That's right. I'm not signing a fucking thing, and you better tell Tabitha to be happy with her divorce. If I hear from you again, I'm just going to kill you."

The FBI would have been appalled, but paralegal

extraordinaire Mike Marvich would have been proud: the terrified lawyer never bothered me again. I can't say the same for Tabitha. She continued to come in and out of my life as long as I was on the streets, sometimes looking to get back together, the rest of the time asking me to intercede on her behalf with madams, pimps, and thieving business partners.

Since our phone numbers were still one digit apart, I also received her phone calls, which is how I woke up one morning to find a message from *American Idol*'s Simon Cowell trying to set up a rendezvous (paid, if you believe what Tabitha told me) on my message service.

I made a couple thousand selling the Cowell story to the *National Enquirer* and stood to make a further $100,000 if an *Enquirer* hotel-room ambush of Simon in the act succeeded. Unfortunately, Simon was tipped off, and my relationship with Tabitha remained a net loss.

"Tommaso 'Tommy' Gambino, the son of Rosario Gambino, approached Roger Clinton to help win the release of Rosario Gambino from prison. [. . .] Even though he never was successful, Tommy Gambino provided Roger Clinton with $50,000, a gold Rolex watch, and an undisclosed amount of 'expense money.' [. . .] According to Los Angeles law enforcement and press accounts, Tommy Gambino is not only the son of a mobster, he is a reputed underboss in the Los Angeles Mafia currently under investigation for his own criminal activity."

U.S. House Committee on Government Reform
In the report "Justice Undone: Clemency Decisions
in the Clinton White House"
March 14, 2002

The power of the modern gangster is never greater than when he makes a deal to cooperate with the FBI. At that moment, a gangster who has survived day-to-day by his wit and his gun obtains the fleeting opportunity to take command of the FBI's bottomless budget, its thousands of agents, and its *Star Trek* arsenal of electronic surveillance equipment. By his testimony, that cooperating witness who knows what excites the FBI can effortlessly and instantaneously point their crosshairs at anyone else in the underworld, deciding their fate as surely as he would with a high-caliber shot to the head. Every crime an informant has ever heard about, witnessed, or committed becomes currency that he can cash in to send his enemies to jail, or worse.

The ability to wield this level of power on the streets was one of the reasons I was so eager to work with the FBI. I took to their initial pitch with gusto; theoretically, I had enormous power as a jet-setting informant who could proactively seek out and procure actionable information against any gangster across North America. I was good at my job: after the feds tipped me off to the local connected bar/club/strip club, I would take a porn girl like Jill Kelly or Tabitha to the wiseguy hangout and let the gangsters come to me. After I zeroed in on my target, I would quickly establish a mafioso we knew in common to establish my bona fides and, within minutes, they would busily begin to incriminate themselves.

In this way, I was able to deliver to the feds incriminating audiotapes of Mafia made men from Colorado, Las Vegas, Cleveland, Pittsburgh, Philadelphia, Providence, Boston, and New York itself.

Though I delivered the goods on dozens of gangsters, there was a problem: the FBI didn't do a goddamn thing with my evidence. I discovered why pretty soon:

when a warrant was issued for my arrest after I missed a court date, my handlers refused to intervene and just told me "not to get caught" lest it ruin our deal. That's when I realized that I was not considered a particularly high-priority, high-value informant. They wanted my information to provide "deep background," to fill out crime family charts and inter-bureau reports; I wasn't considered important enough for them to use as the basis for building brand-new cases from scratch.

This lack of respect became maddening when the FBI completely ignored a breakthrough I made against America's top Mafia family. With porn star Dayton as arm candy, a connection of mine brought me to some "friends of his" in Pelham Bay in the Bronx at Basalmo's Funeral Home and the nearby Italian American Social Club. Within seconds, it became clear that this was the secret headquarters and hangout of the Genovese Family in the Bronx. During a bustling social club dinner, the local Bronx capo introduced himself to me as the neighborhood "boss" and legendary Pleasant Avenue Connection heroin trafficker Louis "Fat Gigi" Inglese and then asked me if I, as a Californian, could get him a signed photo of Pam Anderson.

Gigi was locally famous as the wisecracking, megaobese wiseguy who Chazz Palminteri used as the basis for the *Bronx Tale* character "JoJo the Whale," and Gigi liked to ham it up and play the part. Even though he was in his sixties and looked to weigh a little less than 600 pounds, Gigi did not hesitate to hit on Jill and regale us with poetic odes to his favorite show, *Baywatch*.

When I let the FBI know that a few bugs planted in the walls of Balsamo's and the Italian American Club would nab dozens of major wiseguys from America's top crime family, they rolled their eyes. "Eh, we think that place is a Lucchese Family hangout; we're not sure."

"No, I'm telling you, it's the Genovese place in the Bronx. Everyone was there. I met the capo and Fat Gigi."

"Nah, we think it's Lucchese. Don't worry about it. Leave it to us."

It would take the feds another six or seven years to independently discover the importance of the Balsamo Funeral Home and the Italian American Club and bust the joints out. Ralph "The Undertaker" Balsamo himself would be charged with labor racketeering, witness tampering, gambling, gun charges and drug dealing. All of these crimes and many others could have been prevented if the feds had just *listened*.

Figuring that I needed to nab nothing less than bona fide Mafia royalty to interest the feds in my work, I targeted guido princeling Tommy Gambino, Louie Caruso's mini-me.

I ran into Tommy while visiting his old nemesis Jimmy Caci in jail. Jimmy happened to be staying in the same prison as Tommy's old man, Sicilian heroin kingpin Rosario Gambino, so Tommy and I would regularly run into each other on visitors' day. With his tan Richard Grieco looks and expensive designer clothes, Tommy seemed to be auditioning for the role of "flashy, ostentatious young wiseguy" at all times, and it sickened Jimmy to see how much he reveled in the attention he received by flouting his association with a supposedly secret society. When Jimmy heard the rumors about Tommy's alleged promotion in the family and his attempt to bribe Bill Clinton's brother in exchange for a pardon for Rosario, I could tell that, for a brief moment, he just wanted to toss the Life in the trash and go live somewhere far away as a normal old retiree.

Regardless of Jimmy's feelings about Tommy, we thought Rosario, who everyone called "Sal," was a pretty cool guy. The quiet, heavily accented little Sicilian liked me as well, and he insisted on sitting with Jimmy and me whenever I visited to chat. We were sometimes joined by Jimmy's old friend from back East, Rene Piccarreto, the imprisoned boss of what was left of the Rochester Mafia Family. Once Sal heard that I had worked in porn and B movies for years, he set up a meeting for me with Tommy and asked me to help his son develop a screenplay he was writing about Chinese triad gangs and heroin-dealing mafiosi.

As a favor to Rosario, Jimmy insisted I call in a favor on his behalf with Gambino payola kingpin Joe Isgro. Following Jimmy's orders, I took lawyer Mark Mazie to a Beverly Hills hair salon called Giuseppe Franco that Joe Isgro supposedly once owned and left him a message there. It was, ironically, right next door to Café Roma, the restaurant where Tommy Gambino to this day holds court. Within two hours, we received a call back from Joe Isgro, who whispered cryptic directions to this secret gated office on Balboa Boulevard in Porn Valley.

Mark and I could scarcely believe the elaborate ceremonies we witnessed at Isgro's mansion. Apparently, Joe fancied himself a James Bond villain and instructed his staff to treat him as such at all times. After we were buzzed through the front gate and escorted inside by armed guards, Mark and I were greeted at a front desk by a pretty blonde surrounded by an entire crew of muscle-bound, Secret Service–style thugs. As we were making small talk with the receptionist, she received a phone call and gestured to the thugs.

In a moment the entire crew whirred into motion in what was clearly a minutely planned and practiced routine. The thugs rushed outside in a set formation and surrounded a large Mercedes that was pulling up to the home. One thug opened the front door, another helped Joe Isgro out, another hopped in to park the car, and the rest formed a tight semi-circle around Joe as he walked into the home.

Needless to say, I thought this entire routine was fucking ridiculous, but Mafia fan Mark Mazie looked like he was on the verge of ejaculating all over the front desk and the receptionist.

Joe was a short, stocky guy in white dress shirt, blue slacks, and a Julius Caesar hairstyle. He strutted and swaggered with a level of confidence rarely seen outside of a movie or a mental ward. Joe escorted us to a back office complete with its own waterfall and two poster-sized prints of Lucky Luciano and Jimmy Hoffa hanging behind his super-sized desk. Even after staging this elaborate display, Joe still felt compelled to say within two minutes of sitting down at his desk, "I'm a wiseguy, y'know, did you know that? Do you know that I'm a wiseguy? Did you know that I'm *with* people?"

"No," I lied. Regardless of his inexplicable insecurity, Isgro had big-time money, and he was eager to ingratiate himself with Rosario Gambino and Jimmy. He not only said he was interested in producing Tommy's script but also a quickie proposal I had cooked up for a low-budget biopic of Joey Avila's life starring Mickey Rourke.

It just so happened that Isgro was a close friend of Rourke's who had allowed the washed-up actor to stay at his place, so Isgro was given the distinct pleasure of acting like a big shot by waving his hand and saying, "Mickey Rourke? *It's done.* Not a problem. One phone call and that's it. We can make this." On my way out, Joe made a point to show me that one of his hired lackeys was Tommy Gambino's own brother, Anthony; the implication was, "Look at me, I'm rich and powerful enough to hire gangland royalty as my help."

I thought I had hit the jackpot: high-profile Gambino Family soldier Joe Isgro tied up with both Tommy and Anthony Gambino in what would surely be a very crooked business arrangement. I even would get to produce my own film adaptation of Joey Avila's life. I was giddy when I told the feds of my grand score, but their response was chastening. "Stay away from Tommy Gambino and Joe Isgro. Completely. Let it drop immediately." They wanted nothing to do with them, possibly because they already knew that digging too much into Tommy would expose his attempt to bribe the Clinton family and embarrass the President further than Clinton was managing to do on his own.

Even if the feds didn't want Tommy Gambino, I assumed there was no way they would be able to turn down Anthony "Tony Ripe" Civella, the boss of the Kansas City Mafia Family and the son and nephew of two preceding Kansas City godfathers. The Civellas were true Mafia royalty, the longtime rulers of Kansas City and major players in the construction of the Mob's Las Vegas empire. Not only did I know Tony Ripe on a first-name basis, I had him dead to rights on stock fraud, money laundering, and a number of other crimes.

Tony was involved in a Las Vegas pump-and-dump operation I had a piece of, which would take worthless stocks and use dishonest telemarketing methods to artificially inflate their price. I met Tony Ripe in a phone room in an industrial section of Vegas along with a few other wiseguys. He was introduced as "Tony C," and the neatly dressed, heavily tanned old man shook my hand with a smile.

After that initial meeting, a code was set up for future meetings: from now on, since Civella received too much law enforcement heat in Las Vegas, a phone call requesting "a strawberry shake" would mean that everyone would convene the next day in the tiny town of Baker, California, right over the Nevada border. In Baker, home of the world's largest thermometer and not much else, I heard Civella clearly stating his part in the multimillion-dollar stock scam, but even the godfather of Kansas City did not interest the feds. They in effect told me to "Go fish."

That was the biggest surprise about working with the FBI: the feds are slow, picky, and so deluged with informants that they will routinely ignore major, slam-dunk cases or let them collect dust for years and years before doing anything. The FBI indictment pipeline is clogged up with backlogged cases, paper pushers, wads of red tape, redundant employees engaging in turf wars, and Byzantine procedural guidelines. Unless you are hunting a terrorist, a political assassin, or the rapist of a high-profile rich white girl, there is no way to expedite the process; you just wait years and years.

I was at a loss: if Tommy Gambino and Tony Ripe did not interest the FBI, how high-profile would a gangster have to be before they would want one of my cases? This high profile: John "Junior" Gotti.

For my thirtieth birthday, Fate gave me the gift of my first big bust for the FBI. I was hired by a homosexual crook honestly named Paul Flamer to extort some debts from some other homo-cons, which I did by stealing Judy Garland's diary from the crook who had purchased it at auction and threatening to rip out the pages and eat them one after the other. The crew of queer gangsters begged for mercy in the face of such terrorism, and I paid some

of my Crip gangbanger buddies to help me collect the
debts and steal their cars.

Afterwards, I drove the Crip crew led by the fittingly
nicknamed "Crazy Larry" to my porn shop to hang out
and unwind. As we were getting out of my car, we noticed five white guys in "wifebeater" tank tops kicking
some dude's ass in the strip mall parking lot, which we
all found amusing until we realized the dude was my
friend Matt. I ran over and told them to cut the shit, but
the white boys told us to "get the fuck out of here, dog!"

Just as we were about to kick the shit out of them,
one of the goons stepped away from Matt to throw up
what appeared to be a gang sign and scream what Crazy
Larry and his Crips heard as "LBC, motherfucker!" In
Los Angeles, "LBC!" is universally recognized as the
gang call of the Long Beach Crips, a faction of the Crip
Nation that, at the time, was a rival with Crazy Larry's
Hoover Crips set. Though these were clearly just confused white boys, ghetto gangbangers like Larry don't
give a shit; if you throw up gang signs in his face, he is
going to fucking kill you. I had to run after Larry, who
had been given his piece by one of his boys and was
planning to shoot all five of these idiots dead in the
parking lot outside of my porn shop. Instead, the Hoover
Crips just beat these guys into bloody, unrecognizable
stumps.

The next day, I answered a phone call from a friend
asking if I knew about the guys who had been beat up
in my parking lot. Naturally, I said "no" and innocently
asked who they were. When my friend told me that they
were the proprietors of a motocross clothing brand with
initials one letter off from "LBC," I couldn't wait to
call Crazy Larry. Of all the people to try to intimidate
with your pretend gangbanger act, these punk fashion

designers had by chance chosen an actual gang of homicidal Crips.

Shortly after the Crip beatdown, Hells Angel Butch and I spotted a blinged-out young Italian guy looking conspicuously out of place in the sleazy strip-mall titty bar near my porn shop. We called over Crazy Larry and Ikon to rob this out-of-towner since he was wearing an extremely expensive Rolex and looked like he was carrying cash or drugs. While we waited, the flashy guido introduced himself as Chris DeCarlo and started bragging about the escort agency he ran in Las Vegas for the Gambino Family. To my surprise, this kid's references checked out, and I introduced myself as someone who had the connections in the West Coast underworld and porn industry to be of use to an aspiring Las Vegas prostitution kingpin.

When Crazy Larry and Ikon arrived, instead of being robbed DeCarlo hired them on the spot to "do some heavy work" for him. I could not imagine that DeCarlo was hiring total strangers to kill people, but my FBI handlers immediately confirmed that he was for real. They had been closely watching DeCarlo and his Gambino associates, who were apparently in the process of making a bid to take control of Las Vegas's escort agencies using the straightforward strategy of murdering the competition. After a decade with the Milano Family, I couldn't believe that actual New York mafiosi were still brazen enough to just start killing people half a continent away from their home territory.

The feds in L.A. kept me in constant contact with DeCarlo in Vegas on my tapped phone to see what he would give up, and to my shock DeCarlo casually started ranting about *another* imminent murder. He wanted me to help a Gambino team of hit men from Tampa find a local computer hacker, Charles Coveney, who was costing the family millions. A rival escort agency was paying Coveney to hack into the telephone company's computers, intercept all the phone calls to DeCarlo's company, and reroute them to the other escort agency. DeCarlo wanted Coveney dead, and the feds wanted DeCarlo on tape admitting that he had arranged it. Mission accomplished.

Unfortunately, while I was on the phone with DeCarlo, Crazy Larry and Ikon were busy fulfilling his orders. The lunatic wanted the Crips to hunt down a Philadelphia Mafia Family associate in Las Vegas who ran a competing agency and also obtain the weaponry the Gambino hit team needed to take out Coveney. I tried to subtly hint to my Crips not to get involved, but ghetto crack-slingers are not known for being perceptive.

For the Coveney hit, the Crips bought hot rifles, bulletproof vests, and silencers from the ghetto black market and packed them in a black duffel bag. In addition, Ikon wanted me to sell him a pistol with a silencer for the hit. Had the Crips been patient, the feds would have provided me with a fake pistol to sell them and thus save them from attempted murder charges, but they were in a rush to fulfill the contract before anyone else. To my immense panic, they jumped in their stolen pickup truck and hightailed it to Vegas to make their delivery and clip their other target.

I tipped off the feds and a few undercover cars pinpointed the Crip truck and began tailing it as it entered Vegas. The feds watched as Larry and Ikon dropped off the duffel bag at Chris's office and then followed them out to see what they would do.

Soon afterwards, the FBI's SWAT team ambushed the crew of hit men that DeCarlo wanted me to lead to

Charles Coveney. One of the goons they captured was a Gambino from Florida named Vincent "Vinnie Aspirins" Congiusti, a "torture expert" whose nickname derived from his gangland specialty: using a battery-powered drill to bore holes into the skulls of his victims. In addition to the cache of semi-automatic rifles, silencers, and bulletproof vests that my Crips provided, the feds found Vinnie Aspirins' infamous power drill in the back of the hit team's Ford Expedition. When they were indicted, the feds revealed that Junior Gotti was ultimately behind the scheme, which added a nice trophy to my wall as an informant.

One of DeCarlo's murder plots self-destructed of its own accord. In the process of looking for their target from Philadelphia, the smoked-out and paranoid Crazy Larry and Ikon crashed their pickup truck on the Las Vegas Strip. Panicking that the cops would soon arrive at the scene of the wreck, the two tripping Crips spun the truck back into traffic and fled. It all happened so fast that the FBI cars tailing their truck lost sight of Crazy Larry and Ikon instantly. They were never caught.

"Everything is on hiatus."
                                   Charles "Bobby Milano" Caci

On January 2, 1999, the most remarkable event in my lifetime occurred: Michael Patrick Marvich died. Iron Mike succumbed to natural causes well into his eighty-third year terrorizing mankind, and though I had avoided his company ever since I left the drug trade in the interest of self-preservation, I took comfort in the knowledge that he died a free, wealthy, and ancient man. If Mike Marvich could escape punishment for the magnificent crimes against humanity he had committed by becoming a federal informant, I sure as hell should be able to skate by as well.

Accompanying Mike Marvich to that maximum-security prison in the sky was the second greatest criminal I had ever known, Jerry Zimmerman. Jerry's kidney failure eerily mimicked the slow and miserable death of our old mark Mel—an uncomfortable coincidence that secretly unsettled us both even though we frequently made light of the irony. Once insulated by 300 pounds of blubber, Jerry had dwindled down to a thin layer of wrinkled, sallow skin stretched over his still gigantic skeleton and garlic bulb of nose cartilage. I was on a tour of strip clubs back East when Jerry finally died, and since Jews are always in a hurry to bury their dead, I missed his funeral. Though I am usually anything but sentimental, I felt particularly sad about missing Jerry's funeral since I owed him my life. Without his calming, civilizing influence, I probably would have been shot in some coke deal or knifed in jail by a Mexican Mafia cholo for not paying prison tax.

A few months after the Wheel stopped turning for Jerry, his soft-touch counterpart in the Los Angeles Family, Louie Gelfuso, also died. Of all the deaths that I witnessed in gangland, Louie's was especially pathetic since it was preceded by the sudden, excruciating death of his beloved son, Michael. I was with Louie and Michael the day both of their lives entered a nosedive: while we were meeting with porno gangster Tony Sposato, Michael was complaining that he had woken up with a scathing pain in his lower back. Louie, who was a worrier and a hypochondriac, hurried his son to the doctor the next day; the diagnosis was late-stage cancer. There had been no warning. Within a couple weeks, Michael was bed-bound and precipitously losing weight; in a few months he was dead. It was the second child Louie had lost.

After I received the phone call from Louie saying, "Michael's gone," I knew so was Louie. The peppy, energetic, quick-talking wiseguy I had known was replaced by a sullen and joyless old man who smoked pack after pack of cigarettes while brooding over his sons' deaths. Both Batman Esposito and Pete Milano tried to comfort Louie and distract him with new rackets, but it was hopeless. One day he missed an appointment, and when I called his house to find out why Louie was late, his sister informed me that Louie would be permanently late: the late Luigi Gelfuso died from a fatal heart attack at the age of seventy-five.

The few members of the Los Angeles Family who weren't in jail from the cooperation of Ori Spado, John Branco, and Tony Angioletti convened on a boat in Ventura Harbor for a seaborne funeral. The star mourner was Louie's best friend and idol, Pete Milano, who made polite small talk with Batman Esposito, Tony Sposato, Sandy Vaccaro, and of course me. Louie's surviving family threw his cremated ashes along with the ashes of his two deceased children into the sea; in memory of Louie, Michael and Tony threw in packs of cigarettes, and I threw in a deck of cards. If Fiato had been there, he probably would have thrown in a dime bag of cocaine and a handkerchief for Louie the Couch's tears.

After the somber ceremony, I was joined below deck by Pete Milano, who was looking fat, frail, and ancient in his high-waist pants. I could tell Pete was distressed. Louie had been his loyal chief of staff and stand-in for over thirty years; without Louie to rely on, Pete stood a far greater chance of heading to jail. There was no one to replace him. As we made small talk, Pete put his hands on the table, and I noticed for the first time that they shook uncontrollably as he spoke. From then on, I dubbed Pete "Shakes Milano," a nickname that quickly caught on. After the ceremony, Stan Ornellas from the FBI bragged that he had snapped some awesome surveillance photos of Pete and me together.

With Louie dead and Jimmy and Steve Cino in jail, the last remaining member of the Los Angeles Family I trusted was Bobby Milano. Mr. Keely Smith was hardly an inspiring gangland general, but I figured he would be good for a score here and there. When I arranged a meeting, Jimmy's little brother unintentionally signaled the end of my association with the Los Angeles Family.

"Sorry, Ken," the fat little man told me with an ill-fitting note of condescension in his voice. "But we're going on hiatus for two years until Jimmy gets out from prison. Everything's on hold until Jimmy comes back."

If I didn't respect his big brother so much, I would have berated Bobby for being a sorrier excuse for a gangster than he was a lounge singer. The Mafia doesn't go on hiatus; crime doesn't have an off-season. Bobby expected the rest of Jimmy's crew of professional criminals to obtain legitimate civilian employment just because Jimmy was imprisoned. Right.

Fuck it, I thought to myself. I was done with the Milano Family. I tapped out; I could take no more self-parody. It was the end of the longest business relationship of my criminal career. In the intervening years, Bobby Milano and Pete's brother Carmen both died of natural causes. Underboss Carmen Milano died in shame: "Flipper" was exposed as an informant against his own brother's Mafia family. In my opinion, the pretty boy that replaced him as underboss may be an even worse choice than a rat to succeed Pete Milano.

For now, the octogenarian big brothers Pete and Jimmy continue to lead the Los Angeles Family, though

Pete is homebound and quiet in comparison to the still very active Jimmy. My gangster grandpa, Jimmy, was suspicious that I had turned rat from the moment he heard that I was no longer working with his brother, and when his fears were confirmed, I was told he was more heartbroken than when he was betrayed by his good friend and occasional roommate Ori Spado.

The fact that I had specifically avoided testifying against him made no difference; it was the blasphemy against the Mafia code that hurt Jimmy, not any personal offense. When I call him, he still speaks to me with affection and respect, but I have no doubt he would leak my whereabouts to the Persicos in Brooklyn if he had any idea where I lived.

As odd as it may seem, the fact that Jimmy would have me killed only makes me love him more. If nothing else, Jimmy is a man defined by his word and his principles, and I respect that. Unlike most everyone else, Jimmy will die having fulfilled his life's goal: to die a "man of honor" who never wavered from the code of criminal chivalry he swore to uphold. Jimmy may be a deluded and sentimental old man, but like Don Quixote there is something heroic and admirable in the purity of his foolishness.

"If anyone has taken [Hollywood madam Heidi] Fleiss' place, it's Nici—otherwise known as Michelle Braun, a 27-year-old mother of two who until recently lived in Bakersfield, 100 miles outside of L.A. Braun claims that she left the company over a year ago and that it was never an escort or prostitution business but a special-appearance booking company that hired out girls for everything from casual meetings to casino openings. 'My service was for people to meet famous

people,' Braun tells me over the phone. 'Not like Julia Roberts, more like B-actress famous.'"

Anna David
Details Magazine
August 20, 2004

When Michelle Braun was one of my then-wife Tabitha's airhead young groupies, I never would have imagined that she would become the most accomplished sex trafficker of the 21st century. Michelle was full of surprises: she also helped me reopen Joey Avila's murder investigation and convince the FBI to send me to New York City against the Colombo Family.

Shortly before our marriage, Tabitha introduced me to the girl that one day would revolutionize the global sex industry. Michelle was a twenty-year-old Jewish girl fresh off the bus from Bakersfield, California, who was interested in getting into porn and escorting. I disliked Michelle on sight: she was one of those insecure, loud-mouth young girls who compensate for their lack of looks by acting like a Quentin Tarantino character—all ego, obscenities, and brash cocaine attitude. Michelle looked Tabitha and me up-and-down with uncomfortable intensity; I wasn't sure if she wanted a threesome or to be cast in one of my films.

The prospects for either scenario were not good: Michelle was just a plain Jewish girl with an obnoxious attitude and a face that somehow incorporated the worst characteristics of both Bette Midler and Joan Cusack, and her hair looked like a wig taken from the *Golden Girls* costume department. Another problem would be that Michelle had a voice more befitting a hard-living transvestite than a porn queen. After Michelle left, I told Tabitha how funny it would be to see Michelle face a merciless casting agent, who would insist on receiving a blowjob before telling her that she was better suited to a dog kennel than the front cover of a porn VHS.

When Tabitha struck up a friendship with Michelle against my counsel, I told her to keep the girl away from me. I considered her an entitled brat with gangster pretensions who would get in over her head with drugs or wannabe dealers and flip like a gymnast as soon as she was in handcuffs. I was preposterously wrong. Within months of my first meeting with Michelle, the annoying Jewish party girl had revolutionized the global sex industry.

Michelle started her escort business, "Nici's Girls," in the conventional L.A. manner, sucking up to established porn stars like Tabitha and frantically hustling to find high rollers to sell them to, making a name in the industry one well-paying trick at a time. Michelle's genius was that she recognized that the Internet's global reach and façade of anonymity had the potential to transform her L.A. sex racket into a multimillion-dollar international VIP sex cartel. Michelle was the first madam to bring Silicon Valley to the Porno Valley. It was a technological paradigm shift; seemingly overnight, every VIP john in the world was ordering his girls online, just as everyone with an interest in the stock market in the late '90s rushed to become an online day trader.

Within months of putting Nici's Girls on the Internet as an expensive membership-only site, college-aged Michelle had locked down the Internet escort market and made herself the de facto top madam in America. Michelle had the clients that no one else had: the international menagerie of "royalty, *Fortune* 500 CEO's, entrepreneurs, doctors, lawyers, celebrities, entertainment moguls, aristocrats and politicians who afford themselves luxuries in life" accurately described by one of her websites. These A-list johns were attracted by Michelle's snobbishness and exclusivity; they felt safer with a madam who made them fill out applications, suffer through interviews and background checks, and pay thousands of dollars down just for the right to sign up to the website.

In exchange for a $1,000-$5,000-per-hour fee, a highroller could have the porn star, model, or actress of his choice sent to his home or favorite hotel with the click of the mouse. Though Michelle was almost immediately the biggest madam in California, her greatest profits came from her online clients in the flyover states and overseas to whom Hollywood-quality prostitutes were never previously available. For those out-of-towners willing to pay a $1,000–$5,000 retainer and an $8,000 delivery fee, all of Nici's Girls were available at their normal rates *anywhere* in the world. The true high-rollers would throw down $100,000 or more on a vacation for two in Paris or Milan booked by Michelle, who took care of the girls, the flights, the hotels, and even the restaurant and theater reservations.

With Michelle paying $20,000–$100,000 for a weekend of work, almost every major star in the porn industry rushed to join the Nici's Girls roster. When rumors of the $50,000 all-expenses-paid weekends in Tokyo and Rome began to spread through Hollywood, Nici's Girls began to attract high-profile call girls from outside of Porn Valley. Michelle pimped out *Playboy* and *Penthouse* centerfolds like Colin Farrell girlfriend Nicole Narain, World Wrestling Entertainment "divas" like Ashley Massaro, cheesecake models like Wonderbra spokesmodel Sophie Anderton, and even familiar Hollywood actresses that I would be stupid to name publicly.

In addition to their stratosphere salaries, the girls loved Michelle because she introduced them to johns with the money and desperation to make ideal sugar daddies. After being set up on "dates" by Michelle, Buck Adams' former crush Kelly Jaye received $14 million in gifts/payments from a crooked mortgage broker, and *Playboy* model Sandy Bentley was given a $1.7 million mansion and six luxury cars by a hedge fund manager who also went to jail for securities fraud. It was a symbiotic relationship: Michelle was a criminal who made introductions between professional prostitutes and professional white-collar crooks.

As Michelle quickly rose to the top of the Hollywood underworld, she wasted her millions trying to compete with her own employees. She asked Tabitha to hook her up with all the usual Porn Valley Dr. Mengeles, the unprincipled plastic surgeons who make their living mangling genetically perfect Playmates with preposterous boob jobs and gallons of Botox. Soon, plain Jewish girl Michelle was sporting huge double-barreled plastic tits, a fish-lipped face made of overworked dimpled putty, and legs hewn by a Gulag health regimen of crash diets and liposuction.

With Michelle's new look and persona came new business practices. Since she now fancied herself an elite Hollywood executive and a gangster, she started to screw girls and clients out of money. At first, I didn't much care since porn girls are born to be exploited, and Michelle was hiring me as muscle to handle collections and settle beefs with other underworld guys. However, Michelle made a mistake and held back $10,000 from my ex-wife, whom I was briefly on good terms with, and $8,000 from my frequent road trip buddy, porn star Dayton Raines. When I called Michelle to straighten things out, she refused to take my call; I'm sure she was savoring the insult.

Since I couldn't talk to Michelle, I decided to look up her family's names, addresses, phone numbers, and e-mails and see if they could put me in touch with her. I gave Michelle's daddy a friendly call and asked him to let his daughter know I'd like to talk, and that was all it took. The money was wired the next day. It was what I call "extortion light"—just making your target aware that you know where their family lives.

I figured we understood each other, but Michelle had a big ego and no sense; she nursed her grudge. Eventually, she realized that my weak point was Tabitha, and it didn't take much money to flip her. Soon, I began hearing through the grapevine that Michelle was encouraging Tabitha to sue me for more money and for control of my porn store; Michelle was even fronting Tabitha money for attorneys. That was it—Michelle was done.

I was with FBI agent Will Clark, my handler on a case I was building against my former attorney and part-time judge, a guy I'll call "Gaspar King." A cokehead and sleaze-ball who hired me to commit countless crimes, Gaspar had pointlessly framed the innocent civilian father of Orange County meth kingpin John Ward by claiming the harmless old man had threatened to blow up a court-house. This didn't sit well with me, so I convinced Will Clark to let me wear a wire against Gaspar to prove that he had sent an innocent man to jail.

I was meeting Will in a parking lot to return the audio equipment I had used against Gaspar when I received a phone call from a madam named Stacy and a pimp named Mike. They were both pissed at Michelle and heard I was on the warpath against her; they wanted to pay me big money to take care of her. Since I was already planning to set up Michelle, this gave me the perfect opportunity to talk a little too loud in front of my FBI agent friend and catch his interest. When I told Will the type of money Michelle was pulling down, he immediately called the IRS and made an appointment for us in Santa Ana. Michelle was done.

It was funny to me: Will kept telling me how this would be a "major case," yet the FBI ignored cases I gave them on literal Mafia bosses like Tony Civella. To me, prostitution wasn't even a crime, but the FBI and IRS loved the escort business cases because it involved tens of millions of dollars in unpaid taxes and seizable assets. It was crime-fighting that paid. To sweeten the pot, I also tossed in New York's top escort agency, known as Exotica 2000 or New York Elites, and its owners, Ukrainian madam Elena Trochetchenkova and her Egyptian boyfriend Rady Abbassy. I brokered introductions to porn stars and did collection work for Elena, so I had no trouble arranging a meeting for an undercover female FBI agent to interview as a prostitute with Exotica 2000.

Michelle was just as easy to take down. She called me up only a few days after I ratted her out to the feds and asked to make peace: apparently she heard that I was so pissed that I might seek revenge. To avoid that possibility, she tried to placate me by offering to partner with me on an escort agency and website based out of Las Vegas called SinSationalCity.com. She wanted to discuss matters further, but first she wanted to give me cash to go to Las Vegas and stop Mike the Pimp from making any other moves against her. Since my friend Dayton was going to Las Vegas for an escort tour and wanted me to come as her chaperone, Michelle's suggestion was a convenient way for me to make some money and set up her and Mike the Pimp at the same time.

Law enforcement moves slowly, but they usually arrive at their destination: Elena and Rady at Exotica 2000 were arrested in 2005 (five years after I ratted them out in detail), and the feds finally nabbed Michelle "Nici" Braun in 2007. Because their cases have not been fully adjudicated, the full story of the fall of America's top millionaire madams will have to be told later.

THIRTEEN
The Impotent Don

"Kenji is a man of his word. He always speaks the truth, and what he writes about the Colombo Mafia Family is unbelievably accurate. Kenji is a tough man who stood up to the scum of the Earth and helped ensure that they will get what they deserve."

William "Billy" Cutolo, Jr.

"Get a new career!
Write the Book! Start to finish!
Start a new Life!
Move on!
Have an adult relationship!
Only do good."

Kenny Gallo
A note-to-self discovered on an old cell phone
From Brooklyn, 2004

The FBI agreement I made in 1997 only removed the adjective "violent" from my profession. I was still a criminal, only not a *violent* criminal. The FBI was fine with me making a living as long as I did not do permanent damage to the American financial system or anyone's body. Though this halfhearted rule dictated a reliance on "extortion light" verbal techniques for collecting my street debts, I hardly felt like a "new," reformed, or particularly decent guy. Though Fiato and the FBI would tell me I was helping mankind with my work, that was hard for me to accept when I spent most of my time committing crimes with the same crew of prostitutes, thugs, and addicts as always. If Tara had seen how I was living, she would have hardly been impressed, and that was the only standard that mattered to me.

For my first five years as an informant, I made the majority of my income as the male escort of female escorts. I was the bodyguard, chauffeur, on-call psychiatrist, hard-negotiating agent, cash collector, substitute boyfriend, and babysitter that accompanied porn stars like Tabitha, Jill Kelly, and Jenna Jameson on their international tours of strip clubs, radio and TV promotional appearances, porn conventions, and escort agencies. In a crew of women who often preferred to lie about and pop pills for twenty hours a day, I was the all-purpose "worker" that did everything besides the stripping, autograph signing, or fucking to keep the tour running. I was tour manager, agent, roadie, and personal assistant all rolled into one.

I made sure the girls were asleep on time to get up in the morning without looking like haggard banshees, cuddled them to sleep if they were the needy type, and pulled them out of bed in the morning like Jesus raising a gaggle of pilled-out Lazaruses. If a girl was working for an escort agency like Exotica 2000 or Nici's Girls over a weekend, that meant she was supposed to be on call all day and all night in a hotel room waiting for the madam to get in touch. That meant I had to somehow make it tolerable for these easily bored, jumpy women to sit in a hotel for seventy-two straight hours. Once they were finished with their tour, I would be sent to pick up their cash *in full* from otherwise reluctant strip club owners and madams like Michelle Braun. As menial as these tasks seemed, I easily made a six-figure salary with this gig—porn girls were about as prudent with their cash as they were with their bodies.

The "ho wrangler" job, as it's known in the industry,

had its definite perks. Most obviously, I got to spend all of my time with hot, barely clothed, and generally pleasant women like Jill Kelly, Kendra Jade, Deven Davis, Jenna Jameson, and Nikki Tyler. I only consented to work with girls I liked. Whether they were escorting or not, I've always been a sucker for hot women, so I generally reveled in my time as the sole man around who wasn't a pathetic paying customer of one variety or another.

Another serious "ho wrangler" perk was that my everyday quality of life was comparable to a millionaire socialite lounging on vacation. I spent most of the year traveling via first-class tickets and private planes to luxury hotel suites around the world—all for free. I never spent a cent of my own money; my tab at the best restaurants, clubs, and bars was always covered by the girls or by the john who was underwriting that night's festivities. When the girls were asleep or otherwise occupied, I could travel anywhere I wanted, exploring new cities on their dime.

When I was paid to watch over a girl's date from a nearby table at an expensive steakhouse like Morton's or Peter Luger, it went without saying that I could order absolutely *anything* and *everything* on the menu. Unless something looked particularly good, I generally ordered the five most expensive things on the menu to make sure I got the most of the experience. After a nibble from each plate, I'd have it all boxed up for the hotel so that I could wake up the next morning and have filet mignon, lobster, and crab cocktail for breakfast.

The final, and to me paramount, advantage of my life on the road was that I could fulfill my duty to the FBI and bring down criminal organizations throughout the world. In addition to the sense of moral satisfaction and relief I felt when I captured a dangerous sociopath incriminating himself on tape, it was also extremely exciting for me to voluntarily put myself in such danger. I loved meeting the most vicious and feared men in every city across North America, sitting down across from them, looking them in the eyes, and sizing them up in comparison to every other predator I had ever known. No one ever matched up to Mike Marvich, and many of the most terrifying thugs turned into nerdy, stuttering teenagers once a pair of tits like Jill Kelly's sat down next to them.

Life wasn't perfect on the road: too many men who patron strip clubs and escort agencies are irredeemable shitheads. Michelle at Nici's Girls kept setting up my girls with Cliff in Florida, the worst john in America who didn't outright slaughter his hookers. Cliff was a pathological control freak: for entire weekends, the girls would live as the tightly regimented, tightly scripted, and obsessively criticized love slaves of Cliff. The girls were not allowed to say or do a single thing without Cliff's permission; in the absence of his precise orders, they were simply to hold his hand and smile at all times. If they failed to obey, Cliff ridiculed them and refused to pay. Though the girls willingly consented to give Cliff what he wanted for $20,000–$50,000 a weekend, there were many nights I spent awake cradling them to sleep.

The type of strip clubs that could afford expensive "feature" dancers like my girls usually boasted very tight security, but not always. When the strip clubs were not effectively secured, it could get very dangerous. Once, I escorted Jenna Jameson, Jill Kelly, Deven Davis, and Nikki Tyler to the grand re-opening of a three-floor strip club in South Carolina. At the climax of the show, all four of the big-name porn stars jumped on stage and started stripping together, which brought the crowd rushing to the stage to toss dollars at them. One high-roller was peeling off $100 bill after $100 bill at Jenna as she did her best to subtly kick the mounds of cash into the center of the stage. Jenna wasn't quick enough since one of the punks leaning over the stage was able to shovel some of the cash into his pocket.

Before Jenna even had time to shriek I rushed from backstage, grabbed the asshole's wrist, and pie-faced him back into the crowd. His fist let go of the cash, so I swept it into the center of the stage only to feel myself yanked backwards off the stage. I fell to the filthy sticky strip club carpet as the cash-stealer and all of his pals laid in kicks to my face and ribcage. I grabbed the lead dickhead's leg and bit down damn near to the bone. He yelped so loud that his friends were too startled to continue the asskicking, giving me time to stand up and blast a few of them in the face. Finally, the bouncers returned from their piss break to escort the entire mess of troublemakers outside to get arrested. Later that night, Jenna insisted we take a picture together, which she signed to her "cash ho" for my tip-rescuing prowess, and we all had a big laugh when we left and saw the thief handcuffed and crying outside, drunkenly babbling that he didn't know why he was going to jail.

The girls were all very sympathetic and worried about me in the aftermath—"Oh, poor baby, you could have gotten hurt! You shouldn't have put yourself at risk like that!" I laughed to myself; when I wasn't risking a black eye or a chipped tooth at a strip club, I was busily infiltrating the most murderous Mafia Family in America.

The Colombo Mafia Family is dominated and defined by the Persico clan, the family's ruling dynasty and Brooklyn's very own case of venereal disease. Persico family patriarch Carmine "Junior" Persico is a street legend—an infamously tough street fighter, a ferocious hit man, a ruthless backstabber, and a mass murderer—who has been the tyrannical godfather of the Colombo Family ever since he arranged the 1971 shooting of Joe Colombo. Nicknamed "The Snake" by his enemies, Carmine has transformed the Colombo Family from a crime family into something of a medieval death cult.

Carmine instituted a feudal family structure that lifted the Persico clan above the rest of the Colombo Family and Brooklyn like nobility that feels entitled to rape, pillage, and kill on a whim. The Colombo Family is arranged so that anyone with Carmine Persico's last name exists above the rules and the official leadership pyramid of the family. The Colombo Family is filled with literally dozens of the extended Persico family at every level, from street bosses to capos to soldiers to hit men to drug dealers, and, like a breed of dogs, each one shares the same trademarked Persico traits: toughness, unswerving family loyalty, phenomenal ignorance of the world outside of Brooklyn, and a flippant willingness to kill.

Imprisoned since 1985, The Snake has intentionally sacrificed the freedom of a couple dozen of his closest relatives in order to maintain his rigor mortis grip on the Colombo Family throne well into his old age. Whenever one Persico goes to jail, Carmine just picks the next in line to be "promoted" into his patsy and enforcer on the street. Carmine in effect systematically ruins every member of his family's life in order to ensure that he retains his power over Brooklyn from a faraway prison cell. The Persico family forms Carmine's personal army, his inexhaustible stable of stand-ins, successors, and soldiers, a flashy horde of gossipy goombah rich kids who all look forward to the day when they can step up in the family hierarchy, kill a few of Carmine's enemies, and go to jail for a couple decades to protect the family's birthright.

Three generations of Persico children have grown up without fathers to protect Carmine's sadistic right to kill. The Persicos are raised to consider themselves as expendable pawns destined to be sacrificed in service of Carmine's criminal empire, and they live to bask in his reflected street glory. They may spend their lives in jail, but they feel compensated because their name inspires terror in Brooklyn. It inspires terror for good reason; since the Persicos value so little their own lives and the lives of their loved ones, killing other people means nothing to the entitled spawn of the Snake. As my friend Fat Gigi Inglese once told me, "The quickest way to get whacked is to have a Persico owe you money." They'll kill their childhood friends over secondhand rumors; they'll kill a loyal mafioso to avenge a bruised ego.

The Colombo rank and file hated the Persicos for being a crew of greedy, selfish, conniving, and needlessly violent idiots who used Carmine's power to steadily co-opt the most profitable rackets in the family for themselves. After twenty years of the recklessly stupid and greedy Persico family putting Carmine's best interests above those of the thousand or so hardcore Colombo wiseguys and associates, the family revolted. In 1991, Colombo acting boss Victor Orena decided that he was no longer going to recognize his long-imprisoned cousin Carmine Persico as the family's official boss. His revolution was joined by William "Wild Bill" Cutolo, the family's best moneymaker and most liked capo, and a majority of the non-Persico Colombos.

In the ensuing Colombo War of 1991–1993, Brooklyn was overrun with carnage and gunfights in broad daylight. As the top general for opposition leader Vic Orena, Cutolo and his crew earned the reputation as the most deadly and fearless gang of shooters in all of New York. Over a dozen people died and many more were wounded in the power struggle.

Unfortunately for Brooklyn, it proved impossible to defeat the outnumbered Periscos; they were such hardcore, suicidal maniacs that Orena and Cutolo's rebel faction could only have achieved victory by exterminating all 100 or so extended Persico relatives. Before that could happen, the FBI decapitated the rebel leadership with indictments, largely thanks to the machinations of AIDS-riddled FBI informant Gregory "The Grim Reaper" Scarpa, a Persico loyalist who was feeding the feds information against the Orena faction when he wasn't shooting them on the street.

In the aftermath of all the indictments and bloodshed, the mauled Colombo Family patched itself up. Carmine Persico and his brood were still in charge, but, under extreme pressure from law enforcement and the other New York Families, they offered amnesty to any rebel who put down his pistol and recognized their supremacy. With no other options besides leaving the Life, the rebels surrendered and made peace—kowtowing to a family they hated and knew full well would try to kill them at the first convenient opportunity. The Persicos would never forgive the disloyal assholes who had colluded to steal their property and kill their family members, and they would get revenge. A Colombo wiseguy was never in more danger than when he was meeting with his own Family.

This was the insane, cannibalistic mob that I began to infiltrate in 1999, and of which I became a fully accredited member in late 2001.

My entry into New York came through the Garofalo family, the Mafia clan that has wasted more potential than any other I've known. I knew various branches of the Garofalo family for years since their cousin, Keith Gordon, was a porn industry executive at Bizarre Video and my girl Jill Kelly's company. Between Keith and my other connections in the Colombo Family, I would gradually be introduced to the entire younger generation of the Brooklyn Garofalos, all of whom were bright but wild party kids who loved the West Coast and loved porn. In the interests of networking, I let Manny Garofalo's two sons and a couple other Garofalo kids from the Bay Ridge neighborhood vacation at my places in California and Vegas. I'd show them around, take them to porn shoots and strip club appearances, introduce them to big name West Coast wiseguys, teach them how to smuggle pills from Mexico—carefully building up their esteem for me so that they could spread word around Brooklyn about what a great guy I was.

When I dished to the feds about the NYC-based Exotica 2000 at the turn of the millennium, I finally gained a valid excuse in their eyes to start operating and informing in New York City. Though they appreciated my work against the more docile Mafia groups around the country, they had previously been dubious that I could do anything but get in trouble around the far more violent, reckless, and racist Five Families of New York. With millions of dollars of Exotica 2000's seizable, untaxed assets as a sweetener, the FBI consented to allow me to work one week out of every month in New York developing information on Exotica and other NYC escort agencies.

Once I was in Brooklyn regularly, it did not take long for the younger Garofalo kids to introduce me to their idol, Edward "Eddie" Garofalo, Jr., who had heard a great deal about me from them. My first thought upon meeting Eddie, if I remember correctly, was *damn*! Eddie was a beast: six-foot-three, maybe 250 pounds, thick and muscular with a jutting caveman face and hard black stare. Though he was always dressed immaculately—his preference was for brand-new, expensive, all-white tracksuits and sneakers that he would wear maybe twice before tossing—Eddie made the impression of a guy who was not overly familiar with civilization. The first impression was partially unfair: though Eddie could barely read, he was still a smart street operator who was making somewhere between $500,000 and a million dollars per year while still in his thirties.

Eddie's story was typical for a Colombo wiseguy of his generation. His father, Edward senior, was a mobbed up contractor, demolitionist, and garbage trucker who made his name in the '80s in a partnership with his two brothers, Manny and Frank. As the most infamous illegal garbage dumpers in New York City, the Garofalo brothers became known as the "James brothers of garbage." Unlike the more subtle and refined brand of racketeering he would later practice with me, in his youth Manny was considered by far the most flagrant polluter and garbage dumper of the three brothers, the sort of careless crook who would toss toxic waste into protected wildlife habitats and loads of refuse onto playgrounds.

As a junior wiseguy growing up in Brooklyn, Eddie was a member of one of the local Italian street gangs that acted as a farm team for the Mafia by engaging in petty drug dealing, robberies, and graffiti "tagging." His running partner and best buddy was Theodore "Teddy" Persico, Jr., an ultra-violent nephew of Carmine Persico. As Teddy's best friend and business partner in trucking and heavy equipment companies, Eddie was a lock to

become a "made guy" and possibly more in the Persico-
dominated Colombo Family.

Though Eddie seemed like a surefire future Colombo
leader, the same could not be said for his father. Edward
Garofalo had done business for years with the Gambino
Family and its underboss, Salvatore "Sammy the Bull"
Gravano, who happened to be the brother-in-law of
Edward's almost identically named cousin, Edward Ga-
rafola. There was a long-standing resentment between
Gravano and Garofalo over some cash that Sammy
believed he was owed on a job, and on August 9, 1990,
the issue was resolved in a manner that calls to mind
the assassinations of both Joey Avila and Joe Peraino,
Jr. After years of extorting payoffs from Garofalo,
Gravano argued that a suspiciously light jail sentence
Garofalo had received was proof that he was an informant. That was enough evidence for John Gotti, who
approved the hit. Having stolen everything he could
from Edward, Gravano enlisted the victim's own cousin,
Edward Garafola, to help arrange the streetside hit in
Brooklyn.

Soon afterwards, Gravano became a rat for the FBI
and got away with that murder and eighteen others.

Already an established and intimidating hood in his
mid-twenties at the time of his father's death, Eddie Jr.
was stopped from retaliating by his uncle Manny, who
cautioned him that it was just how business was done.
Eddie was told that the Mafia's rules dictated that he
had to be polite and cordial even to his cousin Edward
Garafola, regardless of whether he had been involved in
his father's death. With the entire Brooklyn underworld
watching Eddie to see if he had the discipline and toughness to keep his cool under such intolerable conditions,
Eddie sunk to the challenge; he kept his mouth shut, his

head down, and treated Garafola with respect. The Colombo Family was very impressed.

Eddie's brainwashed cult-member loyalty was proven once and for all in 1997 when he completely disowned his own mother and sisters for breaking the Mafia's rules by suing Gravano for the wrongful death of his father. The Mafia does not sue informants; it is an admission of weakness if the Mob needs to resort to government courtrooms to retaliate against rats. Now that Eddie had sacrificed his relationships with his entire immediate family to win the approval of the Mafia, the Colombos embraced Eddie as one of their most trusted young soldiers and future leaders. Eddie was treated with the utmost respect everywhere I visited in the New York underworld.

Eddie and I made a quick friendship. By this point, I was an accomplished charmer: since my "ho wrangler" gig basically called for me to professionalize the art of "hanging out" and keeping poor conversationalists entertained, I very quickly adapted to become what I sensed Eddie's perfect buddy would be. He was a simple guy who was easy to please: he liked cash, new cars and clothes, and Italian, Chinese, and Asian fusion food in huge portions. He reminded me of Jackie di Padova, so I just acted like I did in Florida: I was always up for a meal and a drink, always up to shoot the shit. After hearing from his young relatives about the money I was making on the West Coast, Eddie was intrigued by the idea that I could get him a piece of the big-time escort business and porn money that his cousin Keith was making.

Eddie already had more money than he knew how to spend: between his trucking and heavy equipment companies, contracting work with his uncle Manny, and interests in stock scams and gambling, Eddie was one of the richest soldiers in the Colombo Family. To impress me before he asked me to officially "go on the record" and move to Brooklyn to work for him, Eddie took me on his daily rounds to the garbage dumps and job sites. He wanted me to marvel at the huge seven-figure numbers he was bidding for jobs.

I was more impressed by Eddie's toughness. When contractors and equipment operators told him that they were behind schedule, all it took was one look from Eddie for 250-pound roughnecks to start begging for mercy. Eddie was not bluffing: one day he showed up at my place with his fist spraying blood like a horror movie prop. Apparently someone had been late finishing a job; by the look of Eddie's giant hand, I bet whomever he punched probably needed reconstructive surgery to be recognizable as a human. I liked Eddie's straightforward "strike first, think later" business model: this wasn't the Milano Family anymore. The Colombos were straight, unprincipled gangsters completely lacking in self-awareness. They weren't faking or putting on a show.

Shortly after 9/11, Eddie invited me to Brothers, a barbecue joint in lower Manhattan, for a family meeting. Since so many streets were still closed in the aftermath of the terrorist attack, all the wiseguys drove up in golf carts from construction sites. Everyone was there: I met Manny, John Baudanza, and John's father, Colombo soldier Carmine Baudanza. I fit in just fine, and I quickly caught on to the "test" Eddie and Manny Garofalo had concocted to see if I was Colombo material: Eddie told me that he was "not talking to Manny" with the intent to see if the uncommonly sly and charming Manny could get any information about his nephew out of me. If I shared any of Eddie's business, then I was a potential rat. Since the younger Garofalo cousins had already tipped me off that Eddie considered Manny his adopted father, I passed their test easily.

At this point, I expected Eddie to invite me to stay in Brooklyn full-time as his associate every trip I made to New York. If anything, Eddie was more cautious than the vast majority of wiseguys would 'have been; it took a couple years of knowing him and his family before he decided to make the pitch. He was being smart: if I turned out bad, he would be held responsible as the soldier who vouched for me. Largely thanks to Manny's tutelage, Eddie was careful about vetting me before I joined the family—but clearly not careful enough.

The offer finally came around November of 2001 after a long conversation about Tommy Gambino and the Los Angeles Family. Eddie was feeling out how I felt about the L.A. guys, seeing if I was wedded to them or the guy it was rumored was their heir apparent. As soon as Eddie heard my feelings about Tommy, he could see there would be no conflict there. "Ken, I want you to come down to Brooklyn. Live here full-time and work for me." In Eddie's flat, loud voice, none of this sounded like anything less than an order. The Brooklyn guys were always very bossy. Why even *ask* when any self-respecting criminal would want to work in New York, the big leagues of the Mafia?

"It'd be good. You could take action [bets] for me on the West Coast. We can bust out those Exotica people and have you take over the escort business for me out here, make some real fucking cash. I can talk to Teddy, and he'll get word to Carmine, and Carmine will send word to L.A. They won't have shit to say about it. You'll be with me." Though ticker-tape parades were spontaneously marching down every wrinkle in my brain, I kept my elation to myself. I knew well enough to play hard to get; I told Eddie I'd think about it.

I had an appointment in Hollywood that I couldn't miss, anyway. It also happened to be Colombo Family business: the acting debut of Colombo Family legend Dominic "Donnie Shacks" Montemarano alongside James Caan and Ron Jeremy in *A Night at the Golden Eagle*. My buddy Adam Rifkin, who was close with Tabitha and generally a friend of all porn industry people, directed *A Night at the Golden Eagle,* so I had no trouble getting seats at the special debut at the Paramount Studios lot.

I came to the screening specifically to gawk at what I was positive would be a disastrous performance from Donnie Shacks, whom I fucking despised. Donnie, who I like to call "Pissbag" due to his incontinence, is a well-known woman beater and alleged Colombo Family enforcer. As my good friend Anthony Fiato says, "Shacks is quite a hit with the ladies. He hits the hell out of most of them."

Besides being the top Colombo capo on the West Coast and the shittiest Colombo actor on the planet, Donnie's real claim to fame is that he's the best friend of Carmine Persico. In the '60s, it was rumored that Donnie dressed in drag to accompany Carmine on his many hits and ambushes. After Carmine was imprisoned for life, Donnie relocated to California to take it easy, trade in on his name back East, and break into Hollywood.

To the traditional wiseguys in New York, it was considered something between a disgrace and a violation of the code of omerta for a high profile leader of a secret criminal society to openly play a gangster in a movie. Since Shacks was hyper-homicidal Carmine Persico's blood brother, no one could say anything, but even young guys like Eddie privately mocked Donnie's Hollywood turn as just one more sign that the Mafia had become a parody of itself.

Of course, that had happened long before, especially in California, and Donnie had been trying to infiltrate Hollywood for years. Donnie bragged to me that he had so charmed Congressman Sonny Bono that the former Mr. Cher had allowed him to use his home as his hideout from the feds when he was on the lam. Once Sonny died, Donnie told me that his wife and political successor, Congresswoman Mary Bono, had taken up the Donnie Shacks cause and was busily writing letters to judges and parole officers on his behalf. Speaking of letters, at the same time I pulled a few strings and came into possession of a prison letter from Carmine Persico to Donnie, in which Carmine instructed his friend to refrain from hurting Sean Penn even though the actor was causing trouble with a Hollywood producer the Colombos were trying to cultivate for one of their projects.

The greatest triumph of Donnie Shacks' Hollywood career was not *A Night at the Golden Eagle,* but instead his date for the premiere: *Austin Powers* star Elizabeth Hurley. Once I confirmed that they were a legitimate item and not some type of paid arrangement, the incontinent, cross-dressing hit man and the English model officially became the new all-time oddest wiseguy couple, supplanting the former leader: Ori "Jack LaLanne Juciers" Spado and Tina "Ginger from *Gilligan's Island*" Louise, who I heard dumped Ori over his impotence. My only explanation for Hurley's affair with Donnie is that she may have been trying to win a bet that she could find a boyfriend more embarrassing than Hugh Grant.

While I was ogling L.A.'s hottest new power couple, I caught Donnie's eye, and he brought Tommy Gambino over for a chat. To give you an idea of how highly I was rated at this party, Donnie insisted that I sit in one of the "rows of honor" right by Tommy and Donnie himself.

When I got up to take a leak before the movie started, the insecure Pissbag jumped out of his seat to make sure I wasn't ditching his big-screen debut.

If only! Here is my capsule review of *A Night at the Golden Eagle*—Pissbag Donnie was comprehensively out-acted by Ron Jeremy, which really says it all. The highlight of the event was the bizarre, hagiographic pre-screening speech in honor of Donnie delivered by two of L.A.'s greatest Mob groupies: director Rifkin and billionaire Steve Bing, another ex-boyfriend of Elizabeth Hurley. Though it wasn't Steve Bing money, I made a tidy profit a little later selling video of Donnie and Elizabeth to *The National Enquirer*. A few years after that, Donnie would allegedly be the ringleader in a plot to kill me, but clearly Donnie is nowadays no better at killing people than acting.

After this sojourn in the Neverland of fake wiseguys, I was all too eager to return to Brooklyn and accept Eddie's offer. After a meeting with Eddie where I formally accepted his offer and was told the request would take a while to work through the imprisoned chain of command, Manny's son drove me to his father's home in Seagate, a gated community with an ocean view. Manny and I talked business over coffee. He gave me his all-purpose advice for working in Brooklyn: "The young guys are nice guys, good guys, but they're not good for people like you. Just not a good fit. You have brains. You should be working with people who do business the right way."

It was at that moment that I realized Eddie's sophisticated, wealthy uncle had designs to steal me from his nephew as soon as I moved to Brooklyn. Even Eddie's supposed one true friend and protector in the world was out to screw him for a dollar. I felt for Eddie: I could tell deep down that he was a very lonely and paranoid guy. Who could blame him with his family?

I believe Eddie banished his sisters and mother from his life more to completely eliminate all memories of the pain he had suffered than any real anger over the lawsuit they filed against Sammy Gravano. One night when we were talking about my possible transfer to New York, Eddie's pushy sister Laura called me on my cell phone and asked me to let him know that she missed and loved him. The big man turned on me with a scowl and said "So?" It was a very ugly look.

The next day, I had to get my porn girls up early for a paid, scripted appearance on the *Maury* talk show. On an episode entitled "Secret Crushes," I was paid by Maury Povich's production company and some porn companies to portray a schlub with a secret crush on Tabitha or Dayton—I don't even remember which one. Since I was Tabitha's ex-husband, I hoped it was her because that would have been one hell of a secret. I hooked up some Brooklyn wiseguy kids with roles on the show just to spread around the love. After I successfully held up the producers for more money, I expressed my disappointment that I wasn't booked on one of the "Who's the baby daddy?" paternity test episodes.

On my next visit to Brooklyn, I was called to show up at a truck yard on Butler Street that Eddie was using for his Big R Trucking Company. The truck yard was terrifying: a loud, dark, filthy garbage dump dotted with backhoes digging trenches. The sky was dark; winter was approaching, and the post-9/11 gloom had not yet lifted from the city.

Eddie showed up with a Persico cousin with the last name Cirillo and another heavy wiseguy. He shouted over the noise, "This is Teddy," as he extended a photo taken in prison of an extremely fit, long-faced, canine-looking Italian in his forties with steel-gray hair. "Teddy, as you know, is my partner. He's got four more years to do, but he does 200 push-ups every single day to stay in shape and get ready for when he hits the streets. He's a beast." I nodded appreciatively; you had to play this homoerotic admiration game with members of the Persico family if you wanted to go anywhere in the Colombos.

"I need to know once and for all, for sure, do you want to come out here and be with us?"

"Yes, definitely." Thanks to the cold, I could see the words come out of my mouth in clouds of mist.

"Teddy's a good guy to be with. A real good guy. He'll send word to Carmine to okay your transfer from L.A., and those guys won't have shit to say about it. We'll get you a place in Brooklyn. You'll work with me." As Eddie was talking, a beat-up white van sputtered into the truck yard; my heart rate quickened. It sure looked like the type of disposable van I'd use to transport a dead body. The van came to a stop perilously close to us and out jumped Craig Marino, a young, pint-sized Colombo Family soldier with a Caesar haircut and two Sicilian immigrants in tow. Marino had a reputation as a shooter, and within a couple years he would promise to kill me—but not now. Now he was my friend.

As we were saying our hellos to Craig, Eddie's phone rang; he picked it up with a grunt. It was Teddy Persico from prison. "Hey, Ken, he wants to speak with you." This was the first time I had ever spoken with Teddy, who was a street legend in Brooklyn and almost universally recognized as a future boss of the family. He had the reputation as perhaps the most merciless and trigger-happy of all the younger Persicos, which was an achievement on par with being the sluttiest porn star in the San Fernando Valley.

"Hello," I said, unable to hide the excitement in my voice.

"Hey, it's Teddy. I've heard a lot about you, man. I'm really looking forward to meeting you. You definitely on board?"

"Absolutely."

"Don't worry then. I'll take care of it."

And take care of it Teddy did: he put word out to his also-imprisoned uncle, Carmine, and New York's longest reigning godfather personally okayed my entry into his family and put in the transfer request to Pete Milano.

After I got off the phone, Eddie gave me a little punch on the shoulder. "Hey, now you're playing for the major leagues."

"Meet the Baudanzas.

"There's John, his father Carmine, his uncle Joseph, his brother-in-law Sal, and his father-in-law Danny. . . . [W]hile they may lack the fame of the Gottis, Gigantes, Persicos and other more familiar mob surnames, the Baudanzas have done pretty well in the fortune department. The feds say the Baudanzas—specifically John, Carmine, Joseph and an extended family of seven others—have used good-old-fashioned mob tactics of threats and violence to power a classic pump-and-dump stock scam that ripped off more than $20 million from unsuspecting investors."

Jerry Capeci
GanglandNews.com
May 4, 2006

> *"Johnny Baudanza was on our side in the [Colombo] War. He was always with Craig [Marino] and [Joe] Scopo with their transmitters, on call [for a shootout]. Nonetheless, John to me always was a half-a-fag. Craig, on the other hand, was just a little fucking hoodlum. We were always at block parties and at high school together. He was always a troublemaker, walking around with a pinky in the air and drink in his hand; I'm still shocked he got a badge [button, inducted into the Family]."*

> William "Billy" Cutolo, Jr.

When civilians ask me what life within the New York Mafia is really like, the easy answer is "Not like the movies." There was a time, briefly, when cartoonish cinema-inspired godfather John Gotti really did turn a sizable swathe of the New York Families into a bunch of central casting, pinstripe-and-pinkie-ring-wearing goons, but that's not the reality anymore. Even the backwards Colombo Family strictly instructs its young wiseguys never to wear ostentatious clothing or jewelry; if you meet a Colombo capo, he will most likely be dressed in a pair of khakis and a polo shirt or in a nice tracksuit.

Likewise, most Mafia business is at least supposed to be conducted anywhere *but* connected social clubs, restaurants, bars, strip clubs, and hangouts. Much more common is a "walk talk" in public which is considerably harder to bug. For example, when Eddie Garofalo would have me drive him to see an old Colombo capo in Greenwich Village, I would circle the block as they chatted on the sidewalk until Eddie paged me on my phone to pick him up. The very low-key Colombo capo on Avenue U, whom I only knew by the nickname Jimmy the Gook, had a set spot on the street where visitors were supposed to stand and wait. In a few minutes, one of the Gook's guys would walk by, find out your business, and instruct you where to walk to meet with the Gook. Sometimes it would be outside; sometimes it would be inside in a booth at Joe's on Avenue U or a similar diner.

Another divergence from the Hollywood depictions is the Five Families' size and power, which is drastically smaller than most people imagine. I would estimate over half of the Colombo Family's soldiers and nearly 95% of its top leadership are in prison; at any one time there might be as little as forty or fifty serious Colombo wiseguys on the street in a metropolitan area of twenty million people. The FBI may suck at fighting a lot of criminal organizations, but they have been delivering a ferocious quarter-century beatdown on the New York Mafia.

Of those fifty serious Colombos out at any one time, around thirty are too old or fat to even win a fistfight. Maybe five of the remainder could competently kill anyone, though another 100 neighborhood nobodies who have never held a gun would be eager to try in order to "become someone." Even the competent killers have no reliable guns in storage for a "rainy day"; your average inner-city ghetto gang has exponentially more firepower.

To me, the biggest breach between Mob reality and the average civilian's expectations is to be found in the personalities of most wiseguys. After decades of watching clever, sharp-witted, and generally larger-than-life movie gangsters, a lot of the people that I talk to honestly believe that hanging out with wiseguys all the time would be a laugh riot, a nonstop performance of dirty jokes, hammy storytelling, and exaggerated tempers. To be honest, most mafiosi are just boring, stupid, petty criminals: not crazy stupid, not funny stupid, not *Sopranos* stupid, not charismatic stupid, just fucking plain old uninteresting stupid. Even the guys who won't shut the fuck up usually don't have much to say.

It's almost impossible to exaggerate how provincial and small-minded the guys in Brooklyn were. They were like medieval peasants who were terrified of the mysterious outside world and only felt comfortable in a tiny corner of the neighborhood where they were born. Many of them bragged to me that they had never used the subway in their life; they only traveled to Manhattan or the Bronx under extreme duress. I could never get over the fact that high-ranking, lifelong New York residents in the Colombo Family honestly had no idea where the Empire State Building was or how to get to Times Square. Besides Manny and John Baudanza, I don't remember meeting a single wiseguy with much in the way of an imagination or an active engagement with American society at large. Eddie was considered somewhat avant-garde and progressive, simply for eating at the new Asian restaurants in Brooklyn.

The average New York wiseguy is pretty much indistinguishable from the type of petty crooks Jimmy Caci used to run into at the racetrack. Outside of real heavy hitters like the Baudanzas, Garofalos, or Persicos, there just isn't that much wealth in today's Mafia. Most wiseguys are dealing petty amounts of crap weed or blow or working the bookmaking/loansharking/extortion grind. It's not uncommon for a made guy to be evicted for failing to pay his rent or sent to jail over delinquent child support payments.

The power of the Mafia has fallen so precipitously that even the NYPD views the threat posed by the Five Families as primarily petty street crimes. I know—shortly after I started operating in New York, I had a law enforcement friend make contact with the NYPD so that I had somewhere to send my information in case the FBI proved stubborn or uninterested. I met with Sergeant Fred Santoro of the NYPD organized crime task force, who without hesitation told me exactly who he wanted: Lucchese Family capo John Baudanza and Colombo Family soldier Craig Marino.

"John and Craig are punks that shoot people," Fred said with a scowl. "We are pretty sure they were involved in the death of a law enforcement officer. We want them. They worked for the losing side in the Colombo War, and we're pretty sure they dropped bodies then, too." Fred was elated to hear that I already knew both men. Craig and John were considered rich targets: not only were they very active in street crimes like dealing and loan sharking, but they were also suspected of having high-profile murders in their past that could potentially be uncovered.

John Baudanza, despite his high rank in the equally murderous Lucchese Family, was in fact another Colombo nepotism case: his father Carmine ran some Colombo gambling rackets and his uncle Joe was a fearsome family capo who acted as the liaison with the Russian Mob in Brighton Beach and overseas. John, who I always called "JB," grew up another local street kid and gang member in Brooklyn, kicking around in dealing and petty crime. His running partner was Craig Marino, a tiny Pesci-looking character with a vicious streak. Together, they became known as two of the most volatile and trigger-happy young hang-about kids in Ralph Scopo's Colombo crew.

JB and Craig acted like cracked-out gangbangers; the smart money was that they would kill someone over something petty like a spilled drink at a movie theater and go to jail for life. They weren't considered "made guy material"—too crazy, too petty.

When some poor guy accidentally clipped JB's shoulder at a diner, Craig and John allegedly used the collision as an excuse to beat the guy senseless and shoot him in the back. JB was also known to carry a knife and use it frequently, sticking people in bar fights and petty arguments on a regular basis. When I asked my friend Billy Cutolo, Jr., to explain to me what type of crook JB was in those days, he told a story about Baudanza bursting into the posh Mob restaurant 101 with his ear hemorrhaging blood into a handkerchief and loudly asking for Billy. Once JB found Billy and his wife's table, John barely paused to say hello to Mrs. Cutolo before asking Billy's permission to take out a Cutolo crew wiseguy, Joey Patillo, who had apparently bitten off part of his ear in a fistfight. Billy was disgusted and, on behalf of his then-imprisoned dad, told JB to stop bleeding all over everyone's food and get the fuck out of 101.

In the Colombo War, JB and Craig served as shooters for the rebel faction. For two reckless and impetuously violent kids like JB and Craig, the ability to actually engage in broad daylight Wild West shootouts on the streets of Brooklyn was the most exciting thing to ever happen in their lives. During the struggle, the NYPD told me that Craig obtained the reputation as an "ambush kid," someone who only pulled the trigger when he was looking at someone's back.

Unfortunately for JB and Craig, the Persico family prevailed in the Colombo War, and the two street punks were now tied to a Mafia Family whose own leadership hated their guts. Both JB and Craig knew without being told that the Persicos would never forget and never forgive their "treachery" during the war—it was hard to forget when two local kids shoot your family and get away it.

Though Craig knew he was risking a bullet in his head every time he met with the Persicos, he was one of those guys who had no use for living unless he was in Brooklyn committing crimes. He made his peace with the Persicos and eventually was inducted into the family despite considerable bad blood on both sides. The reasoning was simple: Craig was a moneymaker on par with Eddie. Though, as I would see, the Persicos never abandoned their plans to kill Craig, they saw no reason not to profit from his extremely lucrative loan sharking, weed dealing, and stock scam rackets in the meantime.

JB was different: he had an out. Whether by chance or through a particularly inspired self-preservation ploy, as soon as it became clear the Persicos would triumph, Baudanza successfully courted Danielle Cutaia, daughter of powerful Lucchese Family capo Domenico "Danny" Cutaia. Besides Manny, JB was the smartest New York mafioso I knew, so it was not out of the question that his interest in Danielle was not purely romantic and had a cynical edge to it. Regardless, in 1995 the Colombos happily released JB from his obligations, and JB was inducted along with his brother-in-law Sal into the Lucchese Family. By 2001, when I met him, JB was the youngest capo in the Lucchese Family at the age of thirty, and his blood-brother Craig was one of the top earning and least popular made guys in the Colombo Family.

I first met John and Craig at get-togethers with the Garofalos, but they were just two Italian guys that I vaguely recognized. It wasn't until I saw JB in Atlantic City at a porn convention party that our friendship began in earnest.

I was escorting Dayton to a party thrown by Eddie's

cousin Keith Gordon after a busy day at the convention. I walked in with Dayton and saw JB by the door. Before I had a chance to say hello, he grabbed me by the sleeve and pulled me over. "*Holy shit*," he said, dousing me with a fine mist of Johnnie Walker scotch. "Who the fuck is that?" he asked pointing at Dayton, whose gigantic breast implants and banana-sized collagen lips were just what JB was looking for. Before I could say anything, Dayton and the other porn girls pulled me along; I was needed in the VIP section upstairs to supervise my girls and make sure none of them overdosed.

Less than a minute later, a wiseguy gopher I knew rushed towards me in a hurry. "Kool wants to see you!" The kid sounded really excited to pass on this message, like he had just said "Elvis."

"Who the fuck is Kool?"

"He's the youngest capo in the Lucchese Family. He's friends with Eddie."

I called up Eddie. "Oh yeah, that's John Baudanza," Eddie explained. "Great guy. Tell him I said hello." With Eddie's approval, I went downstairs and had this wiseguy kid Dennis introduce me formally to JB, who thus knew I was with people. Luckily, he remembered me from the Garofalos anyway, so he was very straightforward about his business.

JB quickly lived up to his nickname "Kool." JB was the type of guy who always makes a slick first impression and then steadily demolishes it the more you know him. At the time, he came across like a real operator—slick, even-tempered, and masterfully in control, much more calm and laidback than you would expect from his reputation. After meeting them, it wasn't surprising to me that John and Craig were into pot distribution together; they definitely seemed to have chilled out since the early '90s.

With JB's dark skin tone, he almost seemed like a Californian, only I would later learn that his round-cheeked face was perpetually reddened from alcohol consumption, not sun exposure.

Laidback surfer attitude aside, JB definitely talked like a New York mafioso—from the 1940s. As the son, nephew, and son-in-law of old-school wiseguys, JB's speech patterns and slang were jarringly old-fashioned; he spoke like a James Cagney character. Every girl he saw was "Doll," "Dollface," or "Sweetheart," and despite his youth JB saw no problem in calling other wiseguys "Sonny" or "Kid" or "Champ." As JB was talking, I thought to myself that he would look just like a younger Fred Flintstone if only he weren't wearing such thick-rimmed black glasses. In honor of those gigantic clunkers, I popularized the nickname "Johnny Goggles" for JB, who, in addition to Kool, was also known as "Sex" on the street.

I quickly found out why: JB wanted Dayton, and he damn sure got her. After I made the introduction, JB had Dayton blushing and fluttering her eyelids within seconds. For a chubby Italian guy in a Yankees jersey, JB had no trouble turning a jaded porn star into a self-conscious teenage girl. As Dayton fell progressively under his spell, JB progressively fell under the spell of his Johnnie Walker scotch and started staggering in place just to stay upright.

With JB occupied with Dayton, the party was boring to me; after all, I was the only attendee who wasn't drinking or flying on cocaine. Unfortunately, as the girls' chaperone, I had no choice but to stay until they were ready to leave, which wasn't until 3 a.m. Just when I thought I could go to sleep, Baudanza and his underling Nicky Vitale insisted on accompanying Dayton and me back to our suite at the Borgata Casino to party.

Luckily for me, Dayton told me she trusted John despite his 1-to-1 scotch-to-blood ratio, and I went to sleep as they went off to party in another room. I passed out almost immediately, only to wake up later to a drunk-as-hell John Baudanza on the edge of my bed, slurring out sweet talk to Dayton.

The next day, Dayton and I returned to Brooklyn, where JB had insisted we get together again. Nicky Vitale picked us up and took us to meet JB at Areo's, which along with 101 is the top Brooklyn wiseguy hangout. I think it was a setup, since soon after I sat down Craig Marino arrived and told me he was having a drink nearby at the Blue Zoo—which I took as my hint to let JB have Dayton to himself. I excused myself to go speak with Craig in depth for the first time, and I found him also to be a surprisingly likeable guy. Due to his permanently scowling face, tough guy reputation, and tiny fireplug body, I expected Craig to have an extremely aggressive Napoleon complex—basically, I thought he would act like Joe Pesci. In reality, Craig was a very quiet, reserved, and secure guy. For a violent criminal, he seemed comfortable with himself. I could tell that he was that rare mafioso who was in no way conflicted about the life he had chosen. He loved it.

Apparently my tact at dinner earned JB's gratitude, since Nicky Vitale picked me up the next day to take me to Bay Ridge Realty next to JB's favorite booze-hole, Plush. JB had ties to the company and arranged for me to rent a great new apartment in Brooklyn at a heavily discounted price. Naturally, Dayton, who was making huge money working for Exotica 2000 every weekend, became my roommate and JB's conveniently close-by mistress. We drove cross-country from California and arrived with all of our stuff on New Year's Day, 2002.

As soon as I arrived in Brooklyn full-time, I found myself hanging out more with John Baudanza, Craig Marino, Nicky Vitale, and Marino's driver Georgie Fanelli than I did with Eddie Garofalo. Obviously, it was not Carmine Persico's intent to negotiate a transfer with the Los Angeles Family to provide Persico-killer John Baudanza with a new buddy, and Eddie told me to watch myself since I was going to get in trouble. The problem was that I liked JB, Craig, and Georgie, and the NYPD and FBI liked the information I was feeding them.

For months after my arrival in New York, every day began with me meeting Georgie at his no-show job at a garage that installed TVs and high-end sound systems into luxury cars. From there, Georgie would drive me to meet with JB, Craig, or Nicky Vitale for lunch or coffee depending on who was available that day, and we'd spend four or five hours doing nothing but sitting around a table and talking. Sometimes, Craig and I would hit the movies together, which drove Georgie nuts with jealousy since I got to go out on "dates" with Craig while he was just a gopher.

Georgie was very frustrated with his lackey station in the New York Mafia. He felt he deserved more since he was physically tougher than anyone else in our circle and made good money from weed and coke dealing. The problem with Georgie was that he was simply nuts, even by JB and Craig's standards: everyone in Brooklyn said that Georgie would punch his mom in the face whenever he got tired of her nagging. As a stocky, pot-bellied ex-con and former boxer, Georgie was useful to tiny Craig as a driver and bodyguard, but the Colombos wanted nothing to do with him.

Georgie had his niche: he was a chauffeur and the muscle charged with protecting Craig in any dispute for as long as it took the little guy to find his gun. With his jealousy, I always thought it would only take the slightest suggestion from the Persicos to convince Georgie to whack Craig in the hope of getting promoted.

It seemed like the only people that took Georgie seriously were the NYPD, who wanted me to set up a sting. They came to me with a plan: I would buy one pound of weed from Georgie. I laughed. "Dude, Georgie would just give me a pound of weed. It's nothing to him. Money isn't his problem; it's respect."

Though I liked Craig and Georgie, I was never particularly close to them. They were just hangout buddies since Georgie was too crazy to get close to, and Craig was too reserved. John Baudanza, on the other hand, seemed to have been waiting for someone to talk to his entire life.

JB had a dilemma: he secretly saw through the Life and his insular Brooklyn subculture, yet there was no one for him to talk to about it. Unlike Craig or Eddie, who were just smart enough to make money, JB was cursed with that extra little bit of smarts that grants self-awareness. His conflicted mental state was the inevitable product of a subculture where fathers indiscriminately force their sons, regardless of their personalities or skills, into a life of violent organized crime. Like me, he realized that his entire life was a pathetic sham, but since his entire family—even his wife—was Mafia to the bone he had no way to escape. He was stuck.

"Ken, I'm going to hell," JB always used to tell me whenever we were alone. It was almost his catchphrase, and he never said it lightly. He said it like a man who honestly believed he would spend eternity engulfed in flames and was terrified. "Some of the things I've done are horrible. I'm going to burn in hell. Jesus Christ."

I think JB chose to confide in me since I was the only person in his circle who was a Brooklyn outsider, who had not been brainwashed from birth. Everyone JB knew was a potential informant—not to the feds, but to the Colombo or Lucchese Family leadership. He could never express his doubts or his guilt because, if word got out that he was going soft, he would be killed as a safety precaution. JB lived in a very paranoid and tiny world; whenever we traveled together, he would have me go ahead of him to ensure there wasn't a hit team waiting for him. He was terrified that the Persicos, known for shooting first and thinking later, would hear the wrong rumor and rub him out. "I'm long overdue, Ken," John told me. "Everyone knows it."

JB explained to me, "The only place I can be myself in the entire world is my basement." The first time he took me down to the tiny basement of his house, I understood: it was filled with books, historical memorabilia from World War II, booze, and a big screen TV left always on the History Channel. JB was a reader, but he was afraid to let anyone know lest they mistake him for weak. JB knew more about the Battle of Midway than other Brooklyn wiseguys know about the entirety of human history.

As we sat in his basement and he drank, JB would open up to an extent that I found shocking for one of the most powerful gangsters in New York City. He was anything but guarded. "I fucking hate my pops," he snarled in between sips. "I spent my entire childhood getting beaten, getting told I was a fuckup, getting told I was too weak. Then I get to become a teenager, and I have to prove to the world that I'm the toughest, most dangerous sonofabitch around." JB turned to me, his hooded, watery eyes communicating intense hatred for both himself and his father.

"And don't think I don't know, Ken. Don't think I don't know. I'll be paying for the things I did back then for the rest of my life. I know I'm going to pay, here and in eternity. I'm fucked. There's no way out.

"You know what I wish? You know what wish I would make if I could have only one granted in the entire fucking world?" John asked me, time and time again, always with the same response. "I just wish I could see my kids grow up. After they're adults, fine, unleash the dogs, get the fuck rid of me. But let me be a real dad so they don't grow up and turn into me, for fuck's sake."

"But I know," John continued, his voice getting lower and dark. "I know. I won't make it that long. One way or another, those guys or the other guys will get me. My kids will grow up fucked up. You know what's the saddest thing, sadder even than that, Ken? I'm too smart for all of this. I'm *smarter* than this shit. I'm the one guy who knows better, but here I am anyway." John shook his head. "You don't get it, or maybe you do, but it's so *much worse* when you know better. I'm going to hell, and I fucking know it. That's hell itself, to know that's where you're headed.

"Just do me a favor. Some people don't like me. Watch out for me when I'm around, will ya?"

There was only one time when I ever came close to compromising my cover on the streets, and it was during one of my many conversations with John. I just wanted to tell him to quit so badly, to *run* to the feds and take whatever jail time they threw at him in exchange for a second chance. It wasn't the reduced sentence John Baudanza needed; it was that restored sense of self-respect and identity, the profound relief that came with becoming yourself again after decades of playing a role on the streets. I wanted him to feel like I did at Kaplan's Deli when, with one deep breath, I exhaled twenty years of Kenny Gallo and became myself again.

John Baudanza is what happens when you shoehorn good, normal guys into a bizarre and sadistic life that doesn't suit them: even when they are gangland "successes," they could not be greater failures as human beings. People like Craig Marino and I were violent sleazebags, but we were voluntary crooks, fully self-aware and self-possessed when we made the decisions we made. We owned our decisions; we had fully coherent identities. Eventually I changed and outgrew my underworld lifestyle, but at one time it perfectly fit my personality.

In comparison, John Baudanza has always been trapped and always will be trapped in the personality and life of someone very different than who he really is. I'm not sure a single person in the world really knows John; he is the most alone person I've ever met.

From then on, watching JB drink himself to death on the streets was no longer amusing. We attended Dayton's birthday party together when JB was in a foul, miserable mood, and after a few hours he was so drunk that he insisted that we ditch the party for another club. Against my objections, John insisted on driving, and we sped across New York City as he screamed, ranted, and slammed his pickup truck through trashcans on the sidewalk.

My last night out on the town with JB was a perfect metaphor for his life. Our usual crew took along Dayton and this spectacularly dirty, gap-toothed porn star named Belladonna to a connected strip club called Privileges. The best way I can describe Belladonna is that I once unexpectedly walked in on her as she was shoving the thick end of a baseball bat up her asshole. She was *that* type of girl, which I'll admit appealed to me at the time.

JB had the hookup with the manager for a private room for us, so we were looking forward to a good time when this guy started to bug Dayton. I gave him a look, and he walked away. I thought that was it, but suddenly I heard screams all around: the stranger bull-rushed John Baudanza with what appeared to be a knife in his hands. Nicky Vitale and I both tackled the attacker as John screamed and back-pedaled; I reached for my knife to stick the kid, but someone dove down and stopped me.

The strip club security pulled up the assailant, who was frothing at the mouth and screaming that we didn't know who he was, who his dad was, how much trouble we were in. He was clearly out of his mind. I looked at John, and though his body language was aggressive, I could see he was terrified. He was thinking, "Why me? Why are even complete fucking strangers after me?"

"You have no idea the shit you're in, buddy? Hear that? Ya understand?" John barked out rather timidly in his old-school wiseguy voice. Security dragged the stranger outside, where we never heard of him again.

The side effect of this display of danger and manliness was that Belladonna was suddenly in heat. She threw me against a booth and started giving me a lap dance that would have been illegal in most states. As she was kissing me, I could see that JB was consoling himself with glass after glass of scotch. I knew then that this night would end horribly, but I had Belladonna to distract me.

By the time we left the strip club, JB was so drunk that his "Goggles" were hanging diagonally across his face without him noticing. In his state, he naturally wanted to go to a nice hotel and fuck Dayton, so that was my next task. The problem, as usual, was that I was a newcomer to New York, and none of the Brooklyn natives knew how to get anywhere outside of their neighborhood. Since we were in Manhattan, I asked everyone in the car if they knew how to get to Times Square or Columbus Circle: nope. Big surprise.

When I finally found our way to the hotel Belladonna was staying at, JB stumbled up to a room with Dayton and, after I searched it for him, flounced inside. I grabbed Belladonna, and seconds later we were naked in our own suite. Before I could get anywhere, though, Dayton knocked on the door and told me that John wanted me to escort Nicky home. I thought she was just jealous and cock-blocking me, but whatever, I had to listen to John.

At 5 a.m. the following morning, my cell phone started blowing up. It was Eddie; my previous experience with early morning phone calls made me very uneasy when I saw his name that early. "Hey, what the fuck happened to Kool?" he asked, clearly annoyed that he was up so early.

"He's getting laid next door. Why?"

"Fucking Danielle is freaking out. We don't need that sort of a problem with her father, get what I'm saying?" I told Eddie I would take care of it, but Dayton and John did not pick up the phone or answer their door. The panic spread through Brooklyn: Georgie and Craig Marino were both dragged out of bed by Danielle to find John. Finally, Craig told me something like "Bang on the fucking door until it falls down!" and, after a steady assault for a few minutes, a greasy, marshmallow-faced creature that was supposedly John Baudanza opened the door. He was still drunk, still slurring his words; he looked like he had been in a car wreck that broke every bone in his face. I took John to the shower so he could clean up.

Of course, during our entire friendship I was ratting on John. I felt immensely guilty, not because I was doing anything wrong but just because I felt like I possibly might have been the one person John had opened up to in his whole life. And I was going to destroy him. If it hadn't been for Anthony Fiato's patient advice, I might have done something stupid to compromise the evidence. John was the first real friend that I ratted on, which was inevitable since I met him wired-up in the first place. Our entire relationship existed specifically to be documented on tape.

Nonetheless, I became perpetually nauseous and ashamed around John and even started to avoid him to try to minimize the damage done, but it was too late. I would go over to his house to watch the History Channel or John Wayne movies or play video games, and the entire time all I could think about was that he would never see his kids grow up.

In 2006, the information I provided and the wiretaps I set up led to the inevitable arrest: John and the rest of the Colombo side of the extended Baudanza wiseguy family were indicted for stealing over $20 million from stock market scams. Today, John is confined in the Brooklyn Metropolitan Detention Center with an expected release date in 2014. Even in prison, he could not escape Brooklyn.

John, if you're reading this, flip before one of your accomplices in the Colombo War sends you to death row. From one father to another, it's not worth it. Give your kids a chance to have a dad.

And I'm sorry. You're the only one I'll ever apologize to. One day, I hope we can be friends again far away from Brooklyn.

> *"Kytel was already up and running when my dad and I got involved. It was making millions of dollars. Greg Kylie wanted to open doors for us to let us do business. Kylie was a smart kid. He got his break when a guy devised a box that would reverse the charges on international calls so that you could make millions of dollars of free calls. Kytel was kicking up money anywhere from $50,000–$75,000 a month to us, and that was at the beginning before they started working with my dad and things really got rolling. What they'd do is get $5 million worth of minutes, pay them back $1 million worth, and just keep that $4 million on the balance and string it along. You could string those companies along for years if you were smart; it was free cash. It was the best racket going in the city."*

> William "Billy" Cutolo, Jr.

> *"Hey I just got off with guinea bissau!! I need to western union them 10k tonight so when they wake up in the a.m. it is there to activate my lines!! This is very important. Can you help me with this 10k tonight as a personal favor to me!!"*
> Greg Kylie
> E-mail to Kenji on September 28, 2004

Though John Baudanza may have been the youngest capo in all of New York, as far as the FBI was concerned he was nobody compared to Manny Garofalo. Manny was making millions overseeing the Colombo Family's construction rackets and representing the Colombos in meetings with the other New York Families over construction and labor disputes, but that wasn't what the feds were really after. They wanted Kytel Communications.

Kytel was a company in Manhattan that sold bulk telecommunications bandwidth to major corporations, international phone card companies, and Internet businesses. Kytel's owner and namesake was Greg Kylie, whose skill as a businessman largely sprung from his coincidental discovery of a tech genius within his company. This hardware hacker allegedly devised a technology in the late 1990s that allowed Kytel to reroute calls from overseas through countries with cheaper phone rates, illegally saving millions of dollars on each bulk sale. Now that Kytel was operating on the black market, it would need underworld protection since it could no longer rely on law enforcement.

So they called in William "Wild Bill" Cutolo, the most respected wiseguy in Brooklyn. Besides Sonny Franzese, Cutolo was the most popular member in the entire Colombo Family, a flashy dresser and charismatic social dynamo who received the hero worship of the generation that came up during John Gotti's peak. Cutolo was the Colombo Family's answer to Gotti in that he was stylish, cool, and cocky—only Wild Bill wasn't a loud-mouthed idiot or homicidal maniac like Gotti.

Wild Bill and his top shooter Joseph "Joe Campy" Campanella were among the only Colombos acquitted of their charges after the Colombo War. That's how brilliant a gangster Wild Bill was: his crew could drop a couple hundred bullets on the street over a period of two years and still avoid jail time. After the truce, Wild Bill was left as one of the very few Colombo heavyweights still on the street. In what was seen as a surprisingly mature peace gesture, Carmine Persico offered Cutolo the job of underboss to placate the majority of the family that had opposed him during the war. Wary, but seeing no way to survive without reconciliation, Cutolo accepted.

Wild Bill and his son Billy took over Kytel's operations and quickly doubled and tripled the company's already mammoth profits. The Cutolos realized that, when Kytel purchased bandwidth from other companies in multimillion-dollar bulk, the other companies were so eager to avoid a default that they would postpone calling in the debt for years. According to Billy, Kytel's new scam was to pay the first installment on a package of millions of telephone card minutes and from then on just pay the bare minimum to keep the rest of the balance from being called due. In the meantime, the scam gave the Cutolos the ability to write themselves checks for millions of dollars of easy-to-sell telecommunications bandwidth; by the time all of the debts were finally called in, they would let Greg Kylie take the fall.

In May of 1999, Cutolo was called to a meeting with Colombo Family acting boss Alphonse "Allie Boy" Persico, the son of Carmine Persico. It was the end of the truce: Cutolo's body would not be found for nine years. Soon thereafter, Wild Bill's top shooter Joe Campy was sprayed with bullets at a Coney Island amusement park; thanks to the Persico family's incompetence, he survived to turn rat along with Wild Bill's son and wife.

At Kytel, the Cutolos were replaced by the Garofalos; under Manny's inspired leadership, the already extremely profitable company was reaching new heights. Unfortunately for Manny, Billy Cutolo was busy ratting out every detail of the operation to the FBI, and the FBI had just the person to take it down. They gave me a call and told me to meet them at a hotel room.

I took the subway to ensure that I wasn't being followed; wiseguys' allergy to the best public transportation system in America always baffled me. When I reached the hotel room, the FBI wasted no time in telling me that they thought I was wasting my time with John Baudanza and Eddie Garofalo. "The best thing is if you could find a way to get with Manny Garofalo at Kytel. Do you think that's possible?"

"Shit." I laughed at the question. "What's today? Thursday? Okay, I'll be in there by Monday."

"Are you serious?" the FBI agent looked at me and then side to side at his coworkers in disbelief.

"Just wait and see."

Manny had been doggedly recruiting me as the only criminal in the Colombo Family with the brains to understand the type of complex crimes being committed at Kytel. I was a priceless find for him, which was why every single weekend at the Garofalo family "Sunday Sauce," Manny sneakily pulled me aside to drop hints about how I "shouldn't be working with those young guys," how I "should keep away from street guys," how I was best suited to "be a racketeer—like me." All I had to do was show interest at Sunday Sauce and, as promised, I was transferred to Manny by Monday morning. Manny was beside himself: he finally had an accomplice that actually knew how to use a computer!

Within a week, the feds were getting the in-depth financial details of multimillion-dollar telecommunication racketeering deals that reached from Cambodia to Venezuela. Since this investigation has not been fully adjudicated, I can't divulge any more details.

"When he walked out of Green Haven [Prison], [Teddy Persico] jumped into a well-stocked stretch limousine that was waiting to take Teddy back to Brooklyn. Among the amenities was a porn star/

> *hooker provided by a family associate with a*
> *lucrative online porn and escort business. . . . Un-*
> *fortunately for Persico, the porn dealer had also*
> *been supplying the FBI information about mob*
> *activities from New York to California . . . and*
> *was wired up and on the scene when Carmine*
> *L. Persico gave brother Teddy a handgun that*
> *triggered his tape-recorded rant about clean and*
> *dirty bullets."*
>
> Jerry Capeci
> August 11, 2005

Being "called for" by Eddie Garofalo was the scariest feeling I had experienced since I stopped visiting Mike Marvich in the early '90s. Eddie was a cold sonofabitch, and he was the only soldier in Brooklyn who I was convinced could have resolved to kill me without giving me any indication whatsoever that it was coming. Any time he sent for me without giving any warning or any details, there was a distinct possibility that I either was going to be killed or expected to kill someone else. The FBI couldn't help me; even in Brooklyn, there was no guy in a van waiting nearby, no backup available. It was a wicked fucking rush to be on my own in such a dangerous situation.

The first call from Eddie, when I distinctly remember feeling like I might die, happened in December of 2003. It was around 4 p.m. on a cold, ugly day. Eddie's number flashed onto my phone: "Get over to the truck yard in Staten Island right away." Dial tone. I remember exactly what I thought: *Oh shit.* Unless you've been on the street, you cannot imagine how quickly and forcefully a phone call like that changes your body chemistry; no amount of crystal meth could ever fuck me up that bad. I was woozy, sweaty, hyperventilating, and high all in a second; I was positive someone was going to get murdered. I wished I had my pistol, but I did not.

On the bridge to Staten Island, I called the FBI to let them know what was happening; unsurprisingly, none of my handlers answered their phone. That seemed to happen a lot when I was in trouble. I called the California offices where it was earlier in the day just to let them know where I was going in case I disappeared.

When I drove up, Eddie was standing outside of a mobile home that he used as an on-site office. A plane flew directly overhead when I exited my car; Eddie looked grim even for him. "It's that time," he began. I felt my bowels prepare to drop their payload. "Christmas time. We're making some moves in the New Year and need to put together a nice gift for the Persicos." Understanding immediately, I wiped the cold sweat from my forehead and handed him $4,000 in cash. He smiled. "Great, anything you ever need, you got it. Don't forget: you're on the record."

That relief was short-lived. A couple months later, Eddie called again. I was in the hospital with Manny visiting his dying mother-in-law when my cell phone rang. "I need you right away." I rushed to Manny, but he decided to pull a power trip on his nephew and told me to make him wait. Eddie wasn't playing games: he called back and told me that he was waiting outside of my apartment and to get my ass over there immediately. Manny got the message and gave me a ride to Brooklyn; a perceptive manipulator like him surely could read my body language.

When we pulled up, Eddie was alone, a big quiet hulk, in his truck. Manny asked if I wanted him to go with me, as if Manny was going to protect me against his own nephew, but I knew better than to look scared. The two of them spoke privately, and Manny took off. I was alone with Eddie.

"This is the most important task you'll ever get. There can be absolutely no fuckups, and you absolutely can't tell anyone," Eddie said as he fixed an extremely merciless stare on me. Shit—I was going to be asked to kill John or Craig or Georgie or some other friend who made the mistake of choosing the other side of the Colombo War.

I braced myself and tried to imagine how I would stab Eddie if he tried to accompany me on a hit. "They changed the Rockefeller Laws [governing criminal sentences in New York]. Teddy's getting out early. He's getting out tomorrow morning. It's your job to find him some hot-ass hooker who will travel the four hours back and forth to Green Haven prison to pick him up and take care of him on the ride over. It's been *sixteen years*."

Eddie's old buddy Teddy Persico had gone away in 1988 on a twenty-years-to-life sentence for conspiracy and three counts of criminal sale of a controlled substance. Teddy was a cocaine dealer just like me; only unlike me he sold his cocaine to an undercover informant and spent his 24th to his 40th years on earth in state prison. Though theoretically Teddy's cocaine beef should have resulted in his summary execution for violating the Mafia's anti-narcotics rules, in reality it worked to his benefit. In the intervening sixteen years, it seemed like everyone else in Teddy's generation of Brooklyn street kids had flipped, and the rest of Teddy's older Persico relatives had been hit with long-term jail sentences. The end result was that Teddy returned to Brooklyn, not as a disgraced coke dealer, but as a legendary stand-up guy and the top-ranking Persico on the street.

As silly as it sounds, there were many dozen wannabes who would have literally killed to be the one given the honor of escorting a limo and hooker to Teddy Persico. Everyone was desperate to impress Teddy. Both Manny and Eddie broke omerta to tell me that Teddy was going to become the new boss once he graduated from prison and got reacclimated to the streets. Since Teddy had last seen daylight in the 1980s, he wouldn't immediately be ready to call the shots in the very different 21st century Mafia, but the combination of The Snake's impatient desire to elevate one of his brood to street boss and the quick turnover in Mob leadership meant that Teddy would be king in months rather than years.

Eddie made it clear that any failure on my part to please the new boss would be shared by him, and that was as clear a message as I could ever get not to fuck up. When the powerful need someone to blame, it's guys like me—guys who aren't Italians and don't have connected family to piss off—who pay the price.

Eddie and I walked up to my apartment to start planning Teddy's homecoming. The first step was to call Elena at Exotica 2000 to see what girls she could offer Teddy. I repeated the names and descriptions of the girls Elena had available to Eddie, but he wanted to see photos to make sure that Teddy received only the best of the best. I told Elena I'd call her back and signed Eddie onto the Exotica 2000 website, going down the list of available girls again. "What the fuck are these bitches supposed to be?" he yelled. "They're all fucking dogs! Who the fuck does she think Teddy is?"

I tried to calm Eddie down or at least redirect his anger completely against Elena. "I think she's lying and covering up her best Russian girls. She doesn't want to send them on an all-night gig this risky."

"Call that Russian cunt up," Eddie countered, "and tell her that she either does the right thing or I'll send some guys to bust up the shitty fucking restaurant she owns in Bay Ridge. How about that?" I called Elena, who immediately understood how much danger she was in; she did not want to get between Eddie and a Persico's approval. Eddie's life literally depended on maintaining goodwill with the new boss, so he was accepting no compromises. Elena promised to call up her best girl and get back to us.

While we were killing time waiting for Elena's call, Eddie for the first time that I had ever seen was nervous and fidgety. The normally slow-moving hulk was manically pacing around my apartment picking up and inspecting everything that wasn't nailed down. One of the items he inspected like Hamlet pondering a skull was a photo of Dayton.

"You know what would be great? Dayton. Teddy really likes her," Eddie said with a look that told me his mind was instantly made up. Regardless of John Baudanza's feelings, I had been steadily sending Teddy photos of Dayton and my other porn girls in the hope that I might gain leverage if he developed a crush on one of them. My plan worked.

Though Dayton wasn't in the neighborhood at the moment, I guaranteed Eddie it could be done. It would take a little work—unlike most brazen porn girls, Dayton had a shy attitude about escorting and became embarrassed when anyone found out how she made her money. She was suffering from Porn Star Derangement Syndrome: a girl who happily promotes her work in such films as *Pussyman's Spectacular Butt Babes* and *The Blowjob Adventures of Dr. Fellatio 20* yet becomes incredibly flustered and offended at the thought of anyone thinking she's a whore.

Dayton would be back at my apartment at any moment, so we decided to wait there for her to show up. While we were sitting together, Eddie took out a piece of paper from his pocket and started reading off the names of made guys in the Colombo Family. He waited a while before telling me it was the "do not associate" list given to Teddy Persico as a requirement of his parole. If Teddy were discovered to have associated with any of the wiseguys on the list, he would be sent right back to jail. The list was a mixed bag: while it contained multiple dead guys and long-flipped rats like Sammy the Bull, it also contained relatively new additions like Eddie and his entire crew. Of course, I knew that Eddie's guys were on the list specifically because of me, and I felt momentarily guilty as I watched Eddie read off his own name and laugh. I was sure I would be responsible for putting Eddie in jail for a very long time.

When Dayton came in, we immediately hit her with the idea of being Teddy's homecoming present. Though she was all for it at first, she then became worried about what John Baudanza would think and started to waver. JB the Mafia capo couldn't possibly be allowed to think that Dayton the porn star had loose morals, God forbid! Just at the right moment, Elena called back and told me that her best Russian girl would be available for the job after all; as soon as Dayton heard that, her competitive hooker instincts flared up and she demanded the honor of escorting Teddy home. Regardless of what John Baudanza thought, Dayton wasn't going to let some Soviet slag suck off her Mafia boss! We had Teddy's girl.

When Eddie and I went outside, he told me that everything was riding on this. "If this goes good, you can have anything you want in Brooklyn. This guy is going to be street boss, and he won't forget. I'm his best friend, and I won't forget either." As soon as Eddie left, a worried Uncle Manny gave me a call to "see" if "everything was okay." Manny and Eddie still played their double-team game with me all the time, pretending like they never talked to each other so that they could see if I would slip up and tell one of them the wrong thing. I got off the phone with Manny and immediately my phone rang with a call from Eddie again, who said he was on his way right back to my apartment to pick me up.

Eddie drove me through Bay Ridge, taking an irregular route to shake any surveillance, and eventually came to a place I'd never been. Teddy's brother, Danny "The Town Drunk" Persico as Eddie called him, and some other Persico cousins were waiting for us. Danny gave me a stern lecture, repeating over and over that Dayton had to be ready at 4 a.m. when the limo arrived and that I would be given a bag with new clothes, shoes, cell phones, and money to give to Teddy. It was my responsibility to make sure Dayton and the goods got into Teddy's hands with no trouble.

After I made it clear, through careful reiteration and unwavering eye contact, that I understood what was expected of me, Eddie Garofalo drove me back to my place and let me go. When I got up to my apartment, I was almost too exhausted to speak from all the excitement, but Dayton was all over me with questions about Teddy. Before I sated her curiosity, Eddie called me again and told me to wait outside of my place. Little did I know I was about to be fed to the entire Persico clan.

Eddie drove me to La Yuen, his favorite Chinese joint on Fourth Avenue in Brooklyn. As soon as we sat down, Eddie ordered about a dozen dishes, and we were joined by Danny Persico, ranking female Danielle Persico, and a handful of interchangeable Persico cousins who probably

each shared their names with three or four other Persicos. All the Persicos look the same, have the same first
names, and refer to every male in the family as their
"brother," so it's fucking impossible to keep anything
straight. The name duplication and "brother" bullshit is
all part of Carmine's brainwashing techniques to deper-
sonalize and devalue each individual Persico in favor of
glorifying the family at large.

Every Persico at the table was gobbling expensive
Chinese food and busting my balls, ramming it home
over and over again that I had to make things go perfectly for Teddy, as if I was expected to jump in and blow
Teddy myself if Dayton failed to live up to expectations.
The Persicos didn't seem to understand that I couldn't
really decide how sex between Dayton and Teddy went.
Danny Persico expanded on what he had hinted at earlier, telling me that the family had a huge lunch planned
for Teddy with all the important members of the family;
the only female in attendance would be the daughter of
Persico favorite Donnie Shacks, news which made my
skin crawl.

As we left, Danny gave Eddie the "bag" that was
meant for Teddy; far from a nice Gucci leather accessory,
they had packed Teddy's stuff into a white garbage bag!
After everyone left, Eddie personally kept me at the restaurant until late to make sure I didn't have time to tell
anyone about Teddy's arrival. When he finally dropped
me off, Eddie once again swore me to secrecy. As soon as
he was gone, I made an emergency call to my FBI handlers, who were incredibly excited and made a late night
date with me. As soon as Dayton passed out from all the
pills she was taking, I sorted through Teddy's gift bag:
white velour tracksuit, Cartier watch, fresh-from-the-
store white sneakers, $1,000, and a cell phone.

It was apparently never too late for a good cardiovascular workout; I threw on my jogging gear, pocketed Teddy's cell phone, and ran out for a pitch-black jog through nighttime Brooklyn. I was one block away from my place when a car pulled up next to me. The window was down, so I simply tossed the phone into the car, and it drove off. I jogged up and down Fourth Ave. After fifteen minutes, I bumped into a nondescript man. It was a brush pass; I had the phone back, instantaneously upgraded with FBI listening devices.

I placed the FBI-model cell phone back into the white garbage bag and crawled into bed with Dayton to make her feel like I cared. I had my own bed, but, especially before a job like this, she needed to think that she was loved and appreciated. I held her and thought about poor Teddy.

I had her up in two hours to shower and put on her porn-star kabuki makeup. We were downstairs when the limo pulled up. It was not from the Persico limo company, Romantic, because the family wanted an outside company to minimize suspicion and surveillance opportunities. I spent most of the ride with Dayton in the limo before getting out and getting into another car right before she arrived at the prison. I figured Teddy would want Dayton to greet him by herself. Dayton went into Green Haven State Prison with Teddy's clothes, which must've created quite a scene if any of the other inmates saw her: a giant-breasted bimbo in a short tan miniskirt, all porned up with heavy makeup, fake lashes, and a towering hairdo. It was over an hour before Teddy emerged, which might have been due to Teddy reveling in the attention Dayton brought him.

Two hours later, I started to receive periodic phone calls from the limo telling me every exit they were taking and what their estimated time of arrival was. This unsettled me—if he was enjoying a good fuck, the last thing Teddy would care about is whether some Japanese associate knew where he was on the road. I suddenly became very interested in their status updates; I was dying to see Dayton to find out what had happened and if I was in trouble.

I had to wait a couple hours after Dayton and Teddy's arrival in Brooklyn to receive the phone call I was waiting for from Eddie. "Okay, come meet us and take Dayton home." I couldn't tell from Eddie's voice if something was wrong or not; I wanted advance warning if things had gone bad so I could get out of town. I met Eddie and Teddy at a Bruno Magli shoe store since, I assume, Teddy wanted some new dress shoes for his formal welcome-back party.

Teddy walked over to me with a brisk pace and his hand extended. "Shit, I can't believe this place don't have pointy dress shoes anymore like we had back in the '80s!" he said to me by way of greeting.

Teddy was a handsome man with steel-gray hair and a nervous smile. Even for someone who had been locked up for sixteen years with nothing else to do but exercise, Teddy was in incredibly good shape. Hs six-foot frame was lean and strong with intricate musculature; he bragged just like Eddie that he boxed and did 200 push-ups every day of those sixteen years—as if he had anything else to do. I could immediately tell he wasn't the normal Persico; though he wasn't exactly brilliant or a visionary, Teddy had the bearing and charisma of a leader, a street leader. He was strong, tough, likeable, no bullshit, and, most importantly, dangerous as hell, even for a Persico. He reeked of death.

As I expected, Eddie rushed over to me after Teddy patted me on the shoulder, thanked me, and walked back into the store. Signaling to Dayton, he asked us what had happened. I told him I knew about as much as he did, and we both eagerly turned to Dayton.

"Well, um, y'know . . . God . . ."

"Okay honey, just spit it out," Eddie said, unintentionally doing his best to intimidate and fluster an already shy girl.

"Well, well, well, um, really. Okay. So he takes off his shirt to show me, uh, his nice abs, and we start drinking champagne. I can tell he's nervous, so I kinda take over you know, with my mouth, y'know, taking off everything but heels, making it sexy, ya know? And, honestly, I don't know . . . I . . . I, well, he just *couldn't.*"

"*Couldn't?*"

"He tried, and it wasn't happening. We tried for an hour. He was very determined, but it just didn't happen. It just wouldn't go, y'know, *up.* I think he was too nervous after being in prison so long." Eddie and I looked at each other as if we didn't know what face to put on. Teddy Persico: the Impotent Don.

This was extremely dangerous information in Brooklyn. After all, a guy who can't get it up for a smoking hot porn star after sixteen years in jail is going to be the target of rumors that would be very damaging to both his and the Persico family's reputation. He certainly couldn't be the Snake's successor if his manhood was in any way suspect. The rules against homosexuality are definitely still upheld.

"Listen, listen, that's enough," Eddie said, speaking very fast in a sharp whisper. "Whatever you do, no matter who you talk to, for the rest of your life, you *cannot tell anyone* this story. Understand? No one?" Dayton nodded; so did I with my most solemn and serious face. Sorry Eddie.

After I took Dayton home, I received a phone call from Teddy's FBI phone. I was uneasy but not too scared; Teddy seemed in an okay mood for an impotent guy. Judging by his reputation, a temperamental Teddy would be hard to miss. "Listen, Ken, I'm going to level with you," Teddy said to me with winning matter-of-factness. He was man enough to admit when he wasn't. "It's been a long time since I got laid. I got married to some chick so I could have conjugals in jail, but it didn't work out, y'know what I mean? I've been out of circulation so long, y'know, that things didn't go the way I'd like for them . . . ugh, to have gone with Dayton." At this point, I felt laughter welling up in my throat, but I bit the corner of my mouth.

"Basically, y'know," Teddy said with almost endearing self-consciousness and nervousness. "Basically, I'd like a do-over. I have a party at my mom's house later tonight, and we have a basement down there. Maybe you could smuggle Dayton down into the basement, and I can excuse myself for a moment, and then we can have that do-over, get my drift?" To this day, my friends know that the phrase "do-over" will make me laugh more reliably than anything else in the world. It is practically automatic.

"Teddy, I'll see what I can do," I said, unsure about Dayton and what Eddie might have to say about smuggling a hooker into Teddy's mom's house.

It didn't take long for me to receive a call from Eddie, who told me that Teddy was up *his* ass about the "do-over" as well. Eddie flatly ordered me not to take Dayton to the Persico family party that night because the heaviest guys in the city were attending, and, if anything went wrong, any act of perceived disrespect in the holy sanctum of a Persico mother's house would result in massive retaliation. I listened to Eddie; I wasn't about to launch a covert commando operation into a Persico family gathering to deliver Teddy some free pussy.

> *"Hey, Dude. Things sound serious. . . . Don't fuck with New York, dude. The older guys will be getting out and they will never let you out of their sights until you're dead."*
>
> Anthony "The Animal" Fiato
> E-mail from 5/31/04

A few days later, Teddy invited me to lunch at 101 Restaurant in Brooklyn. Word had come down from On High that Teddy liked me; I was his guy now. I liked Teddy well enough because, like Mike Marvich or Tony Peraino or Jimmy Caci, he was straightforward: a blunt, honest killer who meant what he said. He may have been a horrible person, but he made no excuses and was fully confident in his identity. Self-confidence and honesty counts for so much with me.

It was funny to watch Teddy bumble around Brooklyn like a 1980s gangster teleported into the future; all manner of modern technology baffled him and gave him a headache. The Internet was as mystical and inexplicable a concept to him as it would have been to an ancient Mayan warrior. Whenever I would finish explaining something he didn't understand, he'd change the subject to something more his style—such as why did all the good clubs start playing shitty music that forty-year-old, gray-haired Teddy did not enjoy? Teddy had been away a long time: the last time he had visited a dance club, Clyde and I were still selling coke out at Joey Avila's club.

Teddy also had trouble with his table manners. After so long in jail, he reflexively ate with a muscular arm encircling his dish and his body menacingly bunched over the plate as if he were a bear shielding its cub. The entire plate of food was hurriedly chopped up and snapped up piece after piece without pause like a wolf. When you asked him a question, he would talk with half a sirloin sticking out of his mouth. Even among other Brooklyn savages, Teddy stood out.

"We got to put some bodies on the street, man," Teddy Persico told me completely without warning after taking a sip from his drink. "We got to send a message that we're back. That I'm back. This ain't no joke anymore.

"People need to know who I am. I have to make my name, y'know, so I can do cool stuff like sell security to rap shows. First people need to know I'm back, so we'll need to drop bodies on the street—*like the old days.*"

Teddy was fucking nuts; he truly was worthy of succeeding Carmine. Carmine's sole pleasure in life came from the knowledge that he had the power to kill people from his tiny jail cell, and Teddy believed that the best part of getting out of jail was the opportunity to *personally* kill a few guys to rebuild his street reputation. Within a week of getting back on the street, when he barely knew me, Teddy was always pointing out places that "would be great to bury someone" and talking, seemingly to himself, about the need to murder someone in broad daylight and "leave them on the street" as a "message."

Teddy had no one in particular in mind and no material objective he sought to obtain; he simply thought it would be a good idea to remind people that the Persico family was in the business of arbitrarily murdering people. The Persicos really don't give a damn about jail; can you imagine being out on the streets for the first time in over a decade and, despite extremely intrusive surveillance, immediately planning to kill someone just for the sake of it?

Teddy was by far the target who made me feel the uneasiest as an informant. Though a perfectly cool and straightforward guy in normal conversation, he was always just a slight provocation away from killing someone. I have a finely honed instinct for this sort of thing, and Teddy was just a murderer. I was positive that someone would end up dead soon; I couldn't understand why the FBI wasn't busting him on a parole violation. I know they would have liked to methodically build a case that would put Teddy away for another sixteen years or so, but every second Teddy was in Brooklyn—feeling inadequate, thinking about the disrespect shown to his family during the Colombo War, thinking about his inability to get a hard-on with Dayton—innocent people were at risk. It looked like New York was going to get its very own Fat Herbie Blitzstein: a human sacrifice through FBI inactivity.

I decided that I could not let that happen again. During the conversation at 101, I felt like I had finally discovered my purpose as an informant. In fact, my entire criminal career seemed to be a crash course to give me the skills to stop Teddy Persico from killing.

I could only stop Teddy if Teddy let me stop him. I needed him to trust me and keep me by his side, so the con man skills I learned from the likes of Officer Jerry and Jerry Zimmerman were deployed to convince Teddy that I was his best friend in the world. I stuck close by Teddy every waking moment—I didn't bug him, I just made myself helpful, ever-available, and accommodating. A decade as a "ho wrangler" had taught me how to be indispensable to psychologically warped and helpless creatures, so I knew just how to offer my help to Teddy without making him feel self-conscious.

My service with Jimmy Caci's crew also made me intimately familiar with the counterintuitive withdrawal and panic longtime prisoners feel when they are finally released, so I helped to keep Teddy's days simple and confined to areas and activities where he was comfortable. I did not want the feelings of chaos to overwhelm his psyche's fragile defenses. When Teddy started talking about murder, I acted impressed but not intimidated— just as I learned from working with Mike Marvich.

After watching John Baudanza's self-destruction, I understood how lonely and isolated Teddy had to feel with all Brooklyn's expectations to live up to. At no time could Teddy allow himself to appear weak, vulnerable, confused, depressed, or even too nice—he had to ape the ultra-aggressive machismo of Carmine if he wanted the acting boss job. Carmine's spies were surely watching his every move and sending detailed progress reports to jail. Teddy was under immense pressure with no outlet for his frustrations—so I gave him one.

As a non-Italian outsider, he had no reason to fear making the wrong impression on me; whenever he admitted that something was troubling or confusing him, I always empathized, understood, and coincidentally shared his every opinion. Soon, I had Mafia royalty Teddy convinced that we were so alike. Teddy had to put on a strong and invincible front to other Brooklyn wiseguys, but Mr. Do-Over clearly had no compunction about embarrassing himself to me.

Though my efforts to ingratiate myself to Teddy succeeded in winning his trust, it certainly did not stop him from planning to commit a murder. In fact, the end product of all of my hard work was simply that Teddy chose to commit a murder *with me*. That was fine—the only potential victim of a Teddy and Kenji hit team would be Teddy himself.

As I said earlier, it was clear from talking with Teddy that he would not need much in the way of motivation to kill. It turns out Teddy did not need *any* motivation. No one had to screw up; no had to challenge or disobey him. Teddy was going to kill for the sake of it.

The nominal cause of the murder conspiracy was Craig's driver Georgie, who stole some of Dayton's cash from our apartment. I didn't mind; I told Dayton not to cocktease any of the wiseguys with the hiding place of her money, but she ignored me and told Georgie the Mother Beater of all people. After the theft, I sat Dayton down, looked into her googly doll eyes, and explained to her that, while what happened was unfortunate, she needed to keep her mouth shut about the theft. With Teddy back on the streets, the tension was extremely high in Brooklyn, and the tiniest dispute could become an excuse to launch a war.

Of course, Mrs. Do-Over promptly ignored my advice and told her would-be boyfriend Teddy that one of his friends had robbed her place. This was most definitely a bad situation: since Teddy had failed to prove to Dayton that he was a worthy man with his dick, he could damn well show her how manly he was with a gun. No one was going to rob Teddy's do-over of her hard-won escort cash!

Teddy set up a meeting with Dayton, Eddie, and me at 101 to discuss the theft over lunch. I feverishly e-mailed the FBI from my phone that Teddy was violating his parole by meeting with Eddie again, but they were otherwise occupied. Teddy had an unusual sharpness in his eyes; his pupils were tiny and focused. He gave the impression of a furious man who was barely keeping his cool for the sake of a woman. Teddy was just the sort of Italian to sulk and obsess over the tiniest slights until he has convinced himself an unforgivable transgression has been committed.

I told Dayton that the best thing she could do was to tell the truth about Georgie—that way, Teddy would have an opportunity to let out his steam at lunch and force Georgie to make a repayment. There was a much better chance of containing Teddy's volatility if we knew which way it was directed and we were able to stop his rage from continuing to take on hot air. I wanted to start deflating Teddy at the table with Dayton present to keep him vaguely under control; he could then make a gradual descent back to what passed for sanity among the Persicos.

Dayton nodded as if she understood what I was saying, but, as soon as Teddy started interrogating her about the lost cash, she clammed up again and said nothing. I could see the hairs rise on Teddy's arms every time he asked a question that did not receive a response. He was boiling. A Persico was supposed to know what was going on in his own neighborhood.

The drive from 101 to our apartment was quiet and steaming with tension. Teddy still was not talking or expressing his frustration, which worried me. He had the look of a man that might swerve into oncoming traffic without warning. I was relieved when we pulled up to our place, and we both jumped out. With Dayton alone, maybe I could work on her and convince her to give Teddy a few do-overs to calm him down. It might be a lifesaving gesture.

As soon as I reached the door of my apartment building, I heard Teddy's voice. It was wild, and it was screaming. "KENNY! GET THE *FUCK* BACK IN THE CAR!"

My instincts took over because my legs were already on their way back to the street before my brain realized what had been said. I briefly made eye contact with Teddy, and I saw a look I hadn't seen since my cocaine cowboy days. This guy was *gacked* and ready to kill. His face and throat were a deep, shining maroon red; his jaw was locked and his eyebrows lowered almost over his eyes. I jumped in the back seat, and Teddy swung his wild face towards me. "It's time to get my piece!

"Kenji, are you *alright*? Are you *down*?" Teddy looked back at me with his tongue pressed into the inside of his cheek—a look that seemed to me to be saying "Are you down or are you going to be first victim?"

"I'm alright. I'm ready. Don't you worry about me."

"You sure?" I nodded and acted as nonchalant as my verging-on-a-meltdown heart rate would allow.

The good news was that my plan worked: I was definitely going to be with Teddy when he tried to commit murder. The bad news, of course, was that I was now an FBI informant trapped in a Mafia hit team . . . that planned to shoot a high-profile mobster . . . in broad daylight . . . in densely populated Brooklyn. I had no backup and no way of letting the FBI know that I or anyone else was immediately in trouble. If I had so much as glanced at my telephone after Teddy's announcement of an imminent gangland murder, I would have been dead.

As we were driving, it dawned on me as I listened to Teddy rant that his chosen target was not Georgie but his boss Craig Marino. This, in other words, had nothing to do with Dayton's money; that had simply been the stimulant that angered Teddy enough to take out his pent-up emotions on a completely unrelated target. The only reason Craig Marino was going to be killed was because he had chosen the wrong side of the Colombo War over a decade earlier. This was not ancient history to Teddy or anyone else in Brooklyn: Teddy believed that Craig attempted to kill his family. Truce or no truce, a guy like Teddy never can forget and forgive bodies on the street. For a Persico, bodies on the street call for more bodies on the street call for more bodies on the street . . . until everyone on one side is dead.

We stopped at the house of Teddy's mom—the site of the proposed do-over was now the site of a murder conspiracy. They told me to keep Mama Persico occupied, so she started showing me fucking baby photos of her Pride and Joy Teddy while he rifled through his stuff looking for a gun. Seeing that I did not look so well, Mama Persico brought me a glass of water; I thanked her and wondered what a special brand of hell it must be to be a Persico mother. Your husband, sons, and brothers are murderers and gangsters locked up in jails thousands of miles apart, and your daughters are all married to other families' imprisoned deadbeats and sociopaths. The family reunions must have a 10-to-1 female-to-male ratio.

Teddy's brother Carmine and a neighborhood kid named Walter arrived at Mama Persico's house with the gear in a little cigar box. Soon afterwards, Danny "Town Drunk" Persico drove up and was pacing outside talking on his cell phone. I rushed to see what was going on along with Teddy and Eddie. Danny was on the phone with Craig, who was chilling out as usual at 101, trying to convince him to come to a meeting in the neighborhood around Mama Persico's house. I couldn't believe it; Teddy cared so little for his family that he was going to kill a man right by his own mother's house.

Craig must have been tipped off about how pissed off Teddy was over Georgie's theft because he adamantly refused to leave 101. Craig was under no delusion about his standing with Teddy and the Persicos; he knew that he would be in danger of being assassinated by his own "Family" for the rest of his life. Regardless of any Mafia rule about always coming to meetings when called, Craig chose to take a risk that whatever the long-term repercussions of refusing to show would be, they definitely would not be as bad as what would happen if he met a furious Teddy in a neighborhood where the Persicos felt comfortable.

With a look of madness in his eyes, Teddy snatched the phone from Danny and started talking to Craig in the most strained "friendly" voice I've ever heard. "Ha, ha, ha!" Teddy was an awful fake laugher. "Craig won't come over because he thinks we're gonna whack him or something! HA, HA, HA!" *Real subtle, Teddy.* This was the equivalent of walking up to a girl at a bar and saying, "Ha, ha, ha! You think I'm gonna rape you or something?"

We all nonetheless followed the cue and joined in with equally fake, unconvincing laughter. Craig was not that stupid, so Teddy motioned for Danny to head over to his natural habitat, the 101 bar, and keep Craig occupied until we got there.

Before we could leave for 101, we had to get our assassination team ready. Inside a room in Mama Persico's house, Teddy opened the precious cigar box to reveal a beat-up Walther PPK, a .38 caliber revolver with no bullets, and a shitty off-brand pistol. I am not exaggerating when I say I have to this day never seen sorrier weapons. One gun had no bullets to shoot, and the Walther PPK looked like it was missing screws and had never been oiled or cleaned. It would jam, and if it shot, it would not shoot straight. The pistol wasn't a good piece, but it looked like it would fire. Carmine started rubbing the

Walther PPK with his shirt before giving it to Teddy, but Teddy thought that a waste of time. "I don't need you to clean it. Just give me the gun!" Teddy growled in a voice that was getting hoarser by the second.

Carmine tried to explain that he needed a minute to wipe DNA and fingerprints off not only the gun but the bullets too. This struck Teddy as the height of stupidity. "How do you keep a pistol with fucking dirty bullets in it in the first place? You got an automatic pistol, you clean the bullets, you put them in the fucking clip, and the clip is ready whenever you are!"

At this point, Carmine or Walter gathered the courage to remind Teddy that none of them had gloves—thereby negating the entire point of cleaning the guns. Teddy shot them a look that convinced me he was close to shooting one of them right in his mother's house. "What? Use your socks then! You assholes don't know to use your socks? Come on!"

Teddy paused his self-righteous hissy fit to roll his eyes at Carmine and look to me for support, never imagining than this entire escapade was completely hilarious as far as I was concerned. I was using brand-new, untraceable AK-47 assault rifles and car bombs when I was seventeen; throughout my career, I always kept a fully prepared, ready-at-a-moment's-notice arsenal complete with masks, bulletproof vests, gloves, and explosives someplace nearby where I was living. I took all these precautions just in case an unforeseen emergency should have arisen; I wasn't actively planning on killing people every single day of my life like Teddy.

Yet Teddy, the most feared man in the Colombo Family, apparently had put so little thought into the actual business of killing as opposed to the concept of killing that his idea of "ready firepower" was a cigar box of dirty bullets and old, piece-of-shit guns smudged with fingerprints. Teddy was more enamored with the image than the reality; he was obsessed with the idea of killing, not with the mechanics of the actual act of murder. Look at how much thought Teddy put into the murder conspiracy that would define his return to the streets: he involved at least five other people in the plot—three of whom were incompetent and one of whom was an FBI rat. He only had three guns.

That's the problem with the Colombo Family; since its soldiers live in a subculture that glorifies people who act as if they do not care if they live or die, if they are free or imprisoned, the young guys never take the time to hone their craft as criminals. It's all a big laugh to them; they are more impressed by impetuous fools like Teddy and Sonny Franzese who are so "fearless" that they always end up in jail, than a methodical, careful, and professional crook like Manny or Jerry Zimmerman. They live by impulse, by image, by what sounds good and feels right; they don't take their work seriously.

This type of comprehensive incompetence, sloppiness, and lack of professionalism is why I scoff at the idea that the Colombo Family may ever kill me. Teddy couldn't find working guns to kill one of his soldiers *in Brooklyn;* how the hell is he going to find a transcontinental hit team that can locate ready weaponry in California, pinpoint my location, and then ambush me with enough speed to stop me from striking first? I guess it's possible, but it's certainly not probable. Besides, the knowledge that there is a small likelihood of it happening provides just enough danger in my life to keep things interesting.

We were in the car to 101—Teddy had the Walther PPK, and I believe Carmine had the pistol and Walter the .38, which he filled with bullets of a different caliber. I was almost hoping that Walter had a chance to fire that thing to see how that little science experiment would turn out. Both Walter and Carmine were wearing their sweaty socks on their hands. Since they only had three guns, Teddy told me to stab anyone who tried to interfere with the hit with my knife. I nodded.

"Hey, why is Kenny so quiet?" Teddy suddenly asked as if I should be an unstoppable chatterbox on the way to a murder. Maybe he was having second thoughts about me, but even as an FBI informant I'm not sure I was the biggest liability on Teddy's assassination team.

"Don't worry about me, Teddy, I'm just chill. There's nothing to say." While I sounded convincingly calm, my body was producing heat and sweat like I had come down with a tropical fever. My mind, however, was remarkably focused: I knew exactly what to do. No matter what happened, I was fucked. If I tried to stop the hit in the car, I would have to take out three idiots with guns and Eddie with just my knife. If I stopped the hit at 101 by ambushing Teddy with my knife and thereby incapacitating the one guy with a working pistol, there's no way the FBI would be able to let me off from an aggressive act of violence. If I let Craig die, then it was a murder conspiracy charge. The only scenario that might save me is if the hit was called off at the last second, and that was out of my hands.

Out of curiosity, I craned my head to see Eddie's face—he was shitting himself. The cold, blank, unreadable Colombo giant was putting on a facial acrobatics act that would have made Jim Carrey proud. He may have been Teddy's closest friend and greatest admirer, but he could clearly see this was a disaster waiting to happen. I caught his eye, and we understood each other completely: *We're fucked. There's no way out. We're all caught up, and it's too late to stop now.*

I knew that Eddie would passively let Teddy do his thing, regardless of the consequences, but I wondered if he thought the same for me. Surely, he knew I was too smart to be a party to a fiasco like this. I wondered if he had any inkling that I had firmly decided to stab Teddy in the throat, grab his gun, and shoot my way out of there? The only question was whether I went on the lam or rolled the dice with the FBI.

When we pulled up to 101, Teddy's dream died in an instant: there were already ambulances and police cars at 101. Someone had called the cops. Craig was standing against the front wall of 101, looking pissed. Suspiciously, Manny was there as well, circling in a white convertible with a worried look on his face. I'm not sure which potential rat I would be more impressed by: Craig for having the sense to create a distraction before Teddy arrived or Eddie for leaking the news to his uncle?

We parked the car, and Teddy by himself disconsolately walked over to Craig and beckoned him to take a walk towards the Verrazano Narrows Bridge. In a moment, Teddy's body language had deflated from rampaging gorilla to sulking, rock-kicking teenager. His anger was gone, and to prevent a fiasco he had to clean up his mess by making nice—for now—with Craig. As they were chatting, I spoke with Danny Persico and Manny, letting them both know everything was okay. Danny cursed Georgie for driving Teddy to do what he almost did, which was pretty hilariously off-target—how did Georgie drive Teddy to attempt to kill a loyal, moneymaking soldier who had nothing to do with Dayton or her money? Whatever, Teddy was a Persico, so anything he did that failed had to be someone else's fault.

As I was starting to breathe normally again and laugh inwardly at the absurdity of the whole situation, I looked to see Teddy and Craig walking back together, apparently reconciled. From them my eyes wandered onto Carmine and Walter—who were in position across the street with their socks on their hands. The dumbfucks were actually planning to go through with the hit in front of the cops!

Without thinking about how I would look, I rushed across the street and started waving for the two idiots to stop. They saw me—and possibly so did Craig. Teddy left Craig by 101 and walked up to me. "Everything should be cool with Craig," Teddy said with his old, easygoing tone.

Then Teddy surprised me: his lips twisted into a surprisingly self-aware smirk. "Just don't turn your back on him. You *never* know," Teddy whispered as the smirk expanded into a smile that I recognized. It was *my* smile, the smile of vicious rapture I have always gotten after I've put my life in danger and survived. I exhaled, and the same smile slithered across my face. I always knew there was something about Teddy I liked.

Regardless of our similarities—or maybe *because* of our similarities—I was honored to be the man that sent Teddy back to jail. Thanks to me, he did a few more years and was released in June of 2008. Though it may not seem like a long time, those few years I kept Teddy off the street may have saved a dozen lives. It is now up to some other Colombo Family rat to put him away for good.

Looking over Teddy's shoulder, I noticed that Craig was staring at me with furious rage. Despite his loyalty to the family, Craig had nearly been killed by his own people, and he was powerless to do anything about it. There was no point in confronting Teddy or his fifty Persico relatives on the streets. Craig just had to pretend that the attempted set-up had never happened.

Enraged at his own impotence and vulnerability, Craig compensated by blaming me for the trouble that Dayton had caused. My good friend Craig, the man who I spent thousands of hours of relaxation and fun with, lifted his hand to his face and extended his thumb and index finger into the shape of a pistol. He nodded in my direction. According to the NYPD, a bona fide cop killer and Colombo Family made man had just promised to kill me.

I couldn't help but laugh. Craig, you were not the first or last person to think they were going to kill me—but you are the first one whose life I was going to risk my own to save. Though I can't expect you to appreciate what I am about to say while you're still pouting in the jail cell at Fort Dix I deposited you in, I want you to know that you played a special part in my life. After a decade of guilt, shame, and self-doubt, I finally felt ready to start over in earnest the moment I realized I was truly willing to put my life on the line to save a thug like you. For the first time since I was a child in Orange County, I knew that I could be a decent person.

When I got home that night, I called my psychiatrist Anthony Fiato and told him how I was feeling. He knew just the right thing to say: "Buddy, it's time for you to get the fuck out of there."

In May of 2009, Kenny Gallo's undercover work contributed to the indictment of America's foremost madam, Michelle Braun of Nici's Girls. Despite making an alleged $8.5 million running her elite escort ring, Braun cut a deal with the government in which she had to forfeit only $325,425, pay a $30,000 fine, and serve six months house arrest. It is widely assumed that Braun agreed to work as an informant against her own clients in return for leniency.

In March of 2010, the Colombo Family plot to execute a kickback and extortion scheme for debris removal at the World Trade Center site was derailed by federal indictments—one year after the plot was first revealed in *Breakshot*. Colombo Family street boss Theodore "Teddy" Persico, Jr., his cousin Michael Persico, Edward "Eddie" Garofalo, Jr., and Garofalo's wife, Alicia, were indicted by the federal government on charges including racketeering conspiracy, wire fraud conspiracy, extortion, and embezzlement of union benefit funds.

During the investigation, Teddy Persico was captured on an FBI recording device saying: "You're not me. If it was up to me, I'd go get a gun and shoot them, or stab them, or beat them up when I see 'em. I got nothing. They can't fuck with me because I got nothing to lose and they got everything to lose. You can't fuck with them because you've got everything to lose and nothing to gain by getting physical. I can get physical all day long. I got nothing to lose, I can get crazy. I don't give a fuck;

what are you going to do, put me in jail? What am I going to lose? My wife, my kids, my house that I own, my two-million-dollar house that I own, or my car? I don't own nothing. I got no wife, I got no kids. I can act like a fool."

Following Kenji Gallo's exit from New York City, the FBI was compelled to inform Eddie Garofalo, Jr., that they had reason to believe that Teddy Persico was planning to kill him as a suspected informant.

Kenji Gallo is still a free man. Since *Breakshot*'s publication, he has appeared widely on TV and radio. He is not in hiding.

ACKNOWLEDGMENTS

Kenji:

I want to thank Arielle for accompanying me on my long and dark journey and having faith that I'd make it through to the other side. Thank you for the many days and long hours we spent together, for our time on Las Ramblas and eating tapas.

Thanks also to Anthony Fiato for doing his best to save my life and get me out of New York alive. You told me the truth, and you were a true friend. You gave me the real scoop on the LCN!

I want to extend my love and condolences to the Avila family, the Cutolo family, and the Clyde family. This is for everything you've lost. Bill Jr., I admire the road you've traveled and want you to know that you did the right thing.

I also need to give it up to my old crew, without whom I'd have no story to tell: Phil (the real American hero), Chuck Browntooth, "Babar," Keith, Greg, Jeff, Mike, Joey, and Clyde.

I probably would not be here if not for the help Rick M., Mike M., Will C., John M., Andre J., and Jake G. gave me. Also, thank you to my friends Adrianne Moore, Kendra Jade, Deven Davis, Heidi, Yvette, Brasco & Gia, Jen Peterson, Mike Maggio, Eman The Greek, Jerry Capeci (Ganglandnews.com), Anna David, Steve Miller (Americanmafia.com), Johnny Fratto at Beverly Hills Choppers, and Eric Lynch for the laughs.

I owe my eternal gratitude to my friends who have

shown me "the way": Ted Lucaylucay, David "Musashi" Miller, and Michael "Joker" Guymon. And finally, I need to give my love to all of the warriors with whom I've shed blood: "Night Night" Aryan, Ryan "Agent One" Gonzales, Chris "Coach" Bielecki, Justin Levens, Luke at LA Boxing, Mark "The Philippine Wrecking Machine" Munoz, Mark "Rocky," Ryan Rogers, Albert Rosales, Brian Sesma, Raj Shippen, "The Mayor" Mitch, Joe "Ice Cream" Shapiro, "Tattoo" Johnny, James Wilkes, Jason Lambert, Tim Mackenzie, BHJJC, and Erik "Bad Apple" for teaching me how to act like a man.

MRV:

I owe everything to my wife Melissa, for sacrificing so much to ensure that this book was completed.

Thanks to Emilia Pisani for believing in and supporting this book, and to J.F. for everything.

I owe a great debt to everyone who volunteered their time and in some cases jeopardized their safety and their jobs to be interviewed for this book. Thanks to MP for all of his help. Lastly, thank you to my friends and family who contributed their time and skill to this project: Melissa, Jeannie, Chad England, James Cobo, Bill Huntington, and Dr. Ranjan Chhibber.

The publisher of the first edition engaged the services of Edward Gelb, an eminent polygraph expert, to conduct a polygraph examination of Kenny Gallo in relation to material he presented in this book.

Mr. Gelb has conducted in excess of 30,000 polygraph examinations since 1969 and has testified as an expert in front of courts and legislative bodies throughout the country. Gelb has served as President, Executive Director, and Chairman of the Board of the American Polygraph Association and is an Honorary Fellow of the Academy of Certified Polygraphists. In addition, he is a recipient of the prestigious Leonarde Keeler award presented by the American Polygraph Association.

Kenny Gallo passed the test.